School, Work and Equality

A Reader

Edited by
**Ben Cosin, Mike Flude and Margaret Hales
of the Open University**

Hodder & Stoughton

A MEMBER OF THE HODDER HEADLINE GROUP
in association with the Open University

This reader is one part of an Open University integrated teaching system and the selection is therefore related to other material available to students. It is designed to evoke the critical understanding of students. Opinions expressed in it are not necessarily those of the course team or of the University.

British Library Cataloguing in Publication Data

School, work and equality.
  1. Education. Equality of opportunity.
  I. Cosin, Ben, *1944-* II. Flude, Michael
  III. Hales, Margaret, *1946-* IV. Open
  University
  370.19

ISBN 0 340 49000 4

First published 1989
Impression number 10 9 8 7 6 5 4 3
Year 1999 1998 1997 1996 1995

Printed in Great Britain for Hodder & Stoughton Educational,
a division of Hodder Headline Plc, 338 Euston Road, London NW1 3BH
by Athenæum Press Ltd, Gateshead, Tyne & Wear.

Contents

Acknowledgments

The editors and publishers would like to thank the following for permission to reproduce material in this volume:

Associated Book Publishers (UK) for 'The Challenge of Economic Utility' reprinted from *Beyond the Present and the Particular* by Charles Bailey published by Routledge and Kegan Paul, and for 'Inside/Out: The School in Political Context' reprinted from *The Micro-Politics of the School* by Stephen J. Ball published by Methuen & Co.; Basil Blackwell and Professor Bernard Williams for 'The Idea of Equality' originally published in *Politics, Philosophy and Society* by Basil Blackwell and reprinted in *Problems of the Self* by Cambridge University Press; Carfax Publishing Company for 'The Expansion of Special Education' by Sally Tomlinson published in *Oxford Review of Education*, Vol. II, No. 2 (1985); The Centre for Educational Sociology for 'Comprehensive Schooling is Better and Fairer' by Andrew McPherson and J. Douglas Willms published in *Forum*, Vol. 30, No. 2; the Editors of *Educational Leadership* and Karen P. Edmonds for 'Effective Schools for the Urban Poor' by Ronald Edmonds published in *Educational Leadership*, Vol. 37 (1979); Falmer Press and Phil Brown for 'Schooling for Inequality? Ordinary Kids in School and the Labour Market' reprinted from *Education, Unemployment and the Labour Market* by Phil Brown, Falmer Press, 1987; Falmer Press, Anthony Hartnett and Michael Naish for '"The Values of a Free Society" and the Politics of Educational Studies' reprinted from *Education and Society Today* by Anthony Hartnett and Michael Naish, Falmer Press, 1987; Hodder and Stoughton for 'The Growth of Central Influence on the Curriculum' by Gordon Kirk reprinted from *The Core Curriculum* by Gordon Kirk, Hodder and Stoughton, 1985; Kogan Page for 'The Side Effects of Assessment' by Derek Rowntree from *Assessing Students: How shall we know them?* by Derek Rowntree, second edition, Kogan Page, 1987; Andy Hargreaves for 'Teaching Quality: A Sociological Analysis' published in *Curriculum Studies*, Vol. 20, No. 3 (1988); J. B. Lippincott, a subsidiary of Harper & Row, for 'Records of Achievement and the GCSE' by Patricia Broadfoot reprinted from her book *GCSE: Examining the New System*, T. Horton, 1986. Robert Moore for 'Education, Employment and Recruitment' reprinted from *Frameworks for Teaching*, edited by Roger Dale, Ross Fergusson and Alison Robinson, Hodder and Stoughton, 1988; The National Union of Teachers for 'Testing, Testing, Testing...' by Desmond L. Nuttall reprinted from *NUT Educational Review*, Vol. 1, No. 2 (1987); the Editors of the *New Statesman* and *New Society* for 'Class in the Classroom' by Anthony Heath reprinted from *New Society*, 17 July 1987; The Open University Educational Enterprises Ltd for 'On the Dole' by Frank Coffield, Carol Borrill and Sarah Marshall reprinted from their book *Growing Up at the Margin*, Open University Press, 1986; Unwin & Hyman for 'The Labour Process and the Division of Labour' by Rob Connell reprinted from his book *Teachers' Work*, Unwin & Hyman, 1985; A. P. Watt for '"As interchangeable as ants"' by Anthony Flew reprinted from his book *The Politics of Procrustes* published by Temple Smith, 1981; the Editors of *Youth and Policy* for 'ESRC – Young People in Society' by Ken Roberts published in *Youth and Policy*, No. 22.

The following pieces have been specially commissioned for this volume:
'The National Curriculum and Improving Secondary Schools' by David H. Hargreaves; 'Local Management of Schools' by Hywel Thomas; the conclusion to 'The Growth of Central Influence on the Curriculum' by Gordon Kirk.

Preface

This Reader is one of two collections of papers published in connection with the Open University course E208 entitled 'Exploring Educational Issues'. The course is primarily intended for all those interested in education, including parents, teachers, school governors and administrators. The companion volume, entitled *Family, School and Society,* edited by Martin Woodhead and Andrea McGrath, is also published by Hodder and Stoughton.

Because the Reader is only part of a total learning package, it does not claim to offer a complete picture of the issues with which it deals. Nevertheless, we believe that there are many connections amongst the papers included, and our introductory paper is designed to bring these connections into prominence.

It is not necessary to become an undergraduate of the Open University to take course E208. Further information about the course may be obtained by writing to: The Associate Student Central Office, The Open University, PO Box 48, Walton Hall, Milton Keynes MK7 6AA.

Introduction and Overview

In *School, Work and Equality* we consider some of the major political problems of education in its social context. The chapters fall into four sections: in **Teaching and Learning** we review the conflicts between various demands on educational institutions, conflicts that have become more clearly defined in recent years. In the section on **The Organization and Control of Schooling**, we change the focus to a slightly wider context, considering in particular the balance between home and school and between local and central government. In the section on **Aspects of Equality**, we consider some of the social divisions and inequalities which have featured in educational discourses and policies; and in the section on **Education and Work**, we raise some of the issues stemming from the employment problems of young people. Below, we spell out the relevance of the readings in a little more detail.

1 Teaching and Learning

The chapters in this section of the reader consider various aspects of teaching and learning that have come under increased official scrutiny by central state agencies in recent years, particularly the curriculum of schools, the assessment of pupil performance in school and the quality of teaching itself. The prospect of a national curriculum with prescribed core and foundation subjects covering about 70 per cent of timetabled time, marks a departure from earlier recommendations that sought to delineate a core of subject studies or areas of experience within the secondary curriculum. Gordon Kirk's chapter (1.1) points to the variable controls over the curriculum from the centre that marked earlier historical periods; the post-war tradition that curriculum matters were largely the subject of professional decision-making and the gradual reassertion of central influence and control over the curriculum since the mid-1970s. The part played by various DES (Department of Education and Science) and HMI (Her Majesty's Inspectorate) curriculum documents in redefining particularly the priorities of secondary schooling is examined, alongside the changes that are seen to represent a substantial shift from local and institutional control to greater central control. The strengthening of this centralist trend, which has also been evident in other aspects of state schooling, is seen to culminate in the government's consultation paper *The National Curriculum 5-16* (DES/Welsh Office, 1987) whose proposals were incorporated in a largely unchanged form in Chapter 1 of the 1987 Education Reform Bill. The legislative route adopted by the government with respect to the curriculum and assessment procedures for schools in England and Wales, contrasts with the situation found in Scotland. Here the restructuring of the curriculum and assessment practice has been gradually introduced, with substantial support from educationalists, following the recommendations of the Munn (SED, 1977a) and Dunning reports (SED, 1977b).

While the main pressure for a common framework for the curriculum emerged from the lead given by DES and HMI, it has also been an issue taken up by academics and some local authorities. The moves made by some LEAs to develop a curriculum framework followed the publication of *Local Authority Arrangements for the School Curriculum* (DES/Welsh Office, 1979). This was critical of LEAs in two important respects. First it was claimed that LEAs had inadequate information about curriculum provision in schools; and, second, that they lacked a clear policy on the curriculum. Subsequently local authorities were asked in 1981 to review their curriculum policy and to plan the curriculum along the lines suggested in *The School Curriculum* (DES, 1981). It was in response to these pressures, and more particularly its commitment to enhancing equality of opportunity and tackling the problem of under-achievement, that the Inner London Education Authority (ILEA) set up a committee of enquiry chaired by David Hargreaves. Its recommendations were made in the document *Improving Secondary Schools* (ILEA, 1984). Following Kirk's analysis of increasing central pressures on the curriculum, David Hargreaves compares and contrasts the government's proposals in its consultation document on the curriculum and subsequent Education Reform Bill, with the recommendations made in *Improving Secondary Schools* (1984). In his chapter (1.2) Hargreaves points to some of the major contrasts in the underlying curriculum philosophies informing these curriculum proposals. Although both Kirk and Hargreaves support a common curriculum they have major reservations about the government's proposals. Kirk sees the national curriculum as potentially circumscribing pupil-centred learning, limiting the exercise of professional autonomy, and inadequately recognizing the cultural and ethnic diversity of our society. Hargreaves is particularly critical of the way in which the national curriculum proposals, and associated age-related testing of pupils, will reinforce traditional subject-centred teaching and restrict pupils learning roles.

Andy Hargreaves' chapter links in with themes raised by the previous contributors. The growing central controls on the curriculum, and other aspects of state schooling, has to a considerable extent been grounded on a concern with the quality of teaching, and the associated view that improving the quality of education is dependent on improving the quality of teaching. In 'Teaching Quality: A Sociological Analysis' (1.3), Andy Hargreaves critically analyses official views of what constitutes good and poor quality teaching. In contrast with the largely psychologistic HMI accounts of teaching quality, emphasizing teachers' personal qualities, technical classroom skills and responsibilities, Hargreaves examines teachers and their practices within a sociological framework. His focus is on teachers' understandings of, and attempts to cope with the situations they experience in schools, and the various pressures and constraints that shape the teaching environment and over which teachers have little control. This is seen to give rise to a culture of teaching as teachers collectively evolve sets of attitudes and responses to their tasks, the content of what they teach and the relationships they have with their colleagues. The major features of the present culture of teaching are seen to pose particular problems for curriculum policy, especially when this is directed at changing the delivery and organization of the curriculum.

Proposals for the regular assessment of pupil performance are contained in the government's consultative document on pupil testing (DES, 1987) and now incorporated into the Education Reform Bill. The third theme discussed in this section of the reader is changes in assessment policy. The chapters by Rowntree, Broadfoot and Nuttall examine a number of key developments in the assessment of pupil performance, and point to the rapid speed and scale of changes that have taken place in recent years. In Derek Rowntree's chapter (1.4) various side effects of the competitive aspects of assessment and the giving of grades are identified, and their implications for pupil motivation discussed. In the next chapter (1.5) Patricia Broadfoot discusses the impact of the introduction of the General Certificate in Secondary Education (GCSE) and examines this alongside the simultaneous introduction of Records of Achievement. While both initiatives are seen as bringing about a closer link between assessment and teaching and learning, and place a greater emphasis than hitherto on teacher assessment, Broadfoot points to various tensions and contradictions between these systems of assessment. Records of Achievement are essentially formative records providing summarizing statements of pupils' personal qualities, including some element of the students own self-assessment. In contrast GCSE remains basically a hierarchical, subject based examination that is non-formative in character and like its predecessor is shaped by the requirements of educational and occupational selection. 'In short, the contradictions between GCSE and Records of Achievement hinges on the question of whether the priority for 16+ assessment should be the provision of reliable information which has high predictability for the purpose of selection or whether the primary purpose should be to reflect what has been achieved in relation to the whole range of goals that a school may set for itself'. In addition to this tension in the purposes of assessment pointed to by Broadfoot, we also have to consider the future impact of proposals to introduce national testing at regular intervals. This is regarded by the present government, along with its proposals for a national curriculum, as a means of enhancing the quality of education, and making schools more accountable to parents in a system of schooling that it is intended will be more consumer oriented. These proposals for a national system of pupil assessment are discussed in Desmond Nuttall's chapter (1.6). Nuttall points to various difficulties with this model and some of its possible effects in narrowing pupils' learning opportunities.

2   *The Organization and Control of Schooling*

The topics and issues covered in this section of the reader are in various ways concerned with different aspects of the organization of schooling, the implications of recent changes for teachers' work, and the wider political and educational significance of moves towards more centralized, state directed systems of control.

A substantial body of educational research in recent years has sought to identify those qualities or practices that make an 'effective' school. A considerable impetus behind this research has been the concern of the DES and HMI to improve the quality of schooling, allied with the efforts of educational researchers and practitioners to tackle the persistent problem of the underachievement of many children attending inner city or urban schools. It is this concern for enhancing or widening the opportunities of children living in inner city areas which underpins Ronald Edmonds' chapter (2.1). Edmonds defines effective schooling in terms of enabling children from economically impoverished backgrounds to acquire those 'basic school skills that now describe minimally successful pupil performance for the children of the middle class'. From his review of American research, and his own work with the School Improvement Project in New York City, Edmonds is convinced about the efficacy of school reform in developing and realizing the potential of pupils in inner city schools. Contrary to some of the conclusions drawn from social scientific research suggesting that it is primarily home or family backgrounds that determines the level of educational performance, Edmonds proceeds to identify those characteristics of effective schools delivering marked improvements in children's educational achievements.

The impending changes in the funding and management of state schools in England and Wales, consequent upon the clauses of the Education Reform Bill that will extend local financial management to all schools, are discussed in the next chapter by Hywel Thomas (2.2). These proposals contrast with the growing importance and assumptions behind 'categorical' (Harland, 1985) or centrally targetted funding on favoured educational projects (e.g. Technical and Vocational Education Initiative, Low Attainers project). Such centrally funded schemes have tended to be supported by claims that it is only by central intervention that particular objectives can be achieved. In contrast the development of local management schemes purportedly seeks to enhance local and community control of schools by bringing financial control closer to the point of professional and institutional decision-making. In his chapter Thomas examines the origins of local management schemes, the innovatory work undertaken on this by a number of local authorities, and the objectives of the local management proposals contained in the Education Reform Bill. Various difficulties in devising formula budgetting for schools are pointed to and the implications of the scheme for school governors and the employment of teachers are discussed. Although it is too soon to draw any firm conclusions about the effects of this scheme, it seems likely that it will have a considerable impact on the culture of schools, and the future structure of schooling itself. The devolving of financial responsibility to schools, not only reduces the power and influence of LEAs, but it may well encourage schools at some future point to consider opting out of local authority control altogether.

The next chapter by Connell (2.3) analyses the work of teachers by drawing on concepts and ideas developed in industrial sociology. In contrast to the predominant tradition of writing that concentrates on teachers' professionalism, Connell examines teachers' labour as work. Drawing extensively on teachers' own reflections and comments he points to various external constraints that structure the tasks teachers are expected to perform, as well as those deriving from the organization of time, space and activities in schools themselves. What is revealed is a complex, although often implicit, division of labour that has a marked effect on the social relations of schooling. Connell also points to the ways in which the teaching work force is also structured by a sexual division of labour. One dimension of this is the under-representation of women in senior positions in schools. 'The association that our society makes between authority and masculinity, more specifically adult heterosexual masculinity, is a significant underpinning of the power structure of a school system where most administrators, principals and subject heads are men' (Connell, 1985, pp. 138-9).

Stephen Ball's chapter (2.4) provides an extensive discussion of the political interrelationships between national and local government and schools. Two specific sets of factors are seen as particularly significant in recent years: falling school rolls and cut backs in educational expenditure. Ball examines the relationship between schools and their wider socio-political context as a dynamic one, emphasizing the variety of ways in which schools cope with and respond to increased external intervention. External pressure for change is seen as mediated through the 'micro-politics' of school life, a term used to refer to the conflicts and struggles between various interest groups within schools. This is illustrated by reference to teachers' responses to various externally sponsored innovations and the teachers' pay dispute of 1985-86.

The final chapter in this section by Anthony Hartnett and Michael Naish considers the growth and significance of increased centralized control and direction of state schooling, particularly its impact in limiting the agenda of political and educational debate. On the basis of their commitment to an open and participatory democracy, Hartnett and Naish raise a number of major moral, social and educational issues arising from the drift to a more centralized system of control, in which managerial and bureaucratic priorities and solutions have been advanced over professional and community concerns. They point also to the fundamental, political and enduring character of educational problems and the dangers within a centralized state of putting these beyond political and democratic scrutiny. Importantly their chapter offers a defence of the role of educational studies in addressing fundamental educational problems and issues, and of the need to sustain independent enquiry at a time when official pressure concentrates on the technical and utilitarian aspects of schooling.

3 Aspects of Equality

In this section we consider some equalities and inequalities as they are manifested in relation to education. Whenever we compare two or more people, we can discover a variety of attributes in respect of which they may be equal or unequal. In this section we outline some ways in which educational inequalities and the pursuit of educational equalities have been studied.

In Williams' chapter (3.1), we may perhaps see a justification of equality of condition or outcome on the basis of equality of opportunity. Equality of opportunity – the idea that everybody should have a fair chance of doing themselves justice – is a notion that has been at the basis of public provision of education and indeed of much educational charity for a long time indeed. Usually, those who have espoused it as a goal have had little interest in the idea of equalizing all the pupils of a school or an educational system, or indeed all the people in a particular country. Williams attempts to show that if we examined the commonplace idea of equality of opportunity thoroughly, we find ourselves carried down a sort of 'slippery slope' towards insisting that only if everybody has succeeded to the same degree can we be sure that there has been genuine equality of opportunity. Thus for Williams there is no difference between the right to enter a competition and the right to win that competition.

Flew (1981) (3.2), in the extract from his book *The Politics of Procrustes*, differs from Williams. For Flew, the track which leads from equality of opportunity (a phrase which he finds ambiguous) to equality of outcome is not a slippery slope at all. Rather, Flew claims that the idea of 'open competition for scarce opportunities' is less ambiguous than that of 'equality of opportunity'; that it is, in our metaphor, a level piece of ground rather than a slippery slope; and that it is clearly distinct from that of absolute equality of outcome. Williams, Flew therefore claims, has failed to show that equality of opportunity entails even a prima facie commitment to equality of outcome. He also points out that a commitment to equality implies also a commitment to a state which will push everybody around until they are equal – Procrustes was a figure in Greek mythology who forced all those he came across to become the same height, either by chopping bits off or by using a rack to stretch their legs.

We can see that in this area of intellectual work even the analysis of concepts carries with it a considerable political and even emotional charge.

The next pair of readings are concerned with what has perhaps been the single most salient political issue in British education in the twentieth century: the issue of inequality of opportunity and inequality of outcome between social classes – particularly between middle and working class children. Heath (3.3) sums up one influential and long-established tradition in the study of class differences in education. He compares three studies, carried out respectively in 1949, 1972 and 1983, but reflecting the educational and social conditions of well before those dates. Very broadly, his conclusion is that class inequalities in education – at least for boys – have changed very little since the First World War. He suggests therefore that perhaps the return of a third successive Conservative administration might not lead to a widening of social class inequalities. He further comments that the very increase in examination successes which has occurred especially since the introduction of CSE has meant that educational attainment has become more, not less, associated with social class.

McPherson and Willms (3.4) emphasize somewhat different aspects of this complex topic in rebutting Heath's major claim; that the introduction of comprehensive education has had no effect in reducing class inequalities in education. They find a process which includes both improvement – the increase in average attainment among all children in their Scottish sample; and equalization – a reduction in class differences. In short a process of levelling up rather than the levelling down anticipated by many critics of comprehensive provision. On the central issue – has comprehensive education led to any equalization between social classes – McPherson and Willms argue simply that Heath's time scale is too short. Because comprehensive education has been introduced too recently for its effects to show up clearly in his Anglo-Welsh sample of boys born in 1960–65, Heath's conclusions are in their view simply premature. The effects of the comprehensive policies of the 1960s, reforms of the 1970s and practices of the 1970s and 1980s are available for serious discussion only in the 1990s. It may be worth noting that Heath himself in another article extends his time-scale further back to include the reforms of the first decade of the twentieth century.

Tomlinson suggests in her chapter on 'The Expansion of Special Education' that if selection by ability was inadmissible, so was selection by disability or inability. Thus she ties together of the reduction of class inequality and the reduction of segregation of those children for whom special education is assumed to cater. But who were and are these children? She gives a wide variety of definitions: 'feeble-minded', 'educable defective', 'educationally sub-normal', 'those having moderate learning difficulties', 'dull and backward', 'remedial', and 'maladjusted and disruptive'. So many, so arbitrary, so variable have these definitions been, she claims, that they provide no basis at all for deciding which children need special education nor for explaining the growth of special education. With Mary Warnock's note that all children have some special needs, the notion of special needs becomes impossible to operate, if not meaningless.

What then is special education about? Tomlinson has an explanation in terms of the interests of particular social groups (especially professionals) and of the requirements of an advanced technological or industrial society – often simply termed capitalist. She aims therefore to switch attention from the alleged psychological problems of 'special needs' children and towards the alleged interests of those whose power and influence is furthered by the expansion of such education. Thus apparent natural and psychological inequalities are replaced by social, political and economic inequalities of power. Considering inequalities once again leads us to consider the political machinery which is expected to deal with them – a machinery which itself contains and reinforces inequalities. The advocates of equality, as well as those more concerned with other goals, are given a cue for reflection on the inequalities of equalization.

4   *After School*

In this last section, we consider what for many, especially working class pupils, has been the consummation or the release from schooling: the labour market. Youth unemployment has since the mid-1970s been a central fact or a central fear of many young people, and has affected many others. It is not surprising, then, that the vocational uses have occupied a central position in the assessment of education for all sectors of the political spectrum. Yet education has never guaranteed employment, and whether it has or has not been expected to, we must also consider the other purposes it may serve.

In 'Education, Employment and Recruitment', Robert Moore sets out some empirical findings on how educational qualifications are used in the labour market. He encourages us to face up to the question how useful educational qualifications really are in getting jobs. We need to remind ourselves of the variations between different types of employer, different types of job and different types of qualification; but also of the difficulties employers may have in understanding the meaning of more than a very few qualifications. How well qualified are employers to evaluate education, or the extent to which young people differ from their elders? Moore does not suggest that employers are wholly blinkered: it might be, for example, that employers are finding increased educational and job opportunities have meant a less able body of pupils are applying for apprenticeships. Thus employers' disappointment might be caused by rising educational and other standards. Another doubt about the relevance of school work experience schemes springs from employers' low valuations of such schemes for appraising applicants. They appear to regard them as useful for acquainting teachers and brighter pupils with industrial life, but to discount them as a means of selecting employees. Again, Moore comments on the tendency of employers to prefer hiring or promoting those whose commitments to family and home will encourage them to be reliable. More broadly, there does not seem to be one simple hierarchy of types of job (running from the most unskilled and casual up to the most responsible and secure), rather there are a number of different labour markets, partitioned from each other, and some operating on a sort of grapevine. Educational vocationalism does not seem to offer much hope for the reform either of education or of the labour market.

Bailey's chapter (4.2) 'The Challenge of Economic Utility', which comes from his book *Challenges of Liberal Education* (1984) sets out to distinguish the liberal goals of understanding from the goals, which he describes as both indoctrinatory and utilitarian, of 'respect for industrial and commercial activity', a view based on the goal of 'helping children properly to appreciate how the nation earns and maintains its standard of living and properly (esteeming) the essential role of industry and commerce in this process'. Bailey sums up this pair of purposes under the head of 'instrumentalism'. He compares various glosses on 'preparation for adult life' and implies that this phrase itself is unduly restricting and illiberal. Is this wholly due to objections to using behavioural objectives or skills as the criterion as to whether pupils have really learnt from their education? Bailey identifies a polemical and rhetorical style which coopts creativity for commercial purposes. Have the creativity of art, music, literature and drama always been opposed to activities responding to patronage or markets? Or is Bailey merely articulating an ideology of Bohemianism for the arts and of undirected radicalism for social and political thought in general? How can 'understanding society' be assessed? The Further Education Unit offers us four headings: examination of what is at stake in a given issue (including vested interests and decision-making procedures); experience of membership of a decision-making group; background knowledge of national and local government; and personal legal rights. Bailey dismisses the sum total of these as having 'little to do with any genuine or profound understanding of society'. But how do we recognize a genuine or a profound understanding of society?

Certainly, a consideration of what wealth is to be used for and how it is to be redistributed is an essential ingredient of Bailey's requirements (readers may be interested to contrast Flew's strictures on the notion that wealth is entirely a collective property, and that its distribution is therefore a matter for collective decision-taking). Further, some activities cannot be judged by assessing their value to wealth-creation, when in fact they are what people use their wealth on. Education is about ends, not merely means. Indeed, Bailey holds up for critical scrutiny the idea that schools can prepare young people for a world of rapid technological change by concentrating on the very technology which is subject to change; rather, he suggests, the best basis for adaptability is a liberal education aimed at generating a wide understanding and the development of reason and autonomy. The fact that the more complex realms of human action and reflection are the most important and valuable should inhibit us in assuming that all education should issue in behaviourally identifiable skills. An emphasis on skill without understanding is an emphasis on passivity and subservience. An emphasis on experience without general knowledge confines pupils rather than educating them.

Brown, in chapter 4.3, considers the relationship between the schooling and motivation of 'ordinary kids' and their prospects in the labour market. 'Ordinary kids' (their own classification) aimed at apprenticeships or at clerical or personal service occupations. In the 1980s this prospect became less realistic than previously. Brown foresees an increase in educational and social inequalities arising from the provision of TVEI (Technical and Vocational Education Initiative) studies effectively dedicated to working-class pupils.

In Chapter 4.4, 'On the Dole', Coffield takes issue with some (relatively optimistic) views of youth unemployment expressed elsewhere by Roberts – that young people suffer less from unemployment than do adults. He suggests that to attribute extra suffering to one particular factor – age, length of unemployment, marital status, etc. – is too crude, as is the emphasis on individual responsibility; the gross disparities between the numbers of jobs and the numbers of those seeking jobs cannot be accounted for in terms of the individual psychological characteristics of the latter, nor can the rapid changes in the former. Methodologically, Coffield suggests that explanations must move from individualistic psychological ones to collectivistic, sociological ones (how economic explanations fit in is somewhat unclear); politically he suggests that a minimum income must be the answer.

Roberts (4.5) surveys the literature on youth, pointing out that the traditional focus on how youth cultures have functioned so as to reconcile young people to adult roles in employment and family life have lost a crucial element – the expectation that young people (especially those with only basic education) would have jobs available. It might be argued that this function has been coopted by such purposive (indeed, allegedly manipulative) schemes as the Youth Training Scheme. Or might the turmoil of schemes and unemployment be preparing youth more thoroughly (as has long been the case in the USA) for better adaptation to eventual permanent employment? Is the development towards a new underclass of unemployables, or towards an enterprise culture of independent striving? Effects on family life probably include contrary tendencies – accelerating or delaying decisions to start families, for example. Changes in strictly (party) political attitudes and behaviour among youth do not seem salient, though attitudes to civil authority in general may be changing. Other topics on which findings are ambiguous are the effects on leisure activity, crime, and degree of dependence on parents. Indeed, we trust that all contributions will be judged not as predictions, but rather as means of analysing a complex and unpredictably changing sphere of social life.

References

BAILEY, C. (1984) *Beyond the Present and Particular*. London: Routledge and Kegan Paul.

CONNELL, R.W., (1985) *Teachers' Work*. London: George Allen & Unwin.

DES/WELSH OFFICE (Department of Education and Science/Welsh Office) (1979) *Local Authority Arrangements for the School Curriculum*. London: HMSO.

DES (Department of Education and Science) (1981) *The School Curriculum*. London: HMSO.

DES/WELSH OFFICE (Department of Education and Science/Welsh Office) (1987) *The National Curriculum 5-16: A Consultative Document*. London: HMSO.

FLEW, A. (1981) *The Politics of Procrustes*. London: Temple Smith.

HARLAND, J. (1985) *TVEI: A Model for Curriculum Change*, Paper presented to BERA Conference, Sheffield.

ILEA (Inner London Education Authority) Committee of the Curriculum and Organization of Secondary Schools (1984) *Improving Secondary Schools*. London: ILEA.

SED (Scottish Education Department) (1977a) *The Structure of the Curriculum in the Third and Fourth Years of the Scottish Secondary School* (The Munn Report). Edinburgh: HMSO.

SED (Scottish Education Department) (1977b) *Assessment for All* (the Dunning Report). Edinburgh: HMSO.

Part One:
Teaching and Learning

1.1 The Growth of Central Influence on the Curriculum
Gordon Kirk

The Historical Context

Who should determine what young people learn at school? That has been a keenly disputed question in Britain for more than a hundred years. As public education developed in the middle of the nineteenth century, and as public funds were allocated for this purpose, it was considered that central government should oversee what was taught in schools. If investment in public education was a necessary political and humanitarian response to the problems of poverty and underprivilege, if it was an appropriate means of fostering and maintaining religious adherence, and if it was calculated to equip young people with the skills demanded by a changing industrial society, then a strategy had to be found for ensuring that value was obtained for the funds invested. According to the Newcastle Commission of 1861, the best means of obtaining that assurance was

> to institute a searching examination by a competent authority of every child in every school to which grants are to be paid with the view of ascertaining whether these indispensable elements of knowledge are thoroughly acquired and to make the prospects and position of the teacher dependent, to a considerable extent, on the results of this examination.[1]

In 1862 the Revised Code instituted a system of grants for schools: 8s. (40p) per year was to be awarded for every pupil who attended more than 200 times. Moreover, all pupils were to be subject to annual tests in reading, writing and arithmetic, administered by HMI, and 2s. 8d. (approximately 14p) was to be deducted from the grant for each test a child failed. Such were the main features of the strategy known as 'payment by results'. Through that strategy the machinery of the state was deployed to control the work of teachers, to prescribe standards of achievement in a narrow range of objectives. Representatives of the central government were required to judge whether or not these standards had been achieved.

The system of payment by results was abolished in 1895. Nevertheless, central control of the elementary school curriculum was maintained through a succession of codes and it was not until 1936 that these regulations were changed in a way that left responsibility for 'a suitable curriculum and syllabus with due regard to the organisation and circumstances of the school' in the hands of teachers. Indeed, as far as secondary schools were concerned, the stranglehold exerted by central government over the curriculum was not relaxed until the 1944 Education Act for England and Wales and the corresponding Scottish legislation of 1945.

While the system of 'payment by results' was formally abolished in 1895 it has continued over the years to represent an enormous affront to the professional consciousness of teachers and a threat to the creation of an effective educational service. There are three grounds for this pervasive professional opposition to the system. First, 'payment by results' demeaned education and reduced it to a mere cramming exercise in which all that is expected of pupils is a capacity for recall. Secondly, the system circumscribed professional activity, constrained initiative, and demanded acquiescence in a curriculum that was so narrowly conceived as to represent a parody of education. Finally, 'payment by results' has been interpreted to exemplify a state-controlled curriculum, the deliberate use of political power to mould the minds of the young. For these reasons, 'payment by results' has remained anathema to teachers and their professional associations. Consequently, any measure which seeks to strengthen central influence on the curriculum and to weaken teachers' autonomy in curriculum matters is still likely to evince the same suspicion and hostility with which teachers responded to 'payment by results'. This deeply ingrained suspicion of central government explains the aversion of teachers to any increase of ministerial involvement in curricular matters.

In the years between 1862 and 1944/45 there was a significant lessening of central control of the school curriculum; the years since then have witnessed an equally significant shift in the opposite direction. The extent of that shift can be illustrated by two ministerial pronouncements. The first, attributed to George Tomlinson, the Minister of Education from 1947 in the post-war Labour government, intimated with concise frankness that the 'Minister knows nowt about curriculum'. The second, uttered by Sir Keith Joseph, the Conservative Secretary of State for Education and Science in the present government, in a speech at Sheffield in January 1984 was no less frank:

I can offer an account of what the minimum level to be attained at 16 by 80%–90% of pupils would entail in a few areas of the curriculum...; in English, pupils would need to demonstrate that they are attentive listeners and confident speakers when dealing with everyday matters of which they have experience, that they can read straightforward written information and pass it on – orally and in written form – without loss of meaning and that they can say clearly what their own views are; in Mathematics, that they can apply the topics and skills in the foundation list proposed in the Cockcroft Report; in Science, that they are willing and able to take a practical approach to problems, involving sensible observations and appropriate measurements and can communicate their findings effectively...; in History, that they possess some historical knowledge and perspective, understand the concepts of cause and consequence, and can compare and extract information from historical evidence and be aware of its limitations; and in CDT [craft, design and technology], that they can design and make something, using a limited range of materials and calling on a restricted range of concepts and give an account of what they have done and the problems they encountered.[2]

The first statement, evoking a tradition of political non-interference in the curriculum, repudiates the locus of central government in such matters. The second, by contrast, is a striking use of ministerial authority to influence what is taught in the schools and is indicative of the assertive pursuit of government policy to wield such influence. This chapter seeks to chart the growth of that government assertiveness and to highlight some of the significant manifestations of its emergence.

James Callaghan's Ruskin Speech, 1976

There is evidence that, traditionally, ministers in successive governments were persuaded to adopt a neutral stance on the curriculum. One indeed, the Conservative Minister David Eccles, is reputed to have alluded to 'the secret garden of the curriculum'. That metaphor of the curriculum as forbidden territory to ministers was directly challenged by Mr Callaghan's speech at Ruskin College, Oxford, in October 1976. The Prime Minister was clearly motivated by growing public concern about education and the work of the schools. His brief for the speech was prepared by the DES and was leaked to the press in advance. The Yellow Paper, as the leaked document came to be called, was critical of teaching in primary and secondary schools. It claimed that some teachers in the primary school had allowed performance in the basic skills of reading, writing and arithmetic to be adversely affected by their inadequate understanding and hence uncritical application of child-centred, or informal, methods. With regard to the secondary school curriculum, the Yellow Paper maintained that too much scope had been given to the principle of pupil choice, with the result that many pupils were following unbalanced programmes and not enough pupils were studying science-based and technological subjects. The antidote to these ills was thought to lie in the institution of a core or common component in the curriculum of all pupils.

The Prime Minister's speech was eagerly anticipated by the educational and wider community and it duly received the full media treatment. However, if people expected a lucid analysis of the ills of contemporary education, together with appropriate and carefully contrived proposals for change, they were disappointed. The speech had more modest objectives. First, it implicity and explicitly asserted that the aims of education and the content of the curriculum were legitimate matters for public discussion and could not be looked upon as the exclusive concern of professionals:

> I take it that no-one claims exclusive rights in this field. Public interest is strong and legitimate and will be satisfied... Parents, teachers, learned and professional bodies, representatives of higher education and both sides of industry, together with the government, all have an important part to

play in formulating and expressing the purpose of education and the standards that we need.[3]

Of course, the very fact that the Prime Minister made the speech at all, and that he had rejected the advice 'to keep off the grass', as he put it, was a powerful reinforcement of the case he was arguing. Secondly, the speech identified issues that, in the Prime Minister's judgement, were the source of public concern and required public debate. Among the issues raised were the following: deficiency in the basic skills among school leavers; the reluctance of many of our best trained students to join industry; standards of literacy and numeracy; the value of informal teaching methods; the place of 'a basic curriculum with universal standards'; and 'the role of the Inspectorate in relation to national standards'. Very clearly, the Prime Minister saw the speech as an opportunity to set the agenda for an extended public discussion of educational issues. The 'Great Debate' followed.

The Great Debate, 1967–77

The Great Debate took place at two levels. First, it was represented by a massive output of articles in the educational and the national press about standards, about the composition of the core curriculum, about the control of the curriculum, and about the role of the schools and other related matters. Secondly, at a more formal level, it took the form of eight regional one-day conferences. To each of these there were invited about 200 representatives of the world of industry and commerce, trade unions, teachers' associations, local education authorities and institutions of higher education. The background paper for these meetings, *Educating our Children: Four Subjects for Debate*, was prepared by the DES. This derived clearly from the issues raised in the Prime Minister's Ruskin speech. The four subjects for debate were:

1 The school curriculum 5–16.
2 The assessment of standards.
3 The education and training of teachers.
4 School and working life.

Among the issues for discussion of the first two subjects were the following:

1 What should be the aims and content of a core curriculum?
2 How best can an agreed core curriculum be put into effect?
3 Do we have adequate means of obtaining reliable information about the performance of pupils in schools and, if not, what further measures are required?

What value was served by these regional conferences? According to one commentator, the format allowed little more than 'a short canter for a stable of hobby horses'.[4] Another verdict was that the Great Debate was 'a unique exercise in contemplating the country's educational navel'.[5] For her part, the Minister, Shirley Williams, expressed satisfaction at this move towards open consultation on the part of the DES. It is not beyond the bounds of possibility that the regional conferences demonstrated such a diversity of views on important aspects of educational policy that the way was left clear for a more decisive lead from the centre. That lead was speedily forthcoming.

Education in Schools: A Consultative Document (The Green Paper), July 1977

The Green Paper from the Department of Education and Science and the Welsh Office demonstrates its relationship to the Ruskin speech and to the issues raised in the Great Debate before moving swiftly to a statement on the partnership between schools, local education authorities and ministers. That statement includes the following justification for central involvement in curriculum matters:

> The Secretaries of State are responsible in law for the promotion of the education of the people of England and Wales. They need to know what is being done by the local education authorities and, through them, what is happening in the schools. They must draw attention to national needs if they believe the educational system is not adequately meeting them.

Then, after alluding to current criticisms of the curriculum, and having asserted the need 'to establish generally accepted principles for the composition of the school curriculum for all pupils', the paper continues:

> It would not be compatible with the duty of the Secretaries of State to 'promote the education of the people of England and Wales', or with their accountability to Parliament, to abdicate from leadership on educational issues which have become a matter of lively public concern. The Secretaries of State will therefore seek to establish a broad agreement with their partners in the educational service on a framework for the curriculum, and in particular on whether, because there are aims common to all schools and to all pupils at certain stages, there should be a 'core' or 'protected' part.

In execution of that policy it was proposed that a circular would be issued to all local authorities asking them to carry out a review of the curriculum in their areas in consultation with their schools and to report the results within about twelve months.

Enquiry into Local Education Authority Arrangements for the Management of the Curriculum

Circular 14.27 was a wide-ranging questionnaire to LEAs covering all aspects of the planning, development, evaluation and resourcing of the curriculum in their schools. Some of the relevant questions were as follows:

- What procedures have the authority established to enable them to carry out their curricular responsibilities under Section 23 of the Education Act (1944)?

- What systematic arrangements, if any, have the authority established for the collection of information about the curricula offered by schools in their area?

- How does the authority help schools decide on the relative emphasis they should give to particular aspects of the curriculum, especially the promotion of literacy and numeracy?

- What contribution has the authority made to the consideration of the problems faced by secondary schools, of providing suitable subject options for older pupils while avoiding the premature dropping of curricular elements regarded as essential for all pupils?

- What curricular elements does the authority regard as essential?

The replies to the circular were reported in 1979. Two significant findings emerged in relation to the questions quoted above. First, 'most authorities do not have systematic arrangements for regularly collecting and monitoring curricular information from their schools'. Secondly, there was very considerable diversity of view as to what the 'essential elements' of the curriculum should be, many authorities regarding such matters as being the concern of the schools themselves. Given the prevailing views about where responsibility for curricula rested, these findings are not perhaps totally unpredictable. Indeed, one critic of the exercise considered that 'the circular was a device which managed to make LEAs look as if they were failing in their duties, and thus allowed the DES to take the initiative'.[6] For their part, the ministers concerned made their intentions clear. They proposed 'to give a lead in the process of reaching a national consensus on a desirable framework for the curriculum'. Such an initiative would 'give central government a firmer basis for the development of national policies and the deployment of resources; and provide a checklist for authorities and schools in formulating and reviewing their curricular aims and policies in the light of local needs and circumstances... Conceived in this way, an agreed framework could offer a significant step forward in the quest for improvement in the consistency and quality of school education across the country.'[7] As a first step in the development of such a framework, HMI would be invited to formulate 'a view of a possible curriculum on the basis of their knowledge of schools'.

Papers from HM Inspectorate

The writings of HM Inspectorate can be seen to reinforce the commitment to a national framework for the curriculum. In 1977 they produced *Curriculum 11-16*. The first section of that document set out a powerful 'case for a common curriculum in secondary education to 16'. Such a common curriculum was thought to derive from eight 'areas of experience':

1 the aesthetic and creative;
2 the ethical;
3 the linguistic;
4 the mathematical;
5 the physical;
6 the scientific;
7 the social and political;
8 the spiritual.

The Inspectorate maintained their attack on the 'unacceptable variety' of curricular provision in their *Aspects of Secondary Education* (1979) and again in *A View of The Curriculum* (1980). The latter document re-emphasized the need for a national curriculum framework and for the delineation of a common core of learning for all pupils. The composition of that core was put forward, rather tentatively, as a series of 'propositions for consideration'. In effect, the inspectorate proposed a core that consisted of English, mathematics, religious education, physical education, modern languages, 'arts and applied crafts', history, and science subjects. Finally, in *The Curriculum from 5 to 16* (1985) the Inspectorate insisted that throughout the period of compulsory schooling all pupils should maintain contact with nine areas of learning – the 1977 list, except that 'technological' learning is added and 'the social and political' is replaced by 'human and social'. In each of these areas of learning schools were urged to cultivate appropriate knowledge, concepts, skills and attitudes, thus ensuring that all pupils received a broadly comparable educational experience.

The National Curriculum Framework

The government made its first attempt at formulating a national curriculum framework in the consultative document *A Framework for the School Curriculum* (1980). In a somewhat terse paper – it being considered that the more substantial analysis of principles had been carried out in the HMI document *A View of the Curriculum* – it was maintained that throughout the period of compulsory schooling, from 5–16, all pupils should undertake study in English, mathematics, science, religious education, and physical education. At the secondary level, the report continued, pupils should study in addition a modern language and the curriculum of all pupils should include what is called 'preparation for adult and working life', a varied programme of activities incorporating craft, design and technology, history and geography, moral education, health education, and 'preparation for parenthood and for a participatory role in adult society'.

The government's thinking was further developed in *The School Curriculum* (1981), which was clearly seen as the culminating point of several years of public discussion. Having reasserted the need for a national framework and having listed a set of general educational aims, the ministers set out 'the approach to the curriculum which they consider should now be followed in the years ahead'. As far as the primary phase of schooling was concerned, the plan of development favoured the same activities as were listed in *A Framework for the School Curriculum*, except that more attention was devoted to history and geography, to expressive arts, and to science, and to the need for clearly structured and progressively demanding work in these areas of the curriculum. The framework for the secondary school curriculum was taken to comprise English, mathematics, science, modern languages, microelectronics, craft, design and technology, religious education, physical education, humanities, practical and aesthetic activities, and 'preparation for adult life'.

The paper was seen as constituting 'guidance for local education authorities' and the ministers proposed to inform themselves in due course about the action taken by LEAs with regard to that guidance. That was reinforced in a subsequent circular to LEAs later in 1981 and two years later Circular 8/83 sought a progress report from LEAs on the formation of a curriculum policy for pupils of all abilities and aptitudes.

While *The School Curriculum* might have been seen as the government's definitive statement on the structure of the national curriculum framework, it was superseded in September 1984 by *The Organization and Content of the 5–16 Curriculum*, although the wording of the latest document conveyed the impression that the final nature and scope of the national framework has not yet been determined. The structure of the curriculum proposed for the primary phase is similar to that set out in earlier documentation but includes the following additional components:

- craft and practical work leading to some experience of design and technology and of solving problems;
- introduction to computers;
- insights into the adult world, including how people earn their living.

The proposed structure for the secondary phase is similar to that in *The School Curriculum* except that specific provision is made in the latest document for Home Economics for all pupils.

There is one feature of these developments that is worth highlighting. Throughout the official documents there is a disclaimer about the government's intention. Repeatedly it is urged that there is no intention to introduce, through legislation, a nationally prescribed curriculum that would be binding on all LEAs and on all schools. Thus, *Curriculum 11–16* (1977) from HMI avers:

We repeat that it is not the intention to advocate a standard curriculum for all secondary schools to the age of 16, not least because that would be educationally naive. One of the greatest assets of our educational arrangements is the freedom of schools to respond to differing circumstances in their localities and to encourage the enterprise and strength of their teachers.

Indeed, the goverment's own document, *The School Curriculum* (1981), includes these words: 'Neither the government nor the local authorities should specify in detail what the schools should teach.' At the same time, there is evidence that the government's interest in the school curriculum was not limited to the institution of a national framework. The White Paper, *Better Schools* (1985), indicated that one of the government's major policy commitments was 'to secure greater clarity about the objectives and content of the curriculum', that being considered a necessary step towards the improvement of standards achieved by pupils. That policy is being pursued in two ways: first, the DES is publishing a series of documents on the objectives to be sought in the different areas of the curriculum. To date, the documentation has appeared on English (DES, 1984)[8] and Science (DES, 1985).[9] Both documents seek to identify the skills and understandings which their respective subjects should seek to achieve at different stages of schooling. Secondly, ministers have approved 'national criteria' for different subject areas. These national criteria have been designed in connection with the new General Certificate of Secondary Education and are intended to 'offer a concise account of the understanding, knowledge and competences which should be developed in the course of following the syllabus'. Without question, these developments will impose very powerful constraints on the schools and mark a decisive shift of power in curricular matters to the centre. It is not surprising that a leading official of the NUT should dismiss the White Paper which collates the present government's curricular initiatives as 'a dose of centralist rhetoric'.[10]

For its part, the government insists that 'the establishment of broadly agreed objectives would not mean that the curricular policies of the Secretary of State, the LEA and the school should relate to each other in a nationally uniform way. In the government's view, such diversity is healthy, accords well with the English and Welsh traditions of school education and makes for liveliness and innovation.'[11]

Arguably, what has occurred is a reinterpretation of the traditional partnership between central government, LEAs and schools which has allowed central government, on the basis of its 'accountability to parliament for the performance of the educational service at all levels', progressively to nudge LEAs into a fuller appreciation of their curricular responsibilities and, through that, to influence the schools. The strategy consisted not of ministerial *diktat* but the progressive application of pressure on LEAs to ensure that the school curriculum in their areas was in line with a real or imagined consensus about what pupils should learn at school. At the same time, there were other events which very considerably strengthened the lead from the centre and made it more likely that LEAs would respond positively to the government's initiatives. These are considered in the remainder of this chapter.

The Demise of the Schools Council

The Schools Council (for curriculum and examinations), was established in 1964 by the Secretary of State for Education and Science as an independent body with the function of 'the promotion of education by carrying out research into, and keeping under review, curricula, teaching methods and examinations in schools'. It was funded jointly by the DES and LEAs and its membership was deliberately designed to achieve a majority of teachers. Over the years, the Schools Council was responsible for a prodigious output of reports and materials on every aspect of the school curriculum. It very definitely constituted the most significant and influential curriculum development agency in the country and many of its projects attracted international acclaim.

In keeping with its standing as an independent body with a built-in majority of teachers, the Council was committed to the thesis that 'each school should have the fullest measure of responsibility for its own curriculum and teaching methods based on the needs of its own pupils and evolved by its own staff'. It saw its function not to produce curricular prescriptions but rather 'to extend the range of possibilities open to teachers, and to provide them with the most detailed research evidence on which their judgement can be exercised'.[12] Indeed, even when the Schools Council diverted its attention to the whole curriculum, in contrast to its preoccupation with individual areas or aspects, it maintained its non-recommendatory stance. *The Whole Curriculum* (1975) and *The Practical Curriculum* (1981) both sought to alert teachers to the complex issues that have to be taken into account in whole curriculum planning, but both eschewed the provision of ready-made answers. The Schools Council could therefore be seen as testifying vigorously to two principles – curriculum diversity and teacher control of the curriculum.

Over the years, the relationship between the DES and the Schools Council was characterized by what one commentator has described as 'captiousness'. The confidential Yellow Paper, indeed, dismissed the achievements of the Council as 'generally mediocre'. Reservations continued to be expressed about the power of teacher unions in the Council and there were those who felt that 'the curriculum was too important to be left to teachers'. In October 1981, the government's review of the Schools Council, conducted by Nancy Trenaman, concluded that, although the Council had been 'too political, too complicated and was over-stretched', it should nevertheless continue in existence, albeit in a slimmer form. Notwithstanding that report, conducted on behalf of the government, Sir Keith Joseph intimated in April 1982 that he proposed to terminate the Schools Council and to institute two new bodies – the School Curriculum Development Committee and the Secondary

Examinations Council – to carry out certain advisory functions relating to the curriculum on the one hand and examinations on the other. Sir Keith made it clear that the membership of the two new committees would comprise 'persons nominated by the Secretary of State for their fitness for this particular important responsibility'. That was the ministerial response to Nancy Trenaman's claim that a nominated body is consistent... with a system of central government control of curriculum and examinations'. In the Commons debate which followed the ministerial announcement, there were some MPs who welcomed the demise of 'a nonsensical curriculum development body that has done nothing but damage education over the years'. Others, however, objected to the replacement of the Schools Council by two unelected bodies; they saw dangers in the minister 'surrounding himself by people of one opinion', and in the 'centralized patronage' which was said to characterize the new arrangements, and they detected the eclipse of the values of curriculum pluralism for which the Schools Council had stood.[13] Indeed, one commentator has maintained that the very success of the Schools Council may have hastened its downfall. 'It is ironic that the Council's projects, most of them in one way or another emphasizing the value of local initiative, teacher involvement, school-level decision-making and various innovations in pedagogy such as inter-disciplinary teaching, should lead to heightened activity nationally to control the curriculum.'[14]

The Rise of the Assessment of Performance Unit (APU)

The APU was instituted by the DES in 1974 'to promote the development of methods of assessing and monitoring the achievements of children at school, and to seek to identify the incidence of under-achievement'. While the birth of the new unit was intimated in a document dealing with educational disadvantage and the educational needs of immigrants, the work of the unit has very clearly been concerned with the more general question of standards of achievement in schools. The proponents of the APU insisted that government is bound to maintain an interest in the quality of education in order to determine whether resources are being rationally deployed and whether the schools are serving the changing needs of pupils and of society. To that end, ways had to be found of monitoring the achievements of pupils.

The initial strategy planned by APU was to examine pupils' performances not in the recognized school subjects but in certain areas of development – the verbal, mathematical, scientific, ethical (subsequently changed to social and personal), aesthetic and physical. To date, surveys of achievement have been undertaken in language (with separate provision for foreign languages), mathematics, and science, but not in the three remaining areas. Jean Dawson, administrative head of APU, summarizes the achievements of the unit in these words:

We have now carried out successfully a total of 27 national surveys without undue disruption to schools, with the general support of the LEAs and teachers concerned... and with the enthusiastic cooperation of the children we have tested... Many of the suspicions which existed when the unit was set up, both about the political motivation for its creation and the likely effects of national monitoring on the curriculum, have been allayed (if not entirely put to rest) by the way in which the exercise has been carried out, by the sensitivities displayed by the monitoring teams, by the way in which groups of teachers up and down the country have been involved in the development, trialling and pre-testing of materials, and by the cool, impartial way in which the results have been presented.[15]

At the same time there were others who were resolutely opposed to the APU and its philosophy. They doubted whether valid measures of *all* of the areas of development could be devised; they maintained that the tests used would have a distorting and trivializing effect on pupils' learning ('this year's test becomes next year's curriculum'): they pointed to the possibility, notwithstanding the assurances that light sampling techniques would be deployed, that superficial comparisons would be made on the basis of inadequate evidence between areas and between schools; and they detected in the paraphernalia of mass testing associated with the APU the most sinister intrusion of central government into the work of the schools and the spectre of state-controlled curricula.

The Reform of the Examination System at 16+

It is widely acknowledged that the school examination system has exerted a powerful controlling effect on school curricula, even if, in more recent times, CSE (Mode 3) has allowed schools to play a significant role on the assessment of their own pupils. While, for many years, there has been discussion, in the Schools Council and elsewhere, about the reform of the examination system and the closer integration of CSE and GCE, Sir Keith Joseph gave notice in January 1984 of much more radical changes in the assessment of pupils at the end of compulsory schooling. He envisaged a shift, in line with modern educational thinking, away from a system in which pupils are assessed in relation to each other (a norm-referenced system) to one in which they would be assessed in relation to certain pre-specified criteria (a criterion-referenced system). In the latter, pupils succeed or 'pass' if they reach certain levels of competence: they are expected to give evidence of having reached a particular level of performance regardless of how they stand in relation to their peers. These features will characterize the new General Certificate of Secondary Education in England and Wales.

Sir Keith Joseph has intimated that 'national' criteria will be established in the main curriculum areas. This development will call for detailed research in order to establish clearly and unambiguously the skills and understandings testified by a given level of achievement. In this way, a system is expected to evolve in which teachers, employers, further and higher education, as well as pupils, can have confidence in what a given award actually means: it will indicate, clearly, what a pupil has been able to achieve. Whether or not a reform of this kind will lead, as Sir Keith Joseph maintained, to a general raising of standards of achievement, it has been interpreted as a further encroachment on the part of central government into what is taught and learned in schools. Indeed, if performance criteria are to be *national*, if they are to have currency throughout the system, and if they are to be as detailed and specific as the proponents of criterion-referenced testing insist, then this reform presages central intervention in the school curriculum of a most emphatic kind.

Government Policy on Standards

As has been noted, signs of a more active interest of central government in the school curriculum were apparent under the Labour administration in the 1970s. It is arguable that this interest has intensified under the present Conservative government. That government made standards in education a principal plank in its election platform and the action undertaken by that government in relation to curriculum and assessment is part of a wider and coherent strategy on standards in education. That strategy incorporates a review of the content of courses of initial teacher training; the establishment of a committee for the accreditation of courses of teacher education; an inquiry into the procedures for the external validation of courses in public sector higher education; an inquiry into selection for teaching; suggestions for regular staff appraisal of teachers, and the public reporting by Her Majesty's Inspectorate of their findings on visits to schools and colleges.

Technical and Vocational Education Initiative (TVEI)[16]

In November 1982 the Prime Minister announced the government's intention to launch TVEI, a five-year project to be conducted by the Manpower Services Commission 'to explore and test methods of organizing, managing and resourcing replicable programmes of general, technical and vocational education for young people between the ages of 14 and 18'. This initiative was designed to stimulate local authorities to mount full-time programmes which would be funded from central funds – to the extent of £400,000 per project – provided that they met certain centrally determined criteria relating to equal opportunities, progression, the specification of objectives, the balance between general, technical and vocational elements of programmes, planned work experience, and assessment. Projects in Scotland had, in addition, to demonstrate their compatibility with national curriculum development initiatives for 14–16 year-olds and 16–18 year-olds.

In the first year of its operation TVEI sponsored fourteen projects; in its second year a further 48 projects were mounted, including five in Scotland. In 1985 a further eleven programmes were introduced in England and Wales and one more in Scotland.

While the schemes are voluntary, in the sense that LEAs are not obliged to mount them and pupils are not compulsorily involved, and while the programmes demonstrate the variety that is to be expected from vigorous local initiatives, the significance of TVEI is unmistakable. As the responsibility of the Department of Employment, TVEI represents a determined government effort, practically by-passing the government department that has traditionally exercised responsibility for the schools and the school curriculum, to effect a swift and decisive orientation of the curriculum towards what is considered to be of immediate relevance to the skills and know-how required by a technological society.

Legislating for the National Curriculum

The discussion so far has sought to trace the progressive involvement of central government in the shaping of the school curriculum and to point to certain other government initiatives which undeniably strengthened the centralist trend. All of these developments and initiatives culminated in the government's consultation paper of July 1987 entitled *The National Curriculum 5-16*,[17] which gave notice that the Secretary of State proposed to introduce legislation to establish a national curriculum. The proposed national curriculum contained many familiar ingredients:

Mathematics
English   }   The Core
Science

Modern/Foreign Language (not in primary schools)
Technology
History
Geography
Art
Music
Physical Education

However, the paper went well beyond the delineation of a framework: it proposed the establishment in each subject area of 'attainment targets' for pupils at age 7, 11, 14 and 16, as well as 'programmes of study' setting out 'the overall content, knowledge, skills and processes relevant to today's needs which pupils should be taught'. Furthermore, 'nationally prescribed tests' would be administered at each of the age levels mentioned to determine the extent to which the prescribed targets had been achieved. Finally, the bodies created by Sir Keith Joseph - the School Curriculum Development

Committee and the Secondary Examinations Council – would be replaced by a National Curriculum Council and a School Examinations and Assessment Council, both appointed by the Secretary of State, with responsibility to offer him advice on the national curriculum and its assessment. These proposals, virtually unchanged as a result of the consultation process, were embodied in the Education Reform Bill placed before parliament in November 1987.

While these features of the proposed legislation were foreshadowed in earlier government papers and initiatives it is worth exploring why it was decided to break from the practice of national consensus seeking through discussion and persuasion and to introduce legislation. There are four sets of consideration that are relevant in this connection.

In the first place, the Conservative government had just been re-elected, in June 1987, with a substantial majority. The opportunity afforded by a third term in office is thought to have induced a 'triumphalist' determination to effect even more remarkable and radical transformations in the social order than were brought about since it first took office in 1979. And what more radical initiative in education could be mounted than one which decisively disturbed the traditional partnership between central and local government in the management of education and which exploded once and for all the myth of 'the secret garden of the curriculum'?

A second set of factors justifying legislation are adduced in the consultation paper itself. There it is maintained that, despite a decade of public discussion on the curriculum and the existence of widespread agreement on its main features, there were significant variations in practice which needed to be eliminated in the interests of equipping all young people 'with the knowledge, skills and understandings that they need for adult life and employment'. Legislation clearly was seen as the only way to bring about that objective quickly. It was also seen as a way of raising standards of attainment: the specification of targets and the systematic assessment of pupils' work on a national basis were thought to constitute a challenge to schools and teachers to raise their expectations, and to channel their efforts to bring about enhanced standards in pupils in the key areas represented by the national curriculum. In this way, individual schools and their teachers would be made more closely accountable for the education they provide since their work will be directly assessable against the results of other schools in the locality and against the national standards. These developments reflect the government's acceptance of the importance of education as the key instrument in the liberation of human talent and as the principal agent of the country's economic regeneration. Since education was such a critical service it was a responsibility of government to determine its content and to ensure that it was effective.

The third feature that needs to be considered in contextualizing the national curriculum legislation is the government's attitude towards local authorities. While the legislation is clearly to be seen as evidence of a government's entitlement to legislate in connection with a national responsibility, it is also interpretable as evidence of the government's impatience with local authorities. There had been a decade of consultation and as recently as 1986 an Education Act had required local authorities to devise policy documentation in relation to the curriculum and its delivery. Even that strategy, however, had still left too much responsibility with authorities. The legislation reflected a judgement that local authorities could not deliver what the national interest required.

It is possible to see the national curriculum legislation as part of the government's strategy to reduce the power of local authorities. Indeed, the years since 1979 have witnessed a continuing struggle between local and national government. While that struggle tended to centre on financial matters – the government's commitment to effect reductions in public expenditure in opposition to local authority commitment to the enhancement of public services – what was at issue was the power of local authorities in relation to the power of central government. Significantly, the Education Reform Bill contains two measures that will curtail local authority powers still further. The first of these will require local authorities to delegate to governing bodies of schools very considerable responsibility for financial management and the appointment of staff. The second allows schools to 'opt out' of local authority control altogether and to be funded directly by central government. At first sight these measures appear to be interestingly decentralist in the sense that they devolve power and responsibility to the local level. In that sense they might be seen to be moving in a different direction from the strongly centralist initiatives in connection with the national curriculum. However, these various measures are perfectly consistent in the sense that they encroach decisively on areas on which local authorities exercise responsibility and, since the Secretary of State will have a key role in connection with financial delegation and 'opting out', the measures must be said to reinforce the centralism which is reflected most obviously in the measures to the national curriculum.

Finally, it is necessary to see the national curriculum legislaton in relation to the teaching profession. For two years prior to 1987 there was unprecedented industrial action by teachers which seriously dislocated the educational service. That dispute, which concerned, among other things, teachers' pay and conditions of service, was sustained partly because teachers could exploit contractual arrangements which were imprecise. There have been three government initiatives which were designed to obviate any similar disruption in the future. The Secretary of State has made regulations specifying teachers' contractual obligations in a comprehensive list of duties; he has decided to scrap the long-established machinery in which teachers' pay and conditions were negotiated and has assumed temporary powers to determine these himself; and he has introduced a national curriculum. The last of these, with its prespecified targets, its programmes of study, and its national testing will exercise a powerful constraint on teachers' work. While the consultation paper claims that 'the legislation should leave full scope for professional judgement' and while it insists that the law will provide a framework, 'not a strait-jacket', there are many who will see the legislation as the culmination of a strategy intended to whip teachers into line.

Developments in Scotland

Scotland is a compact educational entity with long experience of strongly centralized modes of operation. The effectiveness of these centralized procedures is demonstrated in the management of the major programme of changes in curriculum and assessment currently taking place in Scotland.

Two national committees were established in 1974, one by the Consultative Committee on the curriculum, the nominated body responsible for advising the Secretary of State on curriculum matters, to examine the structure of the curriculum for 14-16 year olds (the Munn Committee) and the other by the Secretary of State himself to consider assessment at 16+ (the Dunning Committee). Both committees reported in 1977. Munn advocated a core plus options curriculum pattern, which required pupils to undertake work in each of eight 'modes of activity' as follows:

- linguistic/literary;
- mathematics;
- social studies;
- scientific;
- religious education;
- moral education;
- aesthetic studies;
- physical education.

Dunning recommended a complex pattern of 'assessment for all', covering the whole age range and enabling pupils to reach one of three levels of achievement – merit, general or foundation – in each area of study. Following extensive feasibility studies into timetabling arrangements and the technical aspects of the assessment proposals, the Secretary of State produced his response to the reports in 1980 in the shape of a circular from SED (No. 10/93) which included these words:

> All schools are asked to adopt the curriculum framework provided by the eight modes of study provided by the Munn Committee. Within that framework schools and education authorities are in the best position to judge the particular form which the curriculum should take in the light of each school's individual circumstances and the needs of its pupils. Nevertheless, there are certain overriding priorities and the Secretary of State considers that it is essential that all pupils in the third and fourth years of secondary education should study English, Mathematics and Science.

Thus, a national curriculum framework was introduced without recourse to legislation: the Secretary of State merely exercised a traditional entitlement to influence. The Secretary of State's authority on this matter has been accepted, not out of docility or in the belief that the Secretary of State for Scotland is infallible in curriculum matters: it has been accepted because it is very obviously based on a clear national consensus. That consensus was reflected in the recommendations of the Munn Committee itself, which were, in turn, based on the evidence submitted to the committee. It was also reflected in the public discussion that took place following the publication of the report. Without probing too deeply into the reasons for the emergence of that national consensus – and the cogency of the Munn report's argument and the compactness of Scotland as an educational entity, cannot be disregarded in this connection – the existence of that consensus is beyond question and it undoubtedly made the introduction of a national curriculum framework a relatively unproblematic matter. The Secretary of State's announcement reflected what, in the light of the consultation and public discussion, local authorities and schools wished to see.

When the Secretary of State endorsed the curriculum framework proposed by Munn he also intimated that the assessment proposals foreshadowed in the Dunning report would be implemented. After further piloting of appropriate curriculum and assessment materials the Secretary of State intimated in 1982 that there would be a phased implementation of the proposals, beginning in August 1984. That decision called for the establishment of joint working parties, for each of the subject areas, with responsibility for devising guidelines for the new syllabuses and specifying the detailed criteria relating to their assessment. The activities of these joint working parties was extensive and entailed the substantial involvement of teachers in Scotland in curriculum development work. The intention clearly was to make sure that guidelines developed reflected enterprising classroom practice. Besides, within the central guidelines, schools and teachers themselves were expected to exercise their skills and responsibilities for determining what pupils should learn.

Unfortunately for the government's programme, for most of 1985 and 1986, Scottish teachers conducted a massive programme of industrial action which seriously disrupted the work of the schools. Besides, since the industrial action involved a boycott of curriculum development, the carefully planned implementation of Standard Grade, as the reforms came to be known, was completely undermined. Scottish teachers, like their counterparts south of the border, were seeking better pay and conditions; but the Scottish dispute was also a massive protest at the rapid rate of educational change and at the way in which teachers felt they were expected to carry forward developments without adequate support. The longer the dispute continued the more officialdom in Scottish education recognized that support had to be provided. That took two forms. In the first place, a working party set up to simplify the complex technicalities of the original assessment proposals generated a system which was more intelligible and rational. Secondly, before the dispute ended, for each major area of the curriculum there was established a central support group with responsibility for developing exemplar and other materials relating to the Standard Grade programme. Some of these central support groups worked in collaboration with local support groups of teachers and others in an effort to ensure that the centrally endorsed materials were rooted in classroom experience.

The agreement which marked the end of the dispute late in 1986 concluded that, since the preparation of teaching materials to support curriculum development had been a major burden on individual teachers, henceforth curriculum development should be supported by exemplars and other teacher materials prepared by secondees and voluntary working groups. It is difficult not to see in that agreement what has come to be called the 'cascade' model of curriculum development: materials are prepared centrally and passed down the line for the classroom functionaries to implement. One critic has described the model as 'an unholy alliance of enthusiasts for strong management with a sufficient number of apathetic teachers'.[18]

There are two other developments in Scotland that require to be highlighted. The first concerns the government's 16+ Action Plan. Envisaged as a comprehensive restructuring of educational provision in further education colleges into 40-hour modules, it is rapidly finding its way into the work of the secondary school. What is noteworthy in the present context is that it was an initiative that was energetically directed by SED and it involved the preparation centrally of curriculum materials for every area of work.

The second development represents an even more emphatic instance of the growth of government influence on the curriculum in Scotland. In November 1987 the government produced a consultation paper entitled *Curriculum and Assessment in Scotland: a policy for the 90s*[19]. The paper proposed for each area of the curriculum for pupils 5–14 'a nationally agreed set of guidelines setting out the aims of study, the content to be covered, and the objectives to be achieved'. In addition, there will be national testing of pupils at age 8 and age 12 in language and mathematics. If required, legislation will be invoked to give effect to the changes.

The appearance of the Scottish document at the same time as the appearance of the national curriculum legislation in England and Wales can be interpreted as evidence of the government's determination to bring the educational system of Scotland into close alignment with that of England and Wales and to exercise strong control over what that educational system is expected to deliver.

Conclusion

The developments traced in this chapter demonstrate very clearly a significant shift in the control of the school curriculum both north and south of the border: whereas responsibility for the nature and structure of the curriculum once rested with local authorities and individual schools it will now rest with central government. Moreover, that control, in England and

Wales at least, will be reinforced by legislation.

What is remarkable is that this heavily interventionist stance was developed by a government committed 'to rolling back the frontiers of the state' and to the values of consumerism – 'parents know best'. Indeed, the reform bill which marks the full extent of government control has been heralded by the Minister, Kenneth Baker, as a parents charter, maximizing parental choice in education. Apparently, parents know what is best for their children, but not as much as the Minister!

While the balance of power has decisively shifted, it is worth considering some of the educational implications of the transformation this chapter has attempted to describe. Throughout the period under discussion, successive government initiatives stimulated vigorous public and professional debate, since even the early tentative moves were treated with the suspicion that they presaged even more decisive government 'interference' in what was a local or professional matter. Reviewing a very protracted and at times heated public discussion it is possible to identify three major concerns. It is necessary to consider these in relation to the legislative position in England and Wales and the *de facto* position in Scotland.

The first of these has its roots in the pupil-centred view of education. While this view has various formulations its central stance is that *the* purpose of education is to enable pupils to develop with deeper insight and sophistication activities which *they* value or find interesting in ways and contexts which *they* find amenable. On this view, educational systems need to make maximum provision for pupil choice, for curriculum negotiation, and for pupils themselves to determine the lines of their own educational development. Government control or determination of the curriculum, it has been claimed, is a threat to pupil-centred education of this kind. At best, it could kill interest in learning: at worst it could foster the alienation of the young.

The second concern relates to the impact of a government controlled curriculum on social pluralism. Many see life in the modern context as being characterized by wide diversity. Ours is thought to be a multi-faith, multi-ethnic and multi-cultural society, one in which diversity of life-style flourishes and which tolerates and fosters social and individual differences. Schools, on this view, should protect diversity; they should reflect local variety and the features of widely differing neighbourhoods and subcultures. By contrast, the argument runs, a nationally prescribed curriculum, rigidly dispensed to all, will be a force for dull uniformity in which the vitality and diversity of personal and social experience is homogenized.

Thirdly, the move towards a national curriculum was resisted most strongly by those, mainly teachers and other educationists, who claimed that the nature and scope of the school curriculum was a professional and not a political matter. They defended the entitlement of teachers, by virtue of their education and training if not their professional standing, to shape the learning experience of pupils and to devise a curriculum suited to the characteristics of their own pupils. That assertion of professional autonomy was thought to be reinforced by studies which stressed that curriculum development should be school-based, rooted in the professional context of teachers rather than in distant centres such as Whitehall or Edinburgh. Teachers, it was felt, were the guardians of a politically free curriculum: if they lost their entitlement to control the learning experiences of pupils, not only would their own professionalism be undermined, but, worse, schools could easily become the agents for transmitting 'state-approved knowledge'.

How have these concerns been affected by the government's assumption of control in curriculum matters? Arguably, the concerns highlighted could be allayed if the government initiatives were concerned with the establishment of a national curriculum framework only. Thus, it is conceivable that, within such a framework, pupils could enjoy considerable opportunities for choice, for curriculum negotiation and for pupil-centred learning. It is equally possible that within such a framework schools and communities could offer curricula that reflected the responsiveness and diversity that many value. Finally, if teachers were left to enjoy full responsibility for the specific content and teaching strategies to be deployed within each of the major categories of the national curriculum framework, there would be no infringement of teachers' professional autonomy and the curriculum could be protected from unjustified political interference. That is to say, a national curriculum framework is logically not incompatible with pupil-centred learning, with the protection of cultural diversity, and with the professional autonomy of teachers. However, it is clear that ministerial control will extend well beyond the determination of a national curriculum framework. On both sides of the border there is a clear government commitment to the development of curriculum guidelines, and the specification of curriculum objectives and content in each subject area, all of which will require the approval of a central government agency. That is to say, the initiatives that are under way, far from alleviating concerns repeatedly expressed over the years, appear to be confirming the worst suspicions of teachers and other commentators. The defenders of the new arrangements will no doubt claim that there is still reasonable scope for pupil-centred learning, for cultural diversity, and for the exercise of professional autonomy, even within a nationally determined curriculum framework. It is too easy to slip into a mood of depression at the outset of what promises to be a period of very significant change in education but, in relation to the concerns identified earlier, it would have to be said that the omens are not propitious.

Notes

1   LAWTON, Denis (1980) *The Politics of the School Curriuclum*. London: Routledge & Kegan Paul, pp. 15–16.
2   SIR KEITH JOSEPH (1984) speech to North of England Education Conference, Sheffield, as reported in *Times Educational Supplement*, 13 January.
3   CALLAGHAN, James (1976) 'Towards a National Debate', speech at Ruskin College, October 1976, as reported in *Education*, 22 October.
4   Quoted in DEVLIN, Tim and WARNOCK, Mary (1977) *What must we teach?* London: Temple Smith.

5 Ibid., p. 11.
6 HOLT, Maurice (1983) *Curriculum Workshop: An Introduction to Whole Curriculum Planning.* London, Routledge & Kegan Paul, p. 21.
7 DES (DEPARTMENT OF EDUCATION AND SCIENCE/WELSH OFFICE) (1979) *Local Authority Arrangements for the School Curriculum*, Report on the Circular 14.77 Review. London: HMSO.
8 DES (DEPARTMENT OF EDUCATION AND SCIENCE) (1984) *English from 5–16.* London: HMSO.
9 DES (DEPARTMENT OF EDUCATION AND SCIENCE) (1985) *Science 5–16: A Statement of Policy.* London: HMSO.
10 *The Sunday Times*, 31 March 1985, p. 17.
11 DES (DEPARTMENT OF EDUCATION AND SCIENCE) (1985) *Better Schools.* London: HMSO.
12 THE SCHOOLS COUNCIL (1975) Working Paper 53, *The Whole Curriculum 13–16*, London: Evans/Methuen Educational.
13 *Hansard*, 22 April 1982.
14 SKILBECK, Malcolm (1984) 'Curriculum Evaluation at the National Level', in SKILBECK, Malcolm (ed.), *Evaluating the Curriculum in the Eighties.* London: Hodder & Stoughton.
15 DAWSON, Jean (1984), 'The Work of the Assessment of Performance Unit', in SKILBECK, Malcolm (ed.), *Evaluating the Curriculum in the Eighties.* London: Hodder & Stoughton.
16 *TVEI Review 1984* (1984). London: Manpower Services Commission.
17 DES (DEPARTMENT OF EDUCATION AND SCIENCE/WELSH OFFICE) (1987) *The National Curriculum 5–16*, a consultation document, July.
18 SMYTH, Sydney (1987) 'An Ending', in *Teaching English*, Vol. 20, No. 3, Autumn.
19 SED (SCOTTISH EDUCATION DEPARTMENT) (1987) *Curriculum and Assessment in Scotland: a policy for the 90's*, November.

1.2 | The National Curriculum and Improving Secondary Schools
David H. Hargreaves

A characteristic feature of educational concerns in the 1980s has been quality and the raising of standards, especially in secondary education, combined with a political determination to introduce speedy reforms. Among the many reasons for this are, first, a belief that the spread of the secondary comprehensive school has led to a fall in standards or has failed to lead to the heralded improvement in quality; and secondly, a raising of expectations, among politicians, parents, employers and young people, about what young people, in the light of growing youth unemployment, should be expected to achieve by the end of the period of compulsory education, especially in preparation for life, work and further/higher education.

It is against such a backcloth that the aims and purposes of both the government's national curriculum proposals and the Inner London Education Authority's *Improving Secondary Schools* must be set. From the time of James Callaghan's famous Ruskin speech in 1976, an enormous amount of documentation on the curriculum has issued from the DES and HMI (Chapter 1.1 offers a brief overview of some of the key events and documents). Teachers and LEAs could not keep track of this deluge, little of which can now be recalled by practitioners in any detail. Very few, if any, anticipated in 1976 that the period 1976–88 would lead to a radical rethinking about both the content and the control of the school curriculum and of the relationship between central government and the local education authorities.

The first warning bell was sounded in July 1977 in *Education in Schools: a Consultative Document* issued when Shirley Williams was Secretary of State. The vague and confused distribution of powers in relation to the curriculum between the various partners – the individual school, the LEA, and central government – is noted. Issues which were to influence subsequent events and eventually lead to a national curriculum are specified: first, that the curriculum is overcrowded and the timetable overloaded; secondly, that pupils who move from one school to another are penalized because of curricular variations between schools; thirdly, that curricular arrangements within each school tend to give rise to unequal curricular opportunities for pupils; fourthly, that the school curriculum is not sufficiently relevant for life in a modern industrial society; and fifthly, that there are evident weaknesses in existing assessment procedures and methods of recording pupil progress.

In November 1977 the DES issued Circular 14/77 which called on LEAs to review their curricular arrangements and report to the Secretary of State within seven months their answers to fifty detailed and challenging questions. The results, published in 1979, demonstrate the confusion and disarray about the curriculum at the local level. LEAs showed substantial variations in their approach to curriculum policies and their lack of systematic knowledge of what went on in their schools. The picture to emerge is one in which an LEA typically delegated most curricular matters to the individual school, with the advice and support of local inspectors/advisers. ILEA's own response was probably not unusual. There follows some examples of the ILEA answers to the questions of Circular 14/77, with a comment from me.

Q. What procedures have the Authority established to enable them to carry out their curricular responsibilities under Section 23 of the Education Act 1944?

A. The Authority delegates to governors of primary and secondary schools oversight of the curriculum, and control of it to the head teacher in consultation with his staff...

Comment: The procedures are vague and in practice delegated almost entirely to schools.

Q. What systematic arrangements, if any, have the Authority established for the collection of information about the curriculum offered by schools in their area?

A. The Authority relies mainly on the inspectorate for information...

Comment: There are no *systematic* procedures for collecting and reporting regularly on such information to provide a basis on which the Authority might provide coherent curriculum policies.

Q. How do the Authority help schools to decide on the relative emphasis they should give to particular aspects of the curriculum, especially the promotion of literacy and numeracy?

A. The Authority's main help is given through the inspectorate...

Comment: Though the inspectorate gives advice, it is unclear what this is, whether it is taken and what happens if it is ignored.

Q. What contribution have the Authority made to the consideration of the problem faced by secondary schools of providing suitable subject options for older pupils while avoiding the premature dropping of curricular elements regarded as essential for all pupils?

A. The Authority believes that in addition to English, mathematics, RE and PE it is desirable that all pupils should take science in some form until the age of 16. Social studies and aesthetic subjects should also be included. Inspectors have responsibility for ensuring a suitable curriculum and they provide relevant INSET (Inservice Education for Teachers) for senior staff.

Comment: Although there is a commitment to a broad and balanced curriculum, there are no means of ensuring its implementation to prevent premature dropping of important curriculum elements.

In short, ILEA, no doubt like the vast majority of LEAs, had some sensible ideas about a broad and balanced curriculum, but delegated the responsibility to schools and had developed no systematic means of monitoring school curriculum policies and practice or of taking action where schools deviate from the LEA approach to the curriculum. LEA responses to Circular 14/77 were written with sufficient and skilled vagueness that the flaws and weaknesses were not easy to detect; and a similar picture of diversity and confusion over the curriculum emerged from the HMI secondary survey published in 1979.

Circular 14/77 without doubt aroused some LEAs to their curricular responsibilities. The ILEA published its own excellent statement on the curriculum for pupils aged 5–16 in March 1981. But it did not institute systematic means of monitoring school curricula to check on whether or not inspectorate advice was being followed, nor did it devise systematic means for exerting pressure on schools to follow this advice. In other words, while many LEAs became greatly sophisticated in their thinking about the school curriculum, the variety of curriculum practice between schools remained largely unchallenged and the autonomy of the individual school remained sacrosanct. The way was left open for the initiative to be taken at the national level, since LEAs, both individually and collectively, failed to respond to the national call for change.

This is not the place to summarize the rest of the curriculum debate and many important documents, whether from HMI (*Curriculum 11-16* in 1977, *A View of the Curriculum* in 1980) or the DES (*A Framework for the School Curriculum* in 1980 or *The Organization and Content of the 5-16 Curriculum* in 1984): Chapter 1.1 provides some detail. The requirement of the Education (No. 2) Act 1986 Section 17 that each LEA should formulate a written policy on the range and balance of the school curriculum, and then that each school should consider but not necessarily follow that LEA policy, may be regarded as a brief, and confusing, interlude in the movement towards a national curriculum. The more immediate background to government thinking behind the national curriculum is to be found in *Better Schools* (March 1985) – published precisely one year after *Improving Secondary Schools* and with a curiously similar title – and its introductory paragraphs:

> The government's principal aims for all sectors of education are first, to raise standards at all levels of ability; and second, since education is an investment in the nation's future, to secure the best possible return from the resources which are found for it . . . But the government believes that, not least in the light of what is being achieved in other countries, the standards now generally attained by our pupils are neither as good as they can be, nor as good as they need to be if young people are to be equipped for the world of the twenty-first century.

Better Schools made it clear that the government intended to 'take the lead in promoting national agreement about the purposes and content of the curriculum'.

The means of promoting consensus on the curriculum proved to be *The*

National Curriculum 5-16: a consultation document (hereafter TNC), where it is argued that the national curriculum will help to raise standards by ensuring that all pupils follow a broad and balanced curriculum throughout the compulsory period; by setting clear objectives of what pupils should be expected to achieve; by ensuring that all pupils, irrespective of their sex, ethnic origins or geographical location have access to the same curriculum offer; and by checking on performance and progress at various stages. In addition there is an aim to enhance public accountability of schools and teachers by making the results of regular assessments available to parents and public, not only at the individual level for the parent, but more widely in terms of the achievement of schools and local education authorities. The national curriculum proposals form the first part of the Education Reform Bill, which also contains proposals in relation to open enrolments, financial delegation to schools, the establishment of grant maintained schools and various proposals for higher education.[1]

Improving Secondary Schools (hereafter ISS) is set within the context of the ILEA's determination to tackle the issue of under-achievement by pupils, within a framework of a commitment to enhancing equality of opportunity in relation to sex, race and class: particular attention was to be paid by the committee of enquiry to low achievers and disaffected pupils. (Although ISS is concerned with the 11–16 age group, a later report *Improving Primary Schools* – the Thomas Report – was issued to cover the whole 5–16 age range.)

While there is important common ground between the two documents arising from a shared commitment to raising standards by the national (Conservative) government and local (Labour) government, there are significant differences in approach. TNC consists of government proposals but these were not preceded by any kind of inquiry or the involvement of professional educationists or practitioners. Despite the long history of previous documents from the DES and HMI, dating from Callaghan's famous Ruskin speech of 1976, TNC betrays little evidence of direct contributions by HMI. By contrast, ISS originated in an independent committee of inquiry, chaired by an outside academic and including ILEA inspectors and teachers as well as representatives of industry and trade unions. TNC was given an astonishingly brief period of consultation while teachers were on their summer holidays in 1987; ISS was the subject of a year's consultation in 1984–85 – perhaps too long. Most important, TNC is clearly concerned with curriculum and assessment, somewhat artificially separated from the life and work of the school as a whole. ISS is concerned with school organization, as well as curriculum and assessment, and devotes substantial chapters to the teacher-parent partnership and to staff development for teachers. In this sense ISS is much more holistic in its conception than TNC. ISS believes that standards will be raised, not just by reforms in curriculum and assessment, but by making schools generally more effective. It is for this reason that ISS, in line with HMI views in *Ten Good Schools* (1977), places such emphasis on the quality of leadership. For ISS, the head teacher is the key to improvement; the head's capacity to energize staff and build upon known good practice (which ISS carefully sought to identify) is a prerequisite of school improvement. TNC believes that imposed reform of the curriculum and assessment, by which schools become more accountable to the community, will serve as a powerful device to enhance school effectiveness by increasing the external pressure on the head and staff of underachieving schools.

The Curriculum

TNC adduces arguments for a broad and balanced curriculum but implies that there is no possible justification for the pattern of 'small core plus elaborate option scheme' that is commonly found in secondary schools. ISS sets out in great detail (paragraphs 3.9.3 to 3.9.16) both arguments. In brief, the arguments for a large optional element in the fourth and fifth years are:

1   pupils are able and mature enough to make choices at the age of 13/14;
2   choices are essential to maintain pupil motivation and avoid disaffection;
3   there is little evidence of parental or pupil opposition to option schemes;
4   option schemes prevent ossification of the curriculum and encourage innovation;
5   there are insufficient teachers to make subjects such as science, CDT and languages compulsory;
6   a common curriculum will mean a return to the grammar school curriculum.

The main arguments in favour of a larger common curriculum are:

1   option schemes lead many pupils to follow a narrow and imbalanced curriculum;
2   choices are made by pupils on an irrational, peer-influenced and sex-stereotyped basis;
3   there is hidden selection within option schemes;
4   in practice many pupils have their choices denied;
5   pupils should keep options open for post-16 education and not be denied opportunities at later stages;
6   a common curriculum eases movement of pupils between different secondary schools;
7   pupil motivation is maintained in any subject by high quality teaching.

The Committee concluded, on balance, in favour of the second set of arguments.

TNC has been strongly attacked for taking a very narrow and old-fashioned view of the curriculum as a collection of subjects; and it is certainly true that the more sophisticated thinking of HMI on these matters appears to have been disregarded. However, both TNC and ISS produced controversial curriculum suggestions for the fourth and fifth years (pupils aged 14-16), as Table 2.1 shows. Both consider the curriculum in terms of *subjects*, and were open to the criticism that this is an outmoded view of the curriculum. It is, however, the way in which the vast majority of secondary schools construct their timetables. TNC divides subjects into three types: *core* (English, maths and science); *foundation*; and *additional* (or optional).

Table 2.1   A comparison of curriculum proposals made by DES (1987) and improving secondary schools (1984)

TNC	%	ISS	%
English	10	English language and literature	12.5
maths	10	mathematics	12.5
combined sciences	10–20	science	10
technology	10	at least one technical subject	10
art/music/drama/design	10	at least one aesthetic subject	10
modern foreign language	10	(optional)	
history/geography/or history *or* geography	10	(optional)	
physical education	5	**personal and social education; religious education**	7.5
Total	75–85		62.5

ISS also has three types: *compulsory*; *constrained options* (aesthetic – art, music, dance, drama; craft design and technology; computer studies); and *free options*. There is common ground in relation to English, mathematics, science, and technology. TNC has a more limited view of arts subjects than ISS (indeed drama disappears in the Bill). While languages and history/geography and PE are foundation subjects in TNC, they are free options in ISS. Religious education and personal and social education (broadly defined to include 16 areas such as careers education, community studies, education for parenthood and family life, health education, mass media, moral, political and economic education) are compulsory in ISS: in TNC religious education is assumed (but later given status as a 'basic' subject after pressure from the churches) and elements of personal and social education are to be 'taught through other subjects', though no advice is given on how this might be achieved. In TNC the core and foundation subjects are held to apply throughout secondary education, and with the exception of a modern foreign language, to the primary phase also.[2]

For both TNC and ISS the suggested time allocations have been a source of controversy. TNC, it is said, leaves far too little time for optional and additional subjects, namely 10-20 per cent. The new Act will not lay down time specifications, but there is little doubt that the national testing procedures will act as a heavy constraint on time allocations made in schools, potentially to the detriment of optional/additional subjects as well as on foundation subjects which will not be the subject of national testing – the arts, religious education and physical education. ISS is more modest than TNC in its curricular prescriptions. The recommendation was that at least 62.5 per cent of time should be compulsorily allocated. Within this compulsory allocation, there is room for some autonomous decision-making by individual schools. For instance, schools might make one of the four arts subjects compulsory or might institute modular or combined arts courses to cover two or more of the arts subject. In the technical constrained options, schools might make CDT compulsory or offer a choice between CDT, computer studies or some other technical/vocational subject. The view was taken that, since ISS offered a five-year programme of implementation, the proposals should be ones which could be implemented within that time-scale. Naturally there were protests from some ILEA teachers of languages, history, geography, home economics and physical education that their subjects were not to be made compulsory in the fourth and fifth years: such subjects, it was held, were thereby accorded a lower status. But the assumption was that these matters should continue to be a subject of discussion and debate within the ILEA, leading to new proposals after the five-year implementation period. Take, for instance, the case of languages other than English. To have proposed that a language should be compulsory throughout the five-year period would undoubtedly have led to difficulties in recruiting sufficient teachers and have entailed a massive increase in the teaching of French. Yet in fact ILEA pupils represent 171 different home languages and many pupils are bilingual or multilingual. The issue of the maintenance and development of these home languages, which include many West European languages as well as those of Asia and Africa, is a real one. A multilingual community requires a more sophisticated language policy than merely enlarged provision for French. TNC does not help here, by talking of 'a modern foreign language'; and one's fears of too narrow an approach seem confirmed by the Bill's reference to 'a modern foreign language specified in an order of the Secretary of State'.

There does seem to be general agreement amongst teachers that the school curriculum should be broad and balanced for all pupils. But attempts to define breadth and balance rapidly meet a difficult problem: *all* subjects wish to claim compulsory status; however, it then proves difficult to fit them all into reasonable time allocations. As the Scots noted in their report on secondary education:

> A curriculum becomes congested precisely as a book case does with the passing of the years. New interests emerge, fresh claims are admitted, but old titles are seldom revised and still more rarely withdrawn.[3]

That was written in 1946, since when pressure on the curriculum has vastly increased. We are, it seems, some distance from reaching a consensus on the contents of the school curriculum. Does TNC impose a solution too prematurely? It has been argued earlier that the LEAs, both individually and collectively, failed to generate greater consensus on the school curriculum, but were there not alternative means of bringing together the various partners (the LEAs, schools and their teachers, governors and parents, industry and commerce; the churches) to reach an agreement?

At the same time, there is always likely to be a gap between *reaching* a consensus on the curriculum and *implementing* the consensus once it has been reached. The record at the LEA level is, as we have seen earlier, not a promising one, since LEAs have been much more effective at producing curriculum policies than at monitoring and implementing them at the school level. ISS provides a useful case in point. The ISS curriculum proposals for the fourth and fifth years have been summarized in Table 2.1. By the end of the academic year 1986–87 I instituted, in my capacity as Chief Inspector, a survey of the implementation of the proposals that the Authority *commended* to schools and their governing bodies. In my annual report to the Authority in May 1988 – and ILEA is the only LEA which receives an annual report from its Chief Inspector – I commented on the implemention of the ISS curriculum proposals, that in years four and five science should be compulsory; at least one arts course should be followed; and a technical subject should be a compulsory option. By 1987 10 per cent of secondary schools met all three criteria; 28 per cent fulfilled two criteria; 36 per cent fulfilled one criterion only; and the remaining 25 per cent fulfilled none. It is evident that a relatively small proportion of schools had either chosen or felt able to implement the ISS recommended curriculum and that most schools were not following a broad and balanced curriculum for all pupils.

ISS focused on the fourth and fifth years because it is in these years that pupils tend to narrow their curriculum, as schools frequently have a very small core with large option schemes, with the result that some pupils pursue a curriculum that is neither broad nor balanced. ISS assumed that the first three years would continue with a broad curriculum and would include subjects (such as home economics) which at present few schools consider to be compulsory in the fourth and fifth years. Of course it requires skill in curriculum organization to cover the necessary ground, for example by use of modular schemes and carousels. ISS thus offers a more evolutionary approach to curriculum than does TNC, whose exceptionally tight prescriptions, because they require legislation, will be difficult to change. There is a powerful argument that if there has to be a national curriculum it must leave ample room for variation at the level of the local education authority as well as in the individual school. It is perhaps through experimentation and experience at these lower levels in the government of education that we shall best find imaginative solutions to the problem of getting 'the curriculum gallon into the timetable pint pot' as well as moving towards a greater (and yet flexible) consensus on which ideally a national curriculum should rest. That development work or experiments which involve modification of the national curriculum in a school will require the approval of the Secretary of State may well serve to inhibit some forms of school-based curriculum innovation. There are real dangers, as ISS noted, of curriculum ossification.

The ISS curriculum proposals aroused less controversy in ILEA than those of TNC in part because of the very different curriculum philosophy within which the proposals for the fourth and fifth years were set. A substantial section of the report is devoted to the *curriculum as a whole* and to whole curriculum planning. It examines the considerable difficulties, both intellectual and practical, of taking seriously HMI's view of the curriculum as needing to be broad, balanced and coherent. Particular attention was paid to the concept of *coherence*, that is, the way in which the different parts of the curriculum, the subjects, hang together in the experience of pupils so that the curriculum has meaning for them. It is perhaps significant that DES documents retained the concepts of breadth and balance, but dropped the notion of coherence in favour of two new concepts, relevance and differentiation; these are, of course, very important curriculum concepts, but they are not the same as, or an adequate substitute for, coherence. It is this concept which ISS held to be fundamental to increasing the commitment and achievement of pupils who now underachieve, especially many working-class pupils. In the same spirit, ISS drew attention to the importance of HMI work on 'areas of experience' which seem to have had so little influence on TNC. Areas of experience are a valuable heuristic device for teachers in thinking about the curriculum. In themselves, they do not lead directly to the construction of a subject timetable; but there is no doubt that, under the influence of HMI and some important academic writers on the curriculum, much teacher curriculum thinking has been considerably advanced in the decade since 1976. Whilst most secondary schools continue to be organized in terms of a timetable of subjects, the background thinking of teachers has become wider, less conventional and less secure in terms of single subjects. The outcome has been a major advance in thinking about the curriculum in holistic terms, in which curriculum planning is done not just in terms of subjects and their traditional labels, but also in terms of areas of experience, skills and processes as well as knowledge, and personal and affective aspects as well as the cognitive. ISS sought to add to this by what has become perhaps the most famous aspect of the report, its philosophy of achievement as expressed in what it called the *four aspects of achievement*, namely

Aspect 1 – the retention of propositional knowledge and the capacity to reproduce it in written form.

Aspect 2 – the capacity to apply knowledge; the practical as well as the theoretical; the oral as well as the written.

Aspect 3 – personal and social skills; autonomy and independence; working in teams and leadership.

Aspect 4 – motivation and commitment; interest and perseverance; initiative and enterprise.

All four aspects of achievement should penetrate all areas of curriculum, ISS argued; and all four aspects should be celebrated, rewarded and recorded.

And it is here, on matters of assessment, that TNC and ISS grow further apart.

Assessment

The more controversial aspect of TNC concerns the establishment of programmes of study for each subject, with attainment targets for the three core subjects and some foundation subjects. These targets, says TNC

> will establish what children should normally be expected to know, understand and be able to do at around the ages of 7, 11, 14 and 16 and will enable each child to be measured against established national standards.

It is envisaged that much of the assessment will be done by teachers as an integral part of their normal classroom work. This age-related assessment is thus intended to complement the usual assessment procedures of a school. However,

> at the heart of the assessment process there will be nationally prescribed tests done by all pupils to supplement the individual teachers' assessments... The actual tests and other forms of assessment will be developed and piloted by various organizations on behalf of the government.

A task group on assessment and testing (TGAT) was quickly established and then also two subject working groups, for science and mathematics, to suggest programmes of study and attainment targets. Each of these three groups has made a first report at the time this Chapter was written. Parents will have a right to know, at each testing age, pupils' achievements in each subject in comparison with the range of marks of pupils in the same class. Parents will also be able to know the school's performance in relation to other schools in the same LEA and how each LEA performs in relation to other LEAs. This, it is said, will enable parliament and public to monitor national standards and improvement over time.

Curriculum and assessment are, as every teacher knows, inextricably interwoven. At the *practical* level, a discussion of the one leads quickly to a consideration of the other. (At the *theoretical* level the two are much more readily separated.) When a method of assessment is decided upon, the teacher usually finds this affects curriculum content in various and sometimes subtle ways. When some curriculum content is selected, the teacher has to decide how pupil learning is to be assessed, as well as recorded and communicated (e.g., to parents). TNC is as much about assessment as curriculum, and quite properly so. I believe, however, that it is the assessment proposals which will be more influential upon the work of schools, and more long lasting in their effects. The assessment proposals will have greater effects upon the curriculum than will the curriculum proposals upon assessment.

A deeper insight into this has been suggested by Professor Denis Lawton.[4] He argues that it is TNC's approach to assessment which has determined the approach to curriculum, rather than the other way round. We tend not to notice this because in TNC the curriculum proposals came before the discussion of testing and assessment. The TNC sequence, as I have already described, is as follows:

- curriculum (subjects);

- programmes of study;

- attainment targets;

- testing;

- accountability.

But the sequence should really be read *backwards*, starting with the government's ideological commitment to accountability (see later in this Chapter). Thus, accountability requires test results on pupils, schools, LEAs; testing requires attainment targets which are to be set within programmes of study; and these make sense in terms of the subjects which are, in the view of lay people, the essence of the curriculum. This neatly explains why the curriculum proposals appear so simplistic and old-fashioned and constructed in apparent disregard of the professional approach of teachers, inspectors and academics, for they read the sequence in a *forwards* direction, each step being derived logically from the one before. TNC is *presented* in the professional sequence but *constructed* in the opposite direction.

Not surprisingly, many teachers (and others) foresaw, when they read the assessment proposals in TNC, the possibility of a 'national maths (or science, etc.) day' when all pupils would take the nationally prescribed tests leading eventually to publication of results for each class (and their teacher), each school and each LEA. The possibility of a revived 11-plus, as well as a new 7-plus and 14-plus, in addition to the existing 16-plus public examinations, loomed before an astonished profession. Would children be designated as successes or failures at these ages? Would assessment in the public mind become synonymous with this process, leading all other forms of assessment to pale into significance? Would all the energies and the enthusiasm of the teachers who have taken part in the records of achievement movement be rendered pointless? Would 'teaching to the test' become so commonplace that assessment determines curriculum rather than curriculum determining assessment?

It is, of course, difficult as yet to say whether or not these fears are unduly alarmist or exaggerated or even groundless.

The TGAT report is much more reassuring, for TNC is now read forwards, not backwards. The assessment process, it says at the beginning of its report, should not determine what is to be taught and learned. It should be the servant, not the master, of the curriculum. Yet it should not simply be a bolt-on addition at the end. Rather, it should be an integral part of the educational process, continually providing both 'feedback' and 'feed-forward'. It therefore needs to be incorporated systematically into teaching strategies and practices at all levels.

Following the best of recent professional practice in assessment, it argues for four basic criteria: assessment should be criterion-referenced; formative; moderated; and lead to progression. Throughout the report there is evidence that important lessons have been learnt from recent work on records of achievement and developments in graded assessment. They argue for an attainment profile in each subject, consisting of several components, one of which should have cross-curricular features. More controversial is the proposal for 10 achievement levels between the ages of 7 and 16, with the top four levels bearing a relationship to GCSE grades.

The TGAT report is long and difficult in places, but has made a skilful attempt to match the best of teacher practice in the field of assessment with the general constraints imposed by TNC. I have little doubt that, if it is broadly accepted by the Secretary of State and then implemented through the work of the subject working groups, teachers' assessment skills will be vastly improved. On the other hand, the proposed scheme is going to be extremely costly, both in terms of money and teachers' time. The report openly admits that this is the most ambitious assessment scheme ever attempted in the world. It will all without question make the schools and LEAs more accountable, at least in terms of pupil performance, to parents and public. The more important question is this: will the new approach to assessment, including the new forms of accountability, reach its central goal of improving levels of pupil achievement? Is it also the most effective use of increasingly scarce resources to realize this goal?

The answer is, of course, unknown. Proponents (and opponents) argue fiercely that it will (or will not), but we shall not know until the system is in operation in several years' time. Nor is there much existing evidence, here or in other countries, on which to make a reasonable guess. It is an enormous act of faith. In March 1988 considerable consternation was created, not least among teachers who had generally responded very positively to the TGAT report, by the leak of a letter about the report from the Prime Minister's secretary to Kenneth Baker's secretary. The letter expresses four concerns about the TGAT report: that the assessment proposals require an enormously elaborate and complex system; that there will be heavy reliance on teachers' judgements in addition to the nationally prescribed tests; that the costs will be considerable; and that the new system will take a long time to implement. These 'concerns' place the whole TGAT proposals in doubt. Should the TGAT proposals be abandoned for an almost exclusive reliance on nationally prescribed tests for pupils at 7, 11, 14 and 16, there is no doubt that the assessment procedures would have a much stronger impact on the taught curriculum, and pressures for teachers to 'teach to the test' would be greatly increased. The curriculum would be heavily assessment-led. The decision on the TGAT report thus has enormous implications for the reform of the curriculum.

A specific comparison between ISS and TNC is now in order. An immediate difference is that reforms of TNC are directed to curriculum and assessment: there is very little about pedagogy or teaching method. ISS sees curriculum, assessment and teaching methods as closely related. TNC believes that a clearer specification of the curriculum, combined with attainment targets which are assessed within a framework of greater accountability, is enough to raise levels of achievement – by a combination of a clearer specification of the levels of achievement to be reached, and external pressure on teachers to deliver the results. In this sense TNC, which shares with ISS a conviction that part of the problem is teachers with too low expectations of their pupils, directly addresses the problem by means of externally imposed targets and pressure on teachers to reach them by placing the achievement of a school within a comparative framework, with results on school performance unadjusted for intake. ISS, recognizing that the inner city contains schools in areas of intense poverty and deprivation as well as in leafy suburbs, shies away from such simple comparisons between, say, Hampstead and Hackney. Indeed, the ILEA, precisely because its schools operate in such widely differing circumstances, has published a 'league table' of 16-plus examination results adjusted for intake factors, which shows that schools with a disadvantaged intake can do relatively better than a school with an advantaged intake. It should be noted that the existence of a published league table has not led to an automatic and immediate improvement in schools at the bottom of the table. Such a placing seems as likely to engender angry defensiveness as much as a will to improve. Government belief that 'public exposure' of an underperforming school is an effective means to improvement is probably naive; once again, the importance of the head is gravely underestimated. The ISS approach deals with low expectations more indirectly by seeking to improve in a more general and holistic way the practice of all teachers, including the head. It is for this reason that a major part of ISS is devoted to improving the staff development of teachers, and in the period of implementation of ISS efforts have been directed to improving the Authority's INSET and school self-evaluation procedures. The underlying philosophy has been that schools require more INSET to be school-focused, linking the enhancement of a teacher's individual pro-fessional skills with the defined needs of the school as a whole; and further that the capacities of a school staff to evaluate their own strengths and weaknesses must be improved and result directly in more effective forward planning to remedy recognized weaknesses. In short, enhancing pupil achievement is seen to spring from a more coherent approach to curriculum, assessment and teaching method, seen as an integral whole, and that this is most likely to arise when a school has developed more sophisticated self-monitoring that leads to holistic forward planning, of which INSET is an inherent feature. In this respect, the philosophies of TNC and ISS are very different indeed; TNC has no philosophy of schools as dynamic institutions.

It is within such a context that the specific proposals of ISS with regard to assessment are set. The immediate target is the fourth and fifth years. ISS sees the two-year journey to the public examinations as a nebulous one for many pupils, especially those from the working class. It is a kind of mystery tour, with an unimaginable destination; not surprisingly many pupils fall asleep or jump off during the journey. There is an evident need for a clearer definition of the destination and some significant intermediate stations. ISS therefore proposed that all courses in the fourth and fifth years be broken into half-term units (or modules). And such 'modularization' should be undertaken at school level by the teachers themselves, with advice and support, rather than being provided by outside 'curriculum development' agencies. In each case the aims of the unit would be made explicit and discussed with pupils. Aims and objectives need to be shared with pupils, and on that basis the methods of teaching and learning are to be negotiated between teacher and pupil. This is the ISS version of attainment targets, with the added element about negotiation of pedagogy. ISS makes a pointed contrast between the curriculum and the 'curriculum as it is taught' and places major emphasis on the construction of more *active learning roles* for pupils, thus drawing upon the four aspects of achievement. It follows that assessment procedures – the unit credit which attaches to every unit – should reflect all four aspects of achievement *and* involve an element of pupil self-assessment. By encouraging teachers to assess all four aspects, which many found very difficult, ISS drew the attention of teachers to the fact that the curriculum is frequently too narrow in its definition of achievement, often assessing mainly aspect 1. By insisting upon an element of pupil self-assessment, ISS promoted a shift in assessment from a unidirectional flow from teacher to pupil to a joint enterprise in which the pupil has responsibilities for defining his/her own strengths and weaknesses, and devising strategies for improvement. Active learning roles for pupils, therefore, also mean active assessment roles for pupils. These changes in assessment procedures had evident consequences for the teaching methods adopted. In this regard, the ISS proposals for units and unit credits were consonant with other changes in secondary schools which were being developed at the same time: graded assessment, where the initial belief that it was simply a matter of devising achievement tests soon gave way to much more fundamental re-thinking about allied development work on curriculum content and teaching method; and also work on profiles/records of achievement. Although these began as three separate initiatives, they have over the years been brought closer together. All this work has been undertaken with enthusiasm by teachers and on a voluntary basis, in a period of severe industrial action when teacher morale and goodwill were at unprecedentedly low levels. The result is a marked advance within ILEA schools in teachers' skills in relation to assessment as well as movement towards whole school policies on assessment. It seems very likely that ILEA schools which have been most heavily engaged in these developments will have a distinct advantage if national schemes of assessment are broadly in line with the TGAT report, though many teachers are likely to have reservations about nationally prescribed tests. TNC does not seem to recognize how worthwhile changes in assessment need to be 'slowed' by teachers and to have a wider impact on curriculum and teaching methods if they are to have beneficial consequences for achievement levels; that such reform takes time and considerable teacher commitment; and that a heavy investment in INSET is needed. The experience of GCSE reform demonstrates the dangers of moving too fast with too few resources.

Accountability – Consumers or Partners?

It has already been noted that TNC seeks to increase the accountability of individual teachers and schools to parents. The underlying philosophy is one of parents as *consumers*, who need more accurate information about whether the teacher and the school are doing a good job. If parents are dissatisfied, they are presumably expected to exert pressure on the teacher, the school or the LEA to obtain better results, or to seek to place the child in another school. Information is power; and what parents (and the more powerful governing bodies) will do on the basis of their greatly enhanced knowledge of school – and teacher – effectiveness remains to be seen. It is another act of faith that this will lead to the raising of standards; it may also, of course, lead to considerable conflict between governing bodies/parents and head teachers and teachers. There is no guarantee that a spirit of partnership will prevail. In ISS the underlying philosophy is one of parents as *partners*, working collaboratively with teachers as joint but complementary educators. ISS makes proposals to break down the barriers that often exist beween teachers and parents, to improve the extent and quality of communication between school and home, and to increase parental involvement with the child's learning. (ISS also proposed an increase in parental representation on governing bodies.) One of the sad side-effects of industrial action during the early years of the implementation of ISS has been that work on improving the teacher-parent partnership has been more neglected by teachers than anyone initially expected. Parents are consumers; but they are also potential partners with teachers. It may be that TNC proposals will raise standards by increased accountability; but I remain convinced that the creation of a true teacher-parent partnership has even more to contribute. The wider conception of ISS is shown by the mention of parents in the section on assessment, but not simply as receivers of information about test scores.

> The unit credit should in our view contain, or be accompanied by, such diagnostic and self-assessment materials, which can be made known to parents so that they can play a more informed and supportive part in promoting the education of their children. Units and credits should be an important topic for discussion on parents' evenings and at meetings of our

proposed tutor-group parents' associations. The more parents understand the details of the curriculum content and methods of assessment, the more likely they are to act in partnership with teachers to foster pupil motivation and hard work.

Are the TNC proposals an adequate recipe for partnership?

Continuity and Progression

The lack of continuity and progression for many pupils has been a subject of regular critical comments by inspectors in their evaluations of schools. In my experience as an inspector I have been surprised at the frequency with which there are no or inadequate schemes of work within secondary school departments, with the effect that there is either repetition between the years, or gaps and discontinuities. Nor is it uncommon for there to be such poor recording of achievement (as well as diagnosis of weaknesses) that a teacher has relatively little on which to build from the child's teacher of the previous year. (Similar faults are of course to be found in primary schools.) The problem springs from the high degree of autonomy of individual teachers, a reluctance to engage in joint planning, and a lack of detailed records. There is no doubt that such weaknesses impede proper continuity and progression and so lead to underachievement.

Progression and continuity are particularly at risk during the period of transition between primary and secondary school, not least because poor continuity and progression in terms of the curriculum is often accompanied by even more severe discontinuities in teaching methods. The effects on pupil achievement of poorly managed transitions between primary and secondary schools have been amply documented by Professor Galton and his associates at the University of Leicester.[5] Not surprisingly, ISS devoted a substantial section to this topic. The ISS proposals are sensible, and many ILEA schools have sought to implement them, yet they remain limited in scope. Two major problems stand out. The first is that there are serious impediments to ensuring that full and accurate records accompany each child at the point of transfer – and that the secondary schools make full use of them when the primary teachers undertake their part. The second, and much deeper, problem is that there is still far too little agreement about the themes and content in the curriculum of top juniors so that different primary schools which will 'feed' a secondary school are working on a degree of common curricular ground. And there is even less agreement among secondary teachers of first-year pupils about how they should build upon the curriculum of top juniors. The 'fresh start' philosophy is still very widespread among secondary school teachers and it is a major barrier to continuity and progression. The ISS philosophy was that the transition between primary and secondary school should be as smooth as if there were no institutional break; but the recommendations were too limited to ensure such a goal.

It is one of the greatest strengths of the TNC proposals that this long-standing and deep-seated problem may finally be adequately attended to. Because there will be clearer programmes of work and attainment targets for 11 year olds, as well as records of their assessments, progression and continuity at the transition point are likely to be greatly enhanced. This will apply not only to mathematics and English, but also to areas such as science and arts, where at present progression and continuity are particularly weak. There is real promise that the undoubted achievements of some primary schools in teaching science and the arts will be built upon by their secondary colleagues. In the flurry of controversy that has surrounded TNC this important theme has barely been mentioned.

But nowadays there is another transition point for most pupils – at 16. It is now a minority who enter full-time employment and there has been considerable increase in the numbers who now take some form of further education. Ironically, it is in the best FE – and notably in courses such as CPVE – that the curriculum is likely to be integrated rather than in the form of the traditional subject-based curriculum now being solidified by TNC. And it is in the best FE that new methods of assessment, including pupil self-assessment, are most advanced. TNC pays far too little attention to issues of progression and continuity at this important point of transition, especially for those who (for whatever reasons) have been low attainers at secondary school and do not wish to enrol on A-level courses. ISS proposals for the fourth and fifth years were carefully formulated to ease transition to FE, both in terms of providing students with fuller and positive records of achievement (the unit credits) and by experiences of new forms of curriculum organization, especially in modular form (the units). It remains to be seen whether this aspect of TNC proposals will be sufficiently flexible to aid the transition of a section of the population who perhaps deserve the most attention in our common concern to raise levels of achievement and improve the quality of educational provision.

Notes

1   The curriculum proposals constitute a very small part of the Education Reform Bill. The most significant outcome of the Bill may well be the loss of powers to local education authorities in the face of new powers given both to the Secretary of State and to schools.
2   And it is in the primary phase, where a much more integrated approach to the curriculum is common, that the curriculum as a collection of subjects is more difficult to apply. It is evident that the writers of TNC have little experience of the primary curriculum. On the other hand, it has to be said that even where head teachers of primary schools claim that their curriculum is broad and balanced, they often have considerable difficulty in saying with any precision just how much time is in fact devoted to areas of the curriculum such as science or history/geography. The concept of the integrated primary curriculum is not in itself a good defence against more precise thinking about the time allocated to different areas of the curriculum; at the same time, ways of giving teachers more insight into curriculum coverage should not involve a disintegration of the curriculum.
3   *Secondary Education* (1946) A report of the Advisory Council on Education in Scotland. Edinburgh: HMSO.

4 GALTON, M. and WILLCOCKS, J. (1983) *Moving from the Primary Classroom.* London: Routledge & Kegan Paul.
5 Lecture on 'The National Curriculum' given by Professor Lawton at the London Institute of Education, 16 March 1988.

Teaching Quality: A Sociological Analysis[1]
Andy Hargreaves

In England and Wales, as elsewhere, there has of late been a good deal of concern expressed about improving the quality of teaching in schools. Such concerns are outlined most fully in the White Paper *Teaching Quality*[2] and are reiterated and developed in *Better Schools*.[3] In terms of government action, the concerns and implications of these documents have been taken up most directly through the setting-up of national criteria as a basis for controlling and 'accrediting' programmes of initial teacher training.[4]

Three 'theories' or sets of assumptions concerning the determinants of teaching quality appear to inform the analyses and recommendations contained within these influential government reports. One concerns itself with the sorts of personal qualities that are suited to teaching. It calls for more careful selection procedures to ensure that the 'right' sort of personalities enter training for the profession. The other two explanations appear to rest on somewhat inchoate versions of learning theory in claiming that teaching quality results from learned knowledge, skill, and other technical expertise acquired through initial training and further professional experience. The recommendation following from this diagnosis is that more attention should be directed to developing these kinds of competence in initial training, not least with regard to teachers spending more time on becoming more skilled and knowledgeable in their own subject specialisms.

Both these explanations are broadly psychologistic in nature. They appeal to the characteristics of individuals – to competence, skill and personal qualities – as determinants of teaching quality. And it is on these individuals and those who train them that responsibility for the identification of such qualities and the development of such competences is placed. Poor teaching quality, it is implied, results from an *absence* of the required competences and qualities. What is being proposed here, in effect, is a *deficit* model of teaching where poor quality results from deficiencies in personality, gaps in learning, or weak matching of competences to tasks.[5]

By contrast, I want to argue that much of what we call teaching quality (or its absence) actually results from processes of a social nature, from teachers actively interpreting, making sense of, and adjusting to, the demands and requirements their conditions of work place upon them. In this view, what some might judge to be 'poor' teaching quality often results from reasoned and reasonable responses to occupational demands – from interpretive presences, not cognitive absences, from strategic strength, not personal weakness. Aspects of this more sociological and humanistic interpretation of teaching quality will be developed within the chapter through a discussion of teacher cultures, careers and strategies, and their implications for the maintenance and persistence of those 'transmission' styles of classroom teaching which appear to be incurring official disapproval. But first we need to examine the 'official' interpretation of teaching quality and quality deficits a little more closely.

Teaching Quality and Quality Deficits: the Official View

Official views on what makes good and poor quality teaching have become increasingly apparent in Britain over recent years with the publication of a number of surveys and reports by Her Majesty's Inspectorate (HMI) on various parts of the schooling system. In one of the first of these surveys (of the fourth and fifth year curriculum in secondary schools) in 1979, the HMI noted that secondary teachers made wide use of 'heavily directed teaching, a preponderance of dictated or copied notes, and emphasis on the giving and recall of information, with little room or time for enquiry or explanation of applications'.[6] Later, in their survey of new teachers in school, they argued that teachers who were insecure in their subject material adopted

teaching approaches which maintained an often slavish adherence to the textbook, reliance on narrow questions often requiring monosyllabic answers, an inability to follow up and extend pupils' answers and an overprescriptive method whereby the teacher was able to remain within a constricted, safe pattern of work.[7]

Such poor quality teaching has been described in similar terms in a range of reports by the HMI on different age sectors within the education service – on primary and middle schools, for instance – and continues to be a consistent feature of their ongoing commentary on the quality of the present teaching force.[8]

What the HMI appear to be taking issue with here in a particularly strongly value-laden way is something that other writers have variously called 'formal', 'traditional', 'product', 'production', 'transmission', 'class-enquiry', 'recitation' and 'discipline-based' teaching.[9] Similar views on such teaching have also been expressed in the USA, where researchers have voiced concern about the preponderance of what they call 'frontal teaching'. From her survey of high school classrooms, Barbara Tye, for instance, concludes that 'all classrooms are discouragingly similar'.[10] Their physical layout and time scheduling are similar. The pattern of teacher dominance is remarkably uniform: frontal presentation, closed questioning and deskwork being the most commonly recurring features. There is, she says, little intellectual challenge, hardly any praise, not even much blame. The high school environment, it would seem, is one with few peaks and troughs, undemanding and emotionally flat. Listening and writing predominate as the major pupil activities, there being little opportunity for pupils to contribute to, or take responsibility for, their own learning, to develop self-confidence, independence and similar personal qualities.

In a parallel study of 13 junior high and middle schools, Kenneth Tye found that they too were dominated by listening, writing, quizzes and frontal teaching.[11] Opportunities for choice and exploration were restricted, and the emphasis on control and conformity at this vital stage of children's development was even greater than in the high schools. In their attachment to frontal teaching and related methods it would therefore seem that the junior highs outsinned the devil highs themselves.

What is it that is seen as determining these disapproved-of patterns of teaching? What explains these seeming deficits in teaching quality? In *Teaching Quality, Better Schools* and *Circular 3/84*, the Department of Education and Science (DES) appear to be advancing three broad arguments in relation to teaching quality.

First, they stress the importance of the teacher's personal qualities. Referring their readers to the HMI's survey of teachers in their first year in the profession, they repeat the survey's 'finding' that 'the personal qualities of the teachers were in many cases the decisive factor in their effectiveness'.[12] 'Personality, character and commitment', the DES note, are as important as the specific knowledge and skills that are used in the day-to-day tasks of teaching.[13] The need for teachers to have 'appropriate personal qualities' is reiterated in *Better Schools*[14] since, it is argued, 'the personality of the teacher and his relationships with pupils'[15] promote high standards. Given the importance of such personal qualities, the government have called for improvements in the selection of students for initial teacher training and have urged that only students with the 'requisite personal qualities' should be awarded qualified-teacher status at the end of their studies.

While government has been firm in its insistence upon the importance of personal qualities as a determinant of teaching quality, it has, however, been much less clear about what these particular qualities might be – sense of responsibility, awareness, sensitivity, enthusiasm and ease of communication being the only ones they have specifically identified, and then only in passing.[16] In the main, exactly which personal qualities are likely to make a good teacher are not discussed; nor is there any discussion of whether those qualities might vary according to the age group being taught, the special requirements of a teacher's subject, or the ethos of the school, for instance. And no advice is forthcoming either on *how* these (largely unstated) qualities might be identified through the selection process. The HMI certainly give no indication of the measures and procedures they themselves used for identifying the relevant qualities. All that is recommended is that experienced, practising teachers be increasingly involved in the selection process. It seems, then, that in the absence of more objective procedures and criteria, government is here prepared to place its trust in the process described in a well-known British idiom as 'it takes one to know one'.

This kind of guidance places excessive faith in professional intuition. Not only is this kind of personality-screening process likely to be chancy and unreliable, but – if change and initiative is the goal – downright counter-productive. Qualities that might generate and recoup excellent work in the classroom (including, for instance, risk-taking, creativity, originality, the valuing of independence and initiative, a questioning and critical approach, etc., none of which appear on the DES's own list) might not most endear new teachers to their colleagues; and qualities like 'tidy appearance' that may be essential for staffroom acceptance may be relatively unimportant to children.[17]

Secondly, the government clearly places considerable weight on the technical skills of classroom pedagogy or teaching method as determinants of teaching quality. Good teachers, they say, need to have the appropriate professional skills to teach their subject 'to children of different ages, abilities, aptitudes and backgrounds'.[18] *Better Schools* is more emphatic in *its* statement that intending teachers should be given 'training and practice in classroom skills',[19] and devotes some space to these – the skills of selecting appropriate materials, varying teaching styles to match the nature of the work and the type of pupil, guiding individual pupils, handling written and oral work, cultivating independent learning, using open and closed questions when appropriate, managing diverse opinions on sensitive issues, setting clear objectives, and so on. This is a formidable (and by no means exhaustive) list of relevant professional skills.

Greater involvement of practising teachers in the professional preparation of new recruits, the stipulation that a high proportion of teacher trainers directly involved with pedagogy should themselves have recent and successful experience of teaching and should create opportunities to renew this experience, and the setting of minimum periods for teacher-training courses and the practical elements within them – all these things are seen as ways of providing new teachers with greater and more effective assistance in the development of the necessary practical classroom skills.

The formula for change and improvement in teaching quality being employed here is again both legalistic and psychologistic in nature: more teachers in training, more trainers in schools. Most of the vital questions as to how these skills are acquired, how they are to be selected and adjusted according to context, how easily or not different kinds of school environment can accommodate them and so on, are begged. The government position appears to be that if teacher trainers spend enough time in schools, and if student teachers spend enough time alongside experienced ones and their newly expert trainers, the requisite skills will hopefully be acquired by some kind of osmosis. Such an acquisition of skills from existing practitioners, were it proved to be effective, might *just* be a defensible strategy for *maintaining* present levels of teaching quality (assuming we would be satisfied with that). But it would certainly not be an effective strategy for *raising* those levels – for introducing new, improved and professionally challenging skills, techniques and approaches into the system.

Third, and most centrally, the government draw a great deal of attention to the need to establish a close fit or match between secondary school teachers' specialist subject qualifications, and their teaching responsibilities in school. In their 1979 survey of secondary schools in England and Wales, the HMI had first pointed to what they called 'evidence of insufficient match in many schools between the qualification and experience of teachers and the work they are undertaking'.[20] In their subsequent survey of probationary teachers, the HMI claimed that 'one teacher in ten revealed insecurity in the subject they were teaching',[21] an insecurity that was reflected in their teaching method. And in their survey of 9–13 middle schools, the HMI argued that work was of a higher standard where there was a greater use of subject teachers, and where those subjects had been studied in a major way in higher education by the teachers concerned.[22] In view of such associations, *Teaching Quality* goes on to state that 'the Government attach high priority to improving the fit between teachers' qualifications and their tasks as one means of improving the quality of education'.[23] 'All specialist subject teaching during the secondary phase', they continue, 'requires teachers whose study of the subject concerned was at a level appropriate to higher education, represented a substantial part of the total higher education and training period and built on a suitable A level base'.[24] Moreover, they go on, even areas of the curriculum outside the specialist mainstream, like careers education, remedial work or vocational preparation, should only be undertaken by teachers who already have experience of teaching a specialist subject.[25] The importance that government attach to this link between subject match and teaching quality is further emphasized by their announced intentions to take subject qualifications into account in the selection of student teachers, to consider the relevance of students' subject qualifications to school subject teaching in their procedures for approving or 'accrediting' teacher-training courses, and to undertake five-yearly reviews of selected secondary schools to ensure that subject match is being improved within them and being reflected in the pattern of teacher appointments.

The commitment to improving the extent of subject match through the control of teacher education, and the exertion of influence over teacher appointments, is therefore clearly substantial. There are serious problems with this subject match thesis as we shall see, but the subject match initiative undoubtedly provides one of the major thrusts behind the intended improvement of teaching quality.

To sum up, official government policy on the improvement of teaching quality in England and Wales appears to have identified three areas of influence in which intervention would be worthwhile: personal qualities, pedagogical skills and subject expertise.

Explanations in the Tyes' studies of the reasons for quality deficits in the US teaching force are remarkably similar.[26] Though their studies provide very little direct evidence on *why* teachers teach the way they do (they were not really asked this), explanations are advanced all the same. Perhaps teachers teach badly out of habit, it is ventured, or because they have never learned the skills of mixed-ability work in training. In this way, the personality of the teacher and the level of his or her skill are made central to the Tyes' proposed change strategy. In fairness, it must be said that they do point to other influential factors as well – to the need to raise the status and public worth of the teaching profession, to improve leadership skills among school principals, to restructure the curriculum, and so on. But much of their case rests on a proposed strategy of selecting new entrants to the profession more carefully and providing better initial and in-service training in classroom skills. These two easily (or too easily) targetted objectives of personality and performance are given much more extensive treatment than the more politically contentious issues of professional status and recognition, and the basic conditions of teachers' work. It is not, I suspect, the authors' intention, but in their argument much of the blame for the present state of teaching appears to rest with the teachers themselves and those who train them.

All of these explanations are predominantly psychologistic in their understandings (or misunderstandings) of both teacher thinking and teaching quality; and they are particular kinds of psychologistic explanation that take very little account of how teachers themselves understand, interpret and deal with the demands that their work situation makes upon them. Without such understandings of why teachers do what they do, it is then possible for researchers' and policy-makers' own interpretations to flood into the vacuum. Teachers are seen not to display the observer's own preferred skills; so they are diagnosed as not being competent in their use. Teachers are seen to display personal qualities of which the observer disapproves; so it is assumed they lack more desirable ones. Thus, when preferred skills and qualities are not observed, it is assumed the teachers concerned simply do not have them and should therefore be supplied with them (training), prevented from entering teaching at all (screening), or restricted only to those 'safe' areas in which they are competent (matching).

Explanations of this kind have a certain political attractiveness – by making training, selection and deployment the target of reform, things can be done, they can be *seen* to be done, and they can be done relatively cheaply too. Indeed, one wonders sometimes whether the apparent simplicity of such political remedies has, in some peculiar way, affected the diagnosis of the supposed 'sickness' in the first place (undesirable qualities, low levels of skill, weak subject expertise) to which those remedies were presumably a response; whether the remedies have produced the sickness, rather than vice versa.

Of course, other interpretations of teaching quality which considered how far different techniques and approaches were chosen to match the circumstances in hand, and others rejected as inappropriate or which respected teachers as active and rational interpreters of their task and the conditions in which it is carried out, might suggest policy implications that would be more troublesome to manage, more expensive to implement, less easy to evaluate in the short term. But I would urge that in this case, as in all others, the attractiveness (or otherwise) of the remedy should not be allowed to influence the validity or accuracy of the diagnosis. What, then, might this other diagnosis be? What alternative framework is there for analysing teaching quality?

An Alternative Framework

The framework I want to propose rests upon a regard for the importance of the active, interpreting self in social interaction; for the way it perceives, makes sense of and works upon the actions of others and the situation in which it finds itself; the way it pursues goals and tries to maximize its own (often competing) interests; the way it pursues these things by combining or competing with other selves; the way it adjusts to circumstances while still trying to fulfil or retrieve its own purposes – and so forth. In this view, teachers, like other people, are not just bundles of skill, competence and technique; they are creators of meaning, interpreters of the world and all it asks of them. They are people striving for purpose and meaning in circumstances that are usually much less than ideal and which call for constant adjustment, adaptation and redefinition. Once we adopt this view of teachers or of any other human being, our starting question is no longer why does he/she *fail* to do X, but why does he/she do Y? What purpose does doing Y fulfil for them? Our interest, then, is in how teachers manage to cope with, adapt to and reconstruct their circumstances; it is in what they achieve, not what they fail to achieve.

The different sorts of interpretation of teaching quality this sort of framework suggests can be illustrated by looking at explanations for the development and persistence of transmission teaching that have been presented within that framework. Six such explanations in particular will be discussed (these are not intended to be exhaustive): the exigencies of cohort control, situational constraints, examination pressures, subject-related pedagogies, status and career factors, and teacher isolation. It will be seen that these explanations of transmission teaching and its associated connection with teaching quality (or rather, its lack), suggest a very different set of policy implications than those currently in political fashion.

THE EXIGENCIES OF COHORT CONTROL

Transmission teaching, or 'recitation teaching' as it is more commonly called in the United States, is so pervasive within the school system that it can easily be interpreted as the 'natural' or 'proper' way to teach, as a network of rules and procedures special to the teaching environment which must be learned, rehearsed and developed in a practical way by the new teacher in order to gain competent membership of the teaching community, and of the classroom order in particular. Indeed, it is interesting that a good deal of mainstream American research on teacher thinking and the improvement of teaching quality treats this particular version of transmission teaching by and large as representative of teaching itself. 'Novice' teachers are regarded as different from 'expert' ones only in terms of their abilities to handle transmission-type skills – for instance, in selecting examples, illustrations and analogies that will best 'tell the story' in relation to some part of the curriculum.[27] Within such studies there is a tendency also to concentrate on those 'academic' components of the curriculum which more easily lend themselves to didactic modes of exposition and question-and-answer teaching. It is as if teaching quality is only an issue in subjects like mathematics and science.[28] What teaching quality might look like in drama, physical education, music and art, for instance, scarcely gets a mention. This serves only to reinforce our existing stereotypes of what 'teaching' and 'good teaching' really is. Thus, in trying to change teaching, ironically it is likely that the recommendations arising from this kind of research, like much of the research on teacher effectiveness that preceded it,[29] will help keep teaching the same by failing to look outside the parameters of the transmission model.

Teaching is certainly a matter of competence. But it is competence of a particular kind.[30] It is the competence to recognize and enact the rules, procedures and forms of understanding of a particular cultural environment. What is involved is not *technical* competence to operate in a pre-given, professionally correct and educationally worthwhile way, but *cultural* competence to 'read' and 'pass' in a system with its own specific history, a system once devised and developed to meet a very particular set of social purposes.

For Hoetker and Ahlbrand[31] and Westbury,[32] these purposes have their roots in the nineteenth-century American elementary school. Grace,[33] writing in the British context, fixes those purposes in the urban elementary context of that country, too. For writers such as these, the quick-fire, question-and-answer strategy of the recitation simultaneously solved the problem of mobilizing attention[34] and sustaining control among large numbers of potentially recalcitrant working-class children, while getting information and material across in an environment where resources were in short supply.

The features and functions of this recitation style of teaching have since been identified in greater detail. The funnelling of classroom talk through the teacher effectively reduces a potentially chaotic 'babble' to the carefully structured, question-and-answer pattern of two-party talk[35] where selected pupils act as proxy representatives for the whole class, where the teacher initiates lines of inquiry and the pupils merely respond, and where the teacher evaluates the accuracy, quality and appropriateness of pupil contributions, but not vice versa.[36] The 'hands up' pattern of pupil participation is carefully orchestrated by the teacher – competition is encouraged, attention sustained, some semblance of involvement secured – in the process of getting the pre-decided point across.[37] To lecture the material would bring only boredom and rebellion, which is why outright dictation is usually only practised with the most self-selected, high ability groups.[38] The organization of competitive pupil participation thus avoids excesses of boredom and inattention – especially where false questioning trails can be set in the early stages and the 'answer' or 'point' of the lesson delayed so that pupils have to work hard to discover it.[39]

Within lesson structures of this kind, teachers do not, in fact, orientate themselves so much to the needs of individual students, but tend to treat the whole class as a kind of 'collective student'.[40] The progress of groups of students in the higher (but not the highest) parts of the class achievement range is often monitored particularly closely by the transmission teacher and used to 'steer' his or her judgements about the management and development of the lesson for the class as a whole.[41] In these sorts of circumstances, the teacher's predominant practical concern is not with the learning experiences of individual students, but with the overall 'instructional flow' of the lesson – with how well it is proceeding to its intended conclusion and maintaining order as it does so.[42]

There are more or less coercive versions of this long-standing pedagogical strategy. Webb describes the drill sergeant approach of the secondary modern teacher, with his inflexible regime of parade ground regimentation and uncompromising obedience.[43] Hargreaves discussed 'policing' strategies in an urban middle school, with their detailed control over the talk, bodily movement and gestures of working-class children.[44] Woods reviews the extensive use of 'domination' style survival strategies among secondary modern teachers where control, especially over older and larger pupils, was a salient problem.[45] And Hargreaves has also identified strong traces of these styles and traditions among former secondary modern teachers working in middle schools with younger children, even in middle-class environments.[46]

These, then, are the techniques, rules and procedures which are widely adopted as part of the practical management of large cohorts of pupils.[47] Such patterns of classroom management are, perhaps, more common in secondary modern schools,[48] in the lower bands of comprehensives,[49] or in working-class elementary schools[50] – the most direct and obvious inheritors of the old elementary tradition.[51] As I have already suggested, transmission styles are much more widespread than this, though: so familiar a part of teachers' experience, in fact, that their practice quickly becomes a matter of habit and routine, of taken-for-granted competence, not strategic choice.

But it should be remembered that, historically, within the system as a whole, and biographically, within the unfolding careers of individual teachers, these familiar patterns do arise from, and are adopted through, conscious strategic choice. It is only when they have been thus adopted that conscious strategy turns into habitual rule, coping into culture. It is at this point, where the routines become more closely aligned with the self and where they appear to be dealing reasonably successfully with the ever-present problem of control, that the habit becomes hard to break and that threats to it will be resisted. This is especially so where 'recitation' or transmission patterns of teaching are strongly approved of and supported by other members of the school community, not least the pupils themselves. Where domination strategies are a pervasive feature of the culture of teaching in a school, pupils can be remorseless in their expectations that teachers conform to the 'normal' pattern and can exercise powerful sanctions of disobedience and disruption against those who allow reason or consideration of personal concern to show through, against those who seem to show manifest signs of weakness or softness, that is.[52]

Transmission teaching is indeed sustained through habit, then. But the habit is by no means irrational. It is a habit that has historically enjoyed a measure of success in maintaining control over and transmitting limited knowledge to young people in large numbers in the physically restricted space of the school classroom. If policy-makers wish to kick this habit out of the classroom, it is clear that training in new skills is not in itself the answer. This lies, rather, in formulation and acceptance by teachers themselves of new, less control-centred educational purposes, along with an easing of the constraints and conditions in which those purposes are to be fulfilled. This brings us to a second set of determinants of transmission teaching – those rooted in the situational constraints of the classroom.

SITUATIONAL CONSTRAINTS

All teaching takes place in a context of opportunity and constraint. Teaching strategies involve attempts at realizing educational goals by taking advantage of appropriate opportunities and coping with, adjusting to, or redefining the constraints. Often, the coping strategies that teachers adopt to deal with contextual contingencies can become so habitual, so routinized, that they seem like coping no more, but worthwhile and valid teaching. In this way, provisional adaptations turn into routine commitments.[53] When constraints are particularly heavy and pressing, though, teaching may become not just a matter of coping, which in some senses all teaching is, but of sheer survival. Woods[54] has outlined some of the constraints that appear to induce survival-based patterns of teaching in the secondary school system – the raising of the school-leaving age (to which we would now add growing youth unemployment), which encourages staying-on among those not otherwise especially enamoured of their school experience; the persistence and extension of 16+ examinations against which teachers' own success will be judged (more of this later); continuing high levels of class size and teacher–pupil ratios that make individualized treatment and small-group work difficult; and declining levels of resources, which make experimentation and adjustment of learning tasks to individual needs problematic and leave teachers in the position of having to rely on their own *personal* resources for managing the class.[55] To these things, we might also add the inappropriateness of, and deterioration of standards in, school buildings – the inconvenience of stairs and galleries for those wishing to use overhead projectors and other cumbersome audio-visual aids; the unsuitability of compartmentalized classrooms for team-teaching, resource-based learning etc.; and the general discouragement that dilapidated walls and leaking roofs present to those who might otherwise take pride in improving the display and all-round aesthetic environment of their classrooms.

Material circumstances, then, do affect the standard and quality of teaching, as the HMI have themselves noted in surveys of the effects of public expenditure policies on teaching and learning.[56] Low resourcing and poor material support encourage teachers to adopt a 'survival' or 'make-do' orientation to their work and incline them towards more control-centred, transmission-style patterns of teaching which revolve around the imposition of their own personal authority within the public setting of the classroom.

Teachers, that is, do not just decide to deploy particular skills because of their recognized professional worth and value, or because of their own confidence and competence in operating them. Rather, they make judgements about the fit between particular skills and the constraints, demands and opportunities of the material environment of the classroom; about the appropriateness of particular styles or techniques for present circumstances. Although, in historical and biographical terms, these judgements rapidly become ingrained and routinized as normal practice, their roots in environmental circumstances, and therefore the importance of the character of those circumstances, should not be forgotten.

The implication here for policy-makers who would wish to promote movement away from transmission patterns of teaching is that there is a need to ease and improve those conditions that currently incline teachers towards survival more than mere coping, and towards the control-centred transmission-style pedagogies that follow from it. This suggests not policies of improved training or selection, but of more generous resource allocation to the system to improve the material environment of teaching.

EXAMINATIONS

> The work attempted in the classroom was often constrained by exclusive emphasis placed on the examination syllabus, on topics thought to be favoured by the examiners and on the acquisition of examination techniques.

So wrote Her Majesty's Inspectorate in their survey of the curriculum for fourth and fifth years in secondary schools.[57] Their evidence for this judgement, as with those presented in most of their surveys, was loosely stated and difficult to verify, but the argument has been echoed many times in recent years in Britain by academics and policy-makers alike. In a polemical critique of modern comprehensive school practice, for instance, David Hargreaves has expressed concern about the ways in which public examinations can come to dominate the process of teaching and learning in secondary schools.[58] And a study of a large group of Scottish secondary school leavers, surveyed after taking their 'Highers', found that 'the most common single method of study was "exercises, worked examples, proses, translations" (73%) followed by "having notes dictated to you in class" (60%)'.[59] The researchers concluded that 'one may infer that many felt there had been a conflict between studying for interest's sake and studying for examination success'.[60]

Perhaps this inference, given its grounding in pupil, not teacher data, is a tendentious one. Perhaps David Hargreaves's remarks are also somewhat speculative since they rest on no other evidence than that presented by Her Majesty's Inspectorate (doubts about which have already been raised). Moreover, evidence from recent research by Hammersley and Scarth suggests that patterns of whole-class teacher–pupil talk do not differ significantly between courses that are assessed by terminal examinations, ones that are continuously assessed, and ones that are not assessed at all – even when these differently assessed courses are taught by the same teacher and within the same subject.[61]

In claiming that terminal examinations have little effect on patterns of teaching and learning, Hammersley and Scarth's research does, however, focus on only one tightly defined area of classroom learning (overall patterns of public whole-class talk). It does not consider other features of classroom learning that might be more strongly affected by the presence or absence of examinations. These would include differences in the amount and type of group work and group discussions, the open or closed nature of classroom tasks, and the kinds of homework set.[62]

Until the findings of such research become available, the weight of argument and evidence would appear to fall in the opposite direction. Both Weston and Olson, for instance, found that teachers involved in the Schools Council Integrated Science Project (SCISP), breached the project's guidelines by teaching from the board and encouraging pupils to revise – and that these teachers referred to the presence of examinations as the reason for their continuing use of these transmission-like styles of teaching.[63]

For some teachers, then, the presence of examinations seems to constrain them in their approach to classroom teaching; it limits innovation and inhibits their willingness to explore new teaching strategies. Achievement conscious pupils may conspire with their teachers in this process of limitation too, drawing them back to safer pedagogical ground when exploration threatens to divert them from their examination destination.[64] Not all teachers are closet radicals, though, waiting for the moment when the unbolting of the examination doors will allow them to open up their pedagogical style. As Sikes, Measor and Woods have found in their life history interviews with secondary teachers, many teachers regard examinations not as a constraint but as a resource for motivating pupils at an age when their enthusiasm for school might otherwise be waning.[65] Many teachers, it must be said, though, are not aware of examinations as either constraining or a resource. For them, examinations are just a 'fact of life' – an assumed and taken-for-granted part of the secondary school system to which their practice is routinely directed.[66]

Constraint, resource, excuse, and fact of life – there are clearly a number of ways in which public examinations have a bearing on the maintenance of transmission styles of teaching. Their importance for the teacher is substantial – in a work environment where few other adults directly witness the quality of the teacher's work, examination results provide one of the few public and apparently objective indicators of a teacher's competence.[67] Teachers ignore the importance of these results at their peril. Indeed, since the 1980 Education Act's requirement that all schools publish their examination results, it is not unreasonable to surmise that the influence of examinations upon teaching quality (or its lack) is likely to grow in years to come.

Even so, it should not be assumed that the abolition of public examinations would necessarily put an end to transmission styles of teaching. Such styles, as we have seen, are apparently as pervasive a feature of US high school teaching as of life in British secondary schools. The grade point average and the development of educational testing may in this sense have as much of a backwash effect on the teaching and learning process in the United States as does the public examination system in Britain. So, too, might the mandated curriculum, be it set at national or provincial level, in its fixing of external curriculum objectives and its restriction of teachers' room for manoeuvre. Clearly, examinations, the way they are perceived, oriented to and drawn upon as a source of professional justification by teachers, are but one source of influence on the continuing pervasiveness of transmission styles of teaching in the school system. Their removal or reform will bring no automatic pedagogical shifts, only the creation of opportunity for alternatives to be explored more thoroughly.

SUBJECT SPECIALISM

For the DES, teaching quality at secondary level is enhanced by the possession of specialist subject expertise among those with responsibility for teaching the particular subjects in question. The DES's case for insisting upon more attention to be paid to subject competence in the training and deployment of teachers rests on two kinds of evidence, both of which are somewhat insubstantial.

First, in *The New Teacher in School*, the HMI identified one secondary teacher in ten as revealing insecurity in the subject they were teaching (an encouragingly small proportion, one might have thought).[68] Moreover, as the National Union of Teachers argues in response to the White Paper *Teaching Quality*, the basis of and variation between different HMI ratings of teacher competence is not made clear; and interestingly, these ratings (formed on the basis of only two observations per teacher), are less generous than those provided by the teachers' heads.[69]

Secondly, in their 9–13 middle school survey, the HMI looked at 'associations between particular modes of staff deployment and overall standards'.[70] They concluded that, in schools where a high proportion of teachers spent over half their week teaching one specific subject, and in schools where a high proportion of the teaching was undertaken by teachers who had studied the relevant subject as a major element in their initial training – in other words, where there was a strong degree of subject match – standards of work were better (to a statistically significant degree). This argument, too, as the National Union of Teachers again point out, is empirically weak, however.[71] For one thing, the HMI leave implicit what they mean by, and measure as, standards. For another, statistically significant associations between standards of work on the one hand and resource levels and the strength of a head teacher's influence on the other, which are even *stronger* than those involving subject match, are not developed through discussion or connected to policy suggestions. Once again, it appears that the nature of the available remedies is having some effect on the character of the diagnosis.

But let us assume, for one moment, that the HMI's case is stronger than this; that subject matter *is*, in fact, related to teaching quality. Is the HMI's interpretation, resting as it does on the claim that teachers' possession of knowledge and expertise provides the basis for their classroom confidence, the only possible one? Have they, like good social scientists, been rigorous, robust and balanced in examining alternative possible theoretical interpretations of the evidence to hand? I want to suggest that they have not and that there are equally plausible (though less politically attractive) explanations for the associations they claim to identify. These explanations – ones which recognize and respect the meanings that teachers take from and give to their work – are concerned, in turn, with the effects of subject-based pedagogies, subject commitment and subject fragmentation.

(i) Subject-based pedagogies

When teachers are trained and develop expertise in particular subjects, they do more than merely master appropriate content and gather relevant bodies of technical expertise. Induction into a subject is also induction into a subject culture or community – into a set of assumptions about how school children learn, how they are best taught, how one should relate to them, and so on.[72] Though definitions of what is the appropriate methodology for a subject tend to shift over time,[73] at present, teachers of certain subjects – modern languages in particular – seem strongly inclined to a transmission approach to teaching.[74] The adoption of this approach within certain subjects is based on what Ball calls an academic perspective, where teachers tend to be strongly subject-centred, to view their own subject as setting special intellectual demands because of its allegedly 'linear' quality, to favour homogeneous ability grouping, and to prefer whole-class teaching methods.[75] In the case of certain subjects, then, it would seem that the dominant assumptions about teaching, learning and knowledge held *within* that subject community actually support the spread of those very transmission pedagogies of which government appears to disapprove.

(ii) Subject commitment.

Subject membership is a hard-won achievement – a result of many years of studying and exploring that subject through school, through university and through teacher training. Almost inevitably, then, induction into a subject brings with it the development of commitment and loyalty to that subject too (and, by implication, weakened loyalty and commitment to others). Subject induction, that is, bestows subject identity.[76] Subject mastery is therefore not only a cognitive process – a matter of acquiring knowledge and skill – but a social one also, in which feelings of attachment, loyalty and identification are built up. So strong can these commitments become that teachers not only come to feel diffident about teaching and reluctant to teach subjects very different from their own, like religious education or personal and social education, which would be likely to form but a minor part of their timetable commitment,[77] but some teachers may even feel reluctant to teach subjects that would appear to have a fairly close cognate intellectual relationship to their own – as when physicists are asked to teach chemistry or integrated sciences, for instance.[78] In these circumstances, poor quality teaching that arises from working outside one's own subject is not so much, or excluisvely, due to lack of knowledge and expertise, but to weakened commitment. And this weakened commitment may in turn be a by-product of the intensity of the subject commitments that have been built up elsewhere in the school curriculum. By this interpretation, the problem that appears as subject mismatch may not be due to too little specialism, but to too much.

(iii) Subject fragmentation

These first two interpretations of the relationship between subject membership and pedagogical preference suggest that weakness in out-of-subject duties may well be caused not simply by unfamiliarity with content but by deep-seated divisions within secondary teaching as a whole brought about by strongly institutionalized systems of subject separation which inhibit the development of transferable pedagogic skills, restrict teachers' adaptability and responsiveness to educational challenge and innovation, and limit their commitment to children and to learning in general as against enthusiasm for particular bodies of content.

My own work on middle school teachers provides some support for this view. Teachers with interests in, and commitments to, humanities, English and creative and expressive arts felt ill-at-ease with teaching science and mathematics, not just because of their lack of confidence with the subject (though this was important), but also because of their discomfort with the very different pedagogies, very different ways of relating to children they felt were associated with those other subjects. As one expressive arts teacher put it:

I think anybody who teaches in the creative arts has this [rapport] with kids, because it's emotionally based... whereas if you're dealing with a factual subject, a scientific subject, you're dealing more with things and objects and reactions. Actually how you *feel* about SO_2 [sulphur-dioxide] coming out of a bottle doesn't come into it, you know.[79]

Similarly, in their life history studies of secondary teachers, Sikes, Measor and Woods came across some subject teachers who felt distinctly uncomfortable with the approaches they were required to adopt in other subject areas:

Last year, I took some English. I couldn't teach it. I was nervous, and besides not being able to do it as well, you need a different approach to what you take in art. You couldn't treat the kids as individuals, like you do in art. You had to be a teacher in front of a class and tell everybody what to do.
    Well, I've got two styles of teaching. I've got the one that I deal with in the art room and the other that's formal because I teach part of my

timetable in humanities ... in art, I can relax and go round and talk to them individually ... with the humanities, it's a case of come in in silence and sit down ... definitely teaching from the board.[80]

Other writers have pointed to the pedagogical anxieties art teachers feel when they move from the security of their practical areas into a more conventional classroom environment – even when they are teaching art appreciation.[81] Nor is the phenomenon confined to art. Ball and Lacey, for instance, have pointed to the tendency of non-specialist English teachers to be more attracted to transmission pedagogies than their specialist counterparts are.[82] What matters here is not so much this association between qualification and quality, but how it is explained. The evidence I have reviewed points to the possibility that poor-quality or transmission-style teaching arises in some subject teaching, not because that subject is being taught by poorly qualified generalists, but by *other* specialists whose commitments lie elsewhere and whose preferred pedagogical approaches are seen as incompatible with those required in subject areas other than their own.

Falling rolls and rapid technological and social change are bringing about constant adjustments and shifts in the secondary school curriculum, demanding in turn a degree of flexibility and adaptability on the part of the teaching force. Where subject fragmentation remains strong, where the firm boundaries and pedagogical dissimilarities between different subjects continue to be emphasized (no emotions in science, no objectivity in art, no hypotheses in history), where the subject specialist pattern of teacher training is maintained and strengthened, the chances of creating such flexibility, of developing the necessary degree of transferable pedagogic skills, will not be great. On the basis of this kind of evidence and interpretation, which recognizes the essentially *social* nature of teachers' developing curricular identities, commitments and pedagogical preferences, the improvement of teaching quality would seem better met by training and deployment policies which are less rather than more specialized in nature.

STATUS AND CAREER FACTORS

I think this year I have suffered from what they call teacher burnout. There is very, very little recognition here. Even a dog needs to be patted on the head, but you don't get that here. It makes you question whether it's worth it.[83]

Competence and efficiency are closely tied to personal senses of worth and value. Much of that worth depends, as it does for the teacher cited above, on recognition and status given to one's work by others. The importance of this association is most evident when it is broken, when careers are truncated or 'spoilt', status is withdrawn and recognition seemingly denied. Such denials of worth, whether they occur within the career structure of a particular school, or whether, through such things as pay erosion, they are seen to emanate more diffusely from society at large, lead some teachers to seek an exit from the profession. Where such options are not possible, though, status denial begins to have adverse implications for professional motivation and classroom performance. One teacher I interviewed in my middle school study, for instance, felt she had not been well treated in the reorganization to a middle school set-up and had resisted the head's attempts at change – 'We don't, some of us don't change so easily!' She went on:

> I've considered doing part-time work ... but its almost impossible now with things as they are in this area. So I settled for the fact that you can't devote the time which I feel you would need to give to the job. So I'm settled now. I've abandoned all hopes. I'm just watching and letting things go.[84]

This process of role retreatism that follows from status denial has been described particularly graphically by Riseborough in his study of a group of middle-aged, male secondary modern teachers who had been reorganized into an academically dominated comprehensive.[85] As these teachers realized they were not to get the major posts of responsibility, that their objective career progression had come to an end, that their own subject expertise was being compared unfavourably with that of their colleagues from former grammar schools, and that they were to be allocated the 'dirty work' of teaching the lower-ability groups in the lower streams – they formed a staff counterculture which set about resisting the initiatives of the head, and they withdrew that commitment and enthusiasm in the classroom that had previously been a major part of their secondary modern identity:

> What's happened must affect the teaching. You can't go into the classroom and forget about what's happening to you. I don't work as hard as I used to. I just make sure I'm not snowed under by kids. I've become quite mechanical. They took away what was important, the job I could do.
> Put it this way, if I had children of my own at school, I would be very, very worried if they had a teacher like me. I'm purely a timefiller, a babysitter. You know, I sit in my stockroom half the day with my electric kettle and a fag and a cup of coffee. And I don't care now that everyone else knows.

In this way, we can see how intimately connected teachers' classroom strategies are to teachers' cultures and careers, how what happens in the staffroom has implications for performance in the classroom also. This is a much more subtle (though politically more contentious) diagnosis that those which rest on notions of teacher burnout or personality deficiency and which individualize professional failure and blame individual teachers for it (or those who train and employ them).[86]

Once we recognize how far classroom competence has its roots in status and recognition, how closely the different elements of teachers' lives are tied together in a coherent structure of meaning and motivation, then the policy implications lead us not to personality-based initiatives or more careful selection, compulsory redundancy to remove 'incompetents' from the profession, or redeployment and encouraging early retirement, but to strategies which will improve the levels of reward and recognition in the system in terms of pay, planning time, in-service opportunity and the like, and in terms of positive (not punitive) systems of staff support and development. Much of that kind of support, though, will obviously depend on greater opportunities being created for teachers to share and witness the success of what their colleagues do. This leads me to the last determinant of transmission teaching I want to explore here: that of teacher isolation.

TEACHER ISOLATION

One of the most pervasive characteristics of teaching is that of classroom isolation – the separation of teachers with their classes into a series of egg-crate like compartments, isolated and insulated from one another's work.[87] This creates an often welcome measure of protection from inspection and intrusion. It gives teachers a kind of autonomy which they will guard jealously if pressed. But isolation from colleagues also creates uncertainty. It removes opportunities for praise and support and therefore serves to undermine confidence about the success or otherwise of one's efforts. In circumstances such as these, colleagues are led to rely on the crude, more tangible and visible indicators of classroom performance to evaluate one another's success, like examination results and noise levels.[88]

This rather crude form of collegial evaluation tends to induce a certain kind of conservatism in teachers,[89] an attachment to existing classroom methods which appear to be reasonably successful in keeping results high and noise levels low. Team-teaching, exploration of new methods, collaborative approaches to improved teaching, constructive collegial criticism of classroom performance – none of these things are fostered by the isolation and individualism of the existing culture of teaching.[90]

Where teachers are isolated in this way, working under the weighty pressure of material constraints, and immersed in the practical immediacy of the classroom environment,[91] personal classroom experience becomes increasingly attracted to itself.[92] What has been done supplies the framework of justification for what is to be done. And as existing experience, unchecked by alternative views of collective reflection, becomes sedimented into teachers' consciousness as valued and 'successful' procedure, so pedagogy undergoes petrification. Once that process of petrification is complete, little new pedagogical blood can be squeezed from it. Classroom isolation, therefore, and the culture of teacher individualism which it generates, operates to support the persistence of transmission pedagogies. Such pedagogies appear to meet the crude, externally visible criteria for professional success, and the lack of collegial reflection or criticism provides no impetus for change in them either. If teachers' allegiances to transmission pedagogies are to be loosened, then ways of encouraging their collaboration with colleagues must be found, along with the resources to do this.

Conclusion

In this chapter, I have examined the nature and validity of current 'official' explanations of teaching quality. These, it was found, rested much of their case on the importance of teachers' personal qualities, their technical expertise and their specialist subject competence. I argued that there was a lack of clarity (or clear research evidence) concerning what these appropriate qualities might be, an unfortunate tendency to abstract approved-of skills from consideration of the contextual circumstances in which they might need to be employed, and an inclination to present a one-sided interpretation of the implications of specialist subject expertise for teaching quality. Most of all, it was suggested, these explanations have placed most of the blame for quality deficits onto teachers themselves or those who train them, instead of examining the characteristics of the environment in which teachers operate and trying to understand and interpret the ways in which teachers make sense of, and adjust to, that environment.

Official explanations of deficiencies in teaching quality have tended to equate such deficiencies with tendencies to adopt transmission patterns of teaching. The chapter has also explored possible reasons why teachers adopt transmission patterns of teaching, but has looked at this not in terms of why teachers fail to do something else, but in terms of what purposes transmission teaching serves for them. This more sociological approach to the study of transmission teaching points to the importance not of personality, skill or expertise as such, but to factors such as the following:

1 the control purposes that transmission teaching serves in managing large cohorts of pupils in restricted physical surroundings;
2 its appropriateness for circumstances of low resource levels and severe material constraints;
3 its compatibility with a mandated curriculum, whether this is govern- mentally set or determined by a public examination system;
4 its association with particular subject specialisms and, elsewhere, its availability as a fall-back strategy for those teaching outside the secure boundaries of their own specialism;
5 the minimal effort demands it makes upon teachers who have lowered their investment in teaching due to career blockage and status denial;
6 its suitability for, and protection by, the conditions of teacher isolation, where external criteria of professional competence are ostensibly met and inducements to change are absent.

For those who wish to weaken the hold that transmission teaching has within the educational system, this more sociological approach to understanding the conditions of teaching quality suggests not a tightening-up of selection procedures, an improvement of training, and an emphasis in training and staff deployment on the strengthening of subject expertise, but policies such as the following:

1 re-examination of the control purposes of schooling and the extent to which they pervade the system to the exclusion of other personal and social ends like collaboration, independence and initiative;

2 allocation of improved resources to the system and the alleviation of material constraints in a way that will enhance the development of new pedagogical approaches;

3 weakening of the public examination system and attenuation of its influence on the school curriculum, possibly in favour of more continuous and pupil-centred forms of assessment, recording and review;

4 weakening of teachers' attachment to particular subject specialisms, development of subject competence across a wider range of the curriculum, and development and dissemination of awareness of the similarities in learning objectives and pedagogical approach between different subjects – in short, the easing of subject loyalties and demystification of subject differences;

5 devising, extending and improving systems of staff development and collegial support (not hierarchical and possibly punitive appraisal) for teachers;

6 creating opportunities and providing conditions in which teachers can spend more time working together, sharing problems, commenting on each others' performance, and collaborating in curriculum planning.

Reforms of this kind point to the importance of attending to the purposes and social context of teaching, if teaching itself is to be changed. In that sense, their political attractiveness is not likely to be as great as that of present policies which emphasize training, selecting and matching, and which address themselves to the individual qualities and characteristics of the teachers themselves. It would be sad, though, would it not, if the analysis of teaching quality were to be prejudged by the availability or attractiveness of particular solutions for dealing with it? One can only hope that, in coming years, politicians, bureaucrats and the teaching profession itself will be able to avoid being drawn into that particular trap.

References and Notes

1 An earlier version of this paper was presented to the Third International Conference on Teacher Thinking and Professional Action held at the University of Leuven, Belgium, 14–17 October 1986.

2 DEPARTMENT OF EDUCATION AND SCIENCE (1983) *Teaching Quality*, Cmnd 8836. London: HMSO.

3 DEPARTMENT OF EDUCATION AND SCIENCE (1985) *Better Schools*, Cmnd 9469. London: HMSO.

4 DEPARTMENT OF EDUCATION AND SCIENCE (1984) *Initial Teacher Training: Approval of Courses, Circular 3/84*. London: HMSO.

5 For more extended discussions of the deficit model of teaching, see HARGREAVES, A. (1984) Curriculum policy and the culture of teaching. Paper given at the annual meeting of the American Educational Research Association. New Orleans; and BROWN, S. and

McINTYRE, D. (1985) Research methodology and new policies for professional development and innovation. Paper given to the annual conference of the Scottish Educational Research Association.

6   HMI (1979) *Aspects of Secondary Education.* London: HMSO, p. 262.

7   HMI (1982) *The New Teacher in School.* London: HMSO.

8   See, for example, HMI (1978) *Primary Education in England.* London: HMSO; HMI (1983) *9-13 Middle Schools - An Illustrative Survey.* London: HMSO; and HMI (1985) *Education 8-12 in Combined and Middle Schools.* London: HMSO.

9   See, for example, BENNETT, N. (1976) *Teaching Styles and Pupil Progress.* London: Open Books. GALTON, M., SIMON, B. and CROLL, P. (1980) *Inside the Primary Classroom.* London: Routledge & Kegan Paul; GRACEY, H. (1975) *Curriculum of Craftmanship: Elementary Teachers in a Bureaucratic System.* Chicago: University of Chicago Press; BARNES, D. and SHEMILT, D. (1974) Transmission and interpretation. *Educational Review,* 26 (3); WESTBURY, I. (1973) Conventional classrooms, open classrooms and the technology of teaching. *Journal of Curriculum Studies,* 5 (2); HAMMERSLEY, M. (1976) The mobilisation of pupil attention. In HAMMERSLEY, M. and WOODS, P., *The Process of Schooling.* London: Routledge & Kegan Paul; and BLENKIN, G.M. and KELLY, A.V. (1981) *The Primary Curriculum.* London: Harper & Row.

10 TYE, B. (1985) *Multiple Realities: A Study of Thirteen American High Schools.* Lanham: University Press of America.

11 TYE, K. (1985) *The Junior High: School in Search of a Mission.* Lanham: University Press of America.

12 HMI (1982) (see note 7).

13 DES (1983) (see note 2).

14 DES (1985), p. 44 (see note 3).

15 *Ibid.,* p. 51.

16 See, for example, DES (1984) (see note 4).

17 Such points are made by McNamara in a more extended critique of the 'official' pre-occupation with teachers' personal qualities. See McNAMARA, D. (1986) 'The personal qualities of the teacher and educational policy: a critique', *Journal of Curriculum Studies,* 12 (1). See also RUDDUCK, J. (forthcoming) 'CATE and initial training', in HARGREAVES, A. and REYNOLDS, D. (eds) (1988) *Educational Policy: Controversies and Critiques.* Lewes: Falmer Press.

18 DES (1983), p. 8 (see note 2).

19 DES (1985), p. 44 (see note 3).

20 HMI (1979), (see note 6).

21 HMI (1982), (see note 7).

22 HMI (1983), para. 3. 19 (see note 8).

23 DES (1983), para. 3. 29 (see note 2).

24 *Ibid.,* para. 3.37.

25 *Ibid.,* para. 3.40.

26 TYE, B. (1985) (see note 10); and TYE, K. (1985) (see note 11).

27 See, for example, WILSON, S.M. and SHULMAN, L.S. (1987) '150 different ways of knowing: representations of knowledge in teaching', in CALDERHEAD, J. (ed.)*Exploring Teacher Thinking.* Eastbourne: Holt Saunders.

28 See, for instance, the experimentally based work of David Berliner, which, while not so exclusively concerned with didactic teaching, none the less focuses on subjects in the intellectual-cognitive, rather than the practical or affective domains. For instance, BERLINER, D.C. and CARTER, K.J. (1986) Differences in processing classroom information by expert and novice teachers. Paper presented to the Third International Conference of the International Study Association of Teacher Thinking, Leuven, Belgium, 14-17 October; and BERLINER, D. (1987) 'Ways of thinking about students and classrooms by more and less experienced teachers', in CALDERHEAD (see note 27).

29 The classic example here is Flanders's recommendations concerning 'indirect' teaching which, because it was based on classroom interaction samples of the transmission type,

could consider only variation *within* the transmission model, rather than possible questioning of the appropriateness of that model as a whole. See FLANDERS, N. (1970) *Analysing Teacher Behaviour*. New York: Addison-Wesley.

30 HAMMERSLEY, M. (1980) 'Putting competence into action: some sociological notes on a model of classroom interaction', in FRENCH, P. and MACLURE, M. (eds) *Adult–Child Conversation*. London: Croom-Helm.

31 HOETKER, J. and AHLBRAND, W.P. (1969) 'The persistence of the recitation', *American Educational Research Journal*, 6.

32 WESTBURY (1973) (see note 9).

33 GRACE, G. (1978) *Teachers, Ideology and Control*. London: Routledge & Kegan Paul.

34 On the mobilization of pupil attention, see HAMMERSLEY (1976) (see note 9).

35 EDWARDS, A.D. and FURLONG, V.I. (1978) *The Language of Teaching*. London: Heinemann.

36 SINCLAIR, J.M. and COULTHARD, R.M. (1974) *Towards an Analysis of Discourse*. Oxford: Oxford University Press.

37 HAMMERSLEY, M. (1974) 'The organization of pupil participation', *Sociological Review*, 22 (3).

38 THOMAS, C. (1984) An ethnographic study of sixth form life. M.Phil. thesis, Department of Educational Studies, University of Oxford.

39 HAMMERSLEY, M. (1977) 'The cultural resources required to answer a teacher's question', in WOODS, P. and HAMMERSLEY, M. (eds) *School Experience*. London: Croom Helm.

40 The centrality of the notion of the 'collective student' within teachers' thinking and practice has been discussed by BROMME, R. (1987) 'Teachers' assessments of students' difficulties and progress in understanding in the classroom', in CALDERHEAD (see note 27).

41 The most important work on 'steering groups' has been conduceted by DAHLLOF, U. and LUNDGREN, U.P. (1970) Macro and micro approaches combined for curriculum process analysis: a Swedish education field project. Report from the Institute of Göteborg, Sweden.

42 See CLARK, C.M. and PETERSON, P.L. (1980) 'Teachers' thought processes', in WITTROCK, M.C. (ed). *Handbook of Research on Teaching*, 3rd edn. New York: Macmillan.

43 WEBB, J. (1962) 'The sociology of a school', *British Journal of Sociology*, 13 (3).

44 HARGREAVES, A. (1979) 'Strategies, decisions and control: interaction in a middle school classroom', in EGGLESTON, J. (ed) *Teacher Decision Making in the Classroom*. London: Routledge & Kegan Paul.

45 WOODS, P. (1979) *The Divided School*. London: Routledge & Kegan Paul.

46 HARGREAVES, A. (1986) *Two Cultures of Schooling*. Lewes: Falmer Press.

47 See PAYNE, G. and HUSTLER, D. (1980) 'Teaching the class: the practical management of a cohort', *British Journal of Sociology of Education*, 1 (1).

48 See WILLIS, P. (1977) *Learning to Labour*. Farnborough: Saxon House; WOODS (1979) (see note 45); HAMMERSLEY (1976) (see note 9); HAMMERSLEY (1974) (see note 37); and HAMMERSLEY (1980) (see note 30). A study of a comprehensive school with a secondary modern type intake presents similar evidence. See BEYNON, J. (1985) *Initial Encounters in the Secondary School*. London: Falmer Press.

49 See BALL, S. (1981) *Beachside Comprehensive*. Cambridge: Cambridge University Press.

50 See ANYON, J. (1981) 'Social class and school knowledge', *Curriculum Inquiry*, 11 (3).

51 BLYTH, W.A.L., (1965) *English Primary Education: A Sociological Description*, Vol 2: *Background*. London: Routledge & Kegan Paul.

52 FURLONG, V.J. (1976) Interaction sets in the classroom: towards a study of pupil knowledge. In STUBBS, M. and DELAMONT, S. (eds) *Explorations in Classroom Observation*. Chichester: Willey. TORODE, B. (1978) 'Teachers' talk and classroom discipline', in MARSH, P., ROSSER, J., HARRE, R. (1978) *The Rules of Disorder*. London: Routledge & Kegan Paul. BEYNON (1985) (see note 48); ZEICHNER, K.M., TABACHNICK, B.R. and DENSMORE, K. (1987) 'Individual, institutional and cultural influences on the development of teachers' craft knowledge', in CALDERHEAD (see note 27).

53 Support for this point, and development of the concept of coping strategies more

generally, is available in HARGREAVES, A. (1978) 'The significance of classroom coping strategies', in BARTON, L. and WALKER, S. (eds) *Sociological Interpretations of Schooling and Classrooms: A Reappraisal*. Driffield: Nafferton Books.

54   WOODS (1979) (see note 45).

55   See WESTBURY (1973) (see note 9); POLLARD, A. (1985) *The Social World of the Primary School*. Eastbourne: Holt-Saunders, p. 31 and DENSCOMBE, M. (1985) *Classroom Control: A Sociological Perspective*. London: Allen & Unwin.

56   This they have done in a series of surveys of the effects of local authority expenditure policies on the education service in England and Wales.

57   HMI (1979) (see note 6).

58   HARGREAVES, D. (1982) *The Challenge for the Comprehensive School*. London: Routledge & Kegan Paul.

59   GRAY, J., McPHERSON, A.F. and RAFFE, D. (1983) *Reconstructions of Secondary Education*. London: Routledge & Kegan Paul.

60   *Ibid.*

61   See HAMMERSLEY, M. and SCARTH, J. (1986) The impact of examinations on secondary school teaching. Unpublished research report, School of Education. Milton Keynes: Open University, and SCARTH, J. and HAMMERSLEY, M., (1987) Examinations and teaching: an exploratory study. Unpublished paper, School of Education, Milton Keynes: Open University.

62   At the time of writing, Hammersley and Scarth are analysing their data with respect to some of these factors.

63   WESTON, P. (1979) *Negotiating the Curriculum*. Windsor: NFER; OLSON, J. (1982) *Innovation in the Science Curriculum*. London: Croom Helm.

64   TURNER, G. (1983) *The Social World of the Comprehensive School*. London: Croom Helm.

65   SIKES, P., MEASOR, L. and WOODS, P. (1985) *Teacher Careers: Crisis and Continuities*. Lewes: Falmer Press.

66   SCARTH, J. (1983) 'Teachers' school-based experiences of examining', in HAMMERSLEY, M. and HARGREAVES, A. (eds) *Curriculum Practice: Some Sociological Case Studies*. Lewes: Falmer Press.

67   MORTIMORE, J. and MORTIMORE, P. (1984) *Secondary School Examinations: The Helpful Servant, not the Dominating Master*. Bedford Way Papers No 18, University of London Institute of Education.

68   HMI (1982) (see note 7).

69   NATIONAL UNION OF TEACHERS (1984 a) *Teaching Quality*. London: National Union of Teachers.

70   HMI (1983) (see note 8).

71   NATIONAL UNION OF TEACHERS (1984 b) *9–13 Middle Schools*. London: National Union of Teachers.

72   See BERNSTEIN, B. (1971) 'On the classification and framing of educational knowledge', in YOUNG, M.F.D. (ed.) *Knowledge and Control*. London: Collier-Macmillan; and GOODSON, J. (1983) *School Subjects and Curriculum Change: Case Studies in the Social History of Curriculum*. London: Croom Helm.

73   A point made repeatedly in GOODSON, I. (ed.) (1985) *Social Histories of the Secondary Curriculum*. Lewes: Falmer Press.

74   BARNES and SHEMILT (1974) (see note 9).

75   BALL (1981) (see note 49). See also EVANS, J. (1985) *Teaching in Transition*. Milton Keynes: Open University Press; and HARGREAVES (1986) (see note 46).

76   BERNSTEIN (1971) (see note 72).

77   A point revealed by BAGLIN, E. (1984) A case study of a social education department. Dissertation for the Special Diploma in Educational Studies, Department of Educational Studies, University of Oxford.

78   Examples can be seen in SIKES, MEASOR and WOODS (1985) (see note 65).

79   HARGREAVES (1986), p. 188 (see note 46).

80   SIKES, MEASOR and WOODS (1985), p. 188 (see note 65).

81   HARGREAVES, D. (1983) 'The teaching of art and the art of teaching', in HAMMERSLEY and HARGREAVES (see note 66).

82   BALL, S. and LACEY, C. (1980) 'Subject disciplines as the opportunity for group action', in WOODS, P. (ed.) *Teacher Strategies*. London: Croom Helm.

83   The quotation is from a United States middle school teacher, cited in WEBB, R.B. and ASHTON, P. (eds) (1986) Teacher motivation and the conditions of teaching: a call for ecological reform. Paper delivered to the International Sociology of Education Conference, Westhill College, Birmingham.

84   HARGREAVES (1986) (see note 46).

85   RISEBOROUGH, G. (1981) 'Teacher careers and comprehensive schooling: an empirical study', *Sociology*, 15 (3).

86   For a critical discussion of teacher 'burnout', see FREEDMAN, S. (1986) 'Weeding men out of woman's true profession'. Paper delivered to the International Sociology of Education Conference, Westhill College, Birmingham.

87   These points are made by LORTIE, D. (1975) *Schoolteacher*. Chicago: University of Chicago Press.

88   DENSCOMBE (1985) (see note 55).

89   LORTIE (1975) (see note 87).

90   On the culture of individualism within teaching, see HARGREAVES (1982) (see note 58).

91   The immediacy of teaching is discussed by JACKSON, P.W. (1968) *Life in Classrooms*. New York: Holt, Rinehart and Winston; and JACKSON, P.W. (1977) 'The way teachers think', in GLICKWELL, J.C. (ed.), *The Social Context of Learning and Development*. New York: Gardner Press.

92   I have developed this point in HARGREAVES, A. (1984) 'Experience counts; theory doesn't: how teachers talk about their work', *Sociology of Education*, 57, October.

1.4 The Side Effects of Assessment
Derek Rowntree

The Competitive Aspects of Assessment

The side effects of learning for the sake of extrinsic rewards are bad enough. But what when these extrinsic rewards are in short supply? When there are not enough to go round? The side effects are then worsened by competition. In one sense, of course, there is more than enough knowledge available for everyone to have a sufficiency. As Robert Paul Wolff (1969, p. 66) points out: 'The Pythagorean theorem does not flicker and grow dim as more and more minds embrace it.' Learning is a 'free commodity', but only so long as we are thinking of knowledge as a source of intrinsic, expressive rewards. Think instead of 'approved' knowledge, legitimated and reified as GCE 'passes', admissions to college, university degrees, and the like. No longer is the supply unlimited. For one person to get more, another must make do with less. A great many assessment systems are competitive in that the extrinsic rewards they offer are in short supply and each student who wants them is asked to demonstrate that he or she is more deserving than others, or others are less deserving.

Contesting with others over the extrinsic spoils of learning is one aspect of competitive assessment. Another, upon which it depends and which usually arises early in a child's educational career, before the extrinsic rewards have become so tangible and external, is his or her teacher's public comparison of one student with another. A child will not have been in school many days before he is made aware of individual differences among his classmates. Roy Nash (1973, p. 17) discovered that pupils as young as eight years were able to say which children in the class were better than them at reading, writing and number; and their self-perceived class rank correlated highly with the rankings made by the teacher at the researcher's request (and therefore not explicitly available hitherto for communication to the children).

Such awareness can encourage learning that is motivated (extrinsically) by what John Holt called 'the ignoble satisfaction of feeling that one is better than someone else'. Jules Henry (1969) describes how a classroom atmosphere of competitive assessment fosters such a tendency. Eleven-year-old Boris is out at the blackboard publicly trying to simplify a fraction while his teacher is being excruciatingly patient and restraining the rest of the class who are bursting to put Boris right. Boris is mentally paralysed by the situation, however. So the teacher finally asks Peggy, who can be relied on to know the correct answer:

> Thus Boris' failure has made it possible for Peggy to succeed; his depression is the price of her exhilaration, his misery is the occasion of her rejoicing. This is the standard condition of the American elementary school . . . To a

Zuni, Hopi, or Dakota Indian, Peggy's performance would seem cruel beyond belief, for competition, the wringing of success from somebody's failure, is a form of torture foreign to those noncompetitive Indians... (Henry 1969, p. 83.)

But why should it be that Peggy gets a lift from knowing that she has 'beaten' Boris? To say that she has been publicly compared with him and proved superior in fraction simplification is insufficiently explanatory. No doubt the teacher too is superior, but she would hardly be expected to feel joyful on that account. Why, for instance, does Peggy not get satisfaction instead from trying to eradicate the difference between herself and Boris, e.g. by helping him reach the answer himself rather than telling him? And if she has already enjoyed the satisfaction of having climbed to a new standard of proficiency, higher than she has been before, why should she care one way or another to know that others have not yet reached this standard? Perhaps the reason is that she has been persuaded that teacher approval, and whatever other more tangible extrinsic rewards may follow, are in short supply and to gain what she needs she must not simply (or even necessarily) improve but also get (or merely stay) ahead of others.

Students generally have been led to believe that they cannot all achieve a worthwhile level of learning. They, and for the most part their teachers, often assume that only a few can do very well, the majority doing only moderately well, and a few doing poorly or even failing. This expectation is seen institutionalized among teachers who 'grade on the curve'. (The practice is to be found in education everywhere, although the terminology is American – see Terwilliger, 1971, pp. 74–100 for a discussion of this and related techniques.) Such teachers, marking students' work with, say, the grades A, B, C, D, F, will set out with a predetermined grade-distribution in mind. (E is often skipped over because by 'happy' coincidence, the next letter is the initial letter of failure!) Among 100 students, for example, they may expect to award about 10 As, 20 Bs, 40 Cs, 20 Ds and 10 Fs. (Figure 4.1 shows this expected distribution graphically – and also the underlying 'normal distribution curve' from which the method gets its name, and which we will meet again later.) The teacher who is 'grading on the curve' may, on marking a given set of students, allow himself to vary the proportions slightly. But he would likely feel uneasy if, say, twice as many students as expected appeared to deserve an A or a B. He might also fear being reproached by colleagues for lowering standards. Some teachers guard against this by making it a principle *never* to award an A. According to a French adage quoted by Remi Clignet (1974, p. 349), the maximum of 20 is 'given only to God, 19 to his saints, 18 to the professor's professor, 17 to the professor himself' – so the student of French composition can't be expected to score more than 16!

The expectation that students with A or B (or their equivalents in other systems for dispensing approval) will be in the minority has a strong hold in classrooms. Too easily it becomes a self-fulfilling prophecy: 'We can't expect the majority of students to do very well – so don't blame us for the failures.'

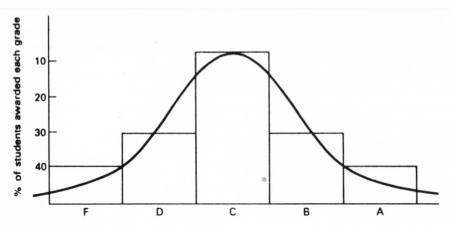

Figure 1.4   Grading on the curve

When year after year the General Nursing Council failed one-third of candidates taking SRN examinations after three years of preparation, few questioned the proportion (*Nursing Times*, 1972). Fear of passing too many students is still preventing the Esperanto Teachers' Association from getting Esperanto examined as a GCE O-level subject. They are told the language is 'too easy'. Too many students would get top grades.

The competitive nature of public examintaions was brutally brought home to me a few years ago when I was first impressed by the instructional potential of programmed learning. In an excess of enthusiasm I suggested to a GCE examiner that with the help of well-written programmes, we would soon enable nearly all students to pass O-level mathematics. 'Oh no you won't,' he said, 'we'll just raise the standard.' Conversely, the Black Paper pessimist (see Pollard, 1969) can accuse this same self-fulfilling mechanism of disguising the fact that standards are falling as the quality of candidates declines!

Such viewpoints I have since found elaborated in Brereton (1944) who records, almost as an educational 'law', that: 'the standard of an examination adjusts itself to the standard of those taking it' (p. 43). While suggesting the possibility that, as a result of the war, children may become more aware of and more knowledgeable about geography, he considers it obvious that School Certificate examinations should continue to give credit only to about half the candidates. He justifies this implicit raising of the required standard partly in order to encourage pupils to continue caring about geography lessons (as opposed to reading the newspapers) and partly because it would be unfair to give pupils taking geography a better chance of reaching university than pupils taking, say, physics under the war-time difficulties caused by shortage of laboratories and physics teachers.

In such situations – where the best X per cent of students are to get the As, the next best nX per cent the Bs, and so on – the grade awarded to a student depends not on the absolute level of performance he or she attains but on how he or she performs *relative to* other students. That is, the student may improve his or her performance by 100 per cent, but if everyone else improves similarly this grade will be no higher than before. To get a better grade the student must take it from one of the students above by out-performing him or her.

What are the side effects of an assessment system believed by students (whether rightly or wrongly) to be competitive? For most students they are centred in the need to come to terms with failure. The psychiatrist Ronald Laing suggested once that 'to be a success in our society one has to learn to dream of failure'. And Bergman's film *Wild Strawberries* shows us an elderly professor at the peak of his career, about to receive the highest academic honour in the land, who dreams the night before of failing an examination.

For a few to emerge as outstandingly successful the majority must fail – to varying degrees. The failure may be only partial. Indeed, had the student been in a different (e.g. less selective) school or college, his/her performance might well have made him/her a success. But, by comparison with those he/she has been led to emulate, he/she has fallen short. Of course, it should be possible for a student who has 'failed' at one learning task to compensate by his/her success on another task. Unfortunately, the ethos of competitive assessment often leads the student who has failed on a few tasks (e.g. learned more slowly than other people) to feel that he/she has failed *as a person*. As a 'failure' he/she may then become less capable of succeeding in subsequent tasks. His/her only consolation may be that most of his/her friends will soon be those who are failing at about the same level as he/she is. Between them they may be able to construct mutually defensive attitudes to those above them and those (if any) below them in the hierarchy.

These defensive attitudes, based on fear, envy, resentment and self-hatred, may be of various kinds. The least active response is what Philip Jackson (1968, p. 27) describes as 'devaluing the evaluations to the point where they no longer matter very much'. Perhaps this attitude of 'cooling it', 'turning off', 'keeping his head down', 'disengaging' on the part of the failing student is a special case of what Roy Cox (1967) had in mind when he said: 'It is clear that where students are assessed in a way which is not seen to be relevant to what they are aiming at they will tend to distort and degrade the assessment so that it does not become a source of esteem.'

More actively, students who cannot 'adjust' equably to being labelled 'failures' may seek alternative sources of esteem. Perhaps through their attempts to pull school (or society) apart out of hours. As Samuel Johnson pointed out: 'By exciting emulation and comparisons of superiority, you lay the foundation of lasting mischief; you make brothers and sisters hate each other.' A US Senate subcommittee survey of 1975 reports the case of a seventeen-year-old Detroit schoolgirl who was awarded massive damages after being beaten up and stabbed with pencils by thirty girl classmates who apparently resented that she was more attractive than they and received better grades. This case may be an example, more physical than usual, of what Arnold Wesker calls 'Lilliputianism – the poisonous need to cut other people down to size.'

Who knows how much of the physical damage done to property and people arises out of the resentment and frustration smouldering on from school-days? (see Hargreaves, 1967, and Lacey, 1970, for accounts of the 'D-stream subculture' in secondary schools).

Peter Vandome and his colleagues (1973) neatly sum up some of the pernicious side effects of competitive assessment at college level:

> Students feel they will gain through the poor performance of others and suffer by imparting their own knowledge to fellow students. In this way, a potentially rich source of knowledge – communication of ideas among students – tends to be stifled. To the extent that it does take place, any exchange is biased by the way in which a student's 'self-image' and his image of his fellows is affected by their grades. A 50% student for instance will think twice before putting forward one of his ideas for discussion with a group of 60% students. This is relevant not only to informal interchange between students but also to tutorial discussion. Competitive rather than co-operative behaviour may be manifested in other ways such as the 'illegal borrowing' of library books.

Sadly, teachers too are sometimes caught up in a competitive assessment system – perhaps even as beneficiaries. While the students compete for honours within their class, the teacher may be looking to the class as a whole, competing with other teachers' classes, to bring *him* esteem and promotion. The following quotation from Norman Conway, a grammar school chemistry teacher interviewed by Brian Jackson and Dennis Marsden (1962), shows how the competition for scarce university places (and ultimately for a better job for the teacher), especially in the context of bureaucratic mass-assessment can allow the instrumental pursuit of extrinsic rewards to drive out the expensive 'educational side':

> I reckon I can do 'A' level chem. in four terms. Four terms flat out mind. We have to go really fast. We have tests twice a week, but we get the results. For instance, last year I got an open at Pembroke, Cambridge, and an exhibition at Trinity Hall, Cambridge, and then I got half-a-dozen places. I've got fourteen places in the last two years and then these opens. I do pretty well; my results are all right. The way we teach, we teach for results. I want the passes, the schols and all those things. Tests all the time, and scrub the teaching methods, forget about the educational side... What I want now is a head of department in a really good school, and then I'd do what our head of department has done. I'd put on the pressure, really hard. Really work those children, tests, tests, tests, and get the results. Get them the results they should have, and that would establish me, wouldn't it? It would give me a reputation. People would know that I could do the job. I might slacken off when I got established – perhaps after ten years or so. I might start looking round and thinking more about the educational side.

But you've got to establish yourself first, haven't you? (Jackson and Marsden, 1972, pp. 36-7.)

The Giving of Grades

Much of the criticism of assessment is aimed at 'the grading system'. Thus we might expect to find that the giving of grades has a crop of side effects peculiarly its own. This, however, is not the case. The side effects usually blamed on grades are, in fact, those we have already seen associated with other aspects of assessment systems – emphasis on the easily-measured, unfairness, standardization, competition, extrinsic rewards. The giving of grades no doubt aggravates and facilitates such effects but mostly they could survive in its absence. So are grades an empty symbol, guilty by association but harmless in themselves? Not quite. Their special 'sin' is simply less obvious, being one of omission. (Remember Sherlock Holmes's clue of the dog that *didn't* bark in the night?) Grades are more to be blamed for what they do not do than for what they do do.

And what grades do not do is tell all that is known about the student's performance or abilities. Information is lost. Consider the assessment process. Someone – teacher, examiner, 'assessor' – observes the student at work, or perhaps interacts with him/her in some way, or more commonly analyses products of the student's work. The assessor forms impressions of the qualities and attainments discernible in the student's work – his interests and aversions, hang-ups and hobby-horses, strengths and weaknesses. These impressions he/she could perhaps spell out, verbalizing them for the benefit of the student and anyone else who has a legitimate interest in knowing how the student is seen by people close to him/her. Sometimes he/she will do this for an individual assessment event (e.g. in commenting on an essay):

You have shown a general understanding of the assignment, but could have improved your answers by closer attention to detail. In the first section (music) you failed to answer the part of the question that asked why the particular form used was appropriate, rather than the other forms available. In the second section, although you noted some of the imagery and discussed it intelligently, you often moved too far away from the imagery itself and relied on an 'outside' view of the poem (what you thought it must be about) to interpret it. In the final section you did pay close attention to detail, but it remained only observation of detail. You failed to connect the various elements together or to move *through* the detail to the larger issues of the painting. See the introductory section in the Unit and its explanation of the movement from meaning to form. It is a matter of working at, responding to the detail, exploring the 'resonances' of the detail and moving from this to a full appreciation of the total effect. (Tutor's comments on an Open University student's assignment, quoted in Kennedy, 1974.)

Such comments are more illuminating, particularly for the student, but also for anyone else concerned, than is a mark or grade or percentage label. (That student's essay, by the way, was graded C.) But when the assessor is expected merely to grade the product he/she will keep such insights to him or herself. Worse still, he/she perhaps never articulates them at all unless he/she expects to have to spell them out. And the tutor's impressions of one student are unlikely to remain vivid after he/she has looked at the work of a few more students. Thus his/her students will probably receive from him/her no feedback of a kind that might help them learn from his/her response to their work. Donald McIntyre (1970) illustrates what is missing when he suggests that the 'result' of a pupil's mathematics exam, *instead of* 40 per cent, might be recorded as a 'diagnostic profile' thus:

> Has mastered ideas of variable and one-to-one correspondence; not yet clear about functions; gets confused with problems of proportions; still has difficulty in structuring verbal problems (lack of grammatical under-standing?); geometry generally competent, but has not learned terminology adequately; considerable skill in analysing visual problems.

Important qualities and features differentiating one student from another are obliterated by the baldness of grades. Thus several students who have all got the same grade may have tackled quite different problems and in quite different ways. As a trivial example, one student may have scored five out of ten on his arithmetic test by answering the five additions correctly and the five subtractions incorrectly while his/her friend is given the same score for precisely the converse performance! Frances Stevens (1970) in reviewing the marking of examiners in A-level English literature, compares the gradings given to two particular scripts and reveals how much information has been lost in labelling the girl C and the boy D:

> Is the more optimistic forecast to be made of the dutiful immature girl who has some mildly appreciative responses, knows her books and has paid careful attention to what she has been told to think, but who has few independent ideas and writes with neither firmness nor joy; or of the mature and independent boy, who may not have studied his notes or perhaps his texts so thoroughly, but who has a sense of relevance, whose judgements are valid, who writes with assurance and betrays in his style ... that he has made a genuine engagement with the literature he has encountered? (Stevens, 1970, p. 130.)

Whether or not the assessor's criteria were exactly the same as Frances Stevens's is neither here nor there. They are unlikely to have been less subjective – or contestable. Translating them into a grade is an act of reification, erecting a pseudo-objective façade on what is a very delicate personal judgement. One effect of this façade is to repel debate. The grade seems god-given and immutable whereas the grounds on which it was decided might seer only too human and open to dispute. If an assessor were to respond to the girl mentioned above in the terms of Frances Stevens's assessment, he might well find her anxious to draw his attention to other qualities of her work which had been overlooked and which might revise his overall assessment. Certainly it could lead to a valuable teacher-learner dialogue. In the con ext of bureaucratic assessment, however, it could only be regarded as 'noise in the system'.

Whether or not we are always aware of the fact, grades act like *averages*. They smooth out and conceal irregularities and variability. One essay may have both first-class and abysmal features and yet be graded neither A nor F; instead it may get a C which fails altogether in letting us know that it differs from another essay graded C which is consistently of that quality in all its parts. Similarly, of two 60 per cent examination scripts, one may contain answers both of failure quality and distinction quality while the other is 60 per cent throughout. And of course, the same variability may lie behind the all-concealing degree class of 'lower second' or a diploma class of 'satisfactory' – for all we know. In short, numbers and labels do not allow us to discriminate even between stable performers and those not infrequently found (see Stevens, 1970, p. 125) 'in whose papers near-brilliance alternates with near-nonsense'.

Grades, percentages and category labels are hopelessly inadequate to convey the load of meaning that we sometimes believe we are putting into them and which other people desperately try to get out from them again. How could a single letter or number possibly tell as much, for example, as is contained in descriptive reports or profiles like those above. There is a well-known Peanuts cartoon by Charles Schulz in which a girl is sitting at her school desk querying the C-grade she's been given for her 'sculpture' made from a coat-hanger. She wants to know whether she was judged on the piece of sculpture itself; and if so is it not true that time alone can judge a work of art? or was she judged on her talent; if so, is it right that she should be judged on a part of life over which she has no control? If she was judged on her effort, then she regards the judgement as unfair since she tried as hard as she could. Was she being judged on what she had learned about the project; and if so, wasn't the teacher being judged on how well he had transmitted knowledge and therefore should he not share the C-grade? And finally, was she perhaps being judged by the inherent quality of the coat-hanger itself out of which her creation was made; and if so why should she be judged by the quality of the coat-hangers on which garments are returned by the laundry her parents patronize – since that's their responsibility shouldn't they share her grade? Her teacher's reply is not recorded.

I cannot applaud the rosy vision of a senior colleague whose spirited defence of grading (and rejection of profiles) climaxed as follows:

Grading is a method of achieving a shorthand synthesis of every possible quality that one might wish to be included in a profile, consolidated into a symbol which examiners understand pragmatically with reference to a platonic point of reference existing in the minds of a group of examiners who have worked together, while a profile, however detailed, can never be more than an attempt to put down all those qualities.

To which perhaps the only reply is St Augustine's lament:

For so it is, O Lord my God, I measure it;
But what it is that I measure I do not know.

References

BRERETON, J.I. (1944) *The Case for Examinations.* Cambridge: Cambridge University Press.

CLIGNET, R. (1974) 'Grades, examinations, and other check-points as mechanisms of social control', ch. 10 in *Liberty and Equality in the Educational Process.* New York: Wiley, pp. 327–58.

COX, R. (1967) 'Examinations, Identity and Diversity'. Talk given at the symposium on Recent Results of Research in Higher Education, organized jointly by South Birmingham Technical College and the Society for Research into Higher Education, Midlands Branch.

HARGREAVES, D.H. (1967) *Social Relations in a Secondary School.* London: Routledge & Kegan Paul.

HENRY, J. (1969) 'In suburban classrooms', in GROSS, R. and B. (eds) *Radical School Reform.* New York: Simon & Schuster.

JACKSON, B. and MARSDEN, D. (1962) *Education and the Working Class.* London: Routledge & Kegan Paul.

JACKSON, P.W. (1968) *Life in Classrooms.* New York: Holt, Rinehart & Winston.

KENNEDY, D. (1974) 'Preliminary Report on case study project in the Yorkshire Region'. Leeds: Open University (limited internal circulation).

LACEY, C. (1970) *Hightown Grammar: The School as a Social System.* Manchester: Manchester University Press.

MCINTYRE, D. (1970) 'Assessment and teaching' in RUBENSTEIN, D. and STONEMAN, C. (eds), *Education for Democracy,* 2nd edn. Harmondsworth: Penguin Books.

NASH, R. (1973) *Classrooms Observed: the teacher's perception and the pupil's performance.* London: Routledge & Kegan Paul.

NURSING TIMES (1972) 'And still they failed', editorial in *Nursing Times,* 27 July 1972.

POLLARD, A. (1969) 'O and A level: Keeping up the standards' in COX, C.B. and DYSON, A.E. (eds) *Black Paper Two.* Critical Quarterly Society.

STEVENS, F. (1970) *English and Examinations.* London: Hutchinson.

TERWILLIGER, J.S. (1971) *Assigning Grades to Students.* Glenview, Ill.: Scott, Foresman.

VANDOME, P. et al. (1973) 'Why Assessment?' Paper given limited circulation in the University of Edinburgh.

WOLFF, R.P. (1969) *The Ideal of the University.* Boston: Beacon.

Records of Achievement and the GCSE
Patricia Broadfoot

The Components of Change

Records of achievement thus rank alongside GCSE as one of the major assessment initiatives of this decade, and the two initiatives are likely to find themselves increasingly running in parallel in individual institutions. This chapter is about the significance of such a concatenation of development activity, and of the potential for links between them. In the first part of the chapter I shall look at some of the similarities which characterize both policies and then turn to some of the contradictions which may well result in significant problems for both of the initiatives.

This analysis will also require us to take into consideration still other developments in assessment procedures which are currently taking place. In particular it is necessary to consider the graded assessment movement, variously called graded tests or graduated assessments, and experiments with modular accreditation techniques.

It is beyond the scope of this chapter to consider in detail the strengths and weaknesses of this whole constellation of assessment initiatives. Rather, the thrust will be to consider not the initiatives themselves, but the interrelationship between them. The need to evaluate the impact of particular innovations is now well recognized. Indeed the DES has currently funded a major research project designed to evaluate the pilot schemes it has funded, for example for developing records of achievement. What is much less likely to be recognized is the importance of considering the *interrelationship between these various initiatives*, and certainly there is no sign as yet that such an evaluation is to take place. What this neglect may mean is the substance of this chapter.

A Growing Consensus

GCSE, records of achievement, graded assessments and modular accreditation schemes are all manifestations of a growing consensus that quite new principles need to be enshrined in certification procedures. The traditional examination emphasized recall of knowledge, external assessment, the ranking of pupils one against another and, perhaps most important of all, the provision of information suitable for selection. However the changes that have taken place in society in recent decades, resulting in the rapid growth of youth unemployment, have also resulted in a greatly reduced importance of certification at 16+ for selection purposes. A small minority of young people now leave school at 16 to go directly into employment. Most will stay on for an extra year at school or go into some form of further training. The choice of that training is often more a question of guidance than of selection. Because of this, wide support has developed for assessment procedures which are more positive and educational in their orientation. In particular, there is a concern to design certification procedures that:

1 allow a much wider range of achievements to be acknowledged;
2 make it possible for all pupils to have some testimony to their achievement;
3 will give information to potential customers which is relevant to both theirs and the pupils' needs;
4 enhance pupils' motivation and self-esteem by providing them with an achievable goal;
5 facilitate large-scale curriculum change by being both formative and summative in its impact.

In place of a 'sudden death', once-and-for-all examination, is growing support for assessment which is an integral part of day-to-day teaching and learning, which helps pupils come to understand themselves better, as well as helping the outside world, subsequently, to understand the qualities of that pupil.

Both the GCSE and records of achievement enshrine many of these principles. They are designed to be positive in their orientation, emphasizing what pupils 'know, understand and can do'. For this reason both are oriented towards criterion-referenced assessment in which achievement is measured against a given level of performance, rather than simply against the performance of other pupils. In many cases, the grade criteria of the GCSE are very similar in format to the comments and grid statements used on many profiles. Both approaches, too, emphasize the importance of teacher assessment. Teacher assessment constitutes a significant part of the assessment in all but one of the 20 principal GCSE subjects. Records of achievement clearly depend fundamentally on teacher-based assessment. Both procedures reflect current government policy concerns with increasing vocationalism and preparation for working life at the pre-16 stage. Thus there is a marked emphasis on the assessment of skills rather than knowledge in both initiatives. For this reason, both the GCSE and records of achievement are likely to require a much wider range of assessment techniques to be employed than was normal for more knowledge-based examinations, with oral and practical components figuring significantly. Finally, both initiatives are capable of incorporating graded assessment information; in the case of the GCSE this is most likely to be in the form of an equation on the graded assessment certificate; in the case of records of achievement such attainment will simply be noted on the record. Nevertheless, both provide the opportunity for such attainments to be formally recognized.

Growing Contradictions

These similarities emphasize the coherence of the contemporary assessment climate. However, if we look a little more closely, we can also detect major contradictions between the two initiatives under discussion. First of all, while records of achievement aim to describe individuals in a sufficiently detailed way to prevent comparison between them, GCSE results are still basically hierarchical in that a series of grades is involved and pupils will still be comparable according to the grade achieved. GCSE, like its predecessors, remains predominantly a 'sudden death' examination, for which there are little or no formative components, whereas the provision of regular feedback and review is becoming increasingly fundamental to profiling schemes. GCSE is also still largely concerned with subject learning and excludes assessment of any personal or work-related qualities and skills, which is a determining characteristic of records of achievement. In addition, while many, if not all, children are likely to take GCSE examinations in the most popular subjects of Maths and English, the examination is primarily designed for the same population as covered by O-level and CSE, namely the top 60 per cent or so. There will still be a significant number of young people who can hope for little success from it, in stark contrast to the commitment that *all* pupils should receive a record of achievement. Lastly, the GCSE requires pupils to wait for the length of a two-year course before they can know whether they have been successful, whereas a record of achievement is only the most recent and perhaps summarizing statement of progress which the pupils themselves have monitored and recorded.

These contradictions between GCSE and records of achievement may be explained quite simply since they reflect a fundamental tension in the purpose of school assessment itself. It is widely recognized among those involved with education that one of the most significant aspects of certification procedures is that aspects of educational endeavour which are not assessed are unlikely to be taken seriously by either teachers or pupils. During the course of the last hundred years or so educationists have progressively sold out to those who have imposed upon the education system the responsibility for attesting attainment and selecting suitable candidates. In the later stages of schooling in particular, examination oriented work in all aspects of the curriculum – aesthetic, physical, intellectual, personal, social, moral and spiritual – and the urgent necessity to cover the syllabus has resulted in many teachers feelng constrained in their choice of teaching method and objectives. As a result, it is common to find many of the widely supported objectives not explicitly recognized in assessment procedures. In consequence, these objectives have been relegated, in many cases, to the hidden curriculum and pastoral concerns.

This argument is well made by the recent report on the curriculum and organization of ILEA secondary schools, which distinguishes between four aspects of achievement (ILEA, 1984). The first – written expression, knowledge retention, organization of material and so on – is that normally measured in conventional examinations. The second relates more to skills – the application of that knowledge, practical, oral and investigative, which figures in some examinations to a greater or lesser extent. The third element covers personal and social skills, communication and relationships, the ability to work in groups and personal qualities such as initiative, responsibility, self-reliance and leadership. The fourth concerns the capacity to understand and cope with one's own experiences in terms of, for example, motivation and commitment, perseverance, self-confidence and the constructive acceptance of failure. Neither of these dimensions are explicitly recognized in public examinations. Yet few educationists would argue that they do not figure in their overall goals for what they wish pupils to achieve or that they do not impinge fundamentally on pupils' potential success or failure. The point at issue is whether such affective, and essentially subjective, aspects of educational and personal development can or should be subjected to formal recognition in the certification process. Those responsible for designing and piloting GCSE have taken the view that such aspects are not appropriate, whereas the records-of-achievement lobby would argue that they are among the most important aspects of progress to record, because in the end they are likely to be the most fundamental.

In short, the contradiction between GCSE and records of achievement hinges on the question of whether the priority for 16+ assessment should be the provision of reliable information which has high predictability for the purposes of selection, or whether the primary purpose should be to reflect what has been achieved in relation to the whole range of educational goals that a school may set for itself. This is essentially a distinction between assessment as an integral part of the curriculum and assessment which is designed primarily to be a form of communication serving the needs of the outside world.

The question therefore arises as to what the implications of this contradiction might be. The answer to this question needs to be couched as much in curriculum terms as in assessment terms. That is to say, whether or not records of achievement can coexist alongside GCSE or will, in the end, be defeated by it or perhaps even itself defeat GCSE will depend very largely on the curricular developments of the next few years. Alongside the current assessment revolution are equally radical curriculum initiatives associated with a whole alphabet soup of acronyms. The Technical and Vocational Education Initiative (TVEI) and the Certificate of Pre-Vocational Education (CPVE) are good examples of this. Both of these curriculum initiatives are associated with trying to increase the component of industrially and vocationally relevant education taking place in schools. Where TVEI is designed to be only a part of a pupil's curriculum in the 14–18 age range, the CPVE has, in contrast, been designed explicitly for that section of the pupil population for whom A-levels are inappropriate, but who wish to achieve some further, more vocationally relevant qualification at school.

Despite their differences, however, both initiatives are associated with an increasing interest in modular-based curriculum provision, and with forms of assessment which can take into account the wide range of outcomes they are designed to achieve. There is considerable variety among different TVEI schemes up and down the country but most, if not all, involve some element of profiling. In the CPVE this element of profiling is explicitly required in the arrangements for the course. The effect of innovations such as TVEI and CPVE is likely to be more far-reaching than is at present possible to envisage. If, as seems likely, the trend continues for the curricular domination of individual subjects to be supplemented or indeed replaced by a more fluid organization of learning in terms of either modular units or work-related competencies, this is also likely to strengthen the support for records of achievement with or without a component of external examination.

Having said this, the question still remains as to whether such records, particularly where associated with unfamiliar curricular approaches, can successfully challenge the status of external examination certificates in the eyes of the world at large, especially parents and employers. Any answer to this question must necessarily be qualified in terms of the type of profile concerned. It is relatively easy, for example, to envisage a complementary relationship between a profiling system which is primarily confined to the pastoral work of a school which will then complement the more conventional assessment procedures. This might be in the form of a joint certificate such as that envisaged in the Oxford Certificate of Educational Achievement (Willmott, 1986), or in the form of a supplementary record such as that provided by 'pupils' personal recording', for example (De Groot, 1986).

It is also possible to envisage successful record of achievement schemes where these are confined to a particular course such as the CPVE or some of the other externally accredited vocational courses. These are essentially isolated from the main curricular work of a school and for those involved in them the profile has its own validity in the same way that, for example, RSA typing examinations have always done. However, the government initiative of 1984, in which it commits itself to a policy of records of achievement for all pupils, states:

> The Secretaries of State believe that the internal processes of reporting, recording and discussion between teacher and pupil should cover a pupil's progress and activities across the whole educational programme of the school, both in the classroom and outside, and possibly activities outside the school as well. Regular dialogue between teacher and pupil will be important for the fulfilment of the first three purposes of records discussed earlier.
>
> The summary document or record which young people take with them when leaving school or college will need to include two main components:
>
> (i) Information, other than academic successes, which throws light on personal achievements and characteristics;
> (ii) Evidence of attainment in academic subjects and practical skills, including any graded results in public examinations.

The summary document will need to be short, clear and concise if employers and others are to make use of it. It cannot reproduce all the recording and reporting which has taken place during a pupil's years of secondary education. It should however be based on this internal recording and the final summary document should help to enhance the motivation and other benefits which pupils derive from the recording system. (DES, Welsh Office, 1984.)

This is likely to mean that this element of coexistence hitherto possible will become increasingly problematic. A brief review of the history of the profiling and records of achievement movement will serve to underline this point.

Going Public: Coexistence or Conflict

At the outset I suggested that there has been considerable grass-roots enthusiasm to initiate profiling schemes. In the late 1970s the early pioneering initiatives such as the Scottish Pupil Profile and the Evesham Personal Achievement Record were subject to considerable diversification by the entry into the field of various further education bodies. The Further Education Unit of the DES itself published a seminal curriculum document in 1979 entitled *A Basis for Choice*, and from this radical approach to curriculum provision for further education a considerable commitment to profiling has emerged. The ideas pioneered in many of the courses which followed on from the ABC document are now central to much of the thinking behind records of achievement. These include the idea of joint review of progress by students and teachers, and the idea of centre rather than pupil accreditation as the basis for the external moderation of records of achievement.

The diversification that followed the entry of further education bodies into the field of profiling was also associated with the move for a more formal institutionalization of records of achievement. In place of the school-based, or perhaps consortia-organized, profiles of the 1970s and early 1980s, there was an increasing tendency for profiling schemes to become more formally institutionalized in either a local authority context and/or in relation to an Examination Board for the purposes of validation. Thus, in the last year or two, many Examinations Boards have become involved with collections of local authorities to form profiling consortia, for example, the Northern Partnership for Records of Achievement, based on the five Examining Boards which constitute the Northern Examining Association and 22 northern LEAs, or the OCEA initiative already referred to. Significant also, in the last year or two, has been a variety of moves to evaluate the impact of records of achievement. Not only has the DES funded a major evaluation programme of its own schemes, many of the local and regional initiatives are also instituting evaluation studies.

All these data will help to inform the stage of development into which the records-of-achievement movement is now moving, namely that of nationalization following the proposals laid out in the 1984 policy statement. It is the escalation of the profiling movement from a diverse and essentially idiosyncratic set of initiatives into a development that looks likely to be rationalized in terms of National Criteria in a very similar way to that imposed on the GCSE itself which makes most problematic the relationship between the two initiatives. If we were simply talking about a supplementary form of school report, with or without external validation, it might be possible to envisage GCSE results as simply one component of such a report. If, however, as seems more likely, the current trend within the profiling movement to give increasing emphasis to the formative dimension of the process continues, then the contradiction will become increasingly pertinent.

Whereas profiles were initially envisaged as a form of school-leaving report or record, and designed to fill a gap in the existing certification procedures, it is now true to say that many, if not the majority, of those involved in such developments place their highest priority on the changes such procedures will bring about within the educational process itself. Many of the schemes currently being developed in various parts of the country are using the establishment of a record-of-achievement procedure to engage teachers in a fundamental review of their curricular goals, their teaching methods and hence their assessment criteria, with a view to stimulating a wide-ranging review of school arrangements. The kind of novel learning environment that is characteristic of the pilot CPVE schemes now being implemented, which breaks down the traditional barriers of subjects, compartmentalized lessons and didactic teaching, may well spread rapidly into other areas of the school's work. Teachers are likely to find themselves increasingly required to engage in one-to-one dialogue with individual pupils as the basis for periodic reviewing of academic and personal progress. Graded assessment and modular accreditation schemes are likely to hasten this process since they too involve the erosion of traditional subject-based teaching and curriculum boundaries and require a much greater degree of organizational flexibility and ongoing review and guidance to be provided through course tutoring if they are to be successful.

Teachers are thus likely to be faced increasingly with divergent pressures. On the one hand, GCSE requires them to develop new ways of teaching the traditional two-year subject course and, in so doing, preparing pupils with the skills required for an external exam. At the same time, they will find themselves caught up in moves to develop new organizational procedures, new teaching situations and new assessment techniques, many of which, such as one-to-one dialogue and negotiation with pupils, they will have had little or no experience of.

The problems this situation is likely to create are considerable. First, and perhaps most fundamental, is the problem of finding sufficient time. This is widely recognized as one of the biggest stumbling blocks to the successful implementation of any innovation, and particularly one such as profiling which requires teachers to find time for a new kind of activity, namely one-to-one discussion with pupils, as well as completing detailed records. In the same way, all examinations make considerable demands on teachers' time in terms of involvement in Examination Board work, running examinations in school and subsequently marking them; but an examination like GCSE, with radically new features, is likely to involve considerably more time over the next few years for teachers to become able and proficient in its procedures. Thus, time taken for GCSE will erode that available for records of achievement and vice versa.

The time problem is also related to the need for in-service training. Teachers readily admit at the present time that in most cases they have had little or no training in assessment procedures, and therefore feel they lack both the skills and the confidence to take on a more responsible role in certification. Not only will the advent of records of achievement and GCSE together make considerable demands in this respect in terms of time, it will also require teachers to engage in in-service activities for a very wide range of different assessment procedures. The potential for confusion therein is therefore considerable.

By the same token, most record-of-achievement schemes now are actively searching for some form of external accreditation through the validation of school procedures and pupils' overall programmes. The model on which GCSE is based is the more traditional one of moderation of individual pupil scripts. Thus, once again, there is considerable potential for teachers to become confused between the relative demands of these two quite different approaches to moderation and caught up in a great deal of additional work. As a consequence, they are likely to be faced with the necessity of balancing priorities – within the various demands being made upon them by the inchoate changes which characterize the present assessment climate.

In this balancing act, a number of factors are likely to be influential. One of these is pupils' attitudes to the various rival innovations, if they cannot be coordinated together. For any institution, it is likely that pupils' attitudes will constitute a significant factor in the success or otherwise of the innovation. As far as records of achievement are concerned, the attitude of pupils is likely to be even more problematic, since pupils' natural concern with the currency of their certificates, and their now well-documented tendency to see schooling largely in terms of its capacity to provide qualifications (see, for example, Turner, 1984), suggests that records of achievement may not have as immediate and enthusiastic support among pupils as they do among many teachers. The problem is one of the continuing dominance of traditional models of assessment at the same time as trying to introduce other models based on quite different educational premises.

Conclusion

The simultaneous introduction of both GCSE and records of achievement is therefore likely to render both innovations more problematic than would otherwise be the case. Goodwill, training, time, skill and pupil support are all likely to be in shorter supply than would be the case if there were not such a plethora of assessment innovations taking place at the same time. Even more fundamental than these pragmatic constraints, however, is the educational philosophy underlying the two initiatives. While two innovations embodying quite different educational values attempt to coexist it is unlikely that both will be successful. Either schools will have to lend the bulk of their support to the organization and teaching forms which are associated with more traditional forms of assessment, or they will have to recognize the full implications of new forms of recording achievement and adjust their procedures accordingly.

In this chapter I have made no attempt to discuss why it should be that the DES has found itself in the situation of promulgating these various initiatives, or indeed how it sees the relationship between them. The principal explanation is likely to be that so characteristic of English educational provision, where the strength of local initiatives is also a weakness; where central government's desire to support and disseminate a variety of innovative practices at the local level can lead to confusion and contradiction in national policy-making. More cynical commentators have suggested that the government's desire to maintain traditional examinations and to introduce records of achievement as well is a re-enactment of the 'sheep and goats' mentality of the earlier tripartite system, with academic exams being preserved for the scholastic elite, and records of achievement serving the needs of the rest (Ranson, 1984). Some would go further and argue that the wide-ranging emphasis of records of achievement on recording a great variety of skills and personal qualities, as well as specific attainments, is a re-enactment of the old elementary school concern with civic virtue and Godliness as well as basic competence in the 'three R's' (Hargreaves, 1986). It is beyond the scope of this chapter to address any of these arguments. It is likely that there is a germ of truth in them all. Rather, what this chapter has been concerned to make clear is that the potential impact of records of achievement, as well as that of the GCSE, cannot be determined without making reference to both initiatives.

It is certainly possible that the confluence of various tides of change in assessment policy will prove instrumental in creating a wave of sufficient magnitude to bring about a revolution in attitudes to 16+ certification: of generating a degree of momentum that no single initiative could achieve by itself. In the wake of such a wave would come the commitment to criterion-referenced, positive statements: to teacher-assessment and to a skills-oriented curriculum, identified earlier as the elements in a new certification consensus; to the principles of curriculum depth, breadth, balance and differentiation integral to the design of GCSE and also central to much of the thinking about records of achievement.

Sadly, it seems more likely that the appeal of the existing examination tradition will remain vastly superior to that of a novel and relatively untried procedure. If this does indeed prove to be the case, one of the most significant outcomes of the GCSE is likely to be the limitations it imposes on the parallel development of records of achievement. Experience with an earlier version of comprehensive 16+ examination north of the border where the cutting edge of educational policy has already elevated modular accreditation into a major component of post-16 certification (SED, 1983) suggests that the GCSE, like the Scottish Standard Grade, may already be obsolete, and that they hybrid offspring of the conjoining of the norm and criterion referencing pedigree that the search for subject and grade criteria represents will satisfy no one (Munro, 1985). Many informed commentators in England also take this view that the GCSE relates to an approach to secondary school curriculum and selection which social change is rapidly rendering inappropriate (see, for example, Nuttall, 1985). If it does indeed prove to be the case that the GCSE becomes outmoded almost before it has begun, for the reasons discussed in this chapter, this will represent a tragic waste of scarce educational resources. It may also prove to be the case that failure to recognize this obsolescence sufficiently early also prevented the development potential of records of achievement being recognized. To avoid this second and ultimately much more fundamental tragedy, the relationship between GCSE, records of achievement and other assessment initiatives needs to become as much a matter for urgent discussion and evaluation as the initiatives themselves.

References

DE GROOT, R. (1986) 'Pupils personal records', in BROADFOOT, P. (ed.) *Profiles and Records of Achievement: A Review of Issues and Practice*. Eastbourne: Holt Saunders.

DES/WELSH OFFICE (DEPARTMENT OF EDUCATION AND SCIENCE) (1984) *Records of Achievement: A Statement of Policy*. London: HMSO.

FEU (FURTHER EDUCATION UNIT) (1979) *A Basis for Choice*. London: DES.

HARGREAVES, A. (1986) 'Record breakers', in BROADFOOT, P. (ed.) *Profiles and Records of Achievement: A Review of Issues and Practice* Eastbourne: Holt Saunders.

ILEA (1984) *Improving Secondary Schools*. London: ILEA.

MUNRO, N. (1985) 'The quiet reform of standard grade', *Times Educational Supplement*. 29 November, p. 5.

NUTTALL, D. (1985) 'Evaluating progress towards the GCSE. Paper given to the annual conference of the British Educational Research Association, Sheffield.

RANSON, S. (1984) 'Towards a tertiary tripartism: new codes of social control and the 17+, in BROADFOOT, P. (ed.) *Selection, Certification and Control*. London: Falmer Press.

SED (SCOTTISH EDUCATION DEPARTMENT) (1983) *16s–18s in Scotland: A Statement of Policy*. Edinburgh: HMSO.

TURNER, G. (1984) 'Pupils' attitudes to examinations', in BROADFOOT, P. (ed.) *Selection, Certification and Control*. London: Falmer Press.

WILLMOTT, A. (1986) 'The Oxford Certificate of Educational Achievement', in BROADFOOT, P. (ed.) *Profiles and Records of Achievement: A Review of Issues and Practice*. Eastbourne: Holt Saunders.

Testing, Testing, Testing...
Desmond L. Nuttall

Assessment, learning and teaching are inextricably linked. Without assessment, the teacher cannot be sure whether learning has taken place and therefore what teaching is appropriate. As the guidance notes to the curriculum working groups say:

> Attainment targets will provide objectives against which pupils' progress and performance can be assessed. The main purpose of such assessment will be to show what a pupil has learnt and mastered, so as to enable teachers and parents to ensure that he or she is making adequate progress and to inform decisions about the next step.

Part of the idea of national assessment is to support teachers in this important task, that is:

> to develop ways of making assessment which teachers might find it helpful to call upon for their own internal assessments. The intention will be to build up a bank of tests, including many of the existing tests already applied by the great majority of schools for assessing pupils' performance at various ages and to make available other means of assessment for use by teachers when they consider them appropriate. (*Consultation Document on the National Curriculum 5–16.*)

So what is there to fear from the assessment arrangements that the Government is proposing to introduce to back the national curriculum? Experience shows that no one is content to use assessment only for the purpose for which it was designed: for example, examinations at 16+ are designed to assess attainment at the end of a two-year course, but they are widely used in selection for employment and further and higher education and to monitor the performance of individual schools. It comes as no surprise, therefore, to read of other purposes of national assessment:

> A National Curriculum backed by clear assessment arrangements will enable schools to be more accountable for the education they offer to their pupils, individually and collectively. The governing body, headteacher and the teachers of every school will be better able to undertake the essential process of regular evaluation because they will be able to consider their school, taking account of its circumstances, against the local and national picture as a whole ... Parents will be able to judge their children's progress against agreed national targets for attainment and will also be able to judge the effectiveness of their school. LEAs will be better placed to assess the strengths and weaknesses of the schools they

maintain by considering their performance in relation to each other and to the country at large, taking due account of relevant socio-economic factors; and the Secretaries of State will be better able to undertake a similar process nationally. (*Consultation Document on the National Curriculum, 5–16*)

The only significant omission from this list is the idea of looking at test results teacher by teacher, not just school by school!

To ensure useful assessment in school, it is vital that all these subsidiary purposes are kept in their place and do not begin to drive the whole process of test design and the reporting of results.

Methods

The Assessment of Performance Unit (APU) is a shining example of where good assessment of a wide range of objectives, including practical and oral ones, was put first and foremost. The result was that the richness and intricacy of the results, avoiding any simplistic reduction to grades, have proved valuable to teachers but of little significance to policy-makers and the public. However, because practical and oral testing is often done individually or in small groups to achieve valid and comprehensive assessment, the cost of testing each pupil is substantially more than the subject entry fee for a 16+ examination. This would become a problem if the techniques were to be used more widely.

The GCSE is another example. It will be considerably more expensive than its predecessors, not least because of the costs of including an element of moderated teacher assessment in every subject – an element that is there, at the government's wish expressed through the national criteria, to ensure that a wider range of objectives, including practical, oral, aural, investigational and expressive objectives, are assessed and taught. So modern good practice involves the assessment of a wide range of skills using a wide range of assessment techniques – at a price.

The GCSE has another lesson for national testing. At the heart of the government's hopes for GCSE was a move away from norm-referenced grading (awarding grades to fixed percentages of the candidates) towards criterion-referenced grading (awarding grades on the basis of what individual candidates know, understand and can do). The Secondary Examinations Council mounted an elaborate exercise to define criteria for the award of grades. For example, for the domain of writing in English under the objective of organization and structure, it is expected that candidates at the grade F/G borderline will 'organize the material in such a way as to enable the reader to follow the train of thought'; a grade E candidate will 'use paragraphs' while a grade C/D borderline candidate will 'organize the writing in paragraphs according to the demands of the task'. For English as a whole, over 50 such criteria were offered for the grade F/G borderline candidate with similar numbers at other grade levels. These criteria must be viewed as models – in fact, the only known model – of attainment targets differentiated for pupils of different ability, around which the national curriculum is to be built.

What have we learnt from the GCSE grade criteria exercise? First, how difficult it is to find language to express and differentiate such objectives, particularly high-level objectives that integrate lower-level skills and knowledge. Secondly, how complicated the assessment is, both technically and for teachers to apply in practice, because of the very large number of separate criteria. Thirdly, the nonsense of having a multiplicity of different targets and then having to report assessment on a single grade scale, so that in practice we cannot be sure that a candidate awarded grade F in English will have mastered all 50 targets. These theoretical, technical and practical objections are so great that the SEC has abandoned (or at the very least put on ice) the attempt to prescribe national grade criteria. Their new research programme starts from the other end by asking examiners to elicit the criteria distinguishing grades by studying scripts from particular examinations. Attempts to specify grade criteria in Scotland and Australia have also run into serious difficulties. Indeed, I know of no working system of differentiated attainment targets for fixed age groups, certainly not one that reports attainment in terms of subject grades. There is more than a hint in the consultation document that the Government is thinking in terms of a crude grading scale (for example 10 per cent got grade 1, 20 per cent grade 2, 30 per cent grade 3 – para. 36). Certainly the much vaunted West German system of the *Notenskala* is not based on a clear statement of criteria; the short descriptions of their six grades range simply from 'very good' to 'very poor', which is then elaborated as 'a performance that does not meet the required standard and indicates that even the basic knowledge is so fragmentary that the deficiencies could not be removed within a foreseeable period'.

The proposed assessment model is put forward in paragraph 29 of the *Consultation Document*:

> The Secretaries of State envisage that most of the assessment at ages 7 (or thereabouts) 11 and 14, and at 16 in non-examined subjects, will be done by teachers as an integral part of normal classroom work. But at the heart of the assessment process there will be nationally prescribed tests done by all pupils to supplement the individual teachers' assessment. Teachers will administer and mark these, but their marking – and their assessment overall – will be externally moderated.

What kind of test might be used? If it is to be readily marked on a reasonably uniform basis by hundreds of thousands of teachers, the test would have to be objective or require short answers and thus very narrow in the coverage of skills. Any broader-based test, modelled on GCSE or APU written papers, would raise major problems for the standardization of marking of a kind that examination boards have solved only with expensive and centralized arrangements. No written test can cover more than a limited range of attainment targets, and would therefore be totally unacceptable for use to moderate teacher assessment statistically. The only professionally acceptable system of moderation would be by visits and discussion, in itself a fruitful staff development device, albeit disruptive to the normal routine of schools. The success of any moderating system is heavily dependent upon a clear understanding of the meaning of the grades or other reporting device (e.g. which individual targets have been achieved), something that is missing at present.

Effects

With the requirement to publish aggregated test results, there would be a great incentive to teach to the test. The narrowing effect of the 11+ on teaching and learning in the primary school is well documented but perhaps the most damning indictment of the effects of 16+ examinations that were almost exclusively written came from Her Majesty's Inspectorate in *Aspects of Secondary Education* published in 1979:

> the effect of the dominating pursuit of examination results was to narrow learning opportunities... Sustained exposition by the teacher and extensive note-taking by the pupil tended to limit oral work... In many subjects writing tended to be stereotyped and voluminous – the result of the wide-spread practice of dictated or copied notes.

It was this critique, as much as any other, that led to the broadening of GCSE courses and assessment, and the requirement for assessing by teachers of objectives not assessable through written or other external tests.

Also well documented, for example by the Cockcroft Report, is the damaging effect of failure. A major feature of the GCSE is the notion of positive assessment, which leads to the need for differentiated assessment, a radical concept that is only just beginning to be worked out. Appropriate positive assessment is critically dependent upon the way in which attainment targets are formulated so that the lowest are genuinely within the reach of all but still expressed in positive terms while the highest offer a challenge. At the same time, the methods of differentiated assessment must avoid being divisive so that failure is not built into the very test taken (as many perceived it to be in the dual system of O-level and CSE). In addition, we must guard against the testing system breeding competitiveness, something that is encouraged by a single grading scale but made less likely by a truly criterion-referenced system and a system that acknowledges the importance of assessing work done cooperatively in groups.

The dangers of reinforcing failure from an early age are particularly acute for the disadvantaged, those with special educational needs and generally for those aged 7 (or thereabouts). The experience of testing such young children with national tests is negligible, and we are only just learning about the manifold aspects of bias in testing and assessment.

Conclusions

Sensitive, comprehensive, positive and valid assessment is in itself a tall order and we cannot yet be sure that we have achieved it in GCSE despite 17 years of intensive research and development (building on the experience of CSE and O level), coupled more recently with the major programme of INSET.

When many of the innovations of the APU and the GCSE (and one of the GCSE's conspicuous failures, namely grade criteria) are generalized to other age groups, where there is no shared understanding of grading systems and no history of moderation, and where the success of the enterprise is dependent upon the hard work and good will of the whole teaching profession, the goal of such high quality assessment must be infinitely harder to achieve.

When the Task Group on Assessment and Testing review the state of the art of testing, they should look particularly at primary record-keeping, Records of Achievement in secondary schools, graded assessment and the reporting of attainment on modules or units of study. For example, the Task Group might pay attention to the philosophy of graded assessment where the assessment is not age-related but based on a progressive set of skills. The assessments are available to all, but are not necessarily taken by every pupil at every level. Parents are, of course, informed about the level for which their child is studying and a Statement of Attainment is presented when a student has mastered all the objectives at a given level. The differentiation is therefore by stage of development, not by objectives at a given age. In this way, it has been possible to deal with the gap – as much as seven years – between pupils in their mathematical attainment at age 11. Differentiated targets and national tests, as outlined in the consultation document, do not seem to be as sensitive and flexible, but it is not too late to try to make them so.

Part Two:
The Organization and Control of Schooling

2.1 Effective Schools for the Urban Poor
Ronald Edmonds

It seems only fair that the reader know what biases, if any, inform the summary remarks I plan to make. Equity will be the focus of my discussion. By *equity* I mean a simple sense of fairness in the distribution of the primary goods and services that characterize our social order. At issue is the efficacy of a minimum level of goods and services to which we are all entitled. Some of us, rightly, have more goods and services than others, and my sense of equity is not disturbed by the fact. Others of us have almost no goods and access to only the most wretched services, and that deeply offends my simple sense of fairness and violates the standards of equity by which I judge our social order.

I measure our progress as a social order by our willingness to advance the equity interests of the least among us. Thus, increased wealth or education for the top of our social order is quite beside the point of my basis for assessing our progress toward greater equity. Progress requires public policy that begins by making the poor less poor and ends by making them not poor at all. This discussion of education will apply just such a standard to public schooling. Equitable public schooling begins by teaching poor children what their parents want them to know and ends by teaching poor children at least as well as it teaches middle-class children.

Inequity in American education derives first and foremost from our failure to educate the children of the poor. *Education* in this context refers to early acquisition of those basic school skills that assure pupils successful access to the next level of schooling. If that seems too modest a standard, note that as of now the schools that teach the children of the poor are dismal failures even by such a modest standard. Thus, to raise a generation of children whose schools meet such a standard would be an advance in equity of the first order. I offer this standard at the outset to note that its attainment is far more a matter of politics than of social science. Social science refers to those formal experiments and inquiries carried out by sociologists, psychologists, educational researchers, and other academicians whose inquiries are described as seeking the relationship among school characteristics, pupil performance, pupil family background, and pupil social class. Politics in this case refers to the substantive and procedural bases for deciding the distribution of educational resources, defining the uses to which the schools are to be put and establishing the criteria by which school personnel are to be evaluated.

Specifically, I require that an effective school bring the children of the poor to those minimal masteries of basic school skills that now describe minimally successful pupil performance for the children of the middle class. [...]

There has never been a time in the life of the American public school when we have not known all we needed to in order to teach all those whom we chose to teach. The discussion of research literature that follows may illuminate that fact, but it cannot change it.

Weber was an early contributor to the literature on the school determinants of achievement. In his 1971 study of four instructionally effective inner-city schools, Weber intended his study to be explicitly alternative to Coleman (1966), Jensen (1969), and other researchers who had satisfied themselves that low achievement by poor children derived principally from inherent disabilities characterizing the poor. Weber focused on the characteristics of four inner-city schools in which reading achievement was clearly successful for poor children on the basis of national norms. All four schools had 'strong leadership' in that their principal was instrumental in setting the tone of the school; helping decide on instructional strategies; and organizing and distributing the schools' resources. All four schools had 'high expectations' for all their students. Weber was careful to point out that high expectations are not sufficient for school success, but they are certainly necessary. All four schools had an orderly, relatively quiet, and pleasant atmosphere. All four schools strongly emphasized pupil acquisition of reading skills and reinforced that emphasis by careful and frequent evaluation of pupil progress. [...]

In 1974, the State of New York's Office of Education Performance Review published a study that confirmed certain of Weber's major findings. New York identified two inner-city public schools in New York City, both of which were serving an analogous, predominantly poor pupil population. One of the schools was high achieving, and the other was low achieving. Both schools were studied in an attempt to identify those differences that seemed most responsible for the achievement variation between the two schools. The following findings were reported:

1 The differences in student performance in these two schools seemed to be attributed to factors under the schools' control.
2 Administrative behaviour, policies, and practices in the schools appeared to have a significant impact on school effectiveness.
3 The more effective inner-city school was led by an administrative team that provided a good balance between both management and instructional skills.
4 The administrative team in the more effective school had developed a plan for dealing with the reading problem and had implemented the plan throughout the school.
5 Classroom reading instruction did not appear to differ between the two schools since classroom teachers in both schools had problems in teaching reading and assessing pupils' reading skills.
6 Many professional personnel in the less effective school attributed children's reading problems to non-school factors and were pessimistic about their ability to have an impact, creating an environment in which children failed because they were not expected to succeed. However, in

the more effective school, teachers were less sceptical about their ability to have an impact on children.

7 Children responded to unstimulating learning experiences predictably – they were apathetic, disruptive, or absent. [...]

For our purposes, these findings reinforce the relevance to pupil performance of the institutional elements of leadership, expectations, and atmosphere. If further evidence for these findings is wanted, the reader is invited to close scrutiny of the 1976 Madden, Lawson and Sweet study of school effectiveness in California. In a more rigorous and sophisticated version of the Weber and New York Studies, Madden and his colleagues studied 21 pairs of California elementary schools, matched on the basis of pupil characteristics and differing only on the basis of pupil performance on standardized achievement measures. The 21 pairs of schools were studied in an effort to identify those institutional characteristics that seemed most responsible for the achievement differences that described the 21 high achieving schools and the 21 low achieving schools. The major findings are the following ten:

1 In comparison to teachers at lower achieving schools, teachers at higher achieving schools report that their principals provide them with a significantly greater amount of support.

2 Teachers in higher achieving schools were more task-oriented in their classroom approach and exhibited more evidence of applying appropriate principles of learning than did teachers in lower achieving schools.

3 In comparison to classrooms in lower achieving schools, classrooms in higher achieving schools provided more evidence of student monitoring process, student effort, happier children, and an atmosphere conducive to learning.

4 In comparison to teachers at lower achieving schools, teachers at higher achieving schools reported that they spent relatively more time on social studies, less time on mathematics and physical education/health, and about the same amount of time on reading/language development and science.

5 In contrast to teachers at lower achieving schools, teachers at higher achieving schools report: (a) a larger number of adult volunteers in mathematics classes; (b) fewer paid aides in reading; and (c) they are more apt to use teacher aides for nonteaching tasks, such as classroom paperwork, watching children on the playground, and maintaining classroom discipline.

6 In comparison to teachers at lower achieving schools, teachers at higher achieving schools reported higher levels of access to 'outside the classroom' materials.

7 In comparison to the teachers of lower achieving schools, teachers at

higher achieving schools believed their faculty as a whole had less influence on educational decisions.

8 In comparison to teachers at lower achieving schools, teachers at higher achieving schools rated district administration higher on support services.

9 In comparison to grouping practices at lower achieving schools, the higher achieving schools divided classrooms into fewer groups for purposes of instruction.

10 In comparison to teachers in lower achieving schools, teachers in higher achieving schools reported being more satisfied with various aspects of their work (pp. 4–9).

My own conclusion is that, aside from intrinsic merit, the California study is notable chiefly for its reinforcement of leadership, expectations, atmosphere, and instructional emphasis as consistently essential institutional determinants of pupil performance.

The Brookover and Lezotte Study

I want to close this part of the discussion with summary remarks about an unusually persuasive study of school effects. In 1977, W.B. Brookover and L.W. Lezotte published their study, *Changes In School Characteristics Coincident With Changes In Student Achievement.* We should take special note of this work partly because it is a formal extension of inquiries and analyses begun in two earlier studies, both of which reinforce certain of the Weber, Madden, *et al.* and New York findings. The Michigan Department of Education's *Cost Effectiveness Study* (1976) and the Brookover, *et al.* study of *Elementary School Climate and School Achievement* (1976) are both focused on those educational variables that are liable to school control and important to the quality of pupil performance. In response to both of these studies, the Michigan Department of Education asked Brookover and Lezotte to study a set of Michigan schools characterized by consistent pupil performance improvement or decline. The Brookover and Lezotte study is broader in scope than the two earlier studies and explicitly intended to profit from methodological and analytical lessons learned in the *Cost Effectiveness* and *Elementary School Climate* studies.

Since the early 1970s, the Michigan Department of Education has annually tested all Michigan pupils in public schools in grades four and seven. The tests are criterion-referenced standardized measures of pupil performance in basic school skills. Over time these data were used by the Michigan Department of Education to identify elementary schools characterized by consistent pupil-performance improvement or decline. Brookover and Lezotte chose eight of these schools to be studied (six improving, two declining). The schools were visited by trained interviewers who conducted interviews and administered questionnaires to a great many of the school personnel. The interviews and questionnaires were designed to identify differences between the improving and declining schools, and which differences seemed most important to the pupil performance variation between the two sets of schools. The following list gives the summary results:

1   The improving schools are clearly different from the declining schools in the emphasis their staff places on the accomplishment of the basic reading and mathematics objectives. The improving schools accept and emphasize the importance of these goals and objectives while declining schools give much less emphasis to such goals and do not specify them as fundamental.

2   There is a clear contrast in the evaluations that teachers and principals make of the students in the improving and declining schools. The staffs of the improving schools tend to believe that *all* of their students can master the basic objectives; and furthermore, the teachers perceive that the principal shares this belief. They tend to report higher and increasing levels of student ability, while the declining school teachers project the belief that students' ability levels are low, and therefore, they cannot master even these objectives.

3   The staff members of the improving schools hold decidedly higher and apparently increasing levels of expectations with regard to the educational accomplishments of their students. In contrast, staff members of the declining schools are much less likely to believe that their students will complete high school or college.

4   In contrast to the declining schools, the teachers and principals of the improving schools are much more likely to assume responsibility for teaching the basic reading and math skills and are much more committed to doing so. The staffs of the declining schools feel there is not much that teachers can do to influence the achievement of their students. They tend to displace the responsibility for skill learning on the parents or the students themselves.

5   Since the teachers in the declining schools believe that there is little they can do to influence basic skill learning, it follows they spend less time in direct reading instruction than do teachers in the improving schools. With the greater emphasis on reading and math objectives in the improving schools, the staffs in these schools devote a much greater amount of time toward achieving reading and maths objectives.

6   There seems to be a clear difference in the principal's role in the improving and declining schools. In the improving schools, the principal is more likely to be an instructional leader, more assertive in his/her institutional leadership role, more of a disciplinarian, and perhaps most of all, assumes responsibility for the evaluation of the achievement of basic objectives. The principals in the declining schools appear to be permissive and to emphasize informal and collegial relationships with the teachers. They put more emphasis on general public relations and less emphasis upon evaluation of the school's

effectiveness in providing a basic education for the students.

7 The improving school staffs appear to show a greater degree of acceptance of the concept of accountability and are further along in the development of an accountability model. Certainly, they accept the MEAP (1976) tests as one indication of their effectiveness to a much greater degree than the declining school staffs. The latter tend to reject the relevance of the MEAP tests and make little use of these assessment devices as a reflection of their instruction (MEAP stands for the Michigan Educational Assessment Program).

8 Generally, teachers in the improving schools are less satisfied than the staffs in the declining schools. The higher levels of reported staff satisfaction and morale in the declining schools seem to reflect a pattern of complacency and satisfaction with the current levels of educational attainment. On the other hand, the improving school staff members appear more likely to experience some tension and dissatisfaction with the existing condition.

9 Differences in the level of parent involvement in the improving and declining schools are not clear cut. It seems that there is less overall parent involvement in the improving schools; however, the improving school staffs indicated that their schools have higher levels of *parent initiated* involvement. This suggests that we need to look more closely at the nature of the involvement exercised by parents. Perhaps parent initiated contact with the schools represents an effective instrument of educational change.

10 The compensatory education programme data suggests differences between improving and declining schools, but these differences may be distorted by the fact that one of the declining schools had just initiated a compensatory education programme. In general, the improving schools are not characterized by a high emphasis upon paraprofessional staff or heavy involvement of the regular teachers in the selection of students to be placed in compensatory education programmes. The declining schools seem to have a greater number of different staff involved in reading instruction and more teacher involvement in identifying students who are to be placed in compensatory education programmes. The regular classroom teachers in the declining schools report spending more time planning for noncompensatory education reading activities. The decliners also report greater emphasis on programmed instruction. (MEAP, 1976, pp. 79–82.)

The Search for Effective Schools Project

Before making summary remarks about the policy import of these several studies, I want to say something of my own research, *Search for Effective Schools: The Identification and Analysis of City Schools that are Instructionally Effective for Poor Children* (Edmonds and Frederiksen, 1978). This discussion will describe our ongoing efforts to identify and analyse city schools that are instructionally effective for poor and/or minority children. I am pleased to note that we have already developed unusually persuasive evidence of the thesis we seek to demonstrate in the research under discussion. Our thesis is that all children are eminently educable and that the behaviour of the school is critical in determining the quality of that education.

The Search for Effective Schools project began by answering the question: Are there schools that are instructionally effective for poor children? In September 1974, Lezotte, Edmonds, and Ratner described their analysis of pupil performance in the elementary schools that make up Detroit's Model Cities Neighborhood. All of the schools are located in inner-city Detroit and serve a predominantly poor and minority pupil population. Reading and maths scores were analysed from Detroit's spring 1973 use of the Stanford Achievement Test and the Iowa Test of Basic Skills. Of the 10,000 pupils in the 20 schools in the Model Cities' Neighborhood, 2,500 were randomly sampled. With minor variation, the sample included eight pupils per classroom in each of the 20 schools. The mean maths and reading scores for the 20 schools were compared with city-wide norms. An effective school among the 20 was defined as being at or above the city average grade equivalent in maths and reading. An ineffective school was defined as one below the city average. Using these criteria, eight of the 20 schools were judged effective in teaching maths. Nine were judged effective in teaching reading, and five were judged effective in teaching both maths and reading.

We turned next to the problem of establishing the relationship between pupil family background and building effectiveness. Two schools among the 20, Duffield and Bunche were matched on the basis of 11 social indicators. Duffield pupils averaged nearly four months above the city average in reading and maths. Bunche pupils averaged nearly three months below the city reading average and 1.5 months below the city maths average.

The similarity in the characteristics of the two pupil populations permits us to infer the importance of school behaviour in making pupil performance independent of family background. The overriding point here is that, in and of itself, pupil family background neither causes nor precludes elementary school instructional effectiveness.

Despite the value of our early work in Detroit, we recognized the limitations of the Model Cities' Neighborhood analysis. Our evaluation of school success with poor children had depended on evaluating schools with relatively homogeneous pupil populations. The numbers of schools were too few to justify firm conclusions. Finally, the achievement tests were normative, as was the basis for determining building effectiveness among the 20 schools. Even so, valuable lessons were learned in Detroit from which we would later greatly profit.

The second phase of the project was a re-analysis of the 1966 Equal Educational Opportunity Survey (EEOS) data Frederiksen, 1975). Our purpose was to answer a number of research questions that required a data base both larger and richer than had been available to use in the Model

Cities' Neighborhood analysis. We retained our interest in identifying instructionally effective schools for the poor, but in addition, we wanted to study the effects of schools on children having different social backgrounds. Such an inquiry would permit us to evaluate school contributions to educational outcomes independent of our ability to match schools on the basis of the socio-economic characteristics of their pupils.

Summarizing and oversimplifying results, we found at least 55 effective schools in the Northeast quadrant of the EEOS. Our summary definition of school effectiveness required that each school eliminate the relationship between successful performance and family background. The effective schools varied widely in racial composition, per-pupil expenditure, and other presumed determinants of school quality.

In our re-analysis of the EEOS, separate evaluations of the schools were made for subgroups of pupils of different races and home backgrounds. Schools were found to be consistently effective (or ineffective) in teaching subgroups of their populations that were homogeneous in race and economic condition. These schools were not found to be consistently effective in teaching children of differing economic condition and race. School effectiveness for a given level on Coleman's home items scale extended across racial lines. The prime factors that condition a school's instructional effectiveness appear to be principally economic and social, rather than racial.

Without seeking to match effective and ineffective schools on mean social-background variables, we found that schools that were instructionally effective for poor and black children were indistinguishable from instructionally less effective schools on measures of pupil social background (mean father's and mother's education; category of occupation; percentage of white students; mean family size; and percentage of intact families). The large differences in performance between the effective and ineffective schools could not therefore be attributed to differences in the social class and family background of pupils enrolled in the schools. This finding is in striking contrast to that of other analyses of the EEOS, which have generally concluded that variability in performance levels from school to school is only minimally related to institutional characteristics.

A very great proportion of the American people believe that family background and home environment are principal causes of the quality of pupil performance. In fact, no notion about schooling is more widely held than the belief that the family is somehow the principal determinant of whether or not a child will do well in school. The popularity of that belief continues partly because many social scientists and opinion-makers continue to espouse the belief that family background is chief cause of the quality of pupil performance. Such a belief has the effect of absolving educators of their professional responsibility to be instructionally effective.

Basic Skills for All Children

While recognizing the importance of family background in developing a child's character, personality, and intelligence, I cannot overemphasize my rejection of the notion that a school is relieved of its instructional obligations when teaching the children of the poor. I reject such a notion partly because I recognize the existence of schools that successfully teach basic school skills to all children. Such success occurs partly because these schools are determined to serve all of their pupils without regard to family background. At the same time, these schools recognize the necessity of modifying curricular design, text selection, teaching strategy, and so on, in response to differences in family background among pupils in the school.

Our findings strongly recommend that all schools be held responsible for effectively teaching basic school skills to all children. We recommend that future studies of school and teacher effectiveness consider the stratification design as a means for investigating the separate relationship of programmes and policies for pupils of differing family and social background. Information about individual student family background and social class is essential in our analysis if we are to disentangle the separate effects of pupil background and school social class make-up on pupil achievement. Moreover, studies of school effectiveness should be multivariate in character and employ longitudinal records of pupil achievement in a variety of areas of school learning. [...]

I offer the following distinguishing characteristics of schools that are instructionally effective for poor children:

- What effective schools share is a climate in which it is incumbent on all personnel to be instructionally effective for all pupils. That is not, of course, a very profound insight, but it does define the proper lines of research inquiry.

- What ought to be focused on are questions such as: What is the origin of that climate of instructional responsibility? If it dissipates, what causes it to do so? If it remains, what keeps it functioning? Our tentative answers are these. Some schools are instructionally effective for the poor because they have a tyrannical principal who compels the teachers to bring all children to a minimum level of mastery of basic skills. Some schools are effective because they have a self-generating teacher corps that has a critical mass of dedicated people who are committed to being effective for all children they teach. Some schools are effective because they have a highly politicized parent–teacher organization that holds the schools to close instructional account. The point here is to make clear at the outset that no one model explains school effectiveness for the poor or any other social class subset. Fortunately, children know how to learn in more ways than we know how to teach, thus permitting great latitude in choosing instructional strategy. The great problem in schooling is that we know how to teach in ways that can keep some children from learning almost anything, and we often choose to thus proceed when dealing with the children of the poor.

One of the cardinal characteristics of effective schools is that they are as eager to avoid things that do not work as they are committed to implementing things that do.

Summary

I want to end this discussion by noting as unequivocally as I can what seem to me the most tangible and indispensable characteristics of effective schools:

1 they have strong administrative leadership without which the disparate elements of good schooling can neither be brought together nor kept together;
2 schools that are instructionally effective for poor children have a climate of expectation in which no children are permitted to fall below minimum but efficacious levels of achievement;
3 the school's atmosphere is orderly without being rigid, quiet without being oppressive, and generally conducive to the instructional business at hand;
4 effective schools get that way partly by making it clear that pupil acquisition of basic school skills takes precedence over all other school activities;
5 when necessary, school energy and resources can be diverted from other business in furtherance of the fundamental objectives;
6 there must be some means by which pupil progress can be frequently monitored.

These means may be as traditional as classroom testing on the day's lesson or as advanced as criterion-referenced system-wide standardized measures. The point is that some means must exist in the school by which the principal and the teachers remain constantly aware of pupil progress in relationship to instructional objectives.

Two final points: first, how many effective schools would you have to see to be persuaded of the educability of poor children? If your answer is more than one, then I submit that you have reasons of your own for preferring to believe that basic pupil performance derives from family background instead of school response to family background. Secondly, whether or not we will ever effectively teach the children of the poor is probably far more a matter of politics that of social science, and that is as it should be.

While it may be improbable that our politics will ever bring us to educational equity for the poor, it is inconceivable that NIE (National Institute of Education) or AERA (American Educational Research Association) should do so. What I am therefore suggesting is that if you genuinely seek the means to educational equity for everyone, you must encourage parents' attention to politics as the greatest instrument of instructional reform extant. You must not for an instant suggest that social science as practiced in AERA or as subsidized at NIE will advance the equity interests of the poor. I mention AERA and NIE in this slightly disparaging manner for a particular reason. Their contribution to our national discourse on educational equity graphically illustrates my point that the poor are far more likely to be served by politics than by any equity interests to be found in the educational research establishment. That is, social-services enterprises like NIE are not substantively different from the schools whose study has been the object of this chapter. Left to their own devices, social services serve those they think they must, and that does not often include the children of the poor. This is not meant to suggest that NIE does not support socially useful projects, carried out by men and women of substance and merit. It is merely meant to suggest that those who get NIE money will, more often than is helpful for our purposes, be white, and of very conventional social science wisdom. Being white and of conventional wisdom is not, of course, an intrinsic disability. However, the combination does preclude repudiation of those of our social science notions that are most pernicious when discussing school reform. Repudiation of the social science notion that family background is the principal cause of pupil acquisition of basic school skills is probably prerequisite to successful reform of public schooling for the children of the poor.

It seems to me, therefore, that what is left of this discussion are three declarative statements: (a) we can, whenever and wherever we choose, successfully teach all children whose schooling is of interest to us; (b) we already know more than we need to do that; and (c) whether or not we do it must finally depend on how we feel about the fact that we haven't so far.

References

BROOKOVER, W.B., *et al.* (1976) *Elementary School Climate and School Achievement.* East Lansing: Michigan State University, College of Urban Development.

BROOKOVER, W.B. and LEZOTTE, L.W. (1977) *Changes in School Characteristics Coincident with Changes in Student Achievement.* East Lansing: Michigan State University, College of Urban Development.

COLEMAN, J.S., CAMPBELL, E.Q., HOBSON, C.J., McPARTLAND, J., MOOD, A.M., WEINFELD, F.D. and YORK, R.L. (1966) *Equality of Educational Opportunity.* Washington, DC: US Office of Education, National Center for Educational Statistics.

EDMONDS, R. and FREDERIKSEN, J.R. (1978) *Search for Effective Schools: The Identification and Analysis of City Schools that are Instructionally Effective for Poor Children.* Cambridge: Harvard University, Center for Urban Studies.

FREDERIKSEN, J. *School Effectiveness and Equality of Educational Opportunity.* Cambridge: Harvard University, Center for Urban Studies.

JENSEN, A. (1969) 'How Much Can We Boost IQ and Scholastic Achievement?' Harvard Educational Review, Winter.

MEAP (RESEARCH EVALUATION AND ASSESSMENT SERVICES OF THE MICHIGAN DEPARTMENT OF EDUCATION) (1976) *Report of the 1974-75 Michigan Cost Effectiveness Study.* Washington, DC: Capital Publications.

STATE OF NEW YORK, OFFICE OF EDUCATION PERFORMANCE REVIEW (1974) 'School Factors Influencing Reading Achievement: A Case Study of Two Inner-City Schools.' March.

TEELE, J. (1973) *Evaluating School Busing.* New York: Praeger.

WEBER, G. (1971) *Inner-City Children Can Be Taught to Read: Four Successful Schools.* Washington, DC: Council for Basic Education.

Local Management of Schools
Hywel Thomas

Introduction

The Education Reform Bill[1] proposes a major re-location of powers, from Local Education Authorities (LEAs) to schools, over the distribution of resources within schools and over the appointment and dismissal of teaching staff. While these changes find their origin with schemes for the delegation of financial control – introduced since 1981 in a small number of LEAs such as Cambridgeshire and Solihull – the current proposals are more fundamental. In the view of a report commissioned by the Department of Education and Science (DES) and intended to offer guidance to LEAs when developing their schemes:

> The changes require a new culture and philosophy of the organisation of education at the school level. They are more than purely financial; they need a general shift in management. We use the term 'Local Management of Schools' (LMS). (Coopers & Lybrand, 1988, p. 5.)

The next section will outline the principal features of the local management proposals in the Education Reform Bill, drawing attention to similarities and differences with existing schemes of financial delegation. This is followed by a section which, drawing upon the experience of delegation schemes in the UK and elsewhere, considers the implications of the local management of schools for groups who are likely to be much affected by the changes.

Proposals for the Local Management of Schools

The government's proposals for the local management of schools (DES, 1987a) have two principal objectives:

1 To ensure that parents and the community know on what basis the available resources are distributed in their area and how much is being spent on each school.
2 To give the governors... freedom to take expenditure decisions which match their own priorities.

By comparison with existing schemes of financial delegation, the first objective is innovative and is better understood as arising from concerns for increasing the accountability of education for the use of public resources. This is made clearer in a later section of the consultation document:

At the end of each year the LEA would be required to publish information on actual expenditure at each school, which could be compared to the original plans. This information together with that required of governors relating to the achievement of the national curriculum would provide the basis on which parents could evaluate whether best use had been made of the resources available to the governors. (DES, 1987a.)

While there may be concern about the nature and quality of the information on performance to which it is being linked, it does seem right and proper that a local community should receive information on the costs of education and the resource decisions of governors. In making this objective operational the Bill requires each LEA to develop a single and public formula for funding its schools, so that the community is made aware of the basis of the budget given to any one school. After allowing an LEA to set aside an amount for central administration, it is proposed that:

the LEA would then be required to allocate the total remaining sum between schools in accordance with a formula to be agreed with the Secretary of State... Legislation, and subsequent regulations, would set out a broad framework within which a formula should be constructed, and would require, in particular, that it should take account of the number and ages of registered pupils at each school. Factors such as differential social need, and different types and sizes of schools, would also require consideration. (DES, 1987a.)

The Bill is less specific about factors such as social need. Clause 27 (3b) states that the formula 'may include provision for taking into account any other factors affecting the needs of individual schools which are subject to variation from school to school'.

Formula budgeting of the type summarized in the consultation paper and the Bill is not a characteristic of existing financial delegation schemes. This much is evident from practice in Cambridgeshire and Solihull who appear to be working effective programmes without using a single funding formula. Moreover, the recently agreed formula for secondary schools in Cambridgeshire – applied for the first time in April 1988 – specifically excludes resources designed to accommodate factors such as social need and school size; these will be covered through 'direct funding' outside the rules of the formula (Cambridgeshire, 1987).

As the formula must also be agreed after consultation with all governing bodies, what seems to be proposed is not only a major change in the techniques and processes for formulating budgets, but also in the cast of characters required to take some part in the decisions, an issue considered more fully in the later section on the implications of the changes.

An initial review of the second objective of the government's proposals suggests a common approach to existing schemes of financial delegation.

Enabling governors to take expenditure decisions which match their priorities seems in harmony with Hudson's (1984) findings, from a survey of the objectives of financial delegation schemes across six LEAs. The emphasis in schemes was a concern for cost-effectiveness and the enhancement of educational capability, findings which mirror my own knowledge and understanding of several schemes. It is an objective which is based upon the 'rationale that the school is closer than the LEA to the children and is, therefore, able to identify resource needs better'. (Davies, 1987.)[2]

However, the proposals also substantially extend the freedoms of governors in the area of employment. In giving powers to the governors of schools over the appointment, suspension and dismissal of staff, the Bill makes changes which have been no part of existing schemes of financial delegation. Decisions over dismissal can be expected as some schools experience a contraction of pupil numbers: a pupil-determined funding formula will leave schools with no alternative but to dismiss teachers as their budgets contract. How this will affect teachers and schools will be discussed further in the following sections on the implications of the local management initiative.

The Implications of LMS

LMS AND THE LOCAL AUTHORITY

By strengthening the direct accountability of schools to the community and in giving schools more control over their budgets and their staff, the LMS proposals weaken the powers of LEAs over their schools. Ironically, the LEAs will have to do much of the work involved in this transfer of power and will also have to bear its consequences over any staff redundancies and its effects on non-educational areas of responsibility. The effects on Local Authorities are discussed below.

Formula-budgeting

At the core of LMS schemes which meet the requirements of the Bill will be formulae for the distribution of resources. Summary statements in consultation documents can avoid the complexities of formula funding, but there can be no doubt that it is an approach to financial delegation which will create great difficulties. The leading exponents of financial delegation in England and Wales (Solihull and Cambridgeshire) have not yet introduced a formula method of the type which seems to be suggested; Solihull resources its schools on a set of conventions which has enabled it to continue using largely historical data.

The move to an explicit and public formula approach, defining the unit cost of a school, will make it almost inevitable that LEAs will have to address the value basis of its resource allocation decisions. It will mean an end to the considerable discretion education officers have often had in allocating resources to different schools.

The change in the people involved in deciding the distribution of resources between schools is also likely to influence spending priorities. Will the change lead to more or less support for younger pupils? Will governing bodies tend to favour generous support for small schools or will they wish to concentrate support on larger schools? Will the process of consultation lead to more or less support for children from socially disadvantaged backgrounds?

Evidence collected by the author from a well-developed formula funding scheme in the Canadian school system of Edmonton, Alberta, suggests a good deal of support for small schools and for pupils with various forms of learning difficulties. However, it is important to be cautious before making assumptions that similar changes will occur in Britain where local circumstances may contribute to quite different patterns of resource distribution.

Financial and management information systems

Debates about the value basis of resource allocation decisions may seem premature when LEAs do not, at present, have the Financial Information System (FIS) to meet the specifications of the government's proposals. Devising such systems will be an enforced priority for local authority education and finance officers in the next two or more years. As such systems emerge, helped by the work of Coopers & Lybrand (1988), the information is likely to support evidence from earlier research (Hough, 1981) that the resourcing of schools is not only unequal but also the differences are not easily explained. It will certainly lead to lengthy transition periods before new schemes are finally in place, enabling those who 'lose' as a result of the change to adjust to lower levels of resourcing; meanwhile the 'winners' will be frustrated that the transition period delays the time before they receive the resources to which they are entitled.

Value for money policies

The different interpretations which can be given to LMS has implications for other value-for-money policies which a local authority may have. In Solihull, for example, LMS is part of a larger value-for-money policy pursued by the Council. This can mean that a school's delegated powers can be set aside if the Council wishes to conclude an Authority-wide contract for the delivery of some goods or services; this has already arisen with respect to policies over the purchase of books. The Bill is no specific on this issue, although it may allow schemes which limit choice to a set of contractors. This is only one area where the government's proposals will give rise to tension between LEAs and schools and within local authorities.

Managing boundary areas

Disagreements over the meaning of regulations is nothing new in local government. The allocation of responsibility over maintenance for voluntary and special agreement schools is indicative of disputes which can occur over budgetary responsibility. LMS will lead to disputes as to whether a job is classified as the responsibility of the school or the maintaining authority. This has been an area which has been the cause of much tension in Solihull (Cambridgeshire continues to exclude maintenance from its budget), although it is also an area where heads have much appreciated their delegated powers. It is also likely that Engineering Departments, Technical Services Departments and DLOs will find these developments unwelcome. Even where they do not, information systems will have to be developed and/or improved if work done is to be accurately linked with the appropriate school cost centre.

LFM AND THE TEACHERS

Commenting on existing experience of financial delegation, the DES notes that it has been 'impressed by the many examples of benefits gained by the schools' (1987a). These will undoubtedly include the evidence of virement between budget heads and items of school-determined spending priorities. A detailed analysis of the 1986/87 budgets of schools involved in Solihull's financial delegation scheme shows the level of planned virement on the current budget. In four selected secondary schools the percentage virement was: 3.3, 3.6, 2.4 and 2.0, and in three selected primary schools the percentage was 5.4, 3.3 and 2.3.

Decisions have led to one school increasing its spending on books by almost 60 per cent in one year, the employment of an extra half teacher in another and of extra foreign language assistance in a third. Freedom to make management decisions and vire funds has resulted in two schools replacing their entire telephone systems with modern installations – and more schools plan to do the same. Not only does this improve communications on large sites but costs are reduced by lower rentals on modern systems, thus increasing efficiency.

What these figures cannot show is the volume and level of staff time involved in the internal management of financial delegation. Where fairly routine work is undertaken by quite senior members of the teaching staff, questions must be raised about the effective deployment of resources. That said, the scheme is viewed favourably by the teaching staff whom I have interviewed in several of the schools. Considerable value is attached to the freedom it gives staff to select their own priorities within a given item of expenditure. For example, the same might be spent on maintenance as budgeted by the LEA but the school can select the projects. Choice on who does the work is also valued because of the flexibility and competition it brings; one school halved the cost of two projects and, compared with the quotations given by the Technical Services Department, saved £4,000. However, the range of possibilities over which this freedom is seen to apply varies greatly between schools and for different reasons.

Set against these largely positive statements, it is important that action is not confused with effectiveness. It may be that, in some cases, virement is evidence of worse use of resources. Much depends upon the abilities of heads as educationists and as effective managers. If heads lack a clear sense of purpose for the school and/or do not have the ability to lead fellow teachers in a chosen direction, extra control over resources is unlikely to enhance effectiveness; the extra responsibilities may even weaken the performance of 'underachieving' heads. As LMS is introduced this problem will become more acute, and the need for appropriate training will become more urgent than has been the case of its more voluntary and gradual extension in Cambridgeshire and Solihull. Even in these cases there is evidence of leadership styles which may run counter to the integration of financial delegation into an effective management structure. A study by Elizabeth Nicholson found that some staff, in one or two schools studied, were not even aware that theirs was a school with financial delegation. She found that a lack of general awareness of the scheme tended to be associated with 'negative opinions... [and]... suspicion of the reasons behind the scheme' (Nicholson, 1986). This problem and these suspicions may well become more common as LMS is introduced, particularly to those schools with heads who may be hostile to the idea and to those LEAs where politicians and officers oppose the proposals.

Added to this are the implications which follow from the joint effect of a funding formula – largely determined by pupil numbers – and the powers over appointment and dismissal, changes which are likely to have greatest impact when schools have falling enrolment. Fewer pupils will mean less money from the formula and will require schools to dismiss teachers in post. Where this happens, the Bill overrides any 'no redundancy' agreements so that the teacher cannot simply be kept in post. Redeployment to another school may save a teacher from redundancy but that is contingent upon finding a school and a governing body willing to take a redeployed teacher. If governors prefer to make a post available to open competition they will be free to do so; it will no longer be possible for an LEA to require a school to take a teacher. Moreover, employing surplus teachers at the centre, without posting them to schools, will be difficult in circumstances where the funding formula requires LEAs to define their need for resources for central administration. It is difficult to avoid the conclusion that LMS will lead to teacher redundancies.

Earlier discussion has already drawn attention to the effect of the funding formula in creating winners and losers in the transition from one system of funding to another, and we might also anticipate that some schools may not be much affected by the changes in the rules. For many schools then, it is important to emphasize the positive reactions to financial delegation from existing practitioners, most of whom have felt that the schemes have enhanced their ability to respond to pupil needs and to get things done on their behalf.

LMS, THE PARENTS AND THE PUPILS

Some of the implications of LMS for parents and pupils are similar to those for teachers, the educational effectiveness of school-based decisions on the budget being dependent upon the organisation's clarity of purpose over objectives and the quality of its decision-making structures. It may follow from this that, because the scope for poor decisions is increased, users of a poorly run school will be further disadvantaged when that school has influence over the budget.

Set against this concern are other threads of the government's strengthened web of accountability. Changes in the powers of LEAs to set admission limits below capacity will enable more pupils to get into popular schools (DES, 1987b). It is a change which complements LMS, ensuring a more effective management response to enhanced power over the budget; in short, more effective schools will attract support and the less effective schools will lose support and eventually close.

This transition from a highly administered system of provision towards one which allows parents and pupils more flexibility in choice of place raises important questions of efficiency and equity for the client group. Will they lead to a *general* improvement in the use to which resources are put in schools? If improvements come about will they be distributed in ways which increase or diminish current levels of educational opportunity? Will the objectives of schools change as a result of this more open environment? That these questions are raised is indicative of the extent of the change in the culture and the philosophy of schools which Coopers & Lybrand anticipate. The questions emphasize the difference in nature between the schemes of financial delegation introduced by a handful of LEAs and the changes included in the Education Reform Bill.

LMS AND THE GOVERNORS OF SCHOOLS

A requirement of Solihull's financial delegation scheme is that governors must give their approval to the school's budget statement and be involved in the year-round monitoring process. In practice only a small number of governors actively participate in the process. This is partly explained by the conjunction of the need to make decisions when problems arise and the infrequency of governors' meetings. However, it is also explained by the greater knowledge of the head about the particular circumstances of the school; in such circumstances, it will be rare that the head does not play the central role. Nevertheless, it is becoming clear that governors of schools with delegated financial authority do show a lively interest in their school finances, partly because they are now presented with more and better information at each meeting. In many schools this increased financial awareness has enhanced the governors interest in school affairs generally, and the value of their interest and support should not be underestimated.

This greater interest in school affairs poses important questions about the effects of LMS on the participation of governors. Given that the Bill protects governors from any legal consequences arising from a poorly managed scheme, will the extra powers which are to be given to governors – over finance and staff – make people more or less willing to serve as governors? How also will the relationship with the head be affected?

One feature of the relationship between heads, governors and the LEA in Solihull offers some modest evidence, at least with respect to the last question. When the delegation initiative was launched in Solihull it had a money-saving objective. While it took over three years to alter this to a value for money objective, it was the view of the teacher professionals which finally prevailed, following lengthy discussions at evaluation sessions which included politicians, officers and teachers. Notably, all the governors gave strong backing to the views of the heads. What this case may illustrate is that, in circumstances where education professionals provide more information on their own activities to their local stakeholders, and offer a reasoned defence of their own point of view, their position may well gain considerable support (Humphrey and Thomas, 1983). The ability to offer such arguments and to present them in appropriate language depends upon the natural talent of heads, or its development through training, a necessary feature if LMS is to be introduced successfully.

Conclusion: LMS in Context

There is an international context to the delegation of greater power to the level of the institution. A recent OECD (1987) seminar summarized the extent of delegated authority over the management of school buildings in Australia, Denmark, Finland, France, Netherlands, Norway, Spain, Sweden, Turkey and the United Kingdom. In an international perspective on 'school-site' management, Caldwell (1988) draws attention to its growth in the United States, Canada and Australia, as well as in Britain.

Caldwell notes that schemes in the United States emphasize administrative rather than political decentralization, 'with decisions at the school level being made within a framework of district, state or national policies and guidelines. The school remains accountable to the school district for the manner in which resources are allocated' (Caldwell, 1988). Much the same applies to the 'lighthouse' scheme (Caldwell's term) in Edmonton, Alberta where there is considerable emphasis on the accountability of the school principal to the school superintendent and the School Board of Trustees. The most developed scheme in Australia (ibid. pp. 13–15) is in the State of Victoria, where school councils representing community interests have a right to be consulted over the programme priorities of schools; however, proposals for making schools 'self-governing' were rejected.

In England and Wales, the Local Management of Schools initiative will give governors of schools a degree of independence on finance and on staffing which will be more extensive than in any other system described here. Pupil-related funding formulae will emphasise the accountability of schools to parents, arising from their greater powers of school choice. The authority of governors over the appointment, suspension and dismissal of staff will strengthen the accountability of staff to governors. It is the role of LEAs which is reduced, the changes making it impossible for them to manage schools in the future as they have done in the past. When the LMS changes are compared with other national developments, what is most significant is not the similarity of an international trend but the more fundamental re-shaping of powers which is taking place between parents, schools and local authorities in England and Wales.

Notes

1 The references to the Government's proposals in this article relate to the consultation papers and not the Education Bill (House of Commons, 1987). As appropriate the discussion will incorporate the contents of the Bill where those differ significantly from the proposals in the consultation papers.
2 'Closeness' presumably means something more than physical proximity and must reflect a good knowledge, understanding and responsiveness to pupil needs. Much of government policy on education rests upon the notion that teachers have been notably unsuccessful in identifying and responding to pupil needs. A fuller discussion of this and other issues assumed within the 'theory' of financial delegation is offered in Thomas (1987).

References

CALDWELL, B. (1988) *An International Perspective on Local Financial Management: Implications for Training in England and Wales.* A monograph commissioned by the National Development Centre for School Management Training, Bristol.
CAMBRIDGESHIRE CC (1987) *LFM News*, No. 7. 3 November.
COOPERS & LYBRAND ASSOCIATES (1988) *Local Management of Schools.* London: HMSO.
DAVIES, B. (1987) 'The Key Issues of Financial Delegation', *Education*, 170 (18), p. 370, 30 October.
DES (1987a) *Financial Delegation to Schools: Consultation Paper.* London: DES.
DES (1987b) *Admission of Pupils to Maintained Schools.* London: DES.
HOUGH, J.R. (1981) *A Study of School Costs.* Windsor: NFER/Nelson.
HOUSE OF COMMONS (1987) *Education Reform Bill*, Bill 53. London: HMSO.
HUDSON, J. (1984) *Financial Devolution to Schools.* Mimeograph. Education Management Information Exchange (EMIE). Windsor: NFER.
HUMPHREY, C. and THOMAS, H. (1983) 'Making efficient use of scarce resources', *Education*, 162, (7) pp. 125-6, 12 August.
NICHOLSON, E.A.J. (1986) *The Effects of Financial Autonomy on the School as an Organization.* B.Phil. (ed.) dissertation. University of Birmingham (unpublished).
OECD (1987) *Greater Institutional Responsibility for Educational Property Management.* Conclusions of a seminar in Cambridge, England. 21-25 September 1986. Paris: OECD.
THOMAS, H. (1987) 'Efficiency and Opportunity in School Finance Autonomy', in THOMAS, H. and SIMKINS, T. (eds) *Economics and Education Management: Emerging Themes.* Lewes: The Falmer Press.

2.3 | The Labour Process and the Division of Labour
Rob Connell

Teachers are workers, teaching is work, and the school is a workplace. These simple facts are often forgotten. Parents often judge teachers as if they were surrogate parents, kids treat them as a cross between a motorcycle cop and an encyclopaedia, politicians and media treat them as punching-bags. Nevertheless they are workers, and in understanding them it is essential to analyse their work.

Recent industrial sociology in studying other industries has emphasized the nature of the labour process and the division of labour. These are useful points of departure for the analysis of teachers' work and are explored here.

The Task and its Circumstances

Helping people to learn is a deceptively simple proposition. Phyllis Howell, Deputy Headmistress of St Margaret's College and a social science teacher of twenty years' experience, explains a basic point: 'You have to like kids, and be prepared to explain things over and over.' Len Johnson, English teacher at Greenway High School, a wry and thoughtful veteran of fifteen years in fairly tough state schools, suspects that however patient you are, teaching is somehow a mission impossible.

> Provided that absolute chaos doesn't reign in the classroom, the capable kid is going to acquire things just as he gets older. I mean, in my subject English, it's *very* difficult to teach a kid English. You can introduce him to different books – which I enjoy doing – and authors, and so on; and you can read them and make them exciting, and actually get them to do what they wouldn't have done themselves. But as to improving their English; I don't think it can be done, quite frankly.

Many teachers would agree. It is a cliché of the trade that you cannot make someone learn, though you can help them if they want to. Yet even that 'helping' is hard to specify. One gestures with phrases like 'explaining things over and over', or 'getting them to do what they wouldn't have done themselves'. Experienced and successful teachers like these often find it difficult to say how it is done, or even what, precisely, they are doing. There is something a little mysterious and evasive at the heart of the business of teaching.

This can be put more formally. Teaching is a labour process without an object. At best, it has an object so intangible – the minds of the kids, or their capacity to learn – that it cannot be specified in any but vague and metaphorical ways. A great deal of work is done in schools, day in and day out, but this work does not produce any *things*. Nor does it, like other white-collar work, produce visible and quantifiable *effects* – so many pensions paid, so many dollars turned over, so many patients cured. The 'outcomes of teaching', to use the jargon of educational research, are notoriously difficult to measure. There is even room for debate whether the quality of teaching has any effect at all: Len Johnson's opinion is not an isolated one.

I do not think it is right; and one reason is the view taken by Len Johnson's own students, who do make clear distinctions between good teaching and bad teaching, and much prefer the good stuff. But the fact remains that it is always difficult to specify the object of the teachers' labour, the raw material they are supposed to be working on. In consequence the definition of the task can expand and contract in quite alarming ways.

The popular image of schoolteaching is of talk-and-chalk in front of a class, and this still is a significant part of the day's work for many, perhaps most, teachers. Apart from principals, we only came across one teacher who never did any talk-and-chalk. But there is much more. Simply to list all the bits of work teachers mentioned to us in describing their relationships with pupils would take pages.

Even talking at a blackboard implies time spent preparing the lesson, time spent getting the class settled and willing to listen, time spent supervising exercises and correcting them. Beyond this, running a class involves keeping order; dealing with conflicts between children; having a joke with them from time to time and building up some personal contact; discussing work with them individually; planning sequences of lessons; preparing handouts and physical materials; collecting, using and storing books and audiovisual aids; organizing and marking tests and major exams; keeping records; liaising with other teachers in the same subject. Most of that has to be done separately for each class; and in the usual high school each teacher is dealing with a number of different classes each day.

That is for conventional classroom work. Beyond it there is a very wide range of jobs to be done to keep a school humming along, or even bumping along. Supervising the kids in playgrounds, at the canteen, at sporting events, onto transport, on excursions. Planning and arranging swimming carnivals, athletics days, football and netball matches, geography excursions, biology excursions and so on outside the school; drama workshops, concerts, gymnastic displays, fetes, speech days, bingo nights and so forth inside it. Going to parent/teacher nights, Parents' and Citizens' Association meetings, union meetings, staff meetings, departmental meetings. Organizing, getting facilities for, and supervizing the school magazine, the chess club, the camera club, the debating teams, the students' council, the end-of-term disco, the farewell to Year 12. Making school rules, policing them, administering punishments. Being class patron (year teacher, form mistress, house master, etc.), and coordinating information about members of the class, doing 'pastoral' work, checking rolls, answering queries. Counselling pupils in trouble, dealing with personal crises, with sexual and ethnic antagonisms, with bullying; and sometimes dealing with agitated parents, welfare officers, police. Modifying curricula, bringing programmes up to date, integrating new materials; getting familiar with new techniques, new machines, new textbooks; attending in-service conferences and courses on new curricula. Planning and taking kids on camps, bushwalking, canoeing, swimming. Writing end-of-term and end-of-year reports, final references and other official documents.

This is far from being the full tally, but it is enough to indicate the enormous range of tasks ordinarily done around a school. There is no *logical* limit to the expansion of an individual teachers' work into this yawning gulf. The more committed teachers consequently work remarkably long hours – 70 to 80 hours a week at peak times – though there is nothing obliging them to do so. Others adopt the survival strategy that makes them, in Jack Ryan's phrase, 'nine-to-three-ers'.

In another direction the lack of an object allows a limitless intensification of teachers' work. 'We teach the individual', Sheila Goffman proclaimed but each individual person is infinitely complex. Here is Mary Coleman, a young teacher at Greenway High, sketching her relationship with Fay McColl, a student she wants to push ahead:

Does she work well all the year?
Up and down – this is in English. In some subjects, in her language subjects, she's been consistently good. In English, a lot of the time, she didn't bother to pass up work, which brought her overall assessment down. When she does her work it's usually at least a B standard. I've written a few rude remarks on her English book, through the year, to the effect that she should start working instead of fiddling about. And for a while after that she's worked. Then she'll slack off again, so she gets another little comment and starts working again! I don't know whether it's just that she doesn't like English, or whether she spends her time with other subjects, and I think she's got a lot of interests outside school. She's interested in horse-riding I think, and boys, and this film-making thing.

The complexity of the relationship and its vicissitudes is obvious. So is the further work Mary could immediately do: check with the teachers in language about Fay's strategies there, find out what Fay's real view of English is, reorganize her allocation of time, try to build on her interests in horses and boys, expand the English curriculum to include films ... And Mary, unlike her colleague Len Johnson, is convinced that her teaching effort counts. She remarks later in the interview:

If I really sit on a kid that's got writing problems, and if I really help them, and if I go over their work again and again, they do learn and they do improve.

The limit is not in that child's capacity to absorb teaching, to use up Mary's labour power; the teaching could become ever more intense. The limit is purely and simply the other demands on Mary's time and energy. She goes on: 'But in the meantime, the rest of the class is playing up or doing something else while you're helping this cne kid.'

In practice, then, the labour-process-without-an-object is not an amorphous mess. It is very firmly shaped by circumstances and demands, both immediate and remote.

The physical and social space of the classroom is the most immediate of these pressures. A great deal of teaching is done with one adult and twenty or thirty children in a fairly bare room together, with the door shut. This situation has a host of consequences for teachers. Joe Milwell, who came late to teaching with a good deal of industrial experience, explains teachers' individualism this way:

Teachers generally don't ever act as a group unless the Minister [pressures them], and they suddenly coalesce and act as a group. And the minute the pressure's off, then they fragment again. This is the nature of teaching, whether it's in a staff meeting or whether it's as a complete profession. This is the nature of the beast.

Are you suggesting that a teacher is in a sense an isolate?

Yes. Because he's professionally bound up in what he's doing in his classroom. This would be different in an open space school. But in a 24×24 type of environment like we've got here, yes. That teacher couldn't care less what's happening next to him, unless it's upsetting his class. So becomes an individualist.

There are other sources of the streak of individualism in teachers' ideology: but there is still a lot of force in what he says. The classroom separates teachers from each other in the ordinary course of their work.

The constraints on their work teachers most often refer to are class sizes and school timetables. Class size both directly defines the teacher's task in whole-class teaching, and limits the teacher's ability to pursue alternatives such as one-to-one work on learning problems. Faye Taylor, a sharply observant maths teacher in one of the working-class schools, notes sadly of a pupil who was not doing 'steady work' in her classes (he was in fact resisting schooling generally at the time): 'I haven't done a very good job on Michael. But you must remember that I had quite a few others leaping around at the same time.' Thus class size has an impact on teachers' stress levels and job satisfaction. The collective memory of our interviewees includes the boom days of the late 1950s, when Ralph Duffy first came to Greenway High to teach science. He expected classes to be smaller than the '55-in-a-room' at the primary school where he had been teaching before. They were not. 'I took them into the lab: they were perched around on the window sills, you know, they couldn't all sit down.' Things are better now;

but they are not equal. Smaller class sizes, and hence easier teaching, is a common reason given by teachers in the elite private schools for preferring to be there rather than in the state system.

The other great engine of constraint is the device that distributes people into those classrooms, the school timetable. In the typical secondary school, classes are organized in about forty-minute 'periods'; at the end of each period, teachers and taught move on to another encounter. There are various modifications to this, but for the most part the classrooms and time-slots form a mighty grid through which both the school's teaching staff and their clients circulate during the week, in opposite directions.

The constraints that govern the construction of the timetable are formidable. Perhaps 800 school children and 70 teachers have to be fitted in (more in many schools), allowing for the subject specializations of each of the teachers; the agreed curriculum for the children; the allowed teacher: pupil ratios in different grades and different subjects; the use of specialized space or equipment in practical subjects, sciences, language labs, and physical eduction; the industrial agreements that lay down the number of 'free' periods in which a teacher is supposed to do marking, preparation, and individual consultation; choice of options by the pupils; streaming, setting, or other ways the school sorts a cohort into classes; differential loads for heads of departments and teachers given special responsibilities outside the classroom; and so on. Making the timetable is traditionally the job of the deputy principal, and takes weeks of work at the begining of each year. Often the mathematics staff are called in to help; and some schools have been trying with varying success, to get the job onto computers. It is hardly surprising that once a year's timetable has gelled, no school looks kindly on any proposal to change it.

Teachers certainly experience it as an absolute constraint on their work. When the bell goes the kids go, no matter what is happening, educationally, at the time. The whole school would seize up otherwise. The forty-minute period becomes a frame governing all technique. Sheila Goffman remarks that by the time you get all the desks shifted around and the pupils settled for a group discussion, half the period has gone. Arlette Anderson has her version of the same problem:

The biggest problem here is just keeping the kids quiet for five minutes so you can actually tell them what you're going to do that lesson. By the time you've done that, 25 minutes of the lesson's gone.

It is no wonder that the timetable confronts working teachers like a mountain, massive and immovable. And in one sense it is. But in another sense it is a particular solution to the problem of organizing the working lives of so many teachers and so many kids. The solution that is more or less standard in Australian secondary schools is dominant for quite specific reasons, including a particular set of divisions among teachers, a particular relation between universities and the curriculum in secondary schools, a particular conception of the process of learning, a particular pattern of control in the education system and of industrial politics on the part of teacher unions.

The Craft of Teaching

Given their situations, how do secondary teachers actually do the job? Many of their practices are versions of a method well adapted to the classroom situation, based on the idea of collective instruction. Here is a brief account of it from a private school history teacher, Julius Abernethy:

> We've just sort of gone through McIntosh, the textbook. We just get them to read round the class and various things. And then I might just elaborate on it; and they'll discuss it if they want to.

Most of the essentials are here. The content to be learnt is decided in advance of the lesson, by the teacher; in this case, on the authority of the textbook. All the pupils in the room are expected to learn the same material at the same time; there is to be only one focus of attention in the room, and the teacher may criticize any pupil whose attention wanders. The material is expounded by the teacher – in Julius' classroom in two steps, directed reading followed by his own commentary – and then worked over by the pupils. The distinctly subordinate place of the kids' initiative is clearly indicated by Julius' phrasing, 'they'll discuss it if they want to'.

Learning how to do this is acquiring the basic skill in high school teaching as it is presently constituted. A teacher who can do this can at least survive in almost all situations the school throws up.

It sounds easy; in fact it is not. It usually takes at least a year of full-time practice, on top of a year or more of teacher training and some years' advanced study of the subject being taught, before a teacher is any good at it. This is a major reason for the trauma of the First Year Out. Margaret Blackall's eloquent description of adjustment after that experience shows her settling into the standard classroom technique, which requires a certain social distance between teacher and taught, a controlled rapport ('friendly but firm'), a good deal of prior organization, and – as Margaret honestly remarks – a touch of professional insensitivity.

Some beginners never do get on top of this method, and they are likely to leave teaching quickly, or be pushed into one of the more marginal specializations around the school. Those who do, learn also to adapt it to the needs of particular subjects and particular classes. Joe Guaraldi, a biology teacher at Greenway High, lays more stress on the pupil-activity end of it, and is supported by the pattern of teaching in his department:

> I try to avoid situations where I'm in front of the class talking for 30 minutes and write up on the blackboard, and the kids are writing notes for 30

minutes. I try to avoid that – not always successfully. I prefer things where the kids are doing something that they would enjoy doing, and that they can see some value in doing, and they can do in their own pace much more. *So how do you organize that?* Well, all unit biology works in a group structure. Biology is the only subject that they do that in. So there's much more things in biology where the kids can talk amongst themselves and discuss questions. There are options in biology where the kids pick their options and do it for three or four weeks. There's set work in the option, but they get to pick which option they want.

The 'set work' still provides the framework, clearly enough. Jeremy Hansen, an experienced science teacher at St Paul's College, a private school for boys, lays the emphasis more heavily on this:

> We believe learning's hard work, and there's nothing else to do but try and make it as enjoyable as you can but at the same time point out to the boys that there's only one way to learn that topic my friend, and that's to sit down and learn it, there's no other way.

Teachers acquiring this technique learn various tricks of the trade to make the work more manageable. One trick is to teach from the back of the room, because you can see better from there who is wasting time and who is working. Jeremy Hansen arranges the seating in his classes so that all his 'problem children' are at the front and under his eye; though he notes ruefully that there is still 'friction' at the back of the room.

As time goes on, more complex and subtle aspects of the technique are learnt. Pacing, for instance. Myra Elsborough, a science teacher at Auburn College, a school making a big push in the science-maths area, concentrates on Year 11 and 12 teaching and preparation for the highly competitive Matriculation exams. However she does enough teaching in Year 10 to get to know the girls who will come on to her. She has developed ways of getting them used to 'the very big jump in standards' from Year 10 to Year 11; and has a well worked out plan for following up this jump with a gradually increasing pace, and teaching them how to handle it.

It is already clear that there is a range of variation within this classroom technique. At one end of the spectrum, 'teacher talk' is what teaching is really about; Julius Abernethy remarks of discussion among his pupils, 'it's not regular teaching'. Collective recitation, repetition, rote learning, and doing things exactly by rule, still happen in the schools, especially the more conservative private schools. John Welton, a teacher at one such, cheerfully describes how one of the boys in our sample had to adjust:

> He began here with very little idea of presentation of work, and with the institution of things like red lines for margins and red-line headings. He's got books now much better than they would have been.

But the climate of professional opinion has changed. Few teachers now would make an issue of red lines for margins, and anyone who did would be regarded in most schools as a bit eccentric.

Broadly speaking, the following is the range of methods for teaching mainstream academic subjects that we encountered. In non-academic subjects like art, music, crafts, physical education, 'personal development' (sex education, social education), part of the teaching follows the classroom model. This is the more so as these subjects get assimilated into the framework of testing for academic certification. Angela Ruskin, art teacher at St Helen's College, notes that there is a 'perennial problem' of the girls seeing art as a 'soft option'. But this is changing now it is a Matriculation subject. It is gaining more prestige, and most of the assessment at higher levels is by written tests on the model of the established academic subjects.

Still, art is far from being completely assimilated, and Angela Ruskin spends most of her time in a workshop situation. She works alongside her students rather than in front of them, physically showing how to do this or that part of the project each has undertaken. She contrasts the effects of this with the usual classroom interactions. The atmosphere is 'more relaxed', the girls speak their minds more, and they talk more freely about their own interests and concerns. It is not only the girls who get satisfaction here. Angela Ruskin herself had wanted to be a full-time artist before she became a teacher, and would still like to be. The workshop situation allows her to practice her trade.

A teacher who survives the baptism of fire, picks up a basic technique and settles down to a career in the schools, may stick at that first phase of learning and stay with tried and true devices for the rest of a working life. But for more reflective teachers the craft can be continually developed and refined. Alison Chant, a mathematics specialist, is a good example of a teacher who is continually reflecting on her methods and their presuppositions.

> Perhaps it takes longer to read, understand and remember than teachers expect. Kids will do it, but they need *time*. If you really want to know something, teach it; it's over-learned. Teachers forget that.

She notes the emotional problems of girls learning maths, and she notes the emotional problems of the maths teacher too:

> You have to face it: teaching anything complicated is an unpleasant experience. Things have to be broken up, and that is unpleasant. It is only when it gets back together that it becomes pleasurable – the things academics just love.

This is refining an existing skill to a very high level. Other teachers acquire new specializations. Glenn Moncrieff, starting out as a history teacher, became more and more interested in the problems of teaching low-stream pupils. He became his school's expert on the question, has put himself through a diploma course and a master's degree in mental retardation', and is even contemplating going overseas to take a doctorate in special education. Len Johnson is doing the same kind of thing but without the benefit of university. Starting out as an English teacher he became the school's unofficial photographer, runs the camera club, and is re-training himself as a official photography teacher.

In such ways individual teachers develop their craft. The changes cumulate, and the craft itself changes. One example has already been mentioned, the decline of drill and the rising emphasis on the pupil's activity in the process of learning. One aspect of the change, a fashion for 'activity teaching', has not always had happy results. Glenn Moncrieff, when teaching Australian history, decided to have his class re-enact in the school grounds the 1854 defence and capture of the Eureka Stockade on the Victorian goldfields. Main result: one pupil with injured leg. Other innovations in method are easier on the nerves. One of the most important in recent years has been the development of audio-visual aids for teaching: records, photographic slides, magnetic tapes, film, and more recently TV, video and stereo recording.

Conscious innovation in method is thus an important fact about the craft of teaching. It can also change in less conscious ways, as a result of wider social changes. Len Johnson, looking back on his fifteen years as a teacher, observes

> Where previously the kids used to just shut up, copy it down and regurgitate it, that's gone. If they don't understand it, or it doesn't interest them, they'll tell you, now. It suits me better in every way.

Not all teachers like it, but they all have to cope with it. Len's observation is one example of a very widespread sense, among the teachers we interviewed, that the conditions in which their craft was exercised had changed, and that the presuppositions of older techniques and traditional attitudes no longer held.

The Division of Labour

Different people do different work; that is a basic fact of industrial organization, and the education industry is no exception. The work of the teachers we studied was divided in quite complex ways, governed by several principles that are not always consistent with each other.

The first pattern is the division of labour crystallized in the school timetable. The collective teaching obligations of the school are divided according to the different contents of learning ('subjects'), the age of the student and difficulty of the content ('grades'), the presumed ability of the students, either generally or in a particular subject ('streams', 'sets'), and a complex set of rules about how much time, and what blocks of time, particular subject grade/set combinations can claim of the pupil's working week.

This carving-up of the total teaching effort of the school's staff already embodies some important educational decisions about what is learnt and under what circumstances. There is an equally complex set of rules, understandings and agreements about which teachers will do what bits of the total. Teachers are very conscious of who does the dishing-out, who has influence on it, what principles govern it, and are often far from pleased by the result.

Rosa Marshall noted how as a new member of staff she got 'all bottom classes'. This is extremely common, and not only in state schools. Allan Watson teaches the Year 12 lower stream in his boys' private school, because the upper stream is monopolized by a teacher who has been there since 1944, and is an expert on exam techniques. This pattern is another of the reasons for the trauma of the first years of teaching. You get the most difficult classes while you are least experienced.

Rosa Marshall noted another important pattern: in the state school she mentioned, all the subject heads, and the principal, were men. Even at St Margaret's College, a school for girls only, the mathematics teachers were all men. That has now changed, though the head of the science department is still a man, and there are no men at all in the English and social science departments. While the school's policy is officially counter-sexist, and 'the students are encouraged to, sort of, not think in terms of sex roles in choosing their subjects, they still see it operating.' Indeed they do. The sexual division of labour is one of the most conspicuous facts about the teaching workforce, operating between sectors of education as well as within schools. Beyond subject specialization, general assumptions about masculine and feminine character and capacities also come into play. As Len Johnson notes, with a touch of bitterness, he gets the tougher Year 8–10 classes 'because I'm male, and I'm big, and they dish out to the women – well, better classes. I don't get on too well with the subject master.'

Beyond the division of labour in teaching, there is a further division of labour among teachers because of non-teaching work, mainly a division between those who do supervisory work and those who do not. Supervisory work is broadly divided between that related to particular subjects and the departments that teach them – which is allocated to department heads (seniors, subject masters, etc) – and the administration of the school as a whole. These tasks are commonly separated in a quite material way by the architecture of the school. The former is based in departmental staff-rooms scattered around the buildings; the latter in 'the school office' or 'the administration' (there are also ruder terms) where principal, deputies, clerks and typists cluster together around the files and the photocopier, and the school nurse, psychologist and careers adviser may also have rooms.

Subtle and sometimes idiosyncratic patterns further subdivide the supervisory and administrative work of the senior teachers. Jeremy Hansen, though not a department head, has been given a subject master's teaching load in the timetable so he can be his school's Director of Extracurricular Activities. As he puts it, if 'it's not sport and it's not academic, it's mine'. He does anything from setting up a work experience programme to organizing flying lessons for senior boys. Margaret Atwill, the only woman among the senior staff at Greenway High, has informally but effectively been landed with the 'problems that involve girls'. She has become the administration's trouble shooter for issues about the emotional and sexual lives of the girls at the school, which are routinely passed over to her – one can almost hear the sighs of relief – by the men: truancies, family dramas, pregnancies, uncontrolled aggression, conflicts with male teachers, and so on and on.

Having got all this nicely laid out, it is now time to take some of it back. The division of labour among teachers is limited in various ways. The distinction between those who do administration and those who do classroom work is far from absolute. Margaret Atwill, even with that management workload, commonly does ten periods of teaching a week. The distinction may be consciously minimized. Phyllis Howell notes the importance of classroom contact hours for her care and maintenance work as deputy, in relation to the other staff as well as the students:

> [In] some schools I think the administration sort of go beyond it. But I think it's important to get the contact, as far as understanding what other staff want. I mean, it's that daily contact. You get to know one bunch of kids quite well; and you can sense the mood of the school in the children you see every day.

The division of labour between departments may also be blurred, not always intentionally. The making of the timetable itself is a force breaking down the division of labour, since the filling up of the slots – especially for the newer teachers who are last in the queue – obliges some people to take classes in subjects outside their own speciality. Roy Clive, in a boys' private school, complains that he only gets half his classes in his own subject, and usually with juniors:

> I'd like to spend more time teaching seniors, but I suppose being only a junior member of staff I can't really pick and choose. In fact even the senior people can't really pick and choose that much.

Doris Willoughby, trained as an English history teacher, found herself teaching maths and physical education. Lots of teachers had similar stories.

The other important qualification is that the division of labour changes historically. Teachers are the most numerous, but are far from being the only group of workers in schools [. . .] a good deal of the clerical work once done by teachers has been hived off and assigned to clerks and secretaries, who are now present in schools in considerable numbers. Cleaners, maintenance workers, caretakers, teaching aides, kitchen workers, psychologists, nurses, and others are there too. As with clerical staff, the division of labour between these workers and teachers is not historically fixed.

Nor is the division of labour within teaching, even the 'subject' divisions that seem so firmly institutionalized, quite fixed. At a couple of points in the research we came upon new subject specializations being constructed. This can be seen most clearly in the story of Andrew Sutting, a maths teacher at Greenway High. He started out teaching maths to lower forms, and science too; gradually he has contracted his teaching to senior maths, where computing is part of the curriculum. He is the school's computer buff. He persuaded the administration to outlay $2,000 on a school computer (a small one, but that was quite a chunk of a high school budget at the time); and his declared aim is to get computing, as a basic skill, on the timetable for all students.

In doing this he is not just constructing a personal niche in a particular school. He and teachers like him in other schools are engaged in redefining the division of labour by producing a new school subject. Given that there are already computing departments in the universities which can give it academic respectability, and there is a labour market demand and new technology to give it economic credibility, there is every prospect that they will succeed. And there is every indication, too, that it will be a strongly masculinized subject – given its growth out of mathematics teaching, its association with sophisticated machinery, and its inevitable association with power. As with the impact of computing in industry, discussed by Game and Pringle (1983), the sexual division of labour is recreated as the labour process is transformed.

Note

This book is an account of the work of a number of Australian secondary school teachers. To preserve confidentiality, real biographies were not published, instead Connell constructed 'composite biographies'. All the quoted material comes from actual interviews, but the teachers named as 'Andrew Sutting' or 'Doris Willoughby' are not real people. However, according to Connell, they are composites of the kinds of teachers who were interviewed.

References

GAME, A. and PRINGLE, R. (1983) *Gender at Work*. Sydney: George Allen & Unwin.

Inside/Out: the School in
2.4 Political Context
Stephen J. Ball

Schools as organizations cannot be conceived of as independent from the environment and they cannot be analysed simply in terms of adaptation to that environment. The national and local state may operate to limit the range of possibilities available to teachers, but at the present time at least, they certainly do not exercise absolute control within that range. As we shall see, in relation to these issues, the 1985–86 teachers' action in the UK may be interpreted as a struggle over where ultimate control over schools is to lie. However, it can be argued that events over the past ten years have already significantly changed the nature of the autonomy available to schools. Beginning with the publication of the first of the so-called Black Papers on education in 1969, teachers have become the butt of powerful criticism, from all parts of the political spectrum. The Black Papers to a great extent succeeded in establishing a publicly accepted view of teachers as responsible for declining academic standards and large-scale illiteracy and increasing violence and indiscipline among school pupils. Further, they conjured up an impression of large numbers of 'left wing' teachers working in schools and concerned solely with the political indoctrination of pupils. In addition, schools were accused of holding on to an academic curriculum ill-suited to modern technological and industrial needs and for generally fostering an anti-industrial ethos among pupils. In other words, schools and teachers were failing the nation. Indeed, for some commentators it was necessary to look no further for the causes of Britain's economic recession, notwithstanding the oil crisis – schools were to blame. In several senses these criticisms are patently ridiculous and internally contradictory, but none the less effective and damning. In effect, teachers were condemned both for hanging on stubbornly to outdated curricula and methods and succumbing to the superficial attractions of 'progressive' theories and thus abandoning traditional and well-tried curricula and methods. What these criticisms indicate perhaps is the profound tension which is built into parental, societal and political expectations of the role and purpose of schooling. The tension is between the moral and the cognitive, or integrative and economic, aspects of schooling. Schools are expected to produce well-behaved and well-adjusted citizens and at the same time select and train those citizens to take up different roles and statuses within the labour force. The increase in school violence and the general level of crime in society is taken as a mark of failure on the first count and is identified with the move away from traditional practices. The decline in British industry in the face of international competition is regarded as an indication of failure on the second count and is identified with schools' slowness to adapt to technological change. School-leavers neither have the right skills for work nor the right attitudes. Teachers find themselves damned if they do change and damned if they do not.

All of this criticism and the national moral panic about education which ensued has provided massive legitimation for greater school and teacher *accountability*. This has become a major watchword for education in the 1980s. The 'failings' of teachers have provided justification for much greater direct intervention into school processes by LEAs, the DES, HMI, the Secretary of State for Education, and other agencies like the MSC. Arguably, the education service has begun to move back towards the form of centralized control which existed until the late 1920s. Dale conceptualizes this move in terms of a shift in the relative autonomy of schools from 'licensed autonomy' to 'regulated automony'. In the first:

> An implicit licence was granted to the education system, which was renewable on the meeting of certain conditions. Just how those conditions could be met was again subject to certain broad limitations... The educational expansion of the decade from the early sixties to the early seventies stretched the terms of the education system's licence to new limits. (Dale, 1979, p. 100.)

> The major source of teachers' authority was that they could expect to be backed up by their employers and their representatives as long as they stayed within certain implicit boundaries of curriculum, pedagogy, and evaluation. (Ibid., p. 105.)

As for regulated autonomy:

> Control over the education system is to become tighter, largely through the codification and monitoring processes and practices previously left to teachers' professional judgement, taken on trust or hallowed by tradition. (Ibid., p. 104.)

In other words, the freedom of manoeuvre available to teachers is reduced. Choices have been removed or pre-empted and certain functions have been withdrawn. In effect, the lines of control are now visible rather than invisible, direct rather than indirect, explicit rather than implicit. Significantly, Dale is not suggesting that autonomy has disappeared; it has been reduced, circumscribed. Intervention and monitoring are making an impact upon the micro-politics of schools, the rules of the game *are* changing, but they have not as yet resulted in a wholesale routinization and homogenization of the system. Schools are responding differently to their changing conditions of work.

The Local Education Authority

Boyd (1976) argues that the acrimony involved in conflicts over redistribution often brings public officials into the fray. Both in attending to their school's public image and their own freedom of action, head teachers must also always look carefully to their relationships with the local education authority (LEA), both officials and council members. However, while good relationships with officials may be necessary, they are insufficient to ensure that a school maintains a good 'front' and continued access to finance and other resources. None the less, much can be achieved through such personal relationships. Discussions on the golf course or over a dinner table can achieve far more on occasion than a more formal approach. Shared allegiance may also lead to preferment for particular institutions. Freemasonry is often suggested as a network of informal influence and communication available to some heads (Burke, 1986). It is difficult to prove, but often stated, that LEAs tend to deliberately favour some schools and neglect others. Fashionable or politically nimble heads may attract special projects or additional funding for their school: 'Some schools were allowed to bloom, others were allowed to wither away. The competition between the schools was a negation of comprehensive education' (a London comprehensive head teacher). However, recent developments in local authority organization suggests that the general movement in relations between the schools and LEA officials may be towards greater formality, as systems of corporate management are introduced (Cockburn, 1978). Wallace, Miller and Ginsburg (1983) certainly found this to be the case in the authority they studied:

> Administrative changes under corporate management had wide implications for negotiative procedures, fragmenting educational interests which were once under the direct control of the Local Education Committee and significantly undermining informal interactions. In the County studied, crucial economic decisions were vested in the powerful Policy, Resources and Finance Committee. Educational buildings became the concern of the property committee and teachers' interests were made part of the task of the Personnel Committee. These shifts in the loci of the decision-making have tended to elevate financial considerations, including such matters as the possible financial return on the sale of school buildings, and to devalue the influence of social and educational criteria in policy deliberations about local schools. (Wallace, Miller and Ginsburg, 1983, p. 114)

Such changes are perhaps indicative of the shift from licence to regulation at the local level. In addition, when head teachers come incorporated into local-authority management structures, which involve 'The placing of administrative responsibility upon heads for carrying out policies made outside of school' (Wallace, Miller and Ginsburg, 1983, p. 130), then changes are also inevitable in institutional relationships. In this situation the headteacher's role as leading professional is superseded by that as manager. The gap between management and workforce is made yet more decisive.

Intervention and the Politics of Response

Two sets of factors have decisively changed school–LEA relations in the 1980s. First, the financial cuts imposed first by the Labour and then the Conservative governments (between 1976 and 1985), and the effects of falling rolls, have led to greater emphasis being placed upon planning decisions at LEA level. Levels of staffing and minimum curricula provisions are now commonly set by the LEA. Hewton (1986) argues that 'the need for resolute action in the face of uncertainty and confusion causes a shift in the locus of power. . . . Crises thus tend to lead towards the centralization of power and autocratic styles of leadership' (p. 49). In 'Shire' County studied by Hewton the response to falling rolls and financial cuts was the working out of a basic 'curriculum model': 'The curriculum model was drawn up by officers but was carefully worked out in detail with heads and unions and was painstakingly explained to councillors' (p. 66). In other words, crucial decisions concerning curriculum planning were now being taken outside the schools. This also relates to the second area of change in school–LEA relations, for LEAs have been encouraged and empowered by central government to take a more interventionist stance towards the school curriculum, albeit within an increasingly tight framework of control based in the DES. Indeed, following the publication of the government's Green Paper *Influence at School* (DES, 1984), Bennett (1985) suggests the following vision of the future of curriculum planning:

> the centre-periphery concept of curriculum creation is articulated in terms of leaving to professionals the task of deciding how to organize and deliver what is required. Curriculum development can therefore be argued to remain in qualified hands. However, the governing body is to define the school's curricular aims and objectives, working within the policy statements of the LEA and therefore the national statements within which those are themselves contained. (Bennett, 1985, p. 160.)

All of this suggests that a comprehensive model of school micro-politics should incorporate both the role of the governing body and LEA. Certainly both need to be taken into account in understanding the constraints within which school-based decision-making is set. However, the data employed in this analysis do not indicate any drastic curtailment of internecine dispute as a result of pre-emption. From the point of view of a theory of school organization, increased environmental constraints on the school and direct intervention by outside agencies must be viewed in two ways: first, as factors that enter into and become part of the existing micro-politics of the institution – these constraints and interventions become subjects of micro-political struggle; their effects are indirect, and mediated through existing micro-political relations. Secondly, as factors that change the structure and nature of micro-political relations in the institution – their effects being direct; for example, in shifting the balance of power between headteacher and staff. No particular new constraint or intervention can necessarily be analysed exclusively in terms of the first or second type of impact but the emphasis may be different. For the purposes of exposition I shall explore these different types of impact in relation to two areas of ongoing change in schools; first, the constraints arising from what Hewton (1986) calls 'the crisis of cuts', and the interventions resulting from the introduction of new curricula and examinations (e.g. TVEI, CPVE, and GCSE); second, the effects, general and specific, of the 1985–86 teachers' pay dispute. In effect, these two areas of activity will provide case studies of the impact of intervention upon school organization and micro-politics.

Survival and Change

The changing articulation of internal and external politics as financial crisis begins to bite is neatly captured by Pettigrew (1982):

> The result is the appearance of the rhetoric of finance, economics and accounting linked to strongly articulated values about efficiency, and all of these harnessed to the new preoccupation of resource management. The old deity of growth has been superseded by the new deity of survival. The language of survival becomes the central legitimating force for action.... The new concern with control puts the spotlight on who governs the system, the new concern with resources releases new energy into the organization's internal and external political processes, as empires created in the rich times are asked to reconsider their role, purpose and share of a shrinking organizational cake. (Pettigrew, 1982, p. 3.)

Thus two somewhat contradictory effects are produced by the onset of financial crisis. One is a pressure for greater centralization, the other is the stimulation of conflict. The first effect is noted by Hewton (1986) in his LEA case study, a reassertion of central control, behind closed doors. Greenwood (1983) studied several local authorities and the procedures which they followed during a period of severe financial constraint and he likens the situation to a form of 'Spanish Inquisition' which relies upon private meetings of the powerful figures outside the committee system (Hewton, 1986, p. 50). The receding locus of control is reflected in the comments of those teachers who find themselves subject to procedures leading to redeployment or redundancy. There is a strong sense of powerlessness, of decisions being made elsewhere, of unknown or unclear criteria being used. One thing that is heightened in this sort of situation, literally, is the sense of them and us. 'They' make the decisions and 'we' have to put up with them. As one of the interviewed heads put it, 'When the chips are down all decisions are made from top management in a school, we pretend very often that we've done it democratically but in the long run decisions are made finally by people in top management positions'.

As organizational 'slack' (Cyert and March, 1963) is wiped out and then core funding reduced, competing demands can no longer be satisfied. The micro-political emphasis is upon survival of the sub-units of the organization; tension increases as some of the competitors lose out in the allocation of reduced monies, posts or resources. Value differences and competing material interests will be directly exposed.

The general effects of cuts on the curricula provision of schools has been monitored since 1978 by annual HMI Inspectorate reports. These reports give some impression of the potential for and outcomes of conflicts in schools. In particular, they note 'an increasing mismatch between the qualifications and experience of teachers and their teaching commitments' and 'the loss of individual subjects' included among which are craft, design and technology, modern languages, general studies, aspects of physical education and music, geology and photography, and remedial provision. In particular institutions these are the empires or parts of empires which have been lost. However, set against these losses, the effects of cuts, there are new 'initiatives' which open up possibilities for some individuals or groups of teachers to gain a greater influence than previously, to develop their careers, enhance their status or make new claims for resources. Proposals like CPVE, TVEI, GCSE or school self-evaluation or school-based in-service work are both subject to and become part of the micro-political arena of the school. Simply because they emanate from outside the school, they do not automatically nullify, negate or eliminate micro-political struggle. Such initiatives, their acceptance, their implementation, become the site as well as the stake of internal dispute. New territories may be staked out, monies earmarked, appointments captured and policies defined. The initiatives themselves may be captured and redefined by particular interests or coalitions, *in* their interest. They are a beginning not the end of conflict inside the school.

The changing political and educational rhetorics which are addressed and in which schooling is embedded can provide new and powerful vocabularies of motives and structures of legitimation for interest groups in the micro-political arena. The advancement of the 'pastoral curriculum' is a case in point. In a broad context of youth unemployment, the restructuring of school-work relationships and a 'moral panic' concerning rising crime and 'youth on the streets', schools are expected to 'take the blame' and 'mend their ways'. The 'educational' responses to these issues are a basis for a change in the distribution of influence inside schools. The emphasis on preparation for work (or employment) and/or adult life has given impetus to pre-vocational courses, and to courses on 'life-skills' and 'personal and social education'. The concomitant changes in forms of assessment – profiling, records of achievement, and graded testing – have created new areas of responsibility and specialist knowledge for the teachers involved, usually pastoral-care staff. Such developments may be seen as contributing, on the one hand, to the overall professionalization of pastoral care and, on the other, they have created a focus for renewed struggle between academic and pastoral interests in schools. Both social education and assessment and guidance offer areas of specialism and esoteric knowledge to pastoral-care teachers. Both enable claims to be made for more timetabled time and more non-timetabled time (free periods) for pastoral work. Both types of time are scarce and critical resources. Furthermore, as new or different skills are legitimated for and demanded of teachers then the system of status and reward begins to change. The introduction of vocationally orientated courses can bring about 'status reversal', moving the marginal 'practical' subjects on to centre stage and reducing the importance of the purely 'academic'. However, the 'initiatives' themselves are not necessarily mutually compatible or coherent. There are choices to be made and emphases to be given. For instance, work on GCSE, with its re-emphasizing of subject specialist teaching, is in direct contradiction to the integration of subjects required in CPVE courses. In ILEA schools developments related to Improving Secondary Schools (ILEA, 1984), like Records of Achievement and modular credits, have to be weighed against GCSE and the ILEA's initiatives on social class, race and gender. In each case there is a potential for conflict, the definition of the school is at stake as certain programmes are prioritized and budgets redistributed. The ideological and the material are again intertwined.

Clearly, the changing context and specific interventions can act to significantly disrupt established institutional ideologies and patterns of preferment. The following teacher, in a sixth-form college, is describing the impact of CPVE work:

> the more we get into integrated and thematic work, the less our subject departments are going to be relevant and I think there is going to be a lot of resistance to the old-style grammar-school teacher (of which we still have many). They are going to find attitude change a difficult one to make. Not too devastating for me because I was primary trained – it does make a difference. And my own degree was an OU degree, so I did eleven subjects over four years, so I'm more used to the integrated approach. But for most of them its 'I'm a chemist and a chemist I will be and this is my department'. So I think there are going to be questions asked about the entire structure of the college when we really get moving.

Here a teacher finds her atypical background and training being validated by new developments, and entrenched positions are being challenged even within the bastion of A-level teaching. A similar point is made by the following teacher in another sixth-form college:

> I can meet those core and option requirements in terms of the thinking that is required to go into them because I have myself, prior to working in a sixth-form college, worked in FE and at a technical college and I therefore have some experience of, for instance, the BTEC and BEC type of structure which is essentially core and option module based and within my own experience therefore I've got past knowledge to rely on.

For teachers like these, prevocational courses open up new avenues of career development and status enhancement. Their skills and experience are in demand. They are advocates of change; they see new developments as worthwhile and as better serving the needs of pupils. They invest their time, energy and beliefs into the construction of new courses. They present a challenge to the established definition of the school.

These sorts of interventions represent radical redefinitions of the nature and purposes of schooling sponsored by external groups and coalitions. They carry within them expectations of thorough-going change. Yet one of the apparent mysteries of the 1980s as far as education is concerned is that the most hectic period of state-initiated change since the 1940s is also a period of massive reductions in school financing and one of acrimonious dispute between teachers and their employers. Change is being promoted in what would seem at first sight to be the most improbable and least conducive economic and political conditions imaginable. The mystery is solved, however, if the terms of the analysis are changed. Both the curricular interventions and the development of the teachers' pay dispute can be reduced to a single issue - control. The interventions represent dramatic examples of an overall attempt by the government both to change the 'ethic' of the school curriculum and to alter the balance of control over the teaching process and the curriculum. The 'conditions' attached by Sir Keith Joseph to the settlement of the teachers' pay dispute is part of a general strategy aimed at asserting greater control over teachers themselves. In general terms this strategy involves extension of the popular notion of 'accountability' towards the direct monitoring and appraisal of the work of individual teachers. At the end of a fifteen-year period during which successive governments have been attempting to convince parents and employers that they should believe in education but should not trust schools, the campaign for 'teacher appraisal' commands considerable support:

> At the heart of the teacher's dispute is not money but management. . . . This dispute is about resistance to change in working practices. The essence of education is discipline. . . . By resisting the discipline of assessment of their own performance, the teachers stand opposed to the renovation of Britain. That is why in this dispute management must win - and there is the beginning and end of the lazy comparison that some people have been tempted to make with the coal strike. (*The Times*' leader, 19 March 1985.)

The introduction of an appraisal system would, it is argued, put teachers on a par with other groups of professional employees:

> The employing authority can only be satisfied that each school is properly staffed if it knows enough about the skills and competencies of individual teachers. Such knowledge can only come from some form of appraisal system. An appraisal system is also needed for the professional enhancement of the individual teacher. Other professions - and some

schools – have found that appraisal interviews provide an opportunity to identify individual and collective training needs. To be fully effective an appraisal system would have to be complemented by better arrangements for the individual teachers' career development – including induction, in-service training, guidance on possible teaching posts and promotion. When I refer to the management of the teaching force I have this whole range of positive activity in mind. I am frequently misquoted in terms that suggest that I am only concerned with the need to dismiss the very small number of incompetent teachers who cannot be restored to adequate effectiveness. That is not the case, I am concerned with the whole range of positive advantages that would flow from applying to the teacher force standards of management which have become common elsewhere. (Speech by Sir Keith Joseph, North of England Education Conference, 4 January 1985.)

The key word in both these extracts is 'management'. In effect, control is to be exerted over teachers' work by the use of techniques of management. In general terms the task of schooling is increasingly subject to the logics of industrial production and market competition. Teachers are increasingly becoming drawn into systems of administrative rationality which exclude them from an effective say in the kind of substantive decision-making that could equally well be determined collectively. As Habermas (1984) suggests, this is a process whereby subsystems of purposive-rational action encroach upon structures of intersubjectivity. Political, ideologically loaded decisions are choked by bureaucratic-administrative systems and attempts are made to displace issues of moral and cultural identity with the imperatives of administrative efficacy. In other words, pragmatism and technologies of control replace ideological dispute. The definition of the school is removed entirely from the hands of teachers. In all this the work of teaching is being proletarianized. The work experience of the teacher is undergoing a significant shift from that of respected professional towards that of beleaguered labourer. The overall effect is a reconstruction of teachers' relationships to their work and their sense of themselves as workers. If such interpretational changes are long-lasting, then the nature of school micro-politics may also shift further towards an industrial-relations/worker-versus-management paradigm. What is being promoted is a shift from the *formal* to the *real* subordination of teachers' work (Braverman, 1974). The conceptual significance of this shift, in its relation to schools, is the appropriation by management of the subjective elements of labour. The worker is reduced 'to a "living appendage" of the production process (instead of being its subject and author)'. The space, the freedom of manoeuvre available for the worker to influence or control production, is closed down. Conception, design and ordering is removed to the responsibility of management 'leaving to the worker only the execution of a pre-set task' (Cressey and MacInnes, 1980, p. 7). To a great extent schools have already succumbed to the ideology of management, as being the one good way to run the organization. The infrastructure of 'real' subordination is already in place in many cases:

> The establishment of management as a separate function... with unique
> expertise and responsibilities, and with major and critical claims to
> authority... upon which the efficiency of the whole enterprise depends...
> is a crucial first step to control over the workforce... because once this
> conception of management had been accepted by workers, they have, in
> effect, abdicated from any question of, or resistance to, many aspects of
> their domination. (Littler and Salaman, 1982, p. 259.)

I am not here suggesting some kind of complex conspiracy against teachers
but rather taking account of the overall effect of the concatenation of
initiatives, constraints, changes in control and decision-making, and changes
in conditions of work which are having their impact on teachers' daily lives.

However, as was the case with previous elements in this analysis, these
developments are not without their own internal contradictions. The pressure
towards greater control over teachers' work and increases in direct
intervention into curriculum matters are accompanied by pressures upon
schools and individual teachers to introduce new curricula, new pedagogies
and new forms of assessment. On the one hand, direct intervention and
prescription of curricula alongside overall reductions in funding are reducing
the possibility of 'initiatory influences' (Offe, 1976) of teachers. On the other
hand, teachers are expected to develop new skills, new ways of working, new
kinds of teacher–pupil relationship. The 'successful' implementation of
externally sponsored curricular changes are making considerable demands
upon teachers' innovatory skills. In this situation the strategy of 'omissive
action' (like non-cooperation with GCSE) is becoming an increasingly
powerful weapon in teachers' political and union struggles.

It also needs to be recognized that these 'interventionary' innovations are
being sponsored by a range of disparate agencies, whose modes of operation
and interorganizational relationships differ considerably (e.g. TVEI schools
are required to enter into contractual relationships with the MSC). Schools
are faced with considerable 'innovation incoherence' and in many cases
'innovation overload'. The messages from different agencies are often
contradictory, schemes are changed during their implementation, documents
fail to appear, key personnel move on suddenly. Speed is of the essence in
many of these schemes; the required pace of change is quite at odds with the
gradualism typically preferred by teachers when grappling with change.
However, schools are set in a 'turbulent environment' where, increasingly,
change is associated with survival. In situations of falling rolls, schools must
compete for pupils. Services must be 'sold' to potential clients. Curriculum
innovations can be crucial factors in the market place. As a result, teachers are
caught between incompatible interpretations of their own self-interest.
Should they resist loss of autonomy and refuse to engage with new 'initiatives'
or underwrite the future security of their job by making a success of these
initiatives? As we have noted individual careers can be made and assured by
commitment to innovation.

Innovation overload as it affects teachers' working conditions is also an aspect of what Apple (1983) calls 'intensification'. Teachers are confronted by increasing and increasingly diverse workloads which destroy sociability and reduce leisure and self-direction. The range of skills required of them may increase, but time and interaction are also under increasing pressure. 'Getting done becomes more important than what was done or how one got there' (Apple, 1983, p. 59.) In several aspects, especially with regard to new assessment procedures, graded-testing, records of achievement, profiling, the new skills being acquired are essentially technical and administrative in character rather than educational. Time spent with pupils and on preparing lesson materials may actually be reduced even though total working hours increase. Apple also points out that the effects of intensification may be contradictory and mystifying 'since teachers thought of themselves as being more professional to the extent that they employed technical criteria and tests, they also basically accepted the longer hours and intensification of work that accompanied the program' (ibid., p. 61). What appears in one respect to be professional enhancement may actually serve to obscure a general worsening of working conditions. As new initiatives in assessment combine with curricular change, the introduction of equal opportunity programmes and greater public involvement in educational debate, many schools have developed a kind of siege mentality, and the pressures involved in coping with conflict and change are beginning to take their toll on the health and tolerance of individual practitioners:

> It's becoming more difficult to do the job. The amount of pressure building up from the LEA, and other groups, over things like the daily act of worship, the ILEA equality initiatives, is enormous. And I'm spending more and more time doing things I don't think I should be doing. The time will come – especially in relation to the amount of work created by the politically committed authority like ours – when we will need a teaching head and an administrative head. I've only been in the job for two and a half years and its become worse in that time. I know colleagues who have been heads for fifteen years who find it intolerable and are getting out. (London infant school head teacher.)

The Micro-politics of Industrial Action

Once again it is important to emphasize the variability of responses to change in different organizations, different schools. While it may be the case that there is a general process of the restructuring of teachers' professional identity and their working conditions, neither the direct effects of these changes nor of the industrial action itself are uniform. The established pattern of micro-political relations, the institutional history of those relations and the perception and identification by participants of their interests (ideological, self and material) all have a direct bearing. It is the articulation of micro-politics with constraints and wider issues that accounts for much of the substance of political contention (or absence of it) within schools.

Again, briefly, I will consider some of the issues raised in teachers' accounts of the effects of the 1985–86 period of industrial dispute in their schools.

The notion of 'dispute' must be recognized in two senses: first, the formal industrial dispute between the teacher unions and their employers; second, the concomitant disputes which have arisen between teachers themselves as a result of the action. Conflicts can emerge in the interpersonal relations of teachers in one school, in the relations between members of different teacher unions, between teachers and their management, particularly the head, and between teachers and the LEA. Which, if any, of these conflicts develop seems to depend to a great extent on (1) the constitution of the staff, particularly the mix and strength of unions represented, and (2) the history of previous micro-political relations in the school. Small schools – infant, junior and nursery schools in particular – seem most likely to achieve unanimity among the staff as a whole:

> Our school is unusual for a primary school. We have 100 per cent union membership and all of those are in the NUT. So if there's a strike nobody's left, so to speak. And membership also includes the headteacher. So if we make a decision that's 100 per cent, the school is automatically closed down and there are no grey areas and that makes it simpler. (Class teacher, a London primary.)

> It's put strains on parent–teacher relationships but it hasn't put any strain on staff relationships because we all agree with the action 100 per cent. And it's put no strain on the staff at all because we've all co-operated with each other and been pleased to co-operate with each other and the nursery nurses who haven't been on strike have understood why we've been on strike and they have found other things to do. (Head teacher, a London nursery.)

In some cases the action has actually been seen to have a positive effect on staff morale and relationships, forging great solidarity and improving morale:

> The NAS chap has always been a militant and he's had us pretty well organized even before the action started, so in fact the head has gone along pretty much in the same way as he always did really, negotiating with us. So it didn't really have that much impact. The solidarity amongst the staff grew. (Sociology teacher, a Midlands comprehensive.)

> I think staff morale is pretty low anyway. It's abysmally low. I think in fact if anything it has boosted them up because it makes us all feel that we're all doing something worthwhile in a positive way to bring about some sort of change and it's brought people together much more and there's a much stronger feeling of pulling together, of doing something as a unit and taking

people on, whoever it is, which is a good feeling, which has been lacking up to now. (Head of PE, a London comprehensive.)

The style and stance of the head teacher clearly emerges as a significant factor in the conduct of the dispute. This is one way in which the existing micropolitics of the institution mediates the meaning and practical realization of the dispute for those involved:

> The head refuses point blank to close the school even when on days such as today there were perhaps only 100 children, out of 900, present in the school. He still insists on lessons continuing and this has led to a number of discipline problems... He's persuaded other members of the teaching staff to break with unions and to support him over supervision of lunches and support him in other ways. He has very obviously rewarded one of these people and that was done very quickly. An interview was set up where this chap was the only candidate and that sort of attitude from the head has caused a lot of bitterness, though he was never popular, he's even less so now and it's just got worse. He's extremely embarrassed to walk into the staffroom. Nobody talks to him. If he sits at a table where staff are sitting, they get up and move away. (Head of drama, a London comprehensive.)

One effect of such antipathy and polarization is the increased feelings of 'them and us' among the staff – the more developed sense of employer–employee type relationships between school management and teachers. The sense of a professional relationship between staff and head teacher is drastically eroded. Furthermore, as the extract indicates, positions adopted in the dispute can have direct career implications. Teachers may find their career prospects damaged or, as here, enhanced by their stance in the dispute. Another respondent suggested also that the list of teachers who withdrew labour, which was required by the local authority, would be used as a blacklist when future promotions or appointments were being made. 'If the list is sent someone will read it... and it's a good way of cutting down the problem of 120-150 applicants for a job' (Head of geography, a south-eastern secondary modern).

> I saw the head this morning. He said everyone seems to be headmaster bashing these days, the teacher representatives on the governing body apparently really had a go at him... I don't know if I can say anything about our head, basically he is a bully and he'll get what he can by bullying people but I think this has sort of shut him up a bit and he realized that he's taking on something quite powerful. Given that he was covering, he and his deputies were covering as hard as they could to slow down the action. (Head of PE, an outer London comprehensive.)

Certainly these data from the dispute highlight once again the contradictions built into the position of headship and particularly the lack of clarity as to where the loyalty as against the responsibility of the head lies. Again the point needs to be made that heads interpret their position differently and work out their handling of dilemmas thrown up by the dispute in different ways.

> if you went to her and said such and such is happening – the NUT has decided X, Y and Z – then her response was, 'OK. Well, if that is the situation I can't operate the school'. She's not the sort of person who would stand at the gates saying, 'I'll run the damn place on my own'. Most provocations arose with the deputy head, who of course was the person more involved in the minutiae of running cover, and that was a major area of confrontation... he would do things he should have known would make people angry. (Head of careers, a London comprehensive.)

> The head's in a difficult position because he's a committed Labour supporter. Secondly, he's about to leave to take up another post. And thirdly, he's got to be seen to be backing the system. So he's in a difficult situation, while understanding the feelings of the lower paid down the scales, of lack of career prospects, stagnation. He's also got to present the front of the school as still operating. (Head of geography, a south-eastern secondary modern.)

Certainly, though, many teachers also experience dilemmas in their feelings about and involvement in the industrial action. The action has implications for the sense of identity of the teacher. This often comes into play in interpretations of the purpose of the actions. That is the question of what the dispute is really about (discussed more fully below).

> There have been moments and times of conflict and there were certainly individual issues that arose which caused problems and people have been put under a certain amount of stress in terms of their trade union loyalties versus what they saw as a kind of professional responsibility and the fact that the action, a lot of people felt anyway, the action in one sense is hurting us and so there was a strong element of self-sacrifice in what we were doing. (Head of drama, a London comprehensive.)

> It's on issues of education under attack, and in that sense it still falls within what I would call the long history of professional sort of actions that teachers take. And teachers have always felt very guilty about striking for pay, about their own conditions. Half the time they feel embarrassed about it. (Head of careers, a London comprehensive.)

Teachers' views and definitions of professionalism and unionism vary considerably (Ginsburg, Meyenn and Miller, 1980). As contrasting ideologies and self-images they can be used to justify all kinds of work-related stances, and they are often a basis for conflict among teachers. This is evident in simple terms in the political standpoints of the different teacher unions; for example, in the case of PAT (the Professional Association of Teachers) strike action is explicitly ruled out by the association's constitution. Union membership can be related to the political affiliations of individual teachers and their views of their own best interests. The unions represent different interests and alliances of interests; they are not necessarily working towards the same ends. Thus, in accounts of the dispute in particular schools, conflicts among the staff were often identified with long-term micro-political divisions *and* different union memberships. The positions articulated by the different unions also reflect different definitions of the school and views of education:

> The souring of the relationships has been in my school largely between the Scale 1 and Scale 2 people, who are mainly NUT, and the senior teachers, heads of department and above, who are by and large AMMA and PAT. And the problem has become almost one of us versus them. And the souring of relationships has come in cover, that is the most definite aspect of the dispute at the moment. Lunchtime supervision has caused problems and the walking off of the premises which has been taking place by the NAS and NUT, who have been walking out at any time . . . The arguments are not so much open as under the surface, so at potential flashpoints like cover the sores are opened up. (Head of geography, a south-eastern secondary modern.)

A variety of issues extant within the institution may be pulled into the dispute. Consciousnesses are raised, disgruntlements focused and old scores settled. Tensions created by issues of race, gender, promotion and patterns of influence are laid bare by the dispute. As with other events (falling rolls, change of head, amalgamation), industrial action embodies the potential for a restructuring of the established patterns of advantage and disadvantage. The pay dispute is neither entirely limited to material concerns nor totally divorced from educational issues. Ideological interests are set against material and self-interests:

> I would say that our staff relationships are extremely strained at this present time. Particularly between unions and between the body of the staff and the management, relationships have deteriorated a good deal in the past term. The main reason for this is that we haven't closed yet although both the NUT and NAS have been taking continual union action. They've failed to agree on the type of action and often the actions have been contradictory so that there are inter-union disputes. In fact the two union reps aren't talking to each other so it's the deputies who are doing the organizing and the talking . . . It's a very high pressure situation, but most people are just totally fed up with what's happening and with what's actually happening to the children. There's a large body of people who wanted the union action to be swift and effective and to get back into a normal routine which we think is the essence of our type of school, but this hasn't been the case and the management hasn't helped so people are just very disenchanted, and

there are lots of other factors to do with the management whose policy, as a child-centred school, ethically is very sound but practically it presents some dangers and a lot of concern by the teaching staff. (Head of drama, a London comprehensive.)

In most cases teachers interviewed linked the conduct of the dispute and the problems arising from it to the organizational and eductional ethos of their school. The primary teachers interviewed also specifically mentioned the effect of the action on their relationships with parents. Their daily routine typically brings them into immediate, face-to-face contact with parents. While this contact can offer a very direct sense of parental concern about the effects of the action on their children – 'their faces dropped and there was a different atmosphere' (nursery teacher) – it also provides a channel for teachers to explain themselves and develop support: 'we can talk to them about the action and the need for it' (primary teacher); 'we talked to them at great length about the reasons why we were doing it... they are very co-operative' (nursery head).

However, coherent explanations of the action are not necessarily easy to assemble. The reasons for the action, and for the length and bitterness of the dispute, offered by teachers I interviewed were typically complex and priorities differed from one school to another. The cutting edge of the dispute seemed to be forged by local conditions and experiences rather than by general principles. The concerns of the teachers were often a reflection of institutional priorities as much as national issues. The following comments illustrate the range:

• The dominant issue is pay absolutely, as the battle has gone on and as Sir Keith Joseph has tried to connect it up with teachers' contracts and conditions of service and so on, it has also become something about teachers' conditions of service, perhaps their professionalism.

• I don't honestly believe in our situation in my particular school that it is actually about pay. I think it's about conditions of service, very much so. In fact, in our first union meeting about strike action pay wasn't mentioned. The percentage was something that everyone was happy to leave to the union to negotiate. The actual thought of changing our contract was pretty horrific. I can see that in some ways assessment could be very useful to teachers, if we were to govern it ourselves, but to place the control over salary and control over us firmly in the hands of the DES and the headmaster, who nobody trusts, fills everyone with grim realization that this could be the end of a bad, bad unhappy career.

• I think that pay is important in the fact that it affects everything else. I don't think it's the actual money I think it's the work that is put on teachers. I think teachers are getting fed up because they are not thought anything of and they are getting more and more responsibility and more and more stick for everything that happens. The government accuses teachers all the time and parents accuse teachers all the time.

• The most important issue is what constitutes the teachers' contract. What precisely are we being paid for and not being paid for. When they're not getting a decent pay rise it's highlighted that they're doing a whole lot of things that they're getting no recognition for. I think the general attitude is we are doing it now, why don't we get paid for it?

• In our school it's about getting a better working situation for teachers. I think all sorts of things, discipline, it's certainly not just money, there's no question of that ... it's being used as a vehicle for all sorts of things, the disruptive kid, the truanting kid. It's opened the way for a whole lot of other things in our school to be brought up which were sort of bubbling away before ... people are now making a stand where they have never made a stand before.

• Professionalism, teacher's morale, the quality of education, the fact that there aren't enough nursery teachers in London. Because they can't afford to live in London.

• That's absolutely clear, I mean it's not really just the pay, I mean it's on issues of education under attack ... you wouldn't get this level of support across the country if it wasn't a general feeling that education, status, their professionalism, their worth, the services themselves, the services to the kids, money for books were not under massive attack. They are fighting a thin-line rearguard action, they're saying this is enough. And certainly the individuals from the school are clearly angry about lots of things. Lots of things get dragged in, redeployment, which is nothing to do with it, the redeployment of teachers within ILEA over falling rolls has been a constant running sore. People have been much more ready to say, 'let's go, let's do it'.

Here again are the mixture of concerns and commitments which have been reiterated throughout this analysis: material interests – pay and conditions of work and conditions of service, control; self-interests – a sense of worth, status and professional autonomy; ideological interests – educational services, teacher numbers and money for books all under attack. These diverse interests and concerns intersect and link national and local with institutional issues. The micro-politics of the school channel and shape the dispute and the dispute provides an outlet for entrenched grievances. Politics, unionism and micro-politics interplay.

Furthermore, these factors within the dispute, diverse and multifaceted as they are, parallel those factors – wages, conditions, control and status (being indicators of structural contradiction) – identified by Althusser and Balibar (1970) as providing the ingredients, when occurring together, for 'ruptural unity' (and thus as capable of producing radical change). In this sense the teachers' dispute and the form it has taken may be regarded as predictable and inevitable and it is possibly far-reaching in its long-term effects on teachers' work roles and political consciousness. Clearly, for many teachers it is an attempt to resist the changes in their work situation that were outlined above and to ensure that the extent of their professional autonomy, such as it is, and their influence in school policy-making are reduced no further.

References

ALTHUSSER, M. and BALIBAR, E. (1970) *Reading Capital*. London: New Left Books.

APPLE, M. (1983) 'Work, Class and Teaching', in WALKER, S. and BARTON, L. (eds) *Gender, Class and Education*. Lewes: Falmer Press.

BENNETT, N. (1985) 'Central Control and Parental Influence: reconciling the tensions in current proposals for school governance and policy-making', *Educational Management and Administration*, 12(3).

BOYD, W.L. (1976) 'The public, the professionals and education policy-making: who governs?' *Teachers College Record*, 77.

BRAVERMAN, H. (1974) *Labour and Monopoly Capital*. New York: Monthly Review Press.

BURKE, J. (1986) 'Concordia Sixth Form College: a sociological case study.' Unpublished D.Phil., University of Sussex.

COCKBURN, C. (1978) *The Local State*. London: Pluto Press.

CRESSEY, P. and MacINNES, J. (1980) 'Voting for Ford: industrial democracy and the control of labour', *Capital and Class*, II, Summer.

CYERT, R.M. and MARCH, J.G. (1963) *A Behavioural Theory of the Firm*. Englewood Cliffs, New Jersey: Prentice-Hall Inc.

DALE, R. (1979) 'The politicisation of school deviance: reactions to William Tyndale', in BARTON, L. and MEIGHAM, R. (eds) *Schools, Pupils and Deviance*. Driffield: Nefferton.

DES (DEPARTMENT OF EDUCATION AND SCIENCE) (1984) *Influence at School*. Government Green Paper. London: HMSO.

GINSBURG, M., MEYENN, R. and MILLER, H. (1980) 'Teachers' Conceptions of Professionalism and Trades Unionism: an ideological analysis', in WOODS, P.E. (ed.) *Teacher Strategies*. London: Croom Helm.

GREENWOOD, R. (1983) 'Changing patterns of Budgeting in English Local Government', *Public Administration*, 61 (Summer).

HABERMAS, J. (1984) *The Theory of Communicative Action, Vol. I: Reason and the Rationalization of Society*. London: Heinemann.

HEWTON, E. (1986) *Education in Question: Crisis in County Hall and Classroom*. Hemel Hempstead: Allen & Unwin.

ILEA (1984) Improving Secondary Schools: Report of the Hargreaves Committee. London: ILEA.

LITTLER, C. and SALAMAN, G. (1982) 'Bravermania and Beyond: revert theories of the labour process', *Sociology*, 16(2).

OFFE, C. (1976) *Industry and Inequality*. London: Edward Arnold.

PETTIGREW, A.M. (1982) 'Patterns of Managerial Response as Organisations Move from Rich to Poor Environments.' Paper delivered to the British Educational Management and Administration Society, Annual Conference, West Hill College.

WALLACE, G., MILLER, H. and GINSBURG, M. (1983) 'Teachers' Responses to the Cuts', in AHIER, J. and FLUDE, M. (eds), *Contemporary Education Policy*. Berkenham: Croom Helm.

2.5 'The Values of a Free Society' and the Politics of Educational Studies
Anthony Hartnett and Michael Naish

Introduction

These are bad times for education. In schools the talk is of falling rolls, reduced resources, increased stress, low pay, low status, redeployment and early retirement. The areas in which teachers have traditionally been able to exercise their own judgement (for example, the curriculum and the assessment of pupils) are becoming smaller and smaller. The interventions of the Department of Education and Science (DES) and of the Secretary of State even extend down to curriculum content (the merits of capitalism) and to syllabus writing. Teachers may soon be subject to regular assessment, and this will bring an increase in the power of 'the management team'. They are being left less and less room to be principals acting in their own right and are constrained more and more to act as agents for others, to be 'no more than an extension of the agency' of their employers, without any purpose of their own in what they do except for that which arises from their desire to make a living (Langford, 1978, pp. 14–15). Scheffler (1964), in a discussion of similar trends in the USA in 1964, notes that they involve a 'view of the teacher as a minor technician within an industrial process. The overall goals are set in advance in terms of national needs ... and the teacher's job is just to supervise the last operational stage, the methodical insertion of ordered facts into the student's mind' (pp. 22–3).

In universities, too, declining resources have been accompanied by increasing central control, direct political pressure, and a severe diminution in autonomy. They are told to be more like Marks and Spencer's, to give good value for money, to provide what the market wants, and to implement 'top-down' management. Vice-Chancellors are to become 'chief executives', professors managers of 'cost centres', lecturers 'trainee managers', and students 'incomplete components' and 'providers of fee income'. The Secretary of State, through the University Grants Committee, is to be the 'chief shareholder' and the talk is of performance indicators, departmental profiles, and management information.

The institutions of teacher education have been particularly badly hit. Large areas of educational studies, particularly at the level of initial teacher training, have effectively been captured by a combination of the government and the DES ('national needs') and the local authorities ('management interests'). The talk is of 'squeezing theoretical studies out of the tube' and of what is taken to be practical relevance. This is the 'new vocationalism' in its teacher education form. At least some of the official leaders of teacher education (the profession's cutting edge) are now taken to be those who, like sheepdogs tamed to the whistle, are tirelessly alert to the demands of the Secretary of State and are ready to implement them, even when these are still corridor talk at Elizabeth House. They have, at best, only half-heartedly defended the independence of educational studies from central control and have failed to support publicly those individuals and groups *within* the centre (in the Department of Education and Science and Her Majesty's Inspectorate, for example) who are opposed to the fashionable currents of the time. Where initial training has led, the rest of educational studies will soon follow. Any independent critique (one as little compromised as possible by particular political or professional interests) of current educational policies and practices will increasingly have to be undertaken by a dwindling band of seemingly eccentric individuals, working within institutions whose orientations are largely determined by whatever set of external interests happen to be dominant at the time.

In general, the picture is one of greater centralization of power; of increasingly hierarchical management structures within educational institutions; of a focus on the requirements of industry and commerce; of leaving politics to the politicians; of teachers as agents for others; and of consultation, where allowed, being given no serious political weight. This is likely to lead to a restricted, controlled and manipulated agenda for public debate, and one that will permit the controversial political and other assumptions of official policies and practices to escape scrutiny. Such a manner of conducting the enterprise of education is likely to be highly damaging. It may work against any improvement in the quality of solutions proposed and implemented to meet educational problems; it is likely to work against the legitimacy of educational institutions in the eyes of their clients; and it is incompatible, in our view, with any adequate conception of democracy.

Educational Problems: Fundamental, Political and Enduring

The central problems of education concern its general direction. Given that it is believed to benefit its recipients and society as a whole, what are these benefits? How are they to be identified? Are the conceptions of education available in society open to amendment and to radical overhaul, as groups within society change and demand to be taken seriously? Do the benefits of education primarily concern the development of rational autonomy or, as Jonathan (1986, p. 138) asks, is this to be 'seen as an unrealistic, wasteful and dangerous aim for the mass of the population, for whom education should be merely a means of acquiring whatever skills and attitudes are appropriate to their allotted social role?' Such questions as these are not merely the central questions of education, but also the prior ones. Without answers to them, more specific educational questions about why we should teach this as opposed to that, or about how we should teach this or evaluate that, or about how we should organize classrooms or schools have little point.

There are three important features of these prior and central educational problems. The first of them is that they are what Maxwell (1980) calls 'fundamental problems' (p. 19). These are 'problems of living which we encounter in seeking to discover and achieve that which is of value in life'. Any conception of education and any policies and practices it sanctions embody an answer to the problem as to how individuals or groups in society are to be put in as favourable a position as possible to live lives that are fulfilling, satisfying, and morally acceptable. They concern how the 'good life' is to be identified and lived, and how we are to know what Fred Inglis (1985) calls 'the good, the true and the beautiful' (p. 27).

Further, as Maxwell (1980) argues, 'it is most improbable – perhaps even undesirable – that there should ever be general agreement as to what is to count as a correct acceptable solution' to any fundamental problem and that 'it is extremely unlikely' that any such problem 'will receive a definitive solution' (p. 33). This has important implications for the debate about education and for the nature and organization of educational studies.

The second feature of these prior and central educational problems is that they are political. Any solution proffered to fundamental problems makes political demands because it will involve issues about the nature, organization, quality, and direction of society; about citizens' interests; and about a just distribution of power, status, wealth and of life-chances in general. Apple (1986) shows how the political philosophy of an alliance of business, industry, and the New Right in the USA yields a view of education embodied in the slogan that 'what is good for business and industry is good for education' and how this has quite specific effects on curriculum content and textbooks. On this view, the 'good life' is possible only in a society predominantly organized on market economy lines. Jonathan (1986) makes a similar point about the UK, when she notes that the new vocationalism in education assumes that 'in an industrial society, the needs of society are to be conflated with the needs of industry, and that, moreover, the needs of each individual are best served by preparing him/her to serve the needs of society, understood in economic terms'. It is reflected in Sir Keith Joseph's remark exhorting schools to 'preach the moral virtue of free enterprise and the pursuit of profit', and the Chairman of the Conservative Party's view that schools 'ought to be places of useful learning where achievement was assessed according to accepted criteria' (*Times Educational Supplement*, 22 November 1985, p. 10.)

But whether a society predominantly ordered along corporate capitalist lines (and the conceptions of the good life for individuals it endorses) are to be preferred to those of other political traditions is a controversial matter and involves debating the criteria by which a justly ordered society is to be identified. To debate such matters is to engage in political theory. The importance of recognizing education's prior and central problems as political and as inseparable from those of political theory is not simply to claim that they cannot be remitted to experts for solution, since recourse to expert opinion is only justifiable where criteria for judging the adequacy of solutions are relatively securely established. It is to claim, in addition, that, in a democracy, the issues are the legitimate concern of all the members of such a society; that they are issues for public debate; and that the debate must have consequences for policy.

The third feature of educational problems is that they are enduring (Kekes, 1976). Kekes contrasts enduring problems with removable problems. A removable problem is one the successful solution of which leads to its abolition. Repairing a broken window by putting in a new pane of glass is to solve a removable problem. However, some problems cannot be removed but have to be lived with. Solving them is a matter of developing, often long-term, strategies of coping which might alleviate the most inconvenient and damaging effects of them. Problems of this kind are enduring problems. An example is having to cope with a deep and chronic tendency to depression or to migraine. Such problems present a series of ever changing challenges and any policy or strategy to cope with them has to be continually interpreted, adapted, revised, adjusted and perhaps even abandoned and replaced by another. The general problem to which the specific problem of education addresses itself – that of preparing members of a society for life in that society – is an enduring one since the circumstances and nature of any society are continually changing. The form education might take will be affected by such factors as how culturally diverse a society is at a particular time; how industrialized or technologically developed it is; and how high the level of unemployment is.

Different individuals and groups will develop and advance different and competing conceptions of education on the basis of their different political and other beliefs, to take account of these changing circumstances (Naish, 1984). Just as believers in corporate capitalism or in certain kinds of liberalism will each endorse and demand the institutionalization of his or her particular conception of education, so will different ethnic, religious, or gender or class-based groups. Much of the argument will be about how, only if this or that particular conception of education is institutionalized (whether for all children or for some group of them) particular groups will best be able to begin to seek 'to discover and achieve that which is of value in life' (Jonathan, 1986, p. 143). The importance of noting that the central and prior problems of education are enduring is that arguments about the form that education should take are open-ended and admit of no last word.

Arguments, then, about the central and prior problems of education are arguments about inherently controversial issues in which the citizenry as a whole has a legitimate role. These arguments are also perennial. All of this has important implications for issues about centralization.

The Limitations of a Centralized Educational System

The question we address here is whether a centralized educational system is, *prima facie*, likely to offer such best solutions as might be had to the prior and central problems of education, given that these are fundamental, political, and enduring.

One preliminary point is that, in any centralized system, the central authority's role and the role of its constituent institutions (for example, the DES) are likely to be put beyond critical scrutiny, even though they themselves may be part of the problem that needs to be tackled. In 1976 the DES was the subject of two critical reports on its own workings which drew attention to a number of serious failings. There have, however, been no scrutinies of its work since then. The control of the agenda is such that Sir William Pile (a former Permanent Under-Secretary at the Department) felt unable to mention these two critical reports, even after his retirement.

Moreover, most centralized systems of educational control are unlikely to be neutral between answers to education's prior and central issues. They will favour some set of political arrangements as opposed to others and, hence, some conceptions of education as opposed to others. Where a system is centralized and where these prior and central issues are not on the public agenda, controversial assumptions and decisions may be put beyond critical scrutiny. And where this happens and where particular groups' views about education are not given adequate political consideration or weight, then general democratic values are threatened. Further, institutions begin to lose their legitimacy in the sense that those over whom authority is exercised cease to feel that the institutions and those who have authority in them, are speaking to their interests, even though it is these very interests that the institutions are, allegedly, there to protect or promote (Reddiford, 1971, pp. 20–1). Where legitimacy is lost, and where there is no forum for or tradition of public politically effective discussion, there is likely to be withdrawal from the institutions (seen, for example, in truancy figures in schools). Where private finance or other resources permit, rival schools are likely to be established. Where they do not permit, there may be recourse to violence or intimidation as a way of gaining what cannot be gained by discussion. Any attempt at coercion and any exercise of power by the state in response to this will simply be taken to provide further evidence of the non-legitimacy of the institutions.

Another equally damaging objection to centralization is that it is incompatible with such problem solving strategies as we have for dealing with fundamental problems and problems in general. The general strategy is one of articulating the problem to be solved as well as possible and then of proposing and of critically assessing possible solutions against each other. This is a collaborative exercise and one which, in the case of political issues in a democracy, is to be taken up by the public at large. To fail to put any proposed solution to public scrutiny is a poor way to treat it since its merits cannot be adequately determined in its absence. A willingness to test canvassable solutions to a problem by public scrutiny is a mark of a genuine interest in seeing a problem solved as well as possible as opposed, say, to simply exercising power or to maintaining, at any cost, a particular political position. Some implications of these points for curricular issues are discussed by Knitter (1985, especially pp. 388–90).

If all of this is true, then there is at least a presumptive case against the kind of centralization under discussion. The nature of education's central and prior problems are such that any solutions to them can only be reasonably judged as the best that can be hoped for if they pass the test set by public scrutiny. Such problems require a tradition of sustained public debate that speaks both to the day-to-day problems of the enterprise, and to the issues about the enterprise's point and purposes. This tradition has to flourish within institutions as well as within society as a whole. [...]

Politics and the Control of Educational Studies

We now turn to the third question, namely the one about the nature and organization of educational studies. The intellectual and cultural resources on which a society can call in the debate about education include its political, social, and other related theories; its art and literature; its religious, historical, and social traditions. Any society should, above all, be able to call particularly on the traditions of educational studies, if these are in good order, as they are institutionalized within higher education. We suggest that educational studies are not, certainly at the institutional level, in good order and, hence, are unable to play the role that they might and should play in the debate about education.

Taylor (1985, pp. 42–3) suggests that, in England and Wales, about £30 million is spent each year on educational research. A good proportion of this sum is used to support the research activities of academic staff in university departments of education. Even before resources were reduced and central control increased, these departments had not established a strong tradition of critical commentary on public issues along the lines of say, the Frankfurt Institute of Social Research. This was established in the early 1920s with an initial endowment that produced a yearly income of about $30,000 US (Jay, 1973, p. 8). For present purposes we suggest a number of factors which may begin to provide an explanation.

To begin with, politicians are interested in educational issues in a way that they are not interested in, say, history, philosophy, music, or, until recently, football. Schools and other educational institutions provide them with ready scapegoats who can be held responsible for any number of social problems. Hence, although these institutions are of interest to politicians, this is often for reasons which have little to do with the prior and central problems of education or with the quality of solutions to them or with the quality of thinking about them in general.

Further, one way of controlling schools is to control educational studies. The government can control the initial training of teachers in such a way as to threaten the survival of the training institutions, and this will have a profound effect on the nature of educational studies in them. This is most immediately seen in thinking and practice on the Postgraduate Certificate in Education course where some academics, apparently led by Professor P.H. Hirst (Hirst, 1985; for additional references see Hartnett and Naish, 1981), have played the Trojan horse to bring into educational institutions a view of educational studies which is incompatible with any adequate conception of independent academic enquiry; which takes no account of the political aspects of educational practice and policy; which is narrowly practice focused; which has no adequate place for serious intellectual reflection on, or understanding of, the nature of the educational enterprise or of its central and prior problems; and which gives no serious weight to the views of student teachers, of children in schools, or of citizens in general.

Educational studies, lacking any rigorous intellectual tradition or resources to fall back on, are an easy victim to a demand to make them 'safe' and 'non-threatening' to governments and other powerful institutions in society, by focussing on issues of day-to-day practice. Educational studies have, to an unparalleled extent, 'taken in' government and other official views about the general direction of policy and practice. They have concerned themselves more with how what has been officially laid down might be better done at the expense of the issue as to whether it should be done at all, and whether it provides as reasonable a solution as can be expected to the problems to which it is allegedly addressed (Jonathan, 1986, p. 139).

To take this practice-focused view of educational studies, however, is to leave unexamined the pattern of practices at any particular time. It is to leave unexamined the question of whether particular practices are compatible with each other; of what conceptions of education they presuppose; of how they relate to the wider societal contexts and to issues of the distribution of power, status and wealth; and of why it is that some sorts of schooling and schools have ceased to speak to some sections of the population (if, indeed, they ever did).

Moreover, practice involves working with simplified models of the social world and of solving problems under conditions of urgency. This leaves little room for reflecting on why the practices are as they are, and this may have an ideological function, in that it may shift attention for educational failure away from wider political issues about the nature and organization of society onto the practices of schools. Further, to focus attention solely on practice is to make it difficult to detect institutional drift, where the aggregate of practices has a tenor which is divorced from, or is even incompatible with, the avowed purposes of particular institutions. To take the particular momentum of an institution for granted and be indifferent to institutional drift is to be bound by an irrational conservatism that precludes reflection about what is going on, and makes adequate action in the face of education's central problems less likely. The weaknesses of this kind of conservative thought are well described by both Mannheim and Hayek.

Mannheim (1953, pp. 102-3) notes how conservative thought 'clings to the immediate, the actual, the *concrete*' and is opposed to 'speculation or hypothesis' and 'therefore does not really trouble itself with the *structure* of the world'. He contrasts this with progressive activity which 'feeds on its *consciousness of the possible*. It transcends the given immediate present, by seizing on the possibilities for systematic change which it offers'. Hayek (1960, p. 404) notes how conservative thought 'tends to harm any cause which allies itself with it' in that it 'fears new ideas because it has no distinctive principles of its own to oppose them; and, by its distrust of theory and its lack of imagination concerning anything except that which experience has already proved, it deprives itself of the weapons needed in the struggle of ideas . . .' It 'is bound by the stock of ideas inherited at a given time. And since it does not really believe in the power of argument, its last resort is generally a claim to superior wisdom, based on some self-arrogated superior quality'.

Educational thinking needs not simply to see the practical but to see the practical in the light of the theoretical and the theoretical in the light of the practical – to see each of them in a way that allows them to illuminate each other. To have theory divorced from practice is, no doubt, as deplorable as it is conventionally taken to be. It is equally deplorable to have practice divorced from theory. Justifications of practice have to be taken back to the political theories out of which they have grown. Criteria of justification and assumptions related to them have to be open to scrutiny. Indeed, it might be argued that in a democratic society, which is opposed to change by violence, it is in its educational institutions above all that traditional, taken-for-granted, conventional answers to fundamental problems in general (and, in this context, the political and social ones raised by education) ought to be subjected to sustained scrutiny.

This is not to suggest there should be no place for practice-focused educational studies, or for some academics in educational studies working closely with politicians, local education authorities and others, in the current fashion. It is to suggest, however, that this is logically secondary to enquiry into education's prior and central problems, and that involvement with the powers should not make up the whole of educational studies. Institutional pressures on autonomous educational studies should be resisted so that the fundamental questions of education do not simply become the concern of a few scattered individuals working, without intellectual and other support, in institutions whose dominant concerns lie largely elsewhere.

A further reason for the failure of educational studies to speak to the fundamental problems of education is that academic careers and advancement are often closely bound up with having well-oiled relationships with central and local government. This would not apply to anything like the same degree in such areas as philosophy or history. Decisions about funding, access to institutions, membership of key committees and institutions are all likely to owe more to narrowly political considerations than they would in mainstream academic disciplines. All of this influences the content, characteristics, and structure of educational studies, and results in certain kinds of text-books, courses, ways of thinking about educational problems, and in certain kinds of academic appointment. Some of those who are, formally, the intellectual leaders listen to the views of the DES or of governments on what educational studies should be about; on what acceptable lines of research are; on what should be taught, and then define the subject accordingly. The role of such institutions as the Universities Council for the Education of Teachers (UCET), the Council for the Accreditation of Teacher Education (CATE), the DES and the research committees are of particular importance here.

Educational studies are also at a disadvantage in the debate about education because they are specialist rather than fundamentalist in focus (Maxwell, 1980). Fundamentalism is the view that intellectual life and academic enquiry should be concerned with helping us discover the best solutions that there are to fundamental problems (see the section of this chapter entitled 'Educational Problems: Fundamental, Political and Enduring'). Specialism is the view that all genuine enquiry must focus on problems that can be sharply defined and that can have agreed solutions reached by the use of agreed procedures. But since the prior and central issues of education (questions about its nature, direction and so on) are decidedly of a fundamentalist and not of a specialist kind, much educational enquiry has simply passed them by. There is a relatively impoverished tradition of discussing them, and this means that much work in educational studies either loses its point, is trivial and isolated from any important problem, or is ideological in that it covertly supports one set of answers to fundamental issues in education, while it believes it is neutral between them. This can be seen in the largely specialist tradition of educational research which, in its search for intellectual respectability, has become empirical, positivist and, apparently, apolitical (see Hearnshaw, 1979; King and Melanson, 1972; Hamilton, 1983).

Specialism has other consequences. It leads to a development of subject areas that takes place independently of fundamental problems. These areas become hermetically sealed off both from fundamental problems and from each other. Within each of them academics speak to one another but not to their fellow academics. A consequence of this is that educational studies usually fails to make connections between social theory and educational research, or between different levels of explanation – for example, between psychological or sociological explanations of what is commonly called 'learning failure'; or between psychology and the philosophical issues raised by and presupposed by much of psychology's view of human nature and of human action (see Schwab, 1978).

Specialism also plays a role (along with other political and cultural factors) in making sure that what audience there is for educational studies predominantly consists of teachers, academics, officials, and civil servants. It consists, that is, of professionals. As Maxwell (1980) points out, specialism is 'almost exclusively a view of professional, expert, scientific, academic inquiry' (p. 31). Hence educational studies are not seen as an intellectual resource which might nourish public discussion of fundamental problems but as a rare claret fit for the palates of connoisseurs. Such a view restricts the debate in respect of those who can take an informed part in it, just as the emphasis on practice restricts the range of questions that are discussed.

Institutions that have given up any serious attempt to defend a view of educational studies as addressed in part to education's prior and central problems are likely to find that policies of trimming, of compromise, of institutional compliance and docility, and of public relations (no doubt all starting as attempts to survive) become a taken-for-granted way of life. This will produce a restricted agenda, a restricted audience, and growing damage to the quality of the public debate about educational issues, to the quality and legitimacy of solutions to them, and to educational studies themselves.

Implications for the Control of Educational Institutions: the Need for Autonomy

The fourth question which we raised concerns the implications of our answers to the first three questions for the control of the institutions of teacher education. It could be argued that, although educational studies might be compromised by the processes outlined above, no society and certainly no democratic society, can have institutions that are immune to the political preferences of elected governments; that in the UK universities are almost all publicly funded and she or he who pays the piper should call the tune; that it is better to have compromised educational studies (perhaps practice-focused) and institutions subject to state control than a non-compromised educational studies with their institutions immune from control. What is actually wrong in having universities and their curricula subject to the kind of party political control that Ten (1975) describes where

> before a student is admitted to the University of Singapore, he has, like students entering all the other institutes of higher learning in Singapore, to obtain a Certificate of Suitability from the Ministry of Education to prove that he is not politically subversive. (Ten, 1975, p. 149.)

A number of things might be said about such an argument. One is that to argue for the institutionalization of autonomous academic enquiry is not to argue that universities and other institutions should be freed from the need to justify what they do. The question is rather why, if at all, societies and hence governments should create and sustain at least some educational institutions whose assigned main function is that of academic enquiry and teaching. In order to answer this question we need to say something about the notion of 'the academic'.

An enquiry is academic when its concern is to get to the truth of some matter, or as near to it as is possible, irrespective of the urgent demands and pressures of the world of practical affairs. As Minogue (1973) puts it, in academic enquiry 'no one has to come to a conclusion upon which a decision must be based' and a person 'can afford the luxury of allowing the evidence to dictate quite precisely what conclusions he will come to...' (p. 86). In the world of practical affairs, by contrast, 'decisions have to be taken and minds made up... on what are, in academic terms, inadequate grounds. There is about the taking of decisions in the practical world an irredeemable element of improvization which renders it necessarily, not contingently, subject to error.'

It is pointless to denounce the approximations, compromises, simplifications, etc., of the world of practical affairs since, without them, timely action is impossible. It is pointless, too, to defend everything that goes on under the heading of 'academic enquiry'. Much of it may be trivial. We agree with Maxwell (1980) and with Popper (1963, p. 72) that academic enquiry takes its value from the importance of problems that have their origins outside it. To say this is to say that any defensible academic enquiry must be fundamentalist. It should, too, be clear from our earlier discussion that there are any number of political, moral, empirical and other assumptions required for action in the social (and educational) world whose reliability cannot be assessed, simply, if at all, by practice. No one can think that practice *tout court*, uninterpreted and without a sustained and unpressured investigation, will establish whether capitalist modes of societal organization and the educational programmes they imply are to be preferred to one or other of their competitors; or whether and to what degree parental attitudes affect school performance; or whether there should be a unitary system of schooling as opposed to different religious or ethnic groups having their own publicly funded schools and so on. What the examples show is that there are plenty of questions about practice which are amenable to academic enquiry and which are not questions of practice (as this is conventionally understood) and yet which are central to the understanding, elucidating, and improvement of it. Further, if such enquiry is to follow the argument wherever it leads, it needs to be free from not simply the pressures of time but from the pressures exerted by particular interest groups which might prejudice the nature of the enquiry and its conclusions, even before it starts. If such enquiry is to be as autonomous as possible, its institutions need to be socially located in such a way as to preserve this autonomy. Where there are a number of competing solutions proffered to fundamental problems, and to the subsidiary problems to which they give rise, institutions are required which are as little beholden as possible to the interest group linked to and advocating one particular solution as opposed to another. These institutions (and universities would be one example of them) need to be independent if they are to be free to follow the argument wherever it leads, to criticize and evaluate the responses of the various interest groups, and to constitute an arena and resource for serious public debate about them. These institutions are themselves interest groups and will expect to be judged by other interest groups. Universities and their departments of education should be judged, on this account, by the extent to which their assessment of ways of meeting fundamental problems in education and elsewhere is more sophisticated and is less adversely affected by particular sets of interests than the responses of the interest groups themselves.

The justification of institutions which are, to some extent, independent and protected from powerful interest groups is an area which is seriously underdeveloped. Some of the consequences of the general failure to articulate the case for such institutions is becoming clear now that many of them are under severe attack. Examples of such institutions include: (a) economics departments or departments of political theory in higher education whose work is independent of whatever happens to be the dominant economic or political views of a particular government; (b) departments in universities or research institutes concerned with human medicine which offer assessments of the claims of drug companies about the efficacy of particular drugs or of tobacco companies' claims about the consequences of cigarette smoking; (c) groups that attempt to examine in a scientifically informed way, the claims of the nuclear energy industry; and (d) broadcasting institutions which are at least partly true of direct government or commercial pressure.

The particular justification of universities (and hence of educational studies) is part of the general justification of institutions which are independent of particular interest groups. What might be called 'the institutional crisis of educational studies', discussed in the section entitled 'Politics and the Control of Educational Studies', is partly a result of pressures on the institutions of teacher education which are forcing them to work hand in hand with a particular government and its agencies and with particular sets of political, social, and economic interests. To subject academic reflection to a particular set of interests in the way that this has happened is to put some inherently controversial positions beyond scrutiny. [...] To be bound in this way to the world of practice is for the academic world to make its norms of epistemological respectability almost entirely political (Kolakowski, 1980, p. 129). It is to abolish any mode of enquiry or any institutions that might play an independent role in assessing claims about the priority or otherwise of particular sets of interests and about the consequences and merits of particular educational policies and practices.

If, then, academic enquiry is to follow the argument wherever it leads, irrespective of time or particular sets of interests, it must be institutionally separate from what we have called 'the world of practical affairs'. Such a particular social location will not *guarantee* that academic enquiry is uncontaminated by particular interests, for universities and other institutions concerned with such inquiry have their interests, just as their individual members do, but they make it likely that their work will be less damagingly contaminated by such interests and by the exigencies of action as they would be, had they a different social location. Part of the value of academic enquiry for practice, it might be said, consists simply in the fact that it is institutionally separate from it.

Educational Studies and Wider Political and Moral Issues

The existence of institutions having the kind of independence discussed above presupposes certain political and societal values of democratic, liberal and non-totalitarian kind (Kolakowski, 1975; and Taylor, C. 1975) so that a defence of fundamentalist educational studies is, in part, a defence of a certain sort of democratic society.

The general defence of such enquiry and the institutions it requires is that it is in the public interest to have institutions concerned with independent academic enquiry into fundamental problems, and to have such enquiry owing as little as possible to particular interests (Benn, 1972; and Maxwell, 1980). For example, a debate controlled by the tobacco industry, about the effects of smoking on health, is less likely to be in the public interest than one informed by considerations that owe something to independent institutionalized enquiry.

If all of this is true, then limiting the agenda of the political and educational debate and restricting those who are deemed fit to take part in it (whether by political exclusion or by giving them an education in schools or in the institutions of teacher education that precludes them from taking part) is a threat to democratic values themselves. If student teachers, teachers, parents, and the citizenry as a whole, or children (Schrag, 1975; and Harris, 1982) are allowed, at best, only a token voice in the debate about education, and if the debate becomes the province of a smaller and smaller group of only indirectly accountable people (politicians, civil servants, and other administrators), to what extent is this compatible with a democratic society? Such a group can, in any case, have no special expertise on the matters in question. And because the central issues of education are political, they are issues on which the citizenry as a whole has a legitimate voice. A consequence of this is that the constituency for educational studies must be wider than politicians, civil servants, academics and teachers. To create such a wider constituency is, in part, to begin to create the political support that any institutionalization of the ideal of independent academic enquiry requires, if it is to be maintained. It also raises questions about access to educational institutions, particularly to those of higher education, by the citizenry as a whole.

Further, where the professional education of teachers (and the educational studies constituting it) are specialist; where the aims of such an education are determined elsewhere and are put beyond critical scrutiny; where such an education encourages intellectual and moral docility; where its content is determined by a particular political ideology (Parekh, 1982, p. 59) and so where professionals in education are ideologically dominated; where they are agents-for-others or alienated from their work; then professional education, far from improving practice, may actually make it worse.

For current purposes it is, we hope, sufficient to note that our view of educational studies presupposes a political position, and one whose defence raises central issues in political and economic theory. It has been argued, for example, that any society organized along predominantly capitalist lines needs to be a society run by a professional political elite with a largely apathetic citizenry, and that the distribution of status, power, and wealth in it will make any genuine participatory democracy impossible (see Pateman, 1970; MacPherson, 1977; and Levine, 1984). There are important questions about whether capitalism and participatory democracy are compatible; whether capitalism is to be taken as a value that is prior to democracy (with democracy and forms of it permitted only to the extent that they do not seriously compromise capitalism's workings); or whether one form or other of participatory democracy is to be taken as the prior value with capitalism as a possible mode of societal and economic organization only to the extent that it does not compromise the form of democracy in question. That our discussion leads to questions of this kind should not be surprising, if our view of the relationship between education and politics is correct. It would, rather, be odd if it did not.

References

APPLE, M.W. (1986) 'Curriculum conflict in the United States' in HARTNETT, A. and NAISH, M. *Education and Society Today*. Lewes: The Falmer Press.

BENN, S.I. (1972) 'Universities, Society, and Rational Inquiry', *The Australian University*, 10, pp. 30–47.

HAMILTON, D. (1983) 'History Without Hindsight: Some reflections on British education in the 1980s, *Australian Educational Researcher*, 10, pp. 24–36.

HARRIS, J. (1982) 'The Political Status of Children', in GRAHAM, K. (ed.) *Contemporary Political Philosophy: Radical Studies*. Cambridge: Cambridge University Press, pp. 35–55.

HARTNETT, A. and NAISH, M. (1981) 'The PGCE as an Educational Priority Area', *Journal of Further and Higher Education*, 5(3), pp. 88–102.

HAYEK, F.A. (1960) *The Constitution of Liberty*. London: Routledge & Kegan Paul.

HEARNSHAW, L.S. (1979) *Cyril Burt Psychologist*. London: Hodder & Stoughton.

HIRST, P.H. (1985) 'Educational Studies and the PGCE Course', *British Journal of Educational Studies*, 23(3), pp. 211–21.

INGLIS, F. (1985) *The Management of Ignorance: A Political Theory of the Curriculum*. Oxford: Basil Blackwell.

JAY, M. (1973) *The Dialectical Imagination*. London: Heinemann Educational Books.

JONATHAN, R. (1986) 'Education and the needs of society', in HARTNETT, A. and NAISH, M. (eds) *Education and Society Today*. Lewes: The Falmer Press.

KEKES, J. (1976) *A Justification of Rationality*. New York: State University of New York Press.

KING, L.R. and MELANSON, P.H. (1972) 'Knowledge and Politics: some experiences from the 1960s', *Public Policy*, 20, pp. 83–101.

KNITTER, W. (1985) 'Curriculum Deliberation: pluralism and the practical', *Journal of Curriculum Studies*, 17(4), pp. 383–95.

KOLAKOWSKI, L. (1975) 'Neutrality and Academic Values', in MONTEFIORE, A. (ed.) *Neutrality and Impartiality: The University and Political Commitment*. Cambridge: Cambridge University Press, pp. 72–85.

KOLAKOWSKI, L. (1980) 'Why an Ideology is Always Right', in CRANSTON, M. and MAIR, P. (eds), *Ideology and Politics*. European University Institute, Publication 5, pp. 123–31.

LANGFORD, G. (1978) *Teaching as a Profession: An Essay in Philosophy of Education*. Manchester: Manchester University Press.

LEVINE, A. (1984) *Arguing for Socialism: Theoretical Considerations*. London: Routledge & Kegan Paul.

MacPHERSON, C.B. (1977) *The Life and Times of Liberal Democracy*. Oxford: Oxford University Press.

MANNHEIM, K. (1953) *Essays on Sociology and Social Psychology*. London: Routledge & Kegan Paul.

MAXWELL, N. (1980) 'Science, Reason, Knowledge and Wisdom: a critique of specialism', *Inquiry*, 23(1), pp. 19–81.

MINOGUE, K. (1973) *The Concept of a University*. London: Weidenfeld and Nicolson.

NAISH, M. (1984) 'Education and Essential Contestability Revisited', *Journal of Philosophy of Education*, 18(2), pp. 141–53.

PAREKH, B. (1982) *Marx's Theory of Ideology*. London: Croom Helm.

PATEMAN, C. (1970) *Participation and Democratic Theory*. Cambridge: Cambridge University Press.

POPPER, K.R. (1963) 'The nature of Philosophical Problems and their Roots in Science', in POPPER, K.R. *Conjectures and Refutations: The Growth of Scientific Knowledge*. London: Routledge & Kegan Paul, pp. 66–96.

REDDIFORD, G. (1971) 'Authority, Education, and Student Power', *Educational Philosophy and Theory*, 3(2), pp. 13–26.

SCHEFFLER, I. (1964) 'Concepts of Education: some philosophical reflections on the current scene', in LANDY, E. and PERRY, P.A. (eds) *Guidance in American Education*. Harvard: Harvard University Press, pp. 20–7.

SCHRAG, F. (1975) 'The Child's Status in the Democratic State', *Political Theory*, 3(4), pp. 441–57.

SCHWAB, J. (1978) in WESTBURY, I. and WILKOF, N. (eds), *Science Curriculum and Liberal Education: Selected Essays*. Chicago: University of Chicago Press.

TAYLOR, C. (1975) 'Neutrality in the university', in MONTEFIORE, A. (ed.) *Neutrality and Impartiality: The University and Political Commitment*. Cambridge: Cambridge University Press, pp. 128–48.

TAYLOR, W. (1985) 'The Organisation and Funding of Educational Research in England and Wales', in NISBET, J. and NISBET, S. (eds) *Research Policy and Practice: World Yearbook of Education 1985*. London: Kogan Page & Nichols Publishing, pp. 42–67.

TEN, C.L. (1975) 'Politics in the Academe', in MONTEFIORE, A. (ed.) *Neutrality and Impartiality: The University and Political Commitment*. Cambridge: Cambridge University Press, pp. 149–64.

Part Three:
Aspects of Equality

3.1 | The Idea of Equality
Bernard Williams

Equality in Unequal Circumstances

The notion of equality is invoked not only in connexions where men are claimed in some sense all to be equal, but in connexions where they are agreed to be unequal, and the question arises of the distribution of, or access to, certain goods to which their inequalities are relevant. It may be objected that the notion of equality is in fact misapplied in these connexions, and that the appropriate ideas are those of fairness or justice, in the sense of what Aristotle called 'distributive justice', where (as Aristotle argued) there is no question of regarding or treating everyone as equal, but solely a question of distributing certain goods in proportion to men's recognized inequalities.

I think it is reasonable to say against this objection that there is some foothold for the notion of equality even in these cases. It is useful here to make a rough distinction between two different types of inequality, inequality of *need* and inequality of *merit*, with a corresponding distinction between goods – on the one hand, goods demanded by the need, and on the other, goods that can be earned by the merit. In the case of needs, such as the need for medical treatment in case of illness, it can be presumed for practical purposes that the persons who have the need actually desire the goods in question, and so the question can indeed be regarded as one of distribution in a simple sense, the satisfaction of an existing desire. In the case of merit, such as for instance the possession of abilities to profit from a university education, there is not the same presumption that everyone who has the merit has the desire for the goods in question, though it may, of course, be the case. Moreover, the good of a university education may be legitimately, even if hopelessly, desired by those who do not possess the merit; while medical treatment or unemployment benefit are either not desired, or not legitimately desired, by those who are not ill or unemployed, i.e. do not have the appropriate need. Hence the distribution of goods in accordance with merit has a competitive aspect lacking in the case of distribution according to need. For these reasons, it is appropriate to speak, in the case of merit, not only of the distribution of the good, but of the distribution of the opportunity of achieving the good. But this, unlike the good itself, can be said to be distributed equally to everybody, and so one does encounter a notion of *general* equality, much vaunted in our society today, the notion of equality of opportunity.

Before considering this notion further, it is worth noticing certain resemblances and differences between the cases of need and of merit. In both cases, we encounter the matter (mentioned before in this chapter) of the relevance of reasons. Leaving aside preventive medicine, the proper ground of distribution of medical care is ill health: this is a necessary truth. Now in very many societies, while ill health may work as a necessary condition of receiving treatment, it does not work as a sufficient condition, since such treatment costs money, and not all who are ill have the money; hence the possession of sufficient money becomes in fact an additional necessary condition of actually receiving treatment. Yet more extravagantly, money may work as a sufficient condition by itself, without any medical need, in which case the reasons that actually operate for the receipt of this good are just totally irrelevant to its nature; however, since only a few hypochrondriacs desire treatment when they do not need it, this is, in this case, a marginal phenomenon.

When we have the situation in which, for instance, wealth is a further necessary condition of the receipt of medical treatment, we can once more apply the notions of equality and inequality: not now in connexion with the inequality between the well and the ill, but in connexion with the inequality between the rich ill and the poor ill, since we have straightforwardly the situation of those whose needs are the same not receiving the same treatment, though the needs are the ground of the treatment. This is an irrational state of affairs.

It may be objected that I have neglected an important distinction here. For, it may be said, I have treated the ill health and the possession of money as though they were regarded on the same level, as 'reasons for receiving medical treatment', and this is a muddle. The ill health is, at most, a ground of the right to receive medical treatment; whereas the money is, in certain circumstances, the causally necessary condition of securing the right, which is a different thing. There is something in the distinction that this objection suggests: there is a distinction between a man's rights, the reasons why he should be treated in a certain way, and his power to secure those rights, the reasons why he can in fact get what he deserves. But this objection does not make it inappropriate to call the situation of inequality an 'irrational' situation: it just makes it clearer what is meant by so calling it. What is meant is that it is a situation in which reasons are insufficiently *operative*; it is a situation insufficiently controlled by reasons – and hence by reason itself. The same point arises with another form of equality and equal rights, equality before the law. It may be said that in a certain society, men have equal rights to a fair trial, to seek redress from the law for wrongs committed against them, etc. But if a fair trial or redress from the law can be secured in that society only by moneyed and educated persons, to insist that everyone *has* this right, though only these particular persons can *secure* it, rings hollow to the point of cynicism: we are concerned not with the abstract existence of rights, but with the extent to which those rights govern what actually happens.

Thus when we combine the notions of the *relevance* of reasons, and the *operativeness* of reasons, we have a genuine moral weapon, which can be applied in cases of what is appropriately called unequal treatment, even where one is not concerned with the quality of people as a whole. This represents a strengthening of the very weak principle mentioned at the beginning of the paper, that for every difference in the way men are treated, a reason should be given: when one requires further that the reasons should be relevant, and that they should be socially operative, this really says something.

Similar considerations will apply to cases of merit. There is, however, an important difference between the cases of need and merit, in respect of the relevance of reasons. It is a matter of logic that particular sorts of needs constitute a reason for receiving particular sorts of good. It is, however, in general a much more disputable question whether certain sorts of merit constitute a reason for receiving certain sorts of good. For instance, let it be supposed for the sake of argument, that private schools provide a superior type of education, which it is a good thing to receive. It is then objected that access to this type of education is unequally distributed, because of its cost: among children of equal promise or intelligence, only those from wealthy homes will receive it, and, indeed, children of little promise or intelligence will receive it, if from wealthy homes; and this, the objection continues is irrational.

The defender of the private school system might give two quite different sorts of answer to this objection; besides, that is, the obvious type of answer which merely disputes the facts alleged by the objector. One is the sort of answer already discussed in the case of need: that we may agree, perhaps, that children of promise and intelligence have a right to a superior education, but in actual economic circumstances, this right cannot always be secured. The other is more radical: this would dispute the premiss of the objection that intelligence and promise are, at least by themselves, the grounds for receiving this superior type of education. While perhaps not asserting that wealth itself constitutes the ground, the defender of the system may claim that other characteristics significantly correlated with wealth are such grounds; or, again, that it is the purpose of this sort of school to maintain a tradition of leadership, and the best sort of people to maintain this will be people whose fathers were at such schools. We need not try to pursue such arguments here. The important point is that, while there can indeed be genuine disagreements about what constitutes the relevant sort of merit in such cases, such disagreements must also be disagreements about the nature of the good to be distributed. As such, the disagreements do not occur in a vacuum, nor are they logically free from restrictions. There is only a limited number of reasons for which education could be regarded as a good, and a limited number of purposes which education could rationally be said to serve; and to the limitations on this question, there correspond limitations on the sorts of merit or personal characteristic which could be rationally cited as grounds of access to this good. Here again we encounter a genuine strengthening of the very weak principle that, for differences in the way that people are treated, reasons should be given.

We may return now to the notion of equality of opportunity; understanding this in the normal political sense of equality of opportunity for *everyone in society* to secure certain goods. This notion is introduced into political discussion when there is question of the access to certain goods which, first, even if they are not desired by everyone in society, are desired by large numbers of people in all sections of society (either for themselves, or, as in the case of education, for their children), or would be desired by people in all sections of society if they knew about the goods in question and thought it possible for them to attain them; secondly, are goods which people may be said to earn or achieve; and thirdly, are goods which not all the people who desire them can have. This third condition covers at least three different cases, however, which it is worth distinguishing. Some desired goods, like positions of prestige, management, etc., are *by their very nature* limited: whenever there are some people who are in command or prestigious positions, there are necessarily others who are not. Other goods are *contingently* limited, in the sense that there are certain conditions of access to them which in fact not everyone satisfies, but there is no intrinsic limit to the numbers who might gain access to it by satisfying the conditions: university education is usually regarded in this light nowadays, as something which requires certain conditions of admission to it which in fact not everyone satisfies, but which an indefinite proportion of people might satisfy. Thirdly, there are goods which are *fortuitously* limited, in the sense that although everyone or large numbers of people satisfy the conditions of access to them, there is just not enough of them to go round; so some more stringent conditions or system of rationing have to be imposed, to govern access in an imperfect situation. A good can, of course, be both contingently and fortuitously limited at once: when, due to shortage of supply, not even the people who are qualified to have it, limited in numbers though they are, can in every case have it. It is particularly worth distinguishing those kinds of limitation, as there can be significant differences of view about the way in which a certain good is limited. While most would now agree that higher education is contingently limited, a Platonic view would regard it as necessarily limited.

Now the notion of equality of opportunity might be said to be the notion that a limited good shall in fact be allocated on grounds which do not *a priori* exclude any section of those that desire it. But this formulation is not really very clear. For suppose grammar school education (a good perhaps contingently, and certainly fortuitously, limited) is allocated on grounds of ability as tested at the age of 11; this would normally be advanced as an example of equality of opportunity, as opposed to a system of allocation on grounds of parents' wealth. But does not the criterion of ability exclude *a priori* a certain section of people, viz. those that are not able – just as the other excludes *a priori* those who are not wealthy? Here it will obviously be said that this was not what was meant by *a priori* exclusion: the present argument just equates this with exclusion of anybody, i.e. with the mere existence of some condition that has to be satisfied. What then is *a priori* exclusion? It must mean exclusion on grounds *other* than those appropriate or rational for the good in question. But this still will not do as it stands. For it would follow from this that so long as those allocating grammar school education on grounds of wealth thought that such grounds were appropriate or rational (as they might in one of the ways discussed above in connexion with private schools), they could sincerely describe their system as one of equality of opportunity – which is absurd.

Hence it seems that the notion of equality of opportunity is more complex than it first appeared. It requires not merely that there should be no exclusion from access on grounds other than those appropriate or rational for the good in question, but that the grounds considered appropriate for the good should themselves be such that people from all sections of society have an equal chance of satisfying them. What now is a 'section of society'? Clearly we cannot include under this term sections of the populace identified just by the characteristics which figure in the grounds for allocating the good – since, once more, any grounds at all must exclude some section of the populace. But what about sections identified by characteristics which are *correlated* with the grounds of exclusion? There are important difficulties here: to illustrate this, it may help first to take an imaginary example.

Suppose that in a certain society great prestige is attached to membership of a warrior class, the duties of which require great physical strength. This class has in the past been recruited from certain wealthy families only: but egalitarian reformers achieve a change in the rules, by which warriors are recruited from all sections of the society, on the results of a suitable competition. The effect of this, however, is that the wealthy families still provide virtually all the warriors, because the rest of the populace is so under-nourished by reason of poverty that their physical strength is inferior to that of the wealthy and well nourished. The reformers protest that equality of opportunity has not really been achieved; the wealthy reply that in fact it has, and that the poor now have the opportunity of becoming warriors – it is just bad luck that their characteristics are such that they do not pass the test. 'We are not,' they might say, 'excluding anyone for being poor; we exclude people for being weak, and it is unfortunate that those who are poor are also weak.'

This answer would seem to most people feeble, and even cynical. This is for reasons similar to those discussed before in connexion with equality before the law; that the supposed equality of opportunity is quite empty – indeed, one may say that it does not really exist – unless it is made more effective than this. For one knows that it could be made more effective; one knows that there is a causal connexion between being poor and being undernourished, and between being undernourished and being physically weak. One supposes further that something could be done – subject to whatever economic conditions obtain in the imagined society – to alter the distribution of wealth. All this being so, the appeal by the wealthy to the 'bad luck' of the poor must appear as disingenuous.

It seems then that a system of allocation will fall short of equality of opportunity if the allocation of the good in question in fact works out unequally or disproportionately between different sections of society, if the unsuccessful sections are under a disadvantage which could be removed by further reform or social action. This was very clear in the imaginary example that was given, because the causal connexions involved are simple and well known. In actual fact, however, the situations of this type that arise are more complicated, and it is easier to overlook the causal connexions involved. This is particularly so in the case of educational selection, where such slippery concepts as 'intellectual ability' are involved. It is a known fact that the system of selection for grammar schools by the '11+' examination favours children in direct proportion to their social class, the children of professional homes having proportionately greater success than those from working-class homes. We have every reason to suppose that these results are the product, in good part, of environmental factors; and we further know that imaginative social reform, both of the primary educational system and of living conditions, would favourably affect those environmental factors. In these circumstances, this system of educational selection falls short of equality of opportunity.[1]

This line of thought points to a connexion between the idea of equality of opportunity, and the idea of equality of persons, which is stronger than might at first be suspected. We have seen that one is not really offering equality of opportunity to Smith and Jones if one contents oneself with applying the same criteria to Smith and Jones at, say, the age of 11; what one is doing there is to apply the same criteria to Smith as affected by favourable conditions and to Jones as affected by unfavourable but curable conditions. Here there is a necessary pressure to equal up the conditions: to give Smith and Jones equality of opportunity involves regarding their conditions, where curable, as themselves part of what is done to Smith and Jones, and not part of Smith and Jones themselves. Their identity, for these purposes, does not include their curable environment, which is itself unequal and a contributor of inequality. This abstraction of persons in themselves from unequal environments is a way, if not of regarding them as equal, at least of moving recognizably in that direction; and is itself involved in equality of opportunity.

One might speculate about how far this movement of thought might go. The most conservative user of the notion of equality of opportunity is, if sincere, prepared to abstract the individual from some effects of his environment. We have seen that there is good reason to press this further, and to allow that the individuals whose opportunities are to be equal should be abstracted from more features of social and family background. Where should this stop? Should it even stop at the boundaries of heredity? Suppose it were discovered that when all curable environmental disadvantages had been dealt with, there was a residual genetic difference in brain constitution, for instance, which was correlated with differences in desired types of ability; but that the brain constitution could in fact be changed by an operation.[2] Suppose further that the wealthier classes could afford such an operation for their children, so that they always came out top of the educational system; would we then think that poorer children did not have equality of opportunity, because they had no opportunity to get rid of their genetic disadvantages?

Here we might think that our notion of personal identity itself was beginning to give way; we might well wonder who *were* the people whose advantages and disadvantages were being discussed in this way. But it would be wrong, I think, to try to solve this problem simply by saying that in the supposed circumstances our notion of personal identity would have collapsed in such a way that we could no longer speak of the individuals involved – in the end, we could still pick out the individuals by spatio-temporal criteria, if no more. Our objections to the system suggested in this fantasy must, I think, be moral rather than metaphysical. They need not concern us here. What is interesting about the fantasy, perhaps, is that if one reached this state of affairs, the individuals would be regarded as in all respects equal in themselves – for in themselves they would be, as it were, pure subjects or bearers of predicates, everything else about them, including their genetic inheritance, being regarded as a fortuitous and changeable characteristic. In these circumstances, where everything about a person is controllable, equality of opportunity and absolute equality seem to coincide; and this itself illustrates something about the notion of equality of opportunity.

I said that we need not discuss here the moral objections to the kind of world suggested in this fantasy. There is, however, one such point that is relevant to the different aspects of equality that have been discussed in this paper as a whole. One objection that we should feel to the fantasy world is that far too much emphasis was being placed on achieving high ability; that the children were just being regarded as locations of abilities. I think we should still feel this even if everybody (with results hard to imagine) were treated in this way; when not everybody was so treated, the able would also be more successful than others, and those very concerned with producing the ability would probably also be over-concerned with success. The moral objections to the excessive concern with such aims are, interestingly, not unconnected with the ideal of equality itself; they are connected with equality in the sense discussed in the earlier sections of this paper, the equality of human beings despite their differences, and in particular with the complex of notions considered in the second section under the heading of 'respect'.

This conflict within the ideals of equality arises even without resort to the fantasy world. It exists today in the feeling that a thorough-going emphasis on equality of opportunity must destroy a certain sense of common humanity which is itself an ideal of equality.[3] The ideals that are felt to be in conflict with equality of opportunity are not necessarily other ideals of equality – there may be an independent appeal to the values of community life, or to the moral worth of a more integrated and less competitive society. Nevertheless, the idea of equality itself is often invoked in this connexion, and not, I think, inappropriately.

If the idea of equality ranges as widely as I have suggested, this type of conflict is bound to arise with it. It is an idea which, on the one hand, is invoked in connexion with the distribution of certain goods, some at least of which are bound to confer on their possessors some preferred status or prestige. On the other hand, the idea of equality of respect is one which urges us to give less consideration to those structures in which people enjoy status or prestige, and to consider people independently of those goods, on the distribution of which equality of opportunity precisely focuses our, and their, attention. There is perhaps nothing formally incompatible in these two applications of the idea of equality: one might hope for a society in which there existed both a fair, rational, and appropriate distribution of these goods, and no contempt, condescension, or lack of human communication between persons who were more and less successful recipients of the distribution. Yet in actual fact, there are deep psychological and social obstacles to the realization of this hope; as things are, the competitiveness and considerations of prestige that surround the first application of equality certainly militate against the second. How far this situation is inevitable, and how far in an economically developed and dynamic society, in which certain skills and talents are necessarily at a premium, and obstacles to a wide realization of equality might be overcome, I do not think that we know: these are in good part questions of psychology and sociology, to which we do not have the answers.

When one is faced with the spectacle of the various elements of the idea of equality pulling in these different directions, there is a strong temptation, if one does not abandon the idea altogether, to abandon some of its elements: to claim, for instance, that equality of opportunity is the only ideal that is at all practicable, and equality of respect a vague and perhaps nostalgic illusion; or, alternatively, that equality of respect is genuine equality, and equality of opportunity an inegalitarian betrayal of the ideal - all the more so if it were thoroughly pursued, as now it is not. To succumb to either of these simplifying formulae would, I think, be a mistake. Certainly, a highly rational and efficient application of the ideas of equal opportunity, unmitigated by the other considerations, could lead to a quite inhuman society (if it worked - which, granted a well-known desire of parents to secure a position for their children at least as good as their own, is unlikely). On the other hand, an ideal of equality of respect that made no contact with such things as the economic needs of society for certain skills, and human desire for some sorts of prestige, would be condemned to a futile Utopianism, and to having no rational effect on the distribution of goods, position, and power that would inevitably proceed. If, moreover, as I have suggested, it is not really known how far, by new forms of social structure and of education, these conflicting claims might be reconciled, it is all the more obvious that we should not throw one set of claims out of the window; but should rather seek, in each situation, the best way of eating and having as much cake as possible. It is an uncomfortable situation, but the discomfort is just that of genuine political thought. It is no greater with equality than it is with liberty, or any other noble and substantial political ideal.

Notes

1 For this argument, see *Future of Socialism* by A. Crosland.
2 A yet more radical situation - but one more likely to come about - would be that in which an individual's characteristics could be *pre-arranged* by interference with the genetic material. The dizzying consequences of this I shall not try to explore.

3 See, for example, Young, Michael, (1958) *The Rise of the Meritocracy*. London: Thames and Hudson.

3.2 | 'As interchangeable as ants' Anthony Flew

The author of the much discussed article 'The Idea of Equality' has been a Professor of Philosophy in the University of Cambridge, and is now Provost of King's College in that same university. For us the main interest lies in an explosive yet perhaps slightly embarrassed development of 'equality of opportunity' in the direction of equality of outcome.

(i) It is common today, especially perhaps among educational sociologists, to collapse this distinction; and common too to pass from one ideal to the other through various sophisms. Now consider the angry treatment of an imaginary track event by another egalitarian: 'Three of the competitors are forty years old, five are overweight, one has weak ankles, and the tenth is Roger Bannister. What sense does it make to say that all ten have an equal opportunity to win the race? The outcome is predetermined by nature, and nine of the competitors will call it a mockery when they are told that all have the same opportunity to win' (Schaar, p. 233).

Maybe they will. But, if so, then they will show that they are not sufficiently apprised of the ordinary meaning of 'equality of opportunity'; which would, in that sense, be better expressed by 'open competition for scarce opportunities' (Lloyd-Thomas, 1977). It will not do to argue that, because the chances (probabilities) of success for one competitor or class of competitors are different from those for another competitor or class of competitors, therefore these competitors cannot have had equal chances in an open competition. For the equal chance offered by what is usually called equality of opportunity is an equal chance in a fair and open competition. Equal chances in this sense not merely are not necessarily, they necessarily cannot be, equi-probabilities of success. A 'competition' in which the success of all contestants is equally probable is a game of chance or a lottery, not a genuine competition. (When I read a first draft of the present chapter in Ramat-Gan, several Israeli colleagues were misled by the fact that the controlling authorities in many sports take trouble to ensure that contestants are evenly matched, heavyweights boxing only heavyweights and so on. But the aim there is close and exciting contests, not fair and open competition. Those other aims are secured, if at all, in other ways.)

(ii) Williams starts from a similar example. His first conclusion is 'that a system of allocation will fall short of equality of opportunity if the allocation of the good in question in fact works out unequally or disproportionately between different sections of society, if the unsuccessful sections are under a disadvantage which could be removed by further reform or social action' (see Chapter 3.1, p. 174). About the first part of this conclusion, before the proviso, it is enough at this stage to say only that outcome and opportunity are sometimes confused in a way even more scandalous: 'Surely,' it has been suggested, 'we could always define "real chance" in such a way that it becomes analytically true that if two members of a society have the same real chance to achieve equality of economic welfare, then their actual economic welfare level will be the same' (Ericsson, 1976, p. 130: inverted commas supplied). Yes, indeed, nothing easier, nor more arbitrary; nor more obscurantist.

(a) The fresh interest lies in the proviso: 'if the unsuccessful sections are under a disadvantage which could be removed by further reform or social action.' For without exception every feature which differentiates one human being from another must in principle be alterable (if not yet – or ever – alterable in practice). Whatever is in fact determined by the environment could theoretically have been altered by changing that. The same applies to genetic constitutions. Science fiction can easily imagine a society in which all the babies become identical, as products of cloning – too many professing social scientists and practising social engineers assume that we do already (Flew, 1976, Ch. 4). From this it might seem a short step, though one which Williams himself visibly hesitates to take, to the conclusion that there can be no essential difference between Robert and Lucinda, or any other two persons. As the *Encyclopaedia of the Social Sciences* had it, in the days of the Model T: 'at birth human infants, regardless of heredity, are as equal as Fords' (quoted in Hayek, 1978, p. 290).

The move which Williams does make is to say: 'In these circumstances, where everything about a person is controllable, equality of opportunity and absolute equality seem to coincide; and this itself illustrates something about the notion of equality of opportunity' (Chapter 3.1, p. 176). The something which he sees it as illustrating is a tension between ideals of our second and first sorts: 'the feeling that a thoroughgoing emphasis on equality of opportunity must destroy a certain sense of common humanity which is itself an ideal of equality' (3.1, p. 176). What Williams does not recognize is that on his assumptions the notion of equality of opportunity must self-destruct, leaving the field clear for his 'absolute equality'; which belongs, presumably, to our third category, equality of outcome. Since he has effectively collapsed the distinction between opportunity and outcome, he naturally finds no occasion to remark that in any case ideals of these last two sorts are ultimately incompatible.

They must ultimately be incompatible, because, in so far as the outcomes are to be made the same for all, there can not only be no incentive to compete for scarce opportunities but no scarce opportunities for which to compete. The hypothesis requires that the attractions of anything which is inherently and incorrigibly scarce must be artificially offset by compensating disadvantages; otherwise there must remain or emerge that most infamous thing, inequality. Nor again, on the present Williams assumptions, can there be those fair and open competitions presupposed by the ideal of equality of opportunity. For if, following Williams, all the competitive advantages of all the competitors have to be removed, then there can, as we saw in the preceding subsection, be no competition at all; only a game of chance or a kind of lottery – a Lewis Carroll caucus lottery in which all participants have to win equivalent prizes.

(b) Another comment which Williams makes, proceeding from the first passage quoted in the present subsection, is 'that one is not really offering equality of opportunity to Smith and Jones if one contents oneself with applying the same criteria to Smith and Jones at, say, the age of 11; what one is doing there is to apply the same criteria to Smith as affected by favourable conditions and to Jones as affected by unfavourable but curable conditions' (ibid., pp. 245–6).

This too is instructively wrong. For that there should be open competitions for scarce opportunities, with the same criteria applied to all candidates, is precisely what the ideal of equality of opportunity does demand. So if you offer this to Smith and Jones you really are 'offering equality of opportunity'. The genuineness of this proposition is in no way prejudiced by the maybe lamentable truths: first, that in any competition held some time after the birth of the contestants, and where there have been differences between their several environments, some are likely to have become advantaged and some disadvantaged; secondly, that in any competition held at any time, and embracing more than a field of monozygotic single-sex siblings, genetic differences are almost bound to advantage some and disadvantage others; and, third, that if things are so set up that the success of every contestant is equally probable, then we no longer have a competition at all. The protagonist of equality of opportunity, therefore, has no choice but to accept that some competitive advantages must be compatible 'with applying the same criteria' to all candidates; or, in other words, if there is to be any competition at all then competitive advantages cannot all be disqualified as unfair. And, furthermore, unless this protagonist is ready to abolish the family, his tolerance will in practice have to embrace at least some competitive assets which are environmentally conditioned.

(iii) It is essential to grasp exactly how it is that Williams contrives thus to reject equality of opportunity as not really being what it is. The trick is done by refusing to admit to the competition the actual competitors; or, at any rate, by refusing to admit those of them whose prospects are poor. According to Williams the truly legitimate and qualified competitors are not those actual but sometimes rather wretched specimens seen now trooping up to the start line. Instead they are the hypothetical people who might have been competing if only the entire Williams programme for total social transformation had been effectively and successfully implemented. So, referring still to Smith and Jones, he gives his Olympian ruling: 'Their identity, for these purposes, does not include their curable environment, which is itself unequal and a contributor of inequality.' Next, referring to his own stunningly high-handed proceedings, he comments: 'This abstraction of persons in themselves from unequal environments is a way if not of regarding them as equal, at least of moving recognisably in that direction.' It was a pity to offset the impact of this restrained truth by adding the false gloss: 'and is itself involved in equality of opportunity' (Chapter 3.1, p. 175).

Only after he has extended his approach to cover alterable genetic constitutions also does Williams begin to display a little anxiety, even if not nearly enough, about the presuppositions now revealed: 'Here we might think that our notion of personal identity itself was beginning to give way; we might well wonder *who were* the people whose advantages were being discussed in this way... if one reached this state of affairs, the individuals would be regarded as in all respects equal in themselves – for in themselves they would be, as it were, pure subjects or bearers of predicates, everything about them, including their genetic inheritance, being regarded as a fortuitous and changeable characteristic' (3.1, pp. 175–6: italics original).

There is no call now to labour the earlier objection to talk about genetic inheritances: 'Who is the fortunate, or unfortunate, legatee?' The important thing is to recognize that the Williams treatment of equality of opportunity, in effect reducing this to equality of outcome, is leading him towards a conception of the human individual thinner and more etiolated even than that of Rawls. For whereas Rawlsian man is allowed straightforwardly to possess all, but only, the characteristics common to the whole body of his fellow contractors, it looks as if the Williams campaign for equalisation is going to be launched for – or should it be against? – 'pure subjects... everything about them... being regarded as a fortuitous and changeable characteristic'. Both conceptions are very different from those which are, perhaps in a weaker sense, presupposed by ideals of the first or second sorts. In the second case, there surely could be no point in, or possibility of, competition for scarce opportunities where in fact everyone was in all relevant respects equal. And the first ideal, of respecting all persons equally, inasmuch as we are equally entitled to choose our own ends and to do our own things, would lose much of its charm if the only important characteristics of any individual human being were those necessarily common to all mankind.

(iv) Although Williams is by his egalitarian commitments led towards this view of the human individual, he does pull back a short way from the brink: 'Here we might think that our notion of personal identity was beginning to give way; we might well wonder *who were* the people whose advantages and disadvantages were being discussed in this way.' Wait though: 'But... in the end, we could still pick out the individuals by spatio-temporal criteria, if no more' (31, p. 176).

Williams, I suspect, believes that this concession disposes of the difficulty at no cost. Let it be conceded that it does dispose of that difficulty. Yet it still carries costs which must be serious for anyone wanting to present equality of entitlement as 'the first principle of justice'. For those who are going to be picked out as individuals 'by spatio-temporal criteria' are going thereby to be picked out as creatures to whose several individualities various different particular relationships to other individuals of the same kind must be essential. To anyone so reactionary as to be prepared to countenance such infamous diversity, these essential differences will be quite enough to serve as bases for considerable inequalities of entitlement.

The crux arises from the fact that personal identity just *is* the identity of persons. But persons are very complicated and peculiar creatures, having their distinctive way of coming into existence; and with from the very beginning a deal of consequent difference one from another. If they are to be identified and individuated by spatio-temporal criteria, then these criteria cannot but refer to the time and place of each one's origin; and hence to the mating of the particular man and the particular woman of which that birth was a product. Like all human beings all parents have their places within networks of blood relationships. All have their places also within networks of social relationships. So all the children of such parents are born into particular networks of both kinds, which are more or less different from each other. Then again, (almost) every human child is in its genetic constitution different from every other, with all that follows from that. Most important of all, we are all creatures who make and cannot but make choices; conducting our own lives under the guidance of our memories of the past and of our hopes and fears for the future. By that conduct we also to some extent make ourselves. As Aristotle used to insist, dispositions are formed by acting in the ways which become habitual.

If, therefore, we are going to identify individuals by spatio-temporal criteria, then at least some elements of these connections are bound to appear in accounts of what is essential to any particular individual; and, as we have already observed in passing, so in fact they do (Flew, 1981, pp. 101–3). This at once yields plenty of essential differences between individuals, offering purchase for differences of entitlement; and that too before we even begin to take account of the contingent differences brought about by what they later do or do not do. Nor should we overlook the fact that, whereas equal entitlements have to be grounded in necessary or at any rate universal human characteristics, unequal entitlements do not have to be grounded in either these or the essential peculiarities of unequal individuals. The grounds of difference do not have to be common at all; indeed they must not be.

References

ERICSSON, L. (1976) *Justice in the Distribution of Economic Resources*. Stockholm: Almquist and Wiksell.
FLEW, A.G.N. (1976) *Sociology, Equality and Education*. London and New York: Macmillan, and Barnes & Noble.
FLEW, A.G.N. (1981) *The Politics of Procrustes*. London: Temple Smith.
HAYEK, F.A. (1978) *New Studies in Philosophy, Politics, Economics and the History of Ideas*. London: Routledge and Kegan Paul.
LLOYD-THOMAS, D.A. (1977) 'Competitive Equality of Opportunity', *Mind*, LXXXVI.
RAWLS, J. (1971) *A Theory of Justice*. Oxford: Clarendon Press.
SCHAAR, J.H. (1976) '*Equality of Opportunity and Beyond*', in PENNOCK, J.R. and CHAPMAN, J.W. (eds). New York: Atheiton.
WILLIAMS, B. (1962) '*The Idea of Equality*' in *Problems of the Self*. Cambridge: CUP 1973; first published in LASLETT, P. and RUNCIMAN, W.G.: *Politics, Philosophy and Society*. Oxford: Blackwell. 1962. (Partly reprinted in reading 3.1.)

3.3 | Class in the Classroom
Anthony Heath

The Conservatives' election victory (1987) and their proposals for educational reform have raised fears of a return to selection and a widening of social class inequalities in education. The arguments for and against the Conservative proposals obscure, however, what research has shown: that class inequalities in British education have been remarkably stable throughout the century and that the educational reforms that have so far been attempted – the 1944 Act and free secondary education for all, comprehensive reorganization and the raising of the school leaving age – have made little impact on these inequalities.

One of the most widespread myths in contemporary education is that comprehensive schools have sacrificed standards on the altar of equality, with the corollary that selective schools will enhance standards at the cost of greater inequality. There is no hard evidence that either has happened, or is likely to.

A series of national surveys charts the history of class inequalities throughout the present century. The 1949 LSE study (Glass, 1954) looks at pre-war educational history. The 1972 Oxford study (Halsey et al., 1980) compares the pre- and post-war decades and looks at the effects (if any) of the 1944 Act. And the 1983 Oxford/ SCPR study (Heath et al., 1985) enters the era of comprehensive reorganization.

For the authors of the 1949 and 1972 studies, the crucial issue was that of selection for secondary school. Glass and his associates in the 1949 study were concerned to show the great social class inequalities that existed before the war, when many less able children of affluent parents secured fee-paying places at grammar schools and this kept out the more able children of poorer parents. They hoped the 1944 Act, by making all secondary education within the state sector free, would diminish the importance of economic and social background as a determinant of the type of secondary education a child received.

The evidence of the 1972 study showed that the social engineering of the 1944 Act had had no measurable impact on class inequalities. Boys educated before the Act came into force were as divided by social class as those educated afterwards. (The 1972 study covered only men. However, neither the 1949 nor the 1983 studies show any statistically significant class difference between men and women in access to selective schools.)

The crucial evidence is shown in Figure 3.3.1a. This traces class inequalities in access to selective secondary schools (largely grammar and private schools) from the beginning of the century (the group born 1890–99) up until the 1950s (the group born 1940–49). The definitions of social class and of selective schooling are somewhat different in the two studies (for technical details see Heath, 1987) and so the graphs do not coincide.

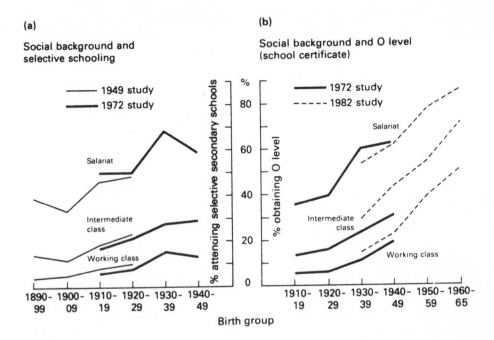

(a)

Social background and
selective schooling

—— 1949 study
—— 1972 study

Salariat

Intermediate
class

Working class

1890- 1900- 1910- 1920- 1930- 1940-
99   09   19   29   39   49

% attending selective secondary schools

(b)

Social background and O level
(school certificate)

—— 1972 study
- - - - 1982 study

Salariat

Intermediate
class

Working class

% obtaining O level

%
80
60
40
20
0

1910- 1920- 1930- 1940- 1950- 1960-
19   29   39   49   59   65

Birth group

Figure 3.3.1

We should not, therefore, make direct comparisons *between* studies, but should limit ourselves to comparing birth groups *within* studies. And here we see that both the 1949 and the 1972 studies tell the same story. The socially and economically advantaged classes conferred on their children great educational advantages and the gap between the classes stayed more or less constant for their respective time spans. There are some fluctuations of the kind that would be expected in sample surveys. But overall there is no consistent trend towards either increasing, or declining, class inequality.

There are serveral possible statistical measures of class inequality that can be used. The simplest is the difference in percentage points between the classes. (There are some technical difficulties with this measure, because of 'floor' and 'ceiling' effects, but more sophisticated statistical techniques yield essentially the same conclusions in the present case.)

So the 1972 study shows that the gap between the salariat and the working class was 47 points for the 1910–19 birth group, who will have received their secondary education before the war when fee-paying places at grammar school were still permitted; it was 45 and 56 points respectively for the next two, transitional, groups; and it was still 46 points for the 1940–49 birth group, who received their secondary education after the 1944 Act when it was, for those within the state system, both universal and free.

Comprehensive reorganization began in 1965. But it was not until the mid-1970s that most schools had been reorganized, and by that time there were two other, perhaps even more important, educational reforms. The school-leaving age was raised to 16 in 1974, bringing all school-children within temporal if not academic reach of the public examinations like the GCE. And the spread of the CSE had also transformed the character of secondary education.

These three changes also mean that the focus of attention necessarily shifts from selection at eleven to attainment (and selection) at 16. In the comprehensive era, then, the focus must shift from access to selective secondary schools to the acquisition of examination certificates. For the pre-war groups, grammar school education gave access to salaried jobs even for school leavers who had not taken their school certificate. In the post-war period, this became less true and it was the acquisition of O-level certificates that became the crucial step on the road to a salaried job.

Figure 3.1.1(b) charts the history of class differences in gaining O-level certificates from the 1972 and 1983 studies. They both tell the same story about trends in class inequalities.

Unlike Figure 3.3.1a, which showed a doubling in the proportion attending selective schools over the period, Figure 3.3.1b shows much larger increases in the proportions, from all social classes, gaining O-level certificates. But despite these differences in the rates of growth, class inequalities in examination success are very similar to those already documented in access to selective schools.

The 1940-49 birth group was one educated in the so-called tripartite system of grammar, technical and secondary modern schools, although our data actually refer to a quadripartite system which included private schools as well. The 1950-59 group was another transitional one, while the 1960-65 group was largely educated in comprehensive schools. (Two thirds of our respondents in this group reported that they have been educated in comprehensive schools.)

Comparisons must again be made between groups within a particular study rather than between studies. So comparing birth groups within the 1983 study shows that the gap between the salariat and the working class moved from 41 points (for the 1940-49 group) to 40 points (the 1950-59 group) and finally to 38 points (the 1960-65 group), a change well within the limits of sampling error.

In this most recent group, the salariat is approaching the ceiling with 91 per cent now obtaining one or more O-levels. If the proportion of children from the working class gaining an O-level continues to increase at the same rate as before, the gap between the classes must narrow decisively. But the likelihood here is that, as fast as the working class catches up at O-level, the qualifications required in the labour market will move upwards with A-levels becoming the key qualification for a successful career in the salariat.

So we have a striking contrast. There has been constantly rising educational attainment (at least as measured by the acquisition of examination certificates, the only measure available to us) during the course of the twentieth century, a silent revolution that has continued throughout both selective and comprehensive eras. But class inequalities first in access to selective secondary schools, then at O and next perhaps at A-level, have shown no overall tendency to decline. Chameleon-like, they seem to reappear in a new guise but fundamentally unchanged as the educational environment changes around them.

In the face of this remarkable resilience of class inequalities, educational reforms seem powerless, whether for good or ill. There are two major reasons for this.

First, the rhetoric of the reforms has often been much bolder than the reforms themselves. Thus the 1944 Act provided free secondary education for all, but many local authorities had already provided the bulk of their places free before the war. The Act merely reinforced a long-standing trend. Similarly some protagonists (and some opponents) of comprehensives talk about a common education (or levelling) but there is substantial differentiation both within and between comprehensives. Class differences between comprehensives (reflecting differences in their catchment areas) may often be as great as the class differences between grammar and secondary modern schools.

Secondly, and relatedly, in a free society educationally ambitious families can adjust their plans so as to maximize their children's chances under any new rules of the game.

This should not be taken to imply that educational reform makes no difference, merely that it has not as yet made any difference to class inequalities in this country. It would be surprising if educational reform did not make life easier for some parents, but more difficult for others. For example, under the selective system it was particularly the affluent parents of less able children (the so-called 11+ failures) who had to turn to private schools if they wanted to secure salaried careers for their children. Under the comprehensive system it is likely to be where you live, not your children's ability to pass selection tests, that is relevant to the decision to opt out of state education.

The private schools will still be patronized by relatively affluent and educationally ambitious parents; but they are likely to be somewhat different subgroups under the selective and comprehensive systems respectively. The differences between the classes stay the same, but the costs and benefits will be redistributed differently within the classes.

To the protagonists of selection, class inequalities may be an irrelevance. But the data of Figure 3.3.1 should also lead to some scepticism about the relation between educational reorganization and standards of attainment. The silent revolution of 'certification' has continued at a steady pace through the last 40 years of educational reform. The rates of growth in the proportions obtaining O-levels seem to be as little influenced by education reform as were the class differences.

No one can tell whether this growth of certification truly measures a rise in educational standards or not. But it is surely of some interest that, while the spread of comprehensives seems to have done little or nothing to reduce class inequalities, it has done nothing either to abate the steady increase in examination successes.

The very increase in examination successes, however, may have important unintended consequences for class inequalities. Even as recently as the 1960s the majority of school-leavers had no academic qualification, and the working class in particular was relatively homogeneous in its lack of qualification.

The subsequent growth in the proportions obtaining O-levels and even more so of those obtaining CSE, means that school leavers are now more heterogeneous in their qualifications. The youngest group has in effect become more stratified in educational terms and there are now new gradations of educational attainment that mirror differences in social background. Whereas most working-class children were once alike in leaving school without qualification, differences are now emerging between the skilled and semi-skilled section of the working class. As a result, educational attainment has become more, not less, associated with social background.

Comprehensive Schooling is Better and Fairer

3.4 Andrew McPherson and J. Douglas Willms

Anthony Heath says that research has shown that comprehensive reorganization, in common with other educational reforms this century, has made little impact on social-class inequalities in British education (*New Society*, 17 July 1987). He is not correct to say this about comprehensive reorganization, nor to conclude that, 'in the face of this remarkable resilience of class inequalities, educational reforms seem powerless, whether for good or ill'.

The view is widespread, of course, that comprehensive schools have failed to improve standards and to reduce social-class inequalities of attainment. Many people, though not Heath, think that they are doomed so to fail. In progressive educational thinking, and in some quarters on the left, this has led to renewed calls for the abolition of public examinations and for a humanist transformation of the secondary school curriculum. On the right, however, a similar pessimism about comprehensive schooling has contributed to the Government's provision for parental choice, to its proposals for the testing of pupils, and to its plan to give parents the right to withdraw a school from local authority control.

Scottish research confirms that social-class differences in attainment have been large and resilient. They remained roughly stable in Scotland for several decades after 1945, as they did in England. But the most recent Scottish study (McPherson and Willms, 1987) has a different and more up-to-date story to tell about comprehensive schooling. Since the mid-1970s, the reorganization that was initiated in 1965 has contributed to a rise in examination attainment and to a fall in the effect on attainment of social class. We call these two trends respectively 'improvement' and 'equalization'. One can infer from the Scottish evidence that there will have been similar, but weaker, trends in England and Wales.

First, the Scottish evidence. A 1983 study has already shown that social-class differences in attainment were higher in areas with selective schooling than in areas served solely by *omnibus* schools (i.e., schools that were non-selective, but streamed). However, this finding came from a sample of pupils who left school in 1976, before the full effects of the post-1965 reorganization could be expected to show. Also, many of the *omnibus* schools long pre-dated 1965. It was not until the mid-1970s that the majority of pupils could start their secondary schooling in a settled comprehensive system. What has happened since then? Could the more egalitarian tradition of the *omnibus* schools be realised in the traditionally selective areas? We can tell by comparing the 'early' cohort of leavers in 1976, with a 'middle' cohort that left school in 1980, and a 'late' cohort that left school in 1984. All three cohorts are representative of the majority of Scottish schools, and the samples are large, totalling around 40,000 members in all.

Figure 3.4.1 shows the average SCE examination attainment of leavers in each of the Registrar General's social classes. We have scaled the attainment measure in order to make meaningful comparisons possible across the years, and we have set the national average of the middle cohort to zero. The figure shows that average attainment increased across all social-class groups. Also, although there are still large social-class differences, attainment has been rising faster among the lower groups. For example, the gap between the

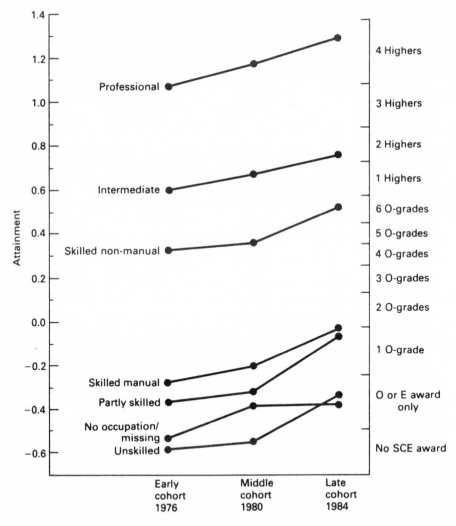

Figure 3.4.1   Average attainment by social class

intermediate and skilled manual fell from .87 to .79, or by roughly half an O-grade award at A-C. (The SCE O-grade is equivalent to the GCE O-level.) Overall, the gap between pupils from middle-class backgrounds (top three categories) and those from working-class backgrounds (bottom three categories) fell by a similar magnitude, from .94 to .87. Put another way, the gap between middle-class and working-class pupils in the percentages getting at least one O-grade award fell by six points between the early and late cohorts, or by almost one percentage point per annum (not shown in the figure). An important point here is that equalization was the result of a levelling-up in working-class attainment, and not of a levelling-down in middle-class attainment.

A private sector survived the reform in Scotland, and continued to 'cream' the state comprehensive schools, mainly in the four major cities. But selection at 12 years (the age of transfer) was eliminated in the public sector, and this reduced the overall incidence of creaming. One effect of this can be seen in Figure 3.4.2. This shows the attainment of a pseudo-pupil who had the nationally average socio-economic status (SES) for the middle cohort. Our

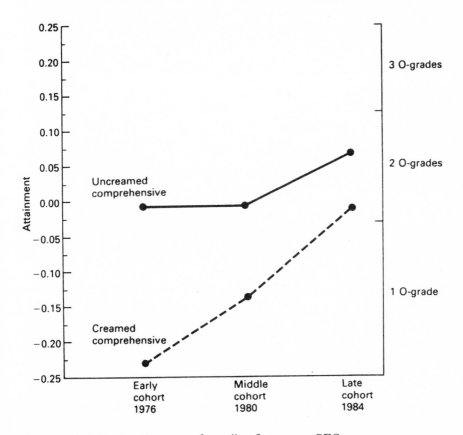

Figure 3.4.2 Attainment of pupils of average SES

SES measure takes account of father's occupation, mother's education, and number of siblings. Not surprisingly, the pupil of average SES performed around the national average in the uncreamed comprehensive sector. But the attainment of the same pseudo-pupil in the creamed sector rose by about one examination pass as the severity of creaming declined over the eight years.

We made similar, carefully controlled, comparisons between other types of schools that had varying histories of reorganization. Other things being equal, the pupil of nationally average SES tended to attain higher

- in uncreamed schools;

- the longer the school had been an all-through comprehensive;

- in schools with 'favourable contexts', that is, with pupil intakes of higher SES or ability.

Fuller details and other findings are in our 1987 article, 'Equalization and Improvement' (*Sociology*).

Why, then, do Heath's data tell a different story? In fact, in spite of his interpretation, it is not clear that they do. They show that both the 'working class' and the 'intermediate class' (Heath uses a different, three-category, classification) have recently been catching the 'salariat' up in respect of the percentage of pupils obtaining at least one O-level award. (The relatively small size of Heath's samples obliges him to treat some of these changes as sampling error.)

In addition, timing is crucial here. Heath's latest time-point is for pupils born 1960–65, who reached 16 years of age between 1976 and 1981. Any effects of reorganization that started to show only after 1976 would be obscured in Heath's averaging for the years 1976–81 (i.e. for pupils born 1960–65). But it was only after 1976 that the effects of reform in Scotland first became apparent. If we averaged our Scottish data across the years from 1976 onwards, as Heath has done with his data, we would underestimate the impact of the Scottish reform. If we stopped the story in the early 1980s, as Heath was obliged to do, we would also underestimate its impact. All in all, Heath's design would probably lead us to conclude that reorganization in Scotland had left inequalities of attainment unchanged. But we would be wrong.

Reorganization in England and Wales has not gone as quickly or as far as in Scotland. Overall, the system south of the border has more selection and creaming, proportionately fewer 'all-through' comprehensives, and proportionately fewer communities that are served by wholly comprehensive systems. The net effects of reorganization will therefore be weaker and later in England and Wales. As Heath says, the rhetoric of reform was bolder than the reality. But this does not mean that the potential for effective reform is any less than in Scotland. What it does mean is that a sensitive and timeous research design is required to evaluate the national significance of the widely varying circumstances of the schools and communities in England and Wales. Because there is no such study, there is little basis in research evidence for the widespread pessimism over the potential of comprehensive schooling outside Scotland.

It would be wrong to dismiss the Scottish experience as non-transferable. It is true that Scotland had more *omnibus* schools before 1965, and also true that the public provision of selective (grammar-school type) schooling was more generous in Scotland. But it was precisely this generosity that convinced professional educational opinion that Scotland did not need comprehensive reorganization. Reorganization was more decisive in Scotland mainly for political reasons. A higher proportion of the local authorities were Labour controlled, and were thus persuaded to implement central-government policy, even though most educational practitioners were sceptical or opposed. It is true, too, that the private sector is smaller in Scotland. But neither Glasgow nor Edinburgh need any lessons from England on how to organize private sector schooling. In both these cities, class inequalities of attainment fell after 1976 (private and public schools combined), and attainment rose.

It would also be wrong to dismiss the size of the change in Scotland as trivial, even though it is small in relation to the class inequalities that remain. A political and historical perspective is essential here. The Scottish system of selective post-primary schooling that was finally ousted in the 1970s had been configured well before the First World War. It subsequently reinforced social-class differences in attainment by shaping expectations both in local communities, and in the national 'policy community' of administrators, school inspectors and leading teachers. The eight years that separate our early and late cohorts was but a brief period in which to unpick the legacy of decades.

How much further could equalization go? Three illustrations are suggestive:

1 In Fife's five largest towns 1976–80, equalization was three times the national average, while attainment rose in four of the five.
2 In Scotland's New Towns, the effect of social class on attainment was only two-thirds as large as the national average, but the level of attainment was at the national average.
3 Scotland's Catholic schools serve a predominantly low SES population. Class inequalities were lower in Catholic schools, but the attainment of our nationally average pseudo-pupil was about two O-grade awards higher.

We conclude that comprehensive reorganization has helped to make schooling better and fairer in the past decade, and could do more in these directions. Current government policies, however, are likely to retard or reverse the recent equalizing trend. Also, as Heath suggests, it is possible that equalization at 16 years will be offset by countervailing trends in post-compulsory education. Indeed, there are some indications in our own data that this might be happening to a limited degree. However, even if the social-class attainment gap were widening after 16 years, this trend would not detract from the educational value of improvement and equalization up to 16 years. Furthermore, the Scottish data support two stronger conclusions. The first is that the equalization of opportunity and attainment between the social classes is perfectly consistent with rising standards for all groups. The second is that social-class inequalities of educational attainment vary considerably across time and community, and are open to change, 'whether for good or ill', through the political process of social democracy.

References

GRAY, J., McPHERSON, A.F. and RAFFE, D. (1983) *Reconstructions of Secondary Education*. London: Routledge & Kegan Paul, chs 12 and 14.

McPHERSON, A.F. and RABB, C.D. (1938) *Governing Education*. Edinburgh: Edinburgh University Press, chs 15–17.

McPHERSON, A.F. and WILLMS, J.D. (1986) 'Certification, Class Conflict, Religion and Community', in KERCKHOFF, A.C. (ed.) *Research in Sociology of Education and Socialization* (Vol. 6). Greenwich, Conn.: JAI Press.

McPHERSON, A.F. and WILLMS, J.D. (1987) 'Equalization and Improvement', *Sociology*, November.

WILLMS, J.D. (1986) 'Social class segregation and its relationship to pupils' examination results in Scotland', *American Sociological Review*, 51, pp. 224–41.

The 1987 research was funded by the ESRC and the Social Science and Humanities Research Council of Canada.

3.5 | The Expansion of Special Education
Sally Tomlinson

Special education in Britain, as in other advanced technological societies, is expanding. In changed forms and rationalized by changed ideologies, notably the ideology of special needs, it is becoming a more important mechanism for differentiating between young people and allocating some to a future which, if not as stigmatized as in the past, will be characterized by relative powerlessness and economic dependency. It is expanding primarily as part of a political response to a crucial dilemma facing education systems in late twentieth-century technological societies. This dilemma is centred round restructuring the education training system to deal with the increasing number of young people who are defined as being unable or unwilling to participate satisfactorily in a system primarily directed towards producing academic and technical elites. Adequate achievements in normal school education or educational training are becoming more important in gaining any sort of employment or income above subsistence level, or exerting any influence on the wider society. The expansion of special education is linked to the question of what sort of education – or preparation for future life-style – can or should be offered to a larger social group who are likely to be partially or permanently non-employed, and thus in traditional industrial society understandings are not economically profitable or 'useful'. As special education expands it is likely to provide both a rationale and a justification for the economic and social position of at least a part of this social group. Although presented in ideological terms as catering for the 'needs' of pupils, the expansion of special education is the result of rational action on the part of those who control and direct education and training, to restructure the education system to fit the perceived needs of a post-industrial, technologically based society.

This chapter examines evidence for the claim that special education is expanding and discusses three reasons for the expansion – professional vested interest, comprehensive school dilemmas and the declining youth labour market – and asserts that the ideology of 'special needs' directs attention away from the social, economic and political concerns which have led to the expansion.

Evidence for Expansion

Legally, special education is defined as the curriculum and pedagogy offered to pupils who pre-1981 had a 'disability of body or mind' calling for special educational treatment, and post-1981 have a learning difficulty which calls for special educational provision. The number of such children rose from nil in the early 1870s – at the beginning of compulsory state education – to some $1\frac{1}{2}$ million in 1981[1]. This argues that a subsystem of special education has been successfully established and has become an important structural component of the educational system. The expansion can be largely accounted for by the number of children who have no physical or sensory handicap, but who are educationally defined as being incapable of participating or unwilling to participate in what is currently defined as the 'normal' curriculum, and being incapable of 'adequate achievements' via this curriculum. Such children have, over the past 100 years, been variously described as feeble-minded, educable defective, educationally subnormal, those having moderate learning difficulties, dull and backward, remedial, and maladjusted and disruptive.

The expansion is linked to enhanced definitions of 'achievement'. There is increasing pressure on schools to raise standards and to credential more and more pupils. This has led to pressures on schools to devise more and more courses leading to lower-level credentials and to seek ways of separating out those who are unable or unwilling to achieve even these lower-level qualifications. In this way the subsystem of special education appears capable of seemingly indefinite expansion. For example, the number of pupils considered to have a disability of body or mind in 1946 was 2 per cent with a futher 8 to 9 per cent likely to be unable to achieve adequately in schools.[2] In 1978, the number in need of special provision was considered by the Warnock Committee to be 20 per cent of the school population. By 1982 the Secretary of State was expressing his concern about the less able 40 per cent and a DES-sponsored programme for lower-attaining pupils was instigated. The ideological differences between the 20 per cent of pupils needing special provision owing to learning difficulties and the learning difficulties of the bottom 40 per cent are problematic, and in practice the programme appears to fill a gap between school definitions of 'special needs' and 'CSE material' (NFER, 1984). In Scotland the system may be expanding faster. A Scottish Inspectorate comment on learning difficulties in 1984 noted that since 'there is a whole range of difficulties faced by very many pupils in the lower half of the ability range ... the progress report was thinking in terms of up to 50%'.[3] Accurate numbers of those in special education provision, or 'in need' of this kind of provision have always been difficult to quantify. One reason for this has been the changing definitions of special education. Another reason is that LEAs have always differed in the kinds and amount of special provision they offered. Perhaps of more interest are the proportional and percentage increases.

Post-war, Booth has worked out that in 1950, 2,402 pupils per million were categorised as ESN-M; by 1977 the proportion had risen to 5,763 per million. Similarly, in 1950, 93 pupils per million were officially maladjusted, by 1977 this had risen to 1,416 per million (Booth, 1981, p. 295). In another entertaining comparison Squibb (1981, p. 47) estimated that in 15 years (1961–76) there was an increase of 150 per cent in pupils classed as ESN, a 237 per cent increase for those classed as maladjusted, a 1,332 per cent increase for those classes as speech defective and an infinite increase (from no pupils in 1961 to 951 in 1976) in those classed as autistic. As Squibb (1981) has noted 'we may all be autistic soon' (p. 48). Further evidence of percentage increases of pupils segregated into special schools and classes under the pre-1981 system of classification by handicap has been provided by Swann who worked out that despite assumptions that integration was occurring and fewer pupils were being physically removed from mainstream schooling, the proportion of pupils segregated in special schools actually increased by 4.8 per cent between 1977 and 82 and he particularly noted the increased segregation into ESN–M and maladjusted provision (Swann, 1984).

From its beginnings special education was concerned to take in those with obvious and definable physical and sensory handicaps and behaviourally troublesome pupils, but from 1889 the most likely candidates for inclusion in an expanding system were those originally classed as feeble-minded or educable defectives – their heirs being the dull and backward, educationally subnormal, remedial, moderate learning and behavioural difficulties, the less-able, etc. I have argued (Tomlinson, 1982) that the persistent connection of this expanding group – and of learning and behavioural problems – with the children of the manual working-class is perennially resilient. The 'social problem' class that worried Cyril Burt continues to worry educationalists from the Secretary of State downwards. Connections between lack of intelligence, inability to learn, bad behaviour, low socio-economic status and a variety of undesirable social attributes continue to ensure that it is largely the children of the lower working class and the unemployed who are candidates for the expanding special education sector. The story of Bill and Daisy included by A.F. Tredgold (1914) in his *Textbook of Mental Deficiency* may still be pertinent:

Bill, we will suppose, had been a pupil in a special [educationally subnormal] school up of the age of 16 . . . and has since been employed in a number of jobs, starting as an errand boy and graduating to simple machine-minding in a factory. Daisy went to an ordinary school but was very backward and like Bill, is scarcely able to read and write. Daisy, before her marriage to Bill, has held a variety of jobs mainly assembling or varnishing small electrical parts.

After joining a gang for acceptance and a sense of importance Bill was . . . impelled to seek a girl friend, but was so unprepossessing that his only chance would be with a girl equally unattractive who might be available. Daisy was unattractive but simple and compliant and an easy date. Between the pair a bond of sympathy grew up. They each provided for the other what had been lacking all the years – comfort and appreciation.

(Daisy became pregnant and they married and went to live in an attic room in an overcrowded house – going down four flights of stairs for water and six for the W.C. Daisy had to give up her job, the couple lacked foresight and planning.)

After the baby's birth, Daisy went out cleaning, Bill lost his job – they had another baby but fear of further pregnancies led Daisy to fail to give Bill comfort and solace. Bill took to staying away from home and he became ripe for any criminal exploitation that might come his way. The children will have a natural backwardness at school, will play truant and delinquent practices will follow. Thus history will have repeated itself. (Tredgold, 1914, p. 394.)

Tredgold's documentation of two ESN school-leavers who found semi-skilled work, married and had a family could be read as a eugenist's warning, or as a libel on a couple who lacked an adequate wage, decent housing and contraceptive advice.

Expansion and Professional Interests

Much of the expansion of special education has been ascribed to accident, spontaneous adjustment, progress and benevolence. These explanations have always proved a stumbling block to the analysis of the emergence and expansion of a special subsystem of education. Archer's (1979) contention that educational structures are the result of the *interests* of those social groups who manage, as a result of conflicts, to achieve educational control, is a more useful starting point. The development and expansion of special education is the result of a variety of conflicting interest groups, both inside and outside education. Indeed, an understanding of the competition and alliances among interest groups in special education is crucial to understanding its expansion.

Pre-1945 (as I have documented in Tomlinson, 1982) educationalists, psychologists and medical practitioners all had vested interests in expanding the numbers of pupils in special education, and government had an interest in the control and direction of numbers of pupils who might prove 'troublesome' in their post-school careers in a variety of ways (principally by unemployment, crime or by requiring resources). Ordinary teachers' interests in the removal of special pupils – who originally interfered with payment-by-results and filled the standard 'O' classes – has proved an enduring and crucial force behind expansion. Then, as now, the public status of ordinary teachers was dependent on their ability to 'raise standards', which called for the removal of defective and troublesome children. This removal coincided with the interests of the new sub-profession of special school teachers who had a vested interest in obtaining clients for their schools. It also coincided with the interests of the eugenists who were concerned to identify and isolate defectives who threatened the 'racial stock'. Psychologists had a crucial interest in developing the tools of assessment for special education, which have proved to be so important in their professional development and claims to specialist expertise. The enduring medical influence in special education has also been well documented (Pritchard, 1963) and the recorded conflicts of educational and medical personnel over the control of access to special education post-1908 provides a good example of the strategic power-play that ultimately determines control of the education system.[4]

Post-1945, medical and psychological interests took precedence over education in vying for control of assessment processes for special education, psychologists partially reaching parity of esteem by 1975 and certainly by 1981. However, by this time all professional interests were becoming united by a suspicion that central and local administrators had annexed control of special education via distribution of resources, control of assessment procedures, parental appeals and decisions on provisions. The 1981 Act did, however, place more control of the expanding sector of special education in the educationalists' area, as its major location became the ordinary school. In particular the expanding sub-profession of 'special needs' heads of departments, teachers and support staff in ordinary schools now has power to shape and control large sectors of special education and in particular to decide who the special clients in the ordinary school will be and what sort of 'special' curriculum and pedagogy they will be offered. The ideology of 'special needs' is currently penetrating the secondary school curriculum and conflicts of interest are developing between 'special needs' specialists and their colleagues. In addition it was not to be expected that teachers in special schools would willingly give up their special expertise or clients as the location changed, and there are currently conflicts of interest between special and ordinary schools over the retention or movements of pupils, particularly in areas where segregated provision was well established.[5] But by the late 1970s 'special' teachers in both segregated and integrated provision had, to some extent, realized that their common interest lay in enhanced professional claims to special expertise. These claims are currently being strengthened and the expansion of special education has created the opportunity for more expert special teachers, support staff, advisers and inspectors to be employed.

Comprehensive School Dilemmas

The expansion of special education cannot be understood without reference to developments and changes in the whole education system, particularly changes since the establishment of state comprehensive education during the 1970s. A common school, underpinned by egalitarian ideologies and attended by middle and working-class children, was envisaged by comprehensive supporters, but comprehensive education is now dogged by a series of dilemmas. One dilemma which was slowly realized during the 1970s was that if selection by ability was inadmissible, so was selection by disability or inability. The 100-year-old principle of segregation gave way to notions of integration and comprehensive schools were expected to incorporate many non-conformist and troublesome children who would previously have been candidates for exclusion. Other dilemmas included the promise to offer equality of opportunity, while explaining away unequal outcomes in what Shaw has termed 'our incorrigibly competitive and hierarchical society' (Shaw, 1983, p. 37); the pressure to raise standards and credential more pupils by expanding the examination system while offering a suitable curriculum to the 'less able'; and the pressure to incorporate a subject-orientated traditional grammar school-type curriculum while incorporating secondary modern-type pupils.

Reynolds & Sullivan (1979) have argued that initially comprehensives were left relatively free to develop their own curriculum, pedagogies and forms of control with little outside interference, and one response to dilemmas posed by the 'less able' and the 'unwilling' (pupils with learning and behavioural problems) whose numbers increased after 1973 and the raising of the school-leaving age, was to segregate them internally within the schools. The rapid development of behavioural units for disruptive pupils from 1974 and the development of large remedial departments created an unofficial expansion of special education in secondary schools. This expansion was noted by the Warnock Committee which recommended that 'children previously regarded as disruptive' and 'children who have hitherto been seen as requiring remedial rather than special education' should be deemed candidates for special education (Warnock Report, 1978, p. 47). Thus the unofficial expansion was given official recognition. Up to the beginning of the 1980s there was little evidence that comprehensive schools had solved the dilemma of providing a curriculum for the 'less able' or the 'remedial-special'. Evidence (HMI, 1979; Reid et al., 1981) indicated that most comprehensives preferred streaming, setting and banding to mixed-ability teaching, and their curriculum for the less able was narrow and inappropriate. Given the pressures to concentrate on the able and the examinable, this is perhaps not surprising.

The incursion of the new vocationalism and MSC activities into secondary schooling and the blurring of the education-training divide has created more dilemmas for comprehensive schools – one of which is how far 'special needs' pupils will be incorporated into technical and vocational courses, or how far they will be offered watered-down palliatives of 'work experience' and 'social and life skills'.

The Disappearng Youth Labour Market

While the comprehensive school curriculum has increasingly become a matter for pressures from political and economic interest groups outside school, a major focus has been on the curriculum for the 'less able'. The DES 14–16 'lower attaining pupils programme', for example, is a direct but little publicised political incursion into this curriculum. DES criticism of the inappropriate curriculum offered to the less able up to the early 1980s was largely a criticism of the apparent slowness of schools to realize the social and political consequences of the disappearance of the youth labour market for less able and special leavers. The pupils to whom the DES and other vocational and educational programmes for the less able are aimed are those who, up the mid-1970s, could be minimally motivated to learn and behave at school by means of the carrot of possible employment. Programmes designed for the less able and special adolescents are part of a political response to the problem of dealing with larger numbers of young people who despite new vocational initiatives, will probably never acquire employment. The expansion of special education to embrace larger numbers of young people, particularly at post-16 level, may provide both a rationale and a justification for the subsequent economic position of this group. I suggested in 1982 that 'to have received a special education – with its historical stigmatic connotations, even a non-recorded special education in an integrated setting, may be regarded unfavourably by potential employers' (Tomlinson, 1982, p. 177). However, this kind of assertion now needs much more careful elaboration. The role of special education in preparing large numbers of young people for a workless future or at least one of sporadic, low-skilled employment needs research and analysis.

Any discussion of the relationship between the expansion of special education and the economic situation must start from the premise that to have 'special needs' is not an individual characteristic; it is the product of interaction between individuals and their social environment. It has been an underlying theme of this article that special education expands, not because of intrinsic qualities or lack of qualities in pupils, but because of the social or educational criteria currently being applied. *Similarly, whether or not the handicapped or the special find employment depends on the current economic conditions rather than on the possession of suitable abilities or skills.* Thus, while the economy was in need of low-skilled labour, the majority of special school leavers found employment, even though their mental or physical capacities were judged to be low. It has been an enduring characteristic of the 'handicapped' (as Barnett (1984) has recently elaborated in an interesting discussion of the economics of mental retardation) that they have often been considered retarded or problematic at school, but not outside school, particularly in employment. In Britain one careers officer wrote in 1974 that in his experience 'the majority of special school leavers found jobs with comparative ease... these included polishing, assembling, building, painting, canteen work and even office work' (City of Birmingham, 1977). A major task of special education has always been to prepare pupils for routine manual work, and some employers came to prefer special school leavers who were often more docile, obedient and punctual than others (see Collman, 1956; Atkinson *et al.*, 1981). By 1975, however, the same careers officer was noting that 'many special school leavers are affected by the recession and those requiring routine or semi-skilled work found most difficulty'. In this, of course, special school leavers were joined by the less able and also leavers with school-leaving certificates. In 1974, 80,000 under-20-year-olds were unemployed; by 1981 this number was 532,000 (although 360,000 were in government schemes or work experience programmes). The kind of work those who had received a special education formerly undertook has now virtually disappeared, although some low-skilled manufacturing or service jobs may continue to be available for them. Although the question of 'specially educated for what?' can only be answered by empirical investigation of the post-school careers of those leaving special education, an examination of some post-16 college courses for special needs students suggests that for those pupils with severe sensory, physical or mental handicaps traditional supervised provision, usually at Adult Training Centres, is envisaged after they have undertaken college courses to the age of 19 or 21. For those with moderate learning difficulties (as the description now runs) further special courses, including special YTS schemes, transfer to a normal YTS place, or even low-skilled employment is the aim, while for more able but handicapped students transfer to mainstream college courses, YTS or particular kinds of employment is the aim. The courses usually include a large component of 'social and life skills', 'coping and independent living' and 'adult responsibility' as well as college or employer-based introductions to basic manual skills. The expansion of special education may have brought more young people in its orbit but the aims of special education may not have changed too drastically over 100 years. Training for self-sufficiency and controlled social behaviour, and training for low-skilled productive work are traditional aims in special education. The major future difference may be that disappearance of low-skilled work will lead to more and more extensive special courses and more carefully planned supervision for those who will never achieve work. The next expansion of special education will undoubtedly be into 'adult special needs' courses.

The Ideology of Special Needs

To study ideology, as Thompson (1984) has recently pointed out, is to study the ways in which the meaning of particular words or ideas serves to sustain relations of domination. The concept of 'special needs' has become an ideological rationalization for those who have the power to shape and define the expanding special education system and have vested interests in this expansion. Those who can define the 'needs' of others and give or withhold provision have great power, yet the benevolent image with which the notion of 'catering for special needs' has become imbued precludes discussion of the supposed needs, or criticism of provision and practice. This, however, is the purpose of ideology – 'ideology is, as it were, the linguistic legislature which defines what is available for public discussion and what is not' (Thompson, 1984, p. 85).

The concept of special needs began to be applied to particular groups of pupils in the 1960s – most notably to ethnic minority pupils whose language and cultural needs were 'special', and to 'disadvantaged pupils'. The liberal child-centred pedagogies of the 1960s focused on children's supposed needs, as did egalitarian programmes to compensate for social disadvantages. The concept was applied to special education in 1965 when a DES report described such education as 'education that is specially well adapted to meet a child's needs'. The Warnock Committee in 1978 adopted the concept both as a rationale for an expanded system of special education ('broader provision', p. 36) and as a more positive description of the clients of special education than description by handicap or disability. While the concept appears to have done the former, all sorts of expansion is now taking place with no further justification than 'the pupil has special needs', the descriptive problem has not been overcome. The child with special educational needs has become the SEN or the SNARC pupil who needs a SNAP![6] The extension of the concept to cover 'gifted' pupils, or indeed *all* pupils, has led Mary Warnock to repudiate the use of the concept for those pupils her report had dealt with (*TES*, 12.11.82, 11.11.83).

The whole concept of special needs is ambiguous and tautological. It has become part of a rhetoric that serves little educational purpose. While it does mainly focus on negative psychogenic properties of individual pupils – their difficulty, disability, incapacity or lack of intelligence, it does not provide any mechanism for deciding who has these properties. The current desperate search for improved assessment procedures is an indication that the concept of special needs is no actual help in deciding who the clients of special education should be. At the same time the concept, with its humanitarian overtones, precludes discussion of the needs and interests actually being served by the expansion of special education. Those who find difficulty in moving beyond humanitarian rhetoric, and insist that 'all children have special needs' still have to explain why a whole subsystem of special education has developed and expanded, which is backed by legal enforcement and caters largely for the children of the manual working class. To do this, attention must turn from the psychogenic focus on individual 'needs' to the social interest groupings, the educational, political and economic 'needs' which an expansion of special education is serving. At the present time the ideological obfuscation provided by the focus on the 'child's special needs' prevents an adequate analysis of this expansion.

Notes

1 In 1981 approximately 200,000 pupils were excluded from mainstream education in special schools and classes plus those unofficially counted and excluded in disruptive units. The Warnock Report's suggestion that remedial and disruptive pupils be officially counted as needing special provision – implicitly accepted by the 1981 Act, and that 1 in 5 children may need special provision, brought the number to $1\frac{1}{2}$ million in 1981 – a fifth of the (then) 8 million pupils in education.

2 *Special Educational Treatment*, Ministry of Education pamphlet no. 5, 1946, pp. 22–23.

3 In *The Concept of Special Educational Needs* by J.H. Thompson HMCI, paper given to the Conference on Special Educational Needs, Dundee, February 1984.

4 See *Report of the Royal Commission on the Care and Control of the Feeble-minded*, Vol. 1, 1980. London: HMSO.

5 See, for example, the conflicting evidence offered to the Fish Committee, set up in 1984 to examine segregated special provision in the Inner London Education Authority.
6 Some schools now have Special Educational Needs (SEN) departments, at least one school has a Special Needs and Remedial Children (SNARC) Department and many schools are adopting the Special Needs Action Programme (SNAP) produced in Coventry.

References

ATKINSON, P. *et al.* (1981) 'Labouring to learn: industrial training for slow learners', in: BARTON, L. and TOMLINSON, S. (eds) *Special Education Policies, Practices and Social Issues.* London: Harper & Row.

ARCHER, M.S. (1979) *The Social Origins of Educational Systems.* London: Sage.

BARNETT, W.S. (1984) The economics of mental retardation, unpublished PhD thesis, State University of Utah.

BOOTH, A. (1981) 'Demystifying integration', in SWANN, W. (ed.) *The Practice of Special Education.* Milton Keynes: Open University.

COLLMAN, R.P. (1956) 'The employment success of ESN pupils', *American Journal of Mental Deficiency*, 60, pp. 247-51.

FISH, J. (1985) *Committee of inquiry into ILEA Special Schools.* London: ILEA.

HMI (1979) *Aspects of Secondary Examination: an HMI survey.* London: HMSO.

NFER (NATIONAL FOUNDATION FOR EDUCATIONAL RESEARCH) (1984) *Lower attaining pupil programme newsletter*, November. Slough: NFER.

PRITCHARD, D.E. (1963) *Education of the Handicapped 1760-1960.* London: Routledge & Kegan Paul.

REID, M.I. *et al.* (1981) *Mixed Ability Teaching: problems and possibilities.* Slough: NFER.

REYNOLDS, D. and SULLIVAN, M. (1979) 'Bringing school back', in BARTON, L. and MEIGHAM, R. *Schools: pupils and deviance.* Driffield: Nafferton.

SHAW, B. (1983) *Comprehensive Schooling: the impossible dream.* Oxford: Blackwell.

SQUIBB, P. (1981) 'A theoretical structuralist approach to special education', in BARTON, L. and TOMLINSON, S. (eds) *Special Education Policies, Practices and Social Issues.* London: Harper & Row.

SWANN, W. (1984) *Statistics of Segregation*, Childright No. 8, pp. 18-19.

THOMPSON, J. (1984) *Studies in the Theory of Ideology.* London: Polity Press.

TOMLINSON, S. (1982) *A Sociology of Special Education.* Henley: Routledge & Kegan Paul.

TREDGOLD, A.F. (1914) *Text-book of Mental Deficiency*, 2nd edn. London: Tindall, Balliere & Cox.

WARNOCK REPORT (1978) *Special Educational Needs.* London: HMSO.

WARNOCK, M. (1982) Personal column, *The Times Educational Supplement*, 12 November, p. 72.

WARNOCK, M. (1983) Personal column, *The Times Educational Supplement*, 11 November, p. 64.

Part Four:
After School

4.1 Education, Employment and Recruitment
Robert Moore

This chapter will consider the way in which educational qualifications are *actually* used in the labour market in the recruitment of young workers. In general, recent studies have found that the use of qualifications varies significantly between different sectors of the labour market and is subject to considerable regional variation. Non-educational criteria almost invariably have priority in recruitment over educational ones and employers tend to have only the vaguest notions as to what particular qualifications entail or imply.

These factors are differentiated by sex and race and also work to reproduce gender and racial differentiation in employment (and unemployment). The findings to be considered here (and the broader body of research of which they are typical) suggest that the link between education and occupation is much more tenuous than is often supposed and call into question many of the assumptions currently held about employers' attitudes to young workers and to educational standards. This is particularly significant given the place of these assumptions within the occupationalist rhetoric of the present assault upon education and liberal education in particular.

Qualifications and Recruitment

A number of illuminating pieces of research have been published recently which look in detail at the way in which qualifications are used by employers in the process of the recruitment of young workers. Cumin, for instance, traces a group of school-leavers from school, through the labour market and into employment. He notes a sharp contrast between the expectations of pupils, parents and teachers about the importance of qualifications and their real significance (Cumin, 1983). A study by Jones (Jones, 1983) provides detailed evidence on the almost complete lack of communication between examination boards and employers and on the uninformed and arbitrary way in which employers use qualifications. Ashton *et al.* (1982, 1986), in an extremely thorough investigation of the relative positions of young workers in contrasting local labour markets, define a number of different recruitment strategies in which qualifications vary in significance, are used in different ways and are almost invariably of secondary importance relative to other factors. It is precisely the subordinate role of qualifications which is the striking feature of this type of detailed work.

EXPECTATIONS AND PRACTICE

The study by Cumin follows a group of school-leavers from their college in Leicestershire out into 'the world of work'. The purpose was to discover precisely how important qualifications were in determining their occupational chances. The study begins by noting the high expectations that the pupils, their parents and their teachers had in this regard. Fifty-seven per cent of pupils and 62 per cent of parents thought that qualifications would be *very important*, and 98 per cent and 96 per cent respectively thought they would be either *very* or *fairly* important. After examining what happened in practice, Cumin concludes that these expectations were not 'based upon actuality' (p. 58).

The study found that 56 per cent of the jobs taken by the young people in fact had no formal educational requirements attached to them. In the end, only 15 per cent of the school-leavers considered that their qualifications had been essential to their getting jobs. Cumin makes the significant point that employers appoint school-leavers to posts *before* examination results are known in any case. It is very rare for young people recruited on that basis to be sacked if they subsequently fail to pass the exam or gain a certain grade. Obviously the simple non-availability of the result must severely limit the significance the employers can place on exam passing *per se*.

However, the limitations upon examinations in shaping recruitment practices are not restricted to the effects of this particular practical exigency. Employers in the main seem to see little direct relevance of education to specific job requirements. This would seem to be the general conclusion of research in this area, and Cumin's conclusion that:

> In terms of the overall needs employers had of young people, it was clear that non-academic criteria, attitudes to work and personal characteristics, and basic skills, essentially those of reading, writing and arithmetic, were far more important to employers than academic qualifications. (Cumin, 1983, p. 57.)

is one widely echoed elsewhere.

EMPLOYERS AND QUALIFICATIONS

The study by Jones (1983) provides information on the use of qualifications by employers in three English regions (London and the South East, the West Midlands, and Yorkshire and Humberside) and also includes some comparisons with other European countries. Fifteen-hundred establishments were surveyed, ranging in size from employing less than 25 to more than 500 and spanning 10 sectors of the Revised Standard Classification of Industry. Five categories of workers were defined: professional and managerial, technician, clerical and sales, skilled manual and operatives. These categories were represented to varying degrees in the various sectors. Employers were found to use five main selection devices: application forms, academic qualifications, school references, performance in aptitude tests, and interviews.

The relative importance of academic qualifications varied between categories, being more significant for non-manual than for manual workers. In all cases the interview was the most important device with qualifications coming second for non-manuals. The level of qualifications varied according to the level of employment. There was particular emphasis upon English and maths. Jones concludes her detailed investigation by saying that:

> These figures suggest that employers, at least with the present education system, largely feel that basic knowledge in a few subjects is all that they find useful for their purpose. Case study experience further suggests that even this use is questionable. Observation... suggest(s) that employers' expectations of the subject content and skills are often very wide of the mark. This appears especially true of Maths, Physics and English, the most frequently required subjects. (Jones, 1983, p. 22.)

The report shows that employers tend to have only extremely vague notions as to what examinations in particular subjects actually involve. There was virtually *no* direct communciation between employers and examination boards. Out of 22 GCE and CSE examination boards, only eight (all CSE) gave out information specific to employers and only nine (eight CSE and one GCE) actively disseminated information to employers. At the same time, only 11 boards (eight CSE and three GCE) reported ever having received requests for information *from* employers. Only three boards (one CSE and two GCE) had an interest in researching employers' views.

Given this, it is probably not surprising that even where qualifications were stipulated, the requirement was not rigidly enforced. Jones (1983) found that although a reasonably high number of employers thought that qualifications were desirable, less than half thought them to be essential. Even where they did, there was a fair degree of flexibility. Interestingly, 'very few' employers saw examinations as essential for specific jobs (p. 23). Rather, they were demanded most rigorously where *further training* involved FE or professional courses where the educational qualification was an entry requirement. In other words, the educational qualification was related to further *educational* needs, not to the needs of jobs as such. Jones concludes that 'These results support the... assertion that desirability of certain qualifications is not closely related to actual job performance' (p. 23).

RECRUITMENT STRATEGIES

The findings of Jones's work are very much in line with those of Ashton *et al.* (1983). Only half of the employers interviewed in Leicester, Sunderland and St Albans thought that qualifications were useful as 'yardsticks of a candidate's ability' (p. 55). Twenty-three per cent of them thought that 'they could possibly be of some use with certain reservations' and 27 per cent considered them to be of no use at all. Forty-five per cent of the first group (i.e.

45 per cent of 50 per cent) thought them to be a true measure of ability and a third saw them as useful indicators of attitude. In the second group, 69 per cent thought that other factors were more important than qualifications and in the third, 75 per cent ignored them altogether or considered them meaningless.

Ashton *et al.* found that employers adopt a range of *recruitment strategies* in which educational qualifications are combined with other attributes to varying degrees. The most common approach was that where 'the balance between academic and non-academic criteria shifts in favour of the non-academic' (p. 52). It is important to note that the educational qualifications are not being treated as an *index* of non-educational attributes (e.g. docility). The other factors which employers take into account (self-presentation, attitude to work, interest in the job, family background) are seen as *independent* from education.

The authors define *five* recruitment strategies which can be summarized as follows:

1 educational qualifications perform a *determinative* function. Here the qualification is the most important criterion in recruitment although other factors might be considered in the interview stage, though in a subordinate role;

2 educational qualifications perform a *screening* function. Qualifications are used to pre-select the sample of candidates. A minimum level is set and those at or above that level are then selected by *non-academic* critieria. Qualifications above the minimum bestow no advantage;

3 educational qualifications perform a *focusing* function. They will be waived if a candidate possesses the appropriate non-academic criteria. This is the point at which non-academic come to take precedence over academic criteria.

4 educational qualifications are *functionless*. Recruitment is based on personality or physical attributes which are seen as having *nothing* to do with education;

5 educational qualifications have a *negative* function. Qualifications *disqualify* the person from being considered (e.g. on the grounds that they will become easily bored or might become a trouble maker). It is, of course, being assumed here that there is some kind of relationship between the qualification level and the nature of the work.

In this study it was the *third strategy* which was most commonly used (53 per cent) followed by the fourth (39 per cent). Hence non-academic criteria have a clear priority over the academic.

The use of strategies varied according to the occupational category: at the *professional and managerial* level, 82 per cent of employers used strategy 2, and at the *technician* level it was used by 74 per cent. Strategy 3 was that most used for *clerical and sales* (57 per cent) and for *skilled manual* (60 per cent). At the *operative level*, strategy four is most common (see Ashton *et al.*, 1983, Table 49).

The use of different strategies relates to the size of the firm. In general, larger firms tended to make more use of qualifications (possibly reflecting the existence of a trained personnel staff who themselves owe their position to qualifications). More reliance was placed upon O than A-levels. The study found that 72 per cent of employers in the top size band saw qualifications as useful as against only 30 per cent in the smallest, where 49 per cent saw them as not useful compared with only 12 per cent in the largest (see Ashton, *et al.*, 1983, Tables 46, 48 and 50).

The size of the establishment could reasonably be expected to affect the number of young people being exposed to the different recruitment strategies (although the relative numbers of small employers would also have to be borne in mind). However, it was found that many large companies took on very few young people (20 per cent of those employing above 1,000 recruited fewer than ten per year (Ashton, *et al.*, 1983, p. 47). Hence, 'the relationship between the size of the employing unit and the number of young people recruited each year was not as close as might have been expected' (p. 47).

Ashton *et al.*'s extremely detailed studies indicate the dangers of generalizing about the education/production relationship. Their more recent work emphasizes the very considerable regional variations which reflect relative unemployment rates. The complex variations and interactions between factors such as recruitment strategies, size of firm, sector, area and local industry mix introduce a wide range of contingencies into the situation which are further complicated by gender and race.

Employers, Educational Standards and Young Workers

A central plank of the current attack upon education and the teaching profession (and one which has grown since Callaghan's Great Debate speech) is that of employers' dissatisfaction with educational standards and with the quality of young workers. This alleged 'failure' on the part of teachers is a main feature of the rhetoric which legitimates the changes which are being imposed. Consequently it is important to critically examine its basis in reality.

The type of detailed empirical research reviewed above suggests that scepticism is to be strongly recommended. Employers, in fact, appear to be not only ill-informed about education but relatively arbitrary in the uses to which they put it. Given the crucial role that the Manpower Services Commission has played in the undermining of education and the construction of its current occupationalist surrogate, its contribution to this debate deserves close scrutiny. It is ironic that the MSC's Holland Report was published in the same year (1977) as the Shirley Williams Green Paper on education which followed on from 'The Great Debate'. The Holland Report looked explicitly at the issue of employers' dissatisfaction with young workers and presented its information in such a way as to support the idea of education's failure in this area. I have suggested elsewhere[1] that their presentation of their evidence benefits from closer examination.

Table 4.1.1 *Employers' evaluations of young workers on 'essential attributes' compared to adults (Holland report)*

Attribute	% of employers agreeing 'essential'	No	% of employers saying that young people are:			Rating (B–W)
			Different Yes	Better	Worse	
1 willingness/attitude to work	81	46	54	11	43	−32
2 good level of general fitness	47	70	30	24	6	+18
3 appearance/tidiness	39	60	40	6	34	−28
4 specific physical attributes	36	72	28	22	6	+16
5 basic 3Rs	21.	46	54	10	44	−34
6 mature/stable	20	40	60	5	55	−50
7 ability to communicate	18	53	47	11	36	−25
8 willingness to join union	16	89	11	8	3	+5
9 good level of numeracy	13	50	50	8	42	−34
10 past experience	7	39	61	2	59	−57
11 good written English/literate	6	40	60	9	51	−42
12 existing union membership	4	85	15	4	11	−7
13 specific educational qualifications	2	49	51	28	23	+5

The Report discusses employers' evaluations of young workers relative to older ones in terms of 13 'essential' attributes. In the case of unskilled/semi-skilled young workers (i.e. the YOP/YTS target group), 81 per cent of the employers listed 'willingness/attitude to work' as the most important attribute. The second most popular one was 'good level of general fitness', mentioned by 47 per cent, followed by 'appearance/tidiness' (39 per cent) and 'specific physical attributes' (36 per cent). The first specifically educational attribute ('basic 3Rs') appears fifth, being mentioned by only 21 per cent of employers. The rest of the 13 essential attributes range between a mention by 20 per cent for 'mature/stable' down to a mere 2 per cent for 'specific educational qualifications'(!)

The discussion which follows in the Report for young people in general is based mainly on a rating which is established by subtracting the number of employers who think that young people are worse than older workers from those who think that they are better on each of these attributes. On this basis they come out very badly with negative marks on nine out of the 13 attributes. However, inspection shows that there are in fact three employer positions: (1) young people are no different/noncomparable, or, if they are different, are (2) better or (3) worse. The *rating* on which young people do so badly is derived only from that fraction of employers who say they are different.

It is a simple arithmetical exercise to reconstitute the original figures. When this is done, a rather different picture emerges. In fact, young people come out worse overall on only three out of the 13 attributes relative to older workers. Two of these are directly age related – 'past experience' (worse: 59 per cent), and 'mature/stable' (worse, 55 per cent). The third is 'good written English/literate' (worse: 51 per cent).

Ironically, the attribute on which young people do best relative to older workers is specific educational qualifications which actually comes *bottom* of the employers' list of essential attributes, being mentioned by only 2 per cent of employers! In fact, employers give *all* the educational attributes a low priority.

Table 4.1.2 *Position of educational 'essential attributes'*

Attribute	Position out of 13	Essential %	Worse %
basic 3Rs	5	21	24
good level of numeracy	9	13	21
good written English/literate	11	6	51
specific educational qualification	13	2	12

(Constructed from *The Holland Report,* Tables 7:1 and 7:2.)

The data corresponds precisely to the situation described by Ashton *et al.*'s recruitment strategies with non-educational criteria taking priority over educational ones. The top four attributes are each of this type. If we take the attribute which employers most often saw as 'essential', willingness/attitude to work (mentioned by 81 per cent), we see that the MSC's poor rating of -32 in fact reflects a negative judgement by less than half of employers (54 per cent said that young workers are different in this respect and 43 per cent said they were worse). In fact, this represents the precise opposite of the MSC position – the majority of employers *think that* young workers are either no different or better! Interestingly this figure is consistent with that most often encountered in the literature in this area where usually between 70 per cent to 80 per cent of employers are favourable to young workers. Ashton *et al.*, for instance, say that:

> Despite the many grumbles and adverse comments, 70 per cent of all employers interviewed claimed to have been satisfied with the standard of work of young people taken on by them in the previous two years, and only 14 per cent expressed dissatisfaction. Indeed, of the respondents in the 60 establishments employing over 5,000 workers, all but one expressed satisfaction. (Ashton *et al.*, 1983, p. 56).

The probable significance of all this is that it is mistaken to attempt to generalize about employers' attitude to young workers. Clearly many are dissatisfied and feel that they can point to declining standards (e.g. in the numeracy of engineering apprentices), but this situation is more likely to reflect changing social patterns of recruitment rather than a real decline in 'educational standards'. Paradoxically it could result from an actual general improvement in standards combined with expanding opportunities in further and higher education. The 'type of lad' who once became an apprentice now goes on to take an engineering degree and is replaced at that qualification level by a different category of young person. In earlier times the former had been underachieving educationally whereas the latter are now near the peak of their attainment level. If these complex changes over time in the relationship between general improvements in attainment, social bases of recruitment and expanded further educational opportunities are not taken into account, the general improvement can appear from the fixed position of an employer as a decline in standards.

WORK EXPERIENCE

As the examination of the Holland Report data indicates, the problem which young people have in the labour market reflects the age-related issue of lack of experience. It is this rather than defective education that disadvantages them. An examination by Richards (1982) of the factors employed in the recruitment of apprentices in the East Midlands illustrates some of the problems in this area, especially in relation to the current occupationalist assertion that young people will benefit from a more 'vocational' education in order to counteract the lack of experience.

Richards asked employers about the factors they took into account when recruiting apprentices. The percentages of employers mentioning the following were: evening classes (92 per cent), holiday jobs (85 per cent), Saturday jobs (84 per cent), hobbies and interests (77 per cent), paper rounds (73 per cent), membership of clubs and social societies (68 per cent), school work experience schemes (52 per cent) (Richards, 1982, Table B, p. 7).

The poor showing of school work experience is striking. The reasons for this are illuminating. The contrast between work experience schemes and informal work experience lies in the fact that the latter are taken by employers as evidence of initiative, an interest in earning money and the ability to sustain regular work discipline (getting up early, etc.). Paper rounds in particular were seen as significant in these respects. Work experience, on the other hand, was seen by employers as part of the school's discipline and as giving little information about the pupil as an individual. Richards says that:

> The feature that impressed these employers about the spare/part-time jobs of young people applying for apprenticeship in their firms were mainly elements which were absent in WE [work experience] schemes. WE schemes did not involve the 'initiative' involved in going out and finding your own part-time job. This was all done by the school following DES and LEA guidelines. The element of 'reliability' (getting up early consistently for a substantial period of time, etc.) was also absent. (Richards, 1982, p. 9.)

Where employers did see value in work experience schemes, it had to do with information about career choices. They felt that such schemes allowed young people to have direct experience of engineering rather than relying purely upon second-hand information (from teachers or the media). If they then still chose to seek engineering jobs, this could be seen as evidence of *commitment*.

This is a central feature of the employers' view.

Richards found a preoccupation among employers with the image of engineering. They were very concerned that pupils, and the 'bright' ones in particular, should be given a positive view of the industry and be attracted to it. This was the main value they attributed to school work experience rather than seeing it in any direct sense as preparation for engineering work. Richard's conclusion is that:

> According to these employers it was teachers who needed WE more than pupils, so that they could get a picture of what engineering was really like (as opposed to media misrepresentations – strikes, redundancies, etc.) and so put across a 'good image' of engineering, hopefully attracting the 'brighter pupils' into the industry. (Richards, 1982, p. 11.)

As far as the actual content of the education was concerned, the employers wanted no more than a solid, old fashioned grounding in 'the basics' and that 'bright pupils' should be positively encouraged to seek jobs in the industrial sector rather than in the academic world or public services. The major problem was seen to be the hostility of teachers towards industrial and commercial values and the way in which this deflected 'bright', traditionally educated pupils away from industry. It was not direct preparation for production that the schools should be providing but image building. Furthermore, this exercise should be aimed at the 'bright' pupils. Richards says that:

> Some writers went on to argue that attracting high ability youngsters into manufacturing industry was one of the conditions for a regeneration of the British economy. Employers making these connections between the 'ignorance' of 'our brightest children', WE, the entry of these youngsters into manufacturing industry and the rejuvenation of British capitalism were clearly *not interested in the notion that WE was essentially concerned with ROSLA or the 'average and below average ability ranges'*. (Richards, 1982, p. 16, my emphasis.)

We can say that the problem being defined here is not so much that the pupils are getting the wrong education (though they might be getting the wrong teachers) as that industry is getting the wrong pupils! The 'high fliers' go elsewhere. This reflects the antipathy towards industry and commerce from traditionally educated, liberal-humanist teachers. It is *they* who need to be changed.

Richards argues that employers' attitudes imply a dual system of work experience – image building for the high-fliers and realism for the rest. In the case of the former, it is a traditional rather than a vocational education which is required, and as to the latter, the evidence suggests that employers are really indifferent to *their* education.

Given that so much of the occupationalist initiative in education and outside (YTS, etc.) is aimed at the lower academic ability bands, it is useful to emphasize certain points:

1 the evidence strongly indicates that employers are not especially concerned with the educational attainment of young workers in those sectors of the labour market in which such individuals tend to seek employment. Non-educational criteria have a clear priority in recruitment strategies;

2 in part this reflects the fact that occupational skill levels are of such a low order that they present no real requirement for educational preparation. Indeed, even training is problematical – as the Further Education Unit, for instance, has conceded.[2] Where extended education or training is provided (e.g. in response to youth unemployment) it tends, consequently, to stress so-called social and life skills or personal effectiveness rather than technical skills. This has the important implication of presenting these young people as personally and socially deficient and incompetent.

3 significantly, pupils of this type tend to have acquired significant degrees of work experience through part-time and spare-time work and also to possess the social skills of network membership which facilitate grapevine recruitment (of course, both of these things are affected by local unemployment levels). These issues will be looked at in more detail below. It is important to stress that (a) this type of work experience is precisely that welcomed by employers, and (b) such young people are socially competent members of labour market social networks.

RECRUITMENT AND THE PROBLEMS OF YOUTH

If young people are not deficient in the ways that current rhetoric suggests, then what is the explanation for the high levels of youth unemployment? The view that they lack work experience is contradicted by a substantial body of evidence. A study by Finn (1987), for instance, illustrates the tendency for non-academic young people to have comparatively more such informal work experience.[3] Lack of conventional school success cannot be seen, in any straightforward way, as indicative of problems in coping with working life. I have suggested elsewhere that difficult behaviour at school can, in fact, reflect a readiness for work and the resentment at having that ambition frustrated (Moore, 1984). Clarke, in a review of the literature on the transition to work, says that it tends to support the view that the 'majority of early leavers adjust fairly painlessly to working life' (Clarke, 1980, p. 10). She concludes a section on young people 'at risk' with the statement that:

This suggests, rather unpalatably, that apart from bright children who do well at both school and work, it is those children who are apathetic about, or even alienated from, school who adjust best to work. (Clarke, 1980, p. 11.)

The major problem that young people suffer is simply that they are *young*. The re-presented Holland Report data showed how young people are judged to be 'worse' by employers on age-related attributes. Obviously, however much informal work experience young people may have acquired, it cannot compete with that of older workers. However, there is a more significant factor. The Holland Report states that:

> Whilst a little over a third of employers thought there was no difference, those employers who did state a preference were, in almost all cases, more likely to prefer other recruits to young people. This was especially true when young people were compared to up-graded existing employees, those recruited from other firms or women returning to work. (Holland, 1977, p. 41.)

Employers' preference for various categories of older workers reflects, in part, the importance of on-the-job training and experience over that of formal education (especially in relation to recruitment within the firm's internal labour market). But it also reflects the fact that older workers are, by virtue of their life situation, more reliable. The significance of attitude to work has been highlighted by numerous studies. It is important to note that this is not simply to do with naturalistic notions of 'emotional maturity'. Blackburn and Mann, on the basis of their extensive study of the labour market for semi and unskilled labour in Peterborough, say that:

> The ideal worker is male, around thirty, married with small children, related to other employees and with a stable educational and work history. He is not necessarily cleverer than other workers, but his commitments are less likely to make him jeopardise his job. (Blackburn and Mann, 1979, p. 13.)

What is signficant about the 'ideal worker' has nothing to do with his (the female 'ideal' is usually somewhat different) education *per se*. It is simply that he *is* a married man, around 30, with wife and children, a car, a mortgage (?) etc. Employers' preferences refer not to personality characteristics developed by a specialized, occupational socializing agency – the school – but to life-cycle characteristics. The difference between the young and the adult worker reflects their different positions on the trajectories of (common) social career paths. It is not 'the dull compulsion of the labour market' which disciplines the worker through the brute necessities of basic subsistence, but the more developed range of needs and commitments which trap them in, what Blackburn and Mann call, 'the life-cycle squeeze' (p. 108). The ideal model helps to differentiate the workforce (by age, sex and colour) according to how far different groups approximate to the model and can be seen as representing its exemplary qualities of commitment and reliability.

This kind of division in the labour market between youth and adults jobs was also investigated by Ashton *et al.* (1986). In a similar fashion, changes in opportunities reflect the development of the social career.

Age barriers also served to structure the young adults' experience of the labour market. This was particularly true of the unemployed. They were too old for most of the jobs which provided training and which only recruit school or college leavers, and too young for many of the adult jobs which required recruits to be over 21, and where employers *preferred those who were married, with a family and a large mortgage.* (Ashton, *et al.*, 1986, p. 104, my emphasis.)

Equally it is the case that the lack of opportunity to participate in employment blocks the development of the social career. Occupational and social careers are mutually facilitating in this respect. Unemployment does not only deny an adequate income, it can create deep crises of social identity.

Recruitment and the Matching Process

Investigation of recruitment strategies indicates that the role of education in occupational allocation is much more contingent than is often allowed. The relationship between qualifications and jobs is attenuated by the complexities of labour market segmentation and this itself is subject to local diversification. The importance of labour market segmentation is emphasized in Ashton *et al.*'s most recent study (1986). This work stresses the fact that there is no simple hierarchy of jobs (matched by a corresponding hierarchy of educational qualifications). The segmentation of the occupational system effectively creates discrete spheres of employment which exhibit radical discontinuities in terms of their structures, processes and possibilities. These in turn are associated with distinctive entry requirements, varying uses of qualifications in recruitment and career development (where career development occurs at all), differing pre- and post-entry orientations to work by young workers and differential effects by age, sex and 'race'.

Ashton *et al.* also stress the importance of *local* labour markets and argue that their variations can have more significant effects than social class differences. They conceptualize these differences in terms of 'separate local labour market cultures' (p. 104). A particularly significant feature of these 'cultures' in respect of occupational recruitment is that of social network or grapevine recruitment. This informal method was found to become increasingly important as individuals moved into second and subsequent jobs. This reflects, the authors argue, an 'increasing awareness of the ways in which employers recruit' (p. 84). Job search, on this basis, is seen as 'more efficient, in that it is more closely aligned to employers' recruitment methods' (p. 84). At the third job level, between 25 per cent and 60 per cent of recruits found their position through 'word of mouth'.

Granovetter (a pioneer of the study of this dimension of recruitment) has argued that sociologists and economists have seriously neglected this aspect of 'the matching process', i.e. the *actual* process whereby individuals come to get the jobs they do (Granovetter, 1975). He stresses the rationality and efficiency of network recruitment for both employers and prospective employees. It is a cheaper and more reliable way of getting information about jobs or workers.

> Furthermore, my empirical work suggests that the signal chosen in the usual models – education – is not actually the main conveyer of information in labour markets. It is true that most jobs have clear cut educational requirements, such that employers assume workers lacking them to be ipso facto unqualified. This is however, a crude sort of screen indeed, and if used alone would leave the employer still with a large and unmanageable information problem. On paper, there are few jobs for which large numbers of people are not qualified; in practice, employers use a more refined and differentiated signal than educational qualifications: they use the recommendations of people personally known to them and prospective employees. Similarly, prospective employees know better than to rely on landscaping or other signals put out by employers and attempt, instead, to find out the inside story from their contacts. (Granovetter, 1981, p. 25.)

He points out that processes of this type are difficult to accommodate within orthodox economics because they are not amenable to 'costing' in the standard economic sense. Because of this, and despite their obviousness to common-sense experience, they have been excluded from formal analysis.

Granovetter's original sample of professional, technical and managerial workers in the Boston, Massachusetts area indicates that these processes are not restricted to either élite 'old boy networks' or to tight-knit working class communities such as dockers or printers. The basic rationality principle of their greater efficiency holds across the occupational system. There is, however, a further dimension to network recruitment which goes beyond the basic exchange of information. This has to do with the way in which network membership involves possession of the social skills and reciprocal relationships which that membership entails.

Grieco (1984), in a fascinating and detailed series of ethnographic studies of working-class networks in this country has pointed to a number of advantages which workers and employers gain from 'the network':

> Firstly, employee referrals provide the cheapest method of obtaining labour. Secondly, employee referrals provide an efficient screening mechanism. Thirdly, recruitment through employees acts as a form of control since responsibilities and obligations hold between workers so recruited: for if the sponsored antagonises the employer, the reputation of the sponsor himself will be damaged; thus, the new worker is constrained by the interests and reputation of his sponsor. (Grieco, 1984, p. 30.)

A number of significant points emerge from these studies:

1 network membership supplies not only information, but also the tacit skills which enable individuals to become competent and accepted members of occupational groups;

2 membership provides a means of social control in the workplace both because those recruited have an obligation to preserve the reputation of their sponsors and also because, in some cases, family authority principles can be transferred from the home to the job, e.g. as with a 'dads' lads' recruitment system.

3 membership also provides a source of social support in the workplace while a newcomer learns the ropes and the tricks of the trade, e.g. network members will make up shortfalls in production while the newcomer settles in. People without access to these support mechanisms can be severely disadvantaged;

4 Grieco's work has also pointed to the wider social importance of women in maintaining and enforcing the system of network reciprocity, even when not themselves in work. She also stresses the strategic, collective role of the network in maintaining employment opportunities *and* a 'family' income. This has important implications for current trends in thinking about the role of the family (and the extended family) in the occupational system of advanced societies and for certain feminist approaches to the issues of women in the labour market which tend to operate from an essentially middle class paradigm of the *individualized* career and salary and the consequent marginalization of women in the domestic context.[4]

Although it is possible to see networks as a mechanism through which workers exercise some degree of control over their labour market, it is important to acknowledge the extent to which they are, by definition, *discriminatory*. Lack of access to network membership can be a major limitation upon employment opportunities and, consequently, a major source of labour market differentiation. As Jenkins and Troyna (and other contributors) have pointed out (in Troyna and Smith, 1983), this has a particular impact upon ethnic minority groups.

> First, in an organisation with an all white or largely white workforce, network recruitment will help to ensure that this stays the case, particularly at a time when large numbers of white workers are unemployed and prepared to re-enter the comparatively poorly paid and less pleasant jobs they deserted in the past few years. At best, this will help to ensure that black workers remain in those employment sectors they entered in the boom years of the 50's and 60's. Secondly and the reasons for this are unclear, there is good reason to suggest that West Indian workers are more likely to use formal or official job-search channels than are white or Asians, who use informal channels to a comparatively greater extent. (Troyna and Smith, 1983, pp. 14–15.)

This indicates a powerful way in which labour market factors can effectively negate educational advances, e.g. in changing the pattern of 'racial' or gender inequalities in attainment. It is striking how even when certain minority groups tend to achieve mean levels of attainment above those of the white majority, they still remain heavily disadvantaged in employment terms.

A similar point about the way in which labour market structures and processes limit educational reform can be made in relation to gender. Crompton and Jones (1984) have highlighted the significance of the relationship between pre-entry academic qualifications and post-entry professional qualifications in shaping the gender inequalities in white collar employment which emerge as occupational careers develop. In their study, young men and women were very similar in their academic qualifications at O and A-level at the point of entry into work. As a result of the bi-modal pattern of female involvement in paid employment (reflecting the demands of child rearing), women tend to be absent from work during the period in which men tend to acquire the post-entry professional qualifications which are required for promotion.

This points to the importance of the relationship of eduation to the articulation between social and occupational career paths and to specific labour market structures such as internal labour markets. It also suggests that educational reforms will be of limited success unless complemented by policies such as contract compliance which act directly upon demand-side institutions. A general implication of the material considered throughout has been the limitation of supply-side analysis.

Conclusion

The material reviewed in this chapter indicates that the manner in which educational qualifications are used in employment is both highly variable and subject to a wide range of contingent factors located in labour market structures and processes. Specifically, the following points can be made:

1 Employers have tended to be extremely ill-informed about the content of educational courses and the significance of qualifications.
2 Little direct relationship is seen to exist between specific qualifications and actual job requirements.
3 Qualifications are invariably used alongside other criteria and these usually take priority in recruitment.
4 Employers tend to use a range of recruitment strategies employing a number of devices. Their use and the relative significance and the role of education varies according to sector, size of firm, level of recruitment and local conditions.
5 Given employers' lack of knowledge about qualifications and the relatively arbitrary way in which they use them, it is difficult to give credence to the widespread notion that they are dissatisfied with the educational levels of young workers. The evidence suggests that they are often indifferent to their educational attainment and are interested in only a narrow range of basic skills or in traditional education for the

'high-fliers'. In general, employers seem to be satisfied with those young workers they employ.

6 This is consistent with the findings which indicate that young people tend to adjust relatively easily to working life and that the less academic tend to do so more than others.

7 Young workers are disadvantaged in the labour market mainly by age itself and the view that, because of their lack of family commitments, the will be unreliable. Evidence suggests that jobs are often distributed according to age life cycle criteria.

The material considered emphasizes the importance of labour market structures and processes in mediating the relationship between education and production and between qualifications and work. It also suggests that they create radical discontinuities between the educational and occupational systems which are a major limitation upon the effectiveness of educational reforms. This both attentuates the force of the current occupationalist attack upon the liberal education tradition and suggests that occupationalist objectives will do little more than merely dilute the quality of the education which pupils might otherwise have received.

It also suggests that teachers should oppose their critics on educational grounds rather than being forced continually onto the sterile terrain of vocationalism. More generally, it can be suggested that the social reforms which have been pursued through educational reform in the post-war period, prior to the collapse of the liberal consensus and its political constituency, need to be approached through a direct assault upon the structural sources of inequality in demand-side institutions.

Notes

1 From Moore, 1983.
2 See *Vocational Preparation* (FEU, 1981) in which it is argued that vocational preparation students present a problem for FE colleges because they are neither academic enough to follow a traditional educational course nor destined for jobs of sufficient skill level for a craft type course. The answer is to turn to 'personal development' based in social and life skills. This is underpinned by a psychological maturation theory which presents these young people as immature and, so, actually requiring this type of approach.
3 See Finn, 1987. This book is an excellent and strongly argued study of the issues relating to the current education and training situation which places their development in an historical perspective.
4 See Grieco and Whipp, 1984.

References

ASHTON, D. *et al.* (1983) *Youth in the Labour Market*, Research Paper No. 34. London: Department of Employment, HMSO.
ASHTON, D. *et al.* (1986) *Young Adults in the Labour Market*, Research Paper No. 55. London: Department of Employment, HMSO.

BLACKBURN, R. and MANN, M. (1979) *The Working Class and the Labour Market*. Basingstoke: Macmillan.

CLARKE, L. (1980) *The Transition from School to Work*. London: Department of Employment, HMSO.

CROMPTON, R. and JONES, G. (1984) *White Collar Proletariat*. Basingstoke: Macmillan.

CUMIN, D. (1983) *School-Leavers, Qualifications and Employment*, mimeo. Nottingham.

FEU (FURTHER EDUCATION UNIT) (1981) *Vocational Preparation*. London: HMSO.

FINN, D. (1987) *Training Without Jobs*. Basingstoke: Macmillan.

GRANOVETTER, M. (1975) *Getting a Job*. Cambridge, Mass.: Harvard University Press.

GRANOVETTER, M. (1981) 'Towards a Sociological Theory of Income Difference' in BERG, I. (ed.) *Sociological Perspectives on Labour Markets*. New York: Academic Press.

GRIECO, M. (1984) *Using the Network*... Paper given to Development Studies Association Annual Conference, University of Bath.

GRIECO, M. and WHIPP, R. (1984) *Women and the Workplace*. Work Organisation Research Centre, University of Ashton.

HOLLAND, G. (1977) *Young People and Work: Report on the feasibility of a new programme of opportunities for unemployed young people* (The Holland Report), Manpower Services Commission.

JONES, J. (1983) *Interim Report*, British Petroleum. London.

MOORE, R. (1983) 'Further Education, Pedagogy and Production' in GLEESON, D. (ed.) *Youth Training and the Search for Work*. London: Routledge & Kegan Paul.

MOORE, R. (1984) *'Schooling and the World of Work'*, in BATES, I. *et al.*, *Schooling for the Dole?* Basingstoke: Macmillan.

RICHARDS, G. (1982) *Work Experience Schemes for School Children: the shape of things to come?* mimeo. University of Warwick.

TROYNA, B. and SMITH, D.I. (eds) (1983) *Racism, School and the Labour Market*. Leicester: National Youth Bureau.

The Challenge of Economic Utility
Charles Bailey

The Challenge Sketched

The view under consideration here takes either a purely instrumental view of education or places so much importance on the instrumental view as to seriously play down any liberal education element even when some form of balance between the two is being nominally advocated. The view has often been tacit or implicit, revealing itself most often in the criteria apparent in criticisms of the alleged shortcomings of the educational system or of its lack of relevance. For a pupil to complain that his education is not relevant to the job he wants to do, or fails to equip him to face unemployment, is to assume that education has a proper instrumental purpose that it has failed to fulfil. For a prime minister to chide the system for failing to produce the scientists and technologists the country needs is to assume that the education system has manpower provision responsibilities that it is neglecting. For a politician to complain that the education system allows pupils to leave school with unfavourable attitudes towards wealth creation or technological growth or competition, is to suggest that there are proper attitudes for an education system to foster.[1]

In recent years, however, the demand for at least a strong instrumental element in the curriculum of secondary education has become more overt, especially from government agencies and from employers or from institutions that speak for employers. This is so much the case that a recent HMI discussion paper on teacher training could open with the statement:[2]

> It has in recent years become 'a truth universally acknowledged' that education should be more closely linked with the world of work and with the country's economic performance; and there has been increasing pressure on schools to assess the relevance of their curriculum to their pupils' future working lives.

Criticism of the Economic Utility Challenge

THE ASSUMPTIONS OF NON-CONTROVERSIALITY

Running through all the discussions of the economic utility model of education is an unspoken assumption of consensus about society, values and education. The assumed consensus is that of continually accepted technological change and development, strangely related to nineteenth-century conceptions of the undoubted good of 'progress', all taking place in the context of a competitive free market economy, and in a wider context of international competitive trade. Also assumed is the undeniable value of wealth creation, ostensibly as a necessary condition of all else that might be valued, but in fact by its emphasis seen as a valued end in itself. Education, in this model, becomes a commodity both for the individual person and for society as a whole, to be assessed like any other commodity in terms of its profitability or usefulness. The education favoured for the individual is one leading to a well-paid job; for the employer it is one producing well-disposed and capable workers and potential managers; and for the state it is one making the country strong in economic competitive power and united around simple ideas of patriotism. Some of these views are explicit in what I have been describing, but most of them are implied or taken for granted. Such a framework of assumed consensus is necessary to give coherence to all the claims and pressures.

That such a consensus exists as anything more concrete than an assumption or necessary presupposition is highly questionable. The value of continued technological growth, especially when dictated and operated by a profit mechanism, is challenged by many people. Not only does such a challenge come from the expected people: ecologists, conservationists and the anti-nuclear lobby, but also from groups like the Council for Science and Society which issued a report in 1981 entitled 'New Technology: Society, Employment and Skill'. The kind of questioning about the advance of technology I have in mind is evidenced by this comment in the CSS Report about the alleged benefits of automation based on computers:

If we look at past experience, it seems likely that possibilities of this kind, if they can be realized profitably with the computer, will be implemented despite any protests by those concerned.

... To follow such a path of increasing automation usually requires an additional expenditure on capital equipment. Profitability then depends upon a reduction of employment for a given output, or at least the substitution of less-skilled, and so cheaper, labour for the more highly skilled. Both courses reduce the demands which are made on human ability, and a classical economic argument sees this as the creation of new opportunity. The human resources set free are available for other needs of society, or to increase the production of goods. Moreover, an economic mechanism will automatically ensure that this opportunity is fully used.

Yet the experience of the last fifty years does little to establish confidence in this self-regulating mechanism. The demoralising unemployment of the 1930s ended only with the beginning of the Second World War, and it is not clear that the depression would have ended without the war. The 1970s, against expectations, saw a renewed increase of unemployment. During the whole period a large proportion of those employed have done work below their capability. What is striking is that very great effort is expended upon the creation of the opportunity which unemployment or underemployment represents, and in comparison almost none upon using that opportunity.[3]

Such a lengthy quotation is necessary to show the kind of detailed critical argument about the benefits or otherwise of technological advance that is completely and naively absent from the statements of those advocating an economic utility model of education. Unemployment has, of course, become much worse since this report was written, and political commentators on unemployment consistently play down the very large technologically structural element within it, hoping instead for some miraculous upturn in international trade to remedy the situation.

The idea of the undoubted good of technological advance is not only thus questionable, it is actively questioned by many people and groups of people in technically advanced societies. Similar detail can be found in literature from the conservationist and anti-nuclear groups, represented as cranks in much of the establishment media, but actually producing complex, sustained and serious argument of a most disturbing kind for those prepared to read it.

It is no part of my present argument to claim that the views now being referred to are necessarily correct, though I believe many of them to be so. The argument here is that views about technological growth are far more controversial than could be inferred from DES documents, HMI documents and other sources referred to earlier. For educators to influence the minds of pupils in the sole direction of the economic utility model of education, in this and other respects, would be highly indoctrinatory and therefore inimical to the development of rational and moral autonomy which is the duty of the liberal educator.

Similarly, the background context of the free competitive market as the determinant of resource allocation is anything but a consensus view of how society should most desirably operate. The Green Paper (*Education in School: A Consultative Document*, 1977), issued by a Labour Party Secretary of State, talked of the mixed economy as the normal state which education must come to terms with, as we might have expected from a government largely in the hands of the right wing of the Labour Party. Conservative politicians and most industrialists are, of course, more stridently supportive of a larger, if not total, free market element, and more directly socialist members of the Labour Party and others too far to the left to be members of that organization would want to see more, or total, central planning of the economy. The numbers of people prepared actually to vote for one or other of these positions when dressed up in various guises in election manifestos varies over time. What is inescapable, however, is the controversial nature of the issue. Politicians and employers have every right in a democracy, to argue their case; but it does not follow from this that any of them have the right, least of all in a democracy, to impose their particular view on the education system. Such a system, in so far as it tries to bring about political and economic understanding in the minds of the pupils entrusted to it, must treat controversial matters *as* controversial matters. The late Lawrence Stenhouse realized this when asked by the Schools Council to propose strategies for teaching the humanities, but the strategy his team constructed and tried so hard to introduce into schools is still only rarely seen in action. The suppression of student opinion in MSC-sponsored courses, already mentioned, stands directly opposed to the thoughtful strategy of neutrality and impartiality advocated by Stenhouse and characteristic of all his work.

If consensus does not actually exist in these areas neither does it exist in the matter of judging the value of activities by their contribution to wealth-creation. What this kind of emphasis leaves out of account is any consideration of what wealth is to be used for and how it is to be distributed. Even nineteenth-century utilitarians made happiness and not wealth-creation the touchstone of value, and were thus concerned about how wealth was used and distributed, and contemporary political philosophers have consistently related these ideas to the justice and morality of the ends to which wealth is put and of its distribution.[4] None of these political theorists appears to believe that a society with more wealth-creation is, in any simple and unqualified way, necessarily better than one with less. It seems particularly one-sided to judge an educational system, or even particular educational practices, by the simple criterion of contribution to wealth-creation for two main reasons. First, because educators must be duty-bound to introduce pupils to controversial matters *as* controversial matters, as I have already said in connection with technological growth; and, secondly, because schools of liberal education must introduce pupils to those activities and practices which can be considered as worthwhile in themselves and therefore fit to be considered as ends rather than as means. To take small but illustrative examples of what I mean here: it would be pointless to judge the value of my listening to music, reading poetry, or even doing my gardening, by assessing their contribution to wealth-creation when these things are for me intrinsically valued ends; when they are, in fact, activities on which I *use* my wealth rather than means to increase it. It is true that for some people the issue becomes confused and wealth-creation becomes an end in itself; but that is but one of the peculiar perversions of modern capitalist society, destructive of justice, morality and a proper humanity, as Erich Fromm and others have pointed out.[5] Education must be concerned with ends, and to the extent that it is so concerned it is improperly judged on the criterion of wealth-creation.

The last important controversial area in the economic utility model of education to be noted here is the emphasis on competition, both individual and national. A full discussion of the place of competition in education cannot be entered into here, but the point must be made that the place of competition, in both education and society at large, is controversial. Some people would favour a much more cooperative society and much more encouragement of cooperation in schools. Similarly some would favour much more international cooperation on trade instead of the present automatic assumptions about national competitiveness. Yet in the model I am criticizing competition is offered as a characteristic of the 'real' world, as though to question competition is like questioning the expansion of metals under heat or the necessity of moisture for growing plants; while cooperation for any other purpose than to defeat the other team, the other firm or the other country, is corrupting idealism, out of touch with the 'real' world. The assumption is as if Kropotkin had never written, the Cooperative Movement had never developed and fraternity had never been a political issue for which men and women had died on the barricades. Team spirit and loyalty have become transmogrified, as R.S. Peters puts it, into instruments of destructive competition instead of universal cooperation among all rational agents.[6]

THE DIVERSION OF RESPONSIBILITY

This criticism of the economic utility model of education is directed to the appropriate allocation of responsibility. Certainly it cannot be denied that there must be efficient and appropriate vocational training in any community. The criticism made by the liberal educator is not against vocational training as such, only against the idea that such training is properly located in schools of general education, or that the needs of such training should dictate the curriculum content and methodologies of schools of general education.

The paradigm notion of training is to do with preparation for some activity of a relatively specific kind which, once trained for, a person will engage in for some time. Such were the reasonable assumptions, for example, of an apprentice; but apprenticeships were features of a craft-orientated economy which has now all but disappeared from the national scene. Preparing people, especially young people, for specific industrial tasks is difficult today for a number of reasons, but two are paramount: first, no one can guarantee that a young person will actually get a job in the task for which he or she has been trained; and, secondly, no one can guarantee that the technical requirements of a task will not change very quickly, even before the young person takes up a job. These difficulties operate profoundly at all levels, as the Council for Science and Society reports in the case of engineers:

> In the university training of engineers, the scientific content is again heavily, and increasingly, stressed. To teach the current technology and procedures of industry is more difficult and less rewarding because they evolve within industry and change rapidly. Only someone directly engaged in the activity can teach it, and what is learned will be rapidly outdated.[7]

Yet employers still complain that graduates do not understand modern industry, and that school-leavers do not understand the particular aspects of work they find themselves in – if they do find themselves in work – as if this was solely the fault of the university or school. The very users of rapidly changing technologies, even the very makers of such technologies, show little signs of grasping these particular social implications, and education policy-makers can naively say that an aim of education should be 'to help pupils to acquire knowledge and skills relevant to adult life and employment in a fast changing world'![8]

Because industry has been unable to cope with these problems itself, and because of the costs of frequently changing training needs, there have been increased demands for national patterns of training and increased blaming of schools for alleged failures to develop appropriate skills and attitudes in young school-leavers. Exactly what these appropriate skills and attitudes are does not appear to have been much discussed outside the literature of the Further Education Curriculum Development Unit, the MSC, and agencies serving them. Inside that literature, however, one finds a flowering of talk about generic skills, social skills and life skills which will have a vocational bias and provide vocational motivation while still being (allegedly) very wide in application. Much of this would not concern us here were it not for the fact that unemployment has brought many more 16- and 17-year-olds under the influence of these training philosophies, and because of the present government's intention to extend these techniques to the 14- and 15-year-old pupils in ordinary schools. In the next subsection I shall look more closely at the characterization of skills in this literature. Here I am concerned to make the point that the very agencies who should tackle the problems of industrial training in the context of modern technology and rapid change, namely the government and industry, have chosen to do so largely by attacking the general education base and attempting, not to put too fine a point on it, to take that base over for purely instrumental purposes. This is a grand passing of the buck and a lamentable shedding of blame and responsibility which has an effect that is doubly disastrous: it fails to provide adequate industrial training that is directly linked with jobs on the one hand, and frustrates, confuses and belittles attempts at a genuine liberal education for all pupils on the other.

Much has been made in some recent discussions on these issues of the need for school-leavers to be very adaptable in the present-day situation. The need is genuine, but there are no magic skills for adaptability. The best basis for adaptability is a liberal education which has encouraged a wide understanding and the development of reason and autonomy, in the fullest sense of those oft-misused words, without any early prejudging of how this understanding might later be put to vocational and career use. The very rate of technological change argues in favour of liberal education for all, and not against it; and only from such an education can come adaptability, if that is what is necessary, or the critical power to work for a social control of technology as that increasingly becomes necessary. Liberal educators should be left to their logically prior task, and only after that should those properly responsible for industrial training see that it is efficiently undertaken.

THE CHARACTERIZATION OF SKILLS

It is odd to note that most of the Further Education Curriculum Development Unit teaching material that is so favoured by the MSC attempts to characterize everything in terms of skills. These are not only skills like being able to use a screwdriver or an electric drill, which would be clear and comprehensible, but much more grandly named skills like 'life skills', 'social skills', 'interpersonal skills' and even 'generic skills' which are supposed to underlie all we do. The oddity comes from the contrast between this view that all that is necessary is to equip people with appropriate skills for work, leisure and life, and the comments on skill that we find in the Science and Society report on 'New Technology: Society, Employment and Skill'. This report traces historically how the advance of technology has generally been accompanied by an *elimination* of skill:

> The historical evidence is not encouraging. Where it was possible to eliminate skill in the past, this was generally done. The opportunities which are being offered by the computer to remove skill from office work, printing, engineering design and other occupations, in general seem likely to be taken.... It will affect the majority of occupations up to and within the professional level. There will be a resistance to this development which will be strong and tenacious.... If it is unsuccessful, then the great majority of people will for the first time find themselves united in the misfortune of work which allows them no control or initiative.[9]

Of course the report notes that developing technology generates a need for new skills, but these are for a smaller number of people, usually different people, from those who are de-skilled.

We seem, then, to have two different accounts. One seems to be saying that education does not concern itself enough with skills: 'We believe schools need to make a conscious effort to ensure that their pupils acquire skills, many of which may prove to have a life-long value.[10] The other appears to be saying that the trend of technological change is generally to make increasingly useless the skills that people have acquired.

Part of the confusion here arises from the way in which the word 'skill' is used. The Schools Council gives as examples of skills: initial reading and number skills, the ability to work alone and the ability to work with others.[11] These are among what I have called the serving competencies because they serve instrumentally the other aims and purposes within a liberal education. Whether they are appropriately called skills is questionable. Further skills mentioned by the Schools Council are: a knowledge of political processes, the ability to interpret scientific data and the ability to make judgements on environmental matters. What is gained by calling these abilities 'skills' is difficult to see. Most writers agree at a superficial level as to the components of a skill.

A skill is more than knowing, and more than knowing how. It is action too. A skill involves the application of knowledge to achieve some anticipated outcome. It needs the capacity and the will to act, as well as knowledge. Skill without knowledge is inconceivable, but knowledge without skill has a long sad history.[12]

There are, however, interesting differences of emphasis. If the above quotation stresses the instrumentality of skills and their connection with action and the will, the following, from the Council for Science and Society report, emphasizes the knowledgeable control aspect of skill and marks off two interesting limiting conditions:

we should prefer to stress 'knowledgeable practice', and to emphasize the element of control without which skill does not exist. . . .

Because control is essential for the exercise of skill, it follows that there can be no skill where everything is completely predictable. Screwing a nut onto a bolt demands at most dexterity, not skill. In a large measure, therefore, skill is a response to the unexpected and unpredictable. The blacksmith so places the red-hot iron on the anvil, and strikes it with such a sequence of blows, that its shape converges to the horse-shoe he desires, even though his actions will never be the same on two occasions.

. . . On one side skill is marked off from more trivial accomplishments such as dexterity or 'knack'. On another it is distinguished from activities which are intended to affect people rather than things. . . 'managerial skill' has a manipulative sound if it is applied to the leadership of people. The 'skilled negotiator' or the 'skilled advocate' seem to contradict this rule, but reflection will show that both operate in situations where human contact is circumscribed and manipulation is sanctioned.[13]

The suggested limiting conditions set in this quotation are, it seems to me, sensible ones which accord with our normal usage of the term 'skill'. On the one hand, it accords with our intuitive idea that skills are never *merely* manual and always have a strong cognitive determination which is sometimes almost entirely determinant, as in the doctor's skills of diagnosis which cannot be disassociated from his knowledge and understanding of anatomy, physiology and pathology, as Ruth Jonathan points out.[14] On the other hand, the limiting conditions accord with our unease when morality, personal relationships and even certain features of communication are characterized as skills. People *can*, of course, be skilfully manipulated by others. The point is that this has usually been seen as a perverted side of human relationships, to be spoken of in derogatory terms, and having nothing to do with those humanistic aspects of morality, personal and social relations which should be the concern of liberal educators.

These concerns for life, persons and society are, however, complex and are only to be understood by the prolonged study of the kind of content discussed in chapter 7 (section s.1) of my book *Beyond the Present and Particular* (Bailey, 1984).[15] The advocates of a skill approach are obviously attracted by a simple view of skills which they then project into matters too complex to make the appellation appropriate. They seem to want the advantages of simplicity which lend themselves conveniently to precise statements of objectives and easily manageable assessment and monitoring:

> In specifying the type and level of skill they intend their pupils to acquire teachers come near to setting themselves precise aims. Schools need to decide and state exactly what skills they do hope to develop in each of the main areas of experience they are concerned with. They could use statements of this kind as a basis for self assessment.[16]

Yet at the same time this simplicity and precision must be injected into complex areas like 'verbal skills as vehicles for thought, feeling and imagination'[17] because the more complex realms of human action and reflection are clearly the most important and valuable.

Perhaps the fallacy of thinking that these complex areas can be characterized as skills arises from the fatal slip from the properly adverbial or adjectival to the improper substantive which is so ready a temptation of language. Because a person can be a thoughtful politician or an imaginative architect it is tempting to think that there are reifications like 'thought' or 'imagination' which can be readily identified, isolated and trained for. Similarly, because it *is* meaningful to talk of someone being a skilful thinker, or expressing their feelings skilfully, we are tempted to believe that there is a 'skill' to be identified, isolated and trained for. This reaches its maximum absurdity in notions like 'life skills', 'social skills' and 'generic skills', as if it were meaningful to think of people as skilful at life, in society or in some universal generic sense. These conceptions are either vacuous or pretentious names for isolated and relatively trivial abilities that might in some sense be subsumed under such titles, in the sense that blowing one's nose efficiently or cutting one's toenails adequately are 'life skills'. Ruth Jonathan puts it very well:

> It begins to look as if we have only to dub any desirable capacity or area of experience a 'skill' in order to suggest it can be easily identified and acquired. Advocates of the teaching of 'life skills' or 'survival skills' either have something utterly trivial in mind (like the ability to change plugs or walk through doorways), or something hopelessly vague (like the ability to be innovative or to work cooperatively) or are simply proffering glib new labels for the old educational aims of moral autonomy, rationality and aesthetic discrimination. If we are serious about the desirability of such goals we must look for advances in epistemology, psychology and ethical argument and be prepared to apply these insights in education, rather than following the blind alley of a behaviourist inspired skill-based approach.[18]

Other people are wary of the skills approach. Bernard Davies, writing for the National Youth Bureau, defends what he sees as a 'social education' orientation of youth workers against the pressure to go over to a skill-based approach. He rightly locates social education in the broad tradition of liberal education:

advocates of social education who wish to resist the drift to social and life skills training may need to be looking for alliances with all those other educators now trying to defend the liberal and personalised traditions of education generally.[19]

He also shares my view, or appears to do so, of the importance of justifying and substantiating a liberal education philosophy if one is to be in any position to resist the encroachment of a crude skills approach:

> youth workers, teachers and others involved in social education need to regain their nerve – their conviction that some of the person-centred, critical and creative goals to which they have been committed are still valid.
> ... If they cannot re-assert what is distinctive about the theory, philosophy and practice of their specialist field of work, they cannot hope to resist, still less to influence, the cruder, often highly mechanistic and behaviourist forms of social and life skills training now being foisted on so many young people.[20]

It was noted in the previous subsection that only one immersed in the practice of a skill, properly so called, can train another person in that skill. This was the long-standing basis of apprenticeships and many other less thoroughgoing types of on-the-job training. If we are speaking of the skills of operating a lathe, a computer, a sailing dinghy or anything where particular processes and performances are to be explained and demonstrated by one person to another who then practises the processes under the eye of the expert, then this is an important part of the paradigm of skills. If it is, however, then even more doubt is cast on the idea of life skills, social skills, moral skills and the like. Who are those arrogant enough to claim the necessary expertise to *train* others in these areas? What qualifications should they possess and what experience should they have had? What is their ongoing practice of the expertise which trainees watch and then practise for themselves? What is the rationale of their explanations? How does it escape the controversy found in these fields for thousands of years by philosophers and other reflective persons? Perhaps it is simply ignorance of all these problems, arising from prolonged immersion in action and the assertion of the will.

I must end this subsection, and lead into the next, with what after all is the liberal educator's main complaint about the emphasis on skills. This is to do with the way in which any emphasis on skills divorces the instruments from their purposes, separates means from ends. Logically, of course, skills are not separable from purposes and ends. It is the characterization of particular purposes that helps us to see the use of a particular skill – ball control in football, say – and there is no performance that is just a skill in any isolated sense. To make this point, obvious though it may seem to be, is immediately to diminish the importance of instrumental skills relative to other considerations like being able to *choose our ends* in some understanding and informed way; like entering into an understanding of the *values* involved in different ends; like considering the *morality* of certain means rather than others, even when the ends are determined; and like *understanding* the varied and multitudinous practices of humankind which might or might not come to be valued ends for us. Ruth Jonathan again makes the point crisply when she says that 'education must logically equip children to make these choices before it equips them to carry them out.'[21] Later in her paper she makes this point more fully:

> Formerly, individuals were either educated or trained. As social divisions became slightly more blurred, the vast mass of young people found themselves at the end of formal schooling neither educated nor trained. The answer does not lie in replacing education by training for all, but in acceptance that all young people require a general education which will open to them as many options of an intellectual, aesthetic and moral kind as they are capable of entertaining and society is able to support, followed by an appropriate period of generic training – not in imitative and obsolescent motor skills, but in the appropriate fundamental principles and general skills of particular technologies, whether industrial, commercial, scientific or service. The more specific our skills the shorter their useful life.[22]

With perhaps some room for negotiation as to where the former ends and the latter begins, few liberal educators would quarrel with that.

THE BELITTLING OF KNOWLEDGE AND UNDERSTANDING

Knowledge and understanding, I have claimed, are proper terms for what a liberal education is trying to develop in pupils. These, however, are the very characterizations belittled by exponents of the economic utility model of education, in favour of characteristics like 'skill', largely of course because of the active and instrumental connotation of the latter as compared with the apparent passivity of the former. Part of the technique of advocating the utility model, whether used deliberately and consciously or not it is difficult to say, is to give false, Aunt Sally, conceptions of knowledge and understanding: 'able to understand but not to act', or 'knowledge without skill has a long sad history'. This polarity supposes there to be a kind of knowledge and understanding disconnected from action and purpose, and therefore easily characterized as 'useless' with all the derogatory force of that word in a mainly instrumental, acquisitive and materialistic society. I want to argue that the polarity is a false one. Not only can you not have skills, properly speaking, without knowledge and understanding, which seems to be grudgingly admitted by those who attack liberal education, but it is also nonsense to suppose there to be *any* knowledge and understanding that does not involve the appropriate exercise of skills. These skills may indeed be mental rather than physical in some, though not all, cases; but then so mainly are the skills of engineers, lawyers, doctors, politicians, business executives and other 'practical men and women'. The point is that to come to know and understand anything in the rich evidential sense I have been arguing for is anything but a passive and purely recipient business. To know and to understand in this sense is to be able to follow and to practise particular kinds of investigative procedures, weigh evidence, make judgements and decide what to believe and what not to believe; to decide how to see things and how not to see things. Being able to explain things to oneself in this kind of a way, with attention to consistency and coherence, is the first step to being able to explain them to others. Seen like this it is not at all surprising that the *leaders* of industry and commerce and their related services usually come from those who have had a rich liberal education, rather than from those who at an early age have been cut off from such an education and directed into narrow vocationalism emphasizing mainly motor skills.

The first complaint, then, against the attempted belittling of knowledge and understanding, is that these ideas are wrongly characterized. The decision-making that is so valued by the exponents of the utility model and by the 'capability' proponents is in fact both a necessary part of knowledge and understanding and would be pure unguided will without them.

The second complaint, also following directly from arguments made earlier in this work, is that only knowledge and understanding on a wide base can liberate a person from the particular restrictions of birth, social class and geography. Without such a base any choices are bound to be restricted because of the limited perspective brought to bear on them. To think that choices of career or life-style can be made solely on the basis of necessarily limited work experience, factory visits and similar experiences to be found in careers education courses, is clearly wrong. The number of places visited, the types of work experienced, the life-styles sampled, would need to be enormous for the choices to be made on that basis. The supposition that the evidence on which choices are made becomes more 'real' because of this kind of experience is a fallacy which might be dubbed the 'concrete fallacy'. Having a broken leg, being stuck in a front-line trench or being unemployed are *not* necessarily the best ways of gaining any extensive *understanding* of bone injury, war or unemployment; neither is working on a conveyor belt, learning to use a lathe or to prepare hotel meals the best way of getting an understanding of the so-called 'world of work'. The direct experience may well be sharp and penetrating, but because it is necessarily of such a limited aspect of what is to be understood its very force becomes a handicap rather than an asset. The emotive impact of an experience is no necessary measure of its contribution to understanding. The very detachment, lack of passion, and abstractness of much of the knowledge and understanding handled in a liberally educative way, which it is now so fashionable to attack, are essentials of a balanced, wide and liberating understanding.

A third complaint against the diminution of the extent of knowledge and understanding in a compulsory education, and its replacement by cruder training elements, is that such diminution reduces the liberating influence of education by reducing the pupil's opportunity to develop a critical framework of thinking. To be capable of critically viewing one's own position, one's own perspective, the demands being made upon one and the opportunities provided or not provided, it is necessary to be able to make comparisons and contrasts against a wide background of actual, possible and imaginable different conceptions of things and of how things might be. This kind of comparative complex is only to be gained by a reasonably extensive study of human practices as delineated in chapter 7 (section s.1) of my book *Beyond the Present and Particular* (Bailey, 1984). These practices included those that manifested themselves in economic, commercial and industrial institutions, and in art, craft and design; and the point was made that understanding these practices would necessarily involve some active participation, but that such participatory activities were to be directed to the end of understanding the practices and not towards training for a future in them. For example, I claimed that a pupil engaged in art at a school of general and liberal education is studying and practising with a different purpose from that of a student in an art school. In a school of liberal education we are not trying to produce an artist, but a human being who has some understanding of the arts as a great and pervasive human practice. I should add here that another characteristic of the place of art, or anything else, in a liberal education is that the particular practice is to be seen in the light of, and as shedding light on, all the other practices studied. What R.S. Peters called 'cognitive perspective' is an important aim of liberal education but does not seem to figure very largely in the economic utility model of education. To foreclose too soon on this process of a widening of cognitive perspective through an individual's growth of knowledge and understanding is to limit the growth of critical power which is a necessary part of individual autonomy.

It is perhaps wrong to claim that exponents of vocational training or emphasis within the period of compulsory education are deliberately seeking to curb critical power and attitude, though the references to MSC course censorship already made would lend weight to such a claim. Nevertheless, the result is the same whether deliberate or not, whether wished for or not. Those who seek to devalue knowledge and understanding, as compared with training, and those who seek to reduce the time involved in school concern for knowledge and understanding as against training, are devaluing the concern for developing the rational autonomy of the pupil which constitutes the main justification for compelling children to be in school at all.

Conclusion

In this chapter I have given a sketch and a criticism of what is perhaps the most overt and immediately pressing challenge which faces the view of liberal education that I have outlined in earlier chapters. What I have sketched here is also, of course, an attack on the education system as it stands in this country today. It is important not to be confused here, since an attempt to develop a genuine liberal education for all pupils up to at least the age of sixteen would *also* be an attack on the system as it exists today. To defend my view of liberal education against alternative conceptions giving emphasis to training and to vocational preparation is *not* to defend the present system. Conversely, arguments pointing to defects in the present system, in schools as they actually exist today, and they are many, are not necessarily arguments against the view of liberal education presented here. I happen to believe that a good deal of what goes on in our schools *is* liberally educating; but not enough of it is. There is not enough concern for evidential teaching and teaching for understanding; there is far too early a narrowing of curriculum spread; there is too much concern for relating the curriculum to career choice and there is too much emphasis on competition and not enough on collaboration. An exponent of the economic utility model of education that I have tried to characterize and criticize would no doubt turn these criticisms of the status quo on their head, claiming there to be too much concern about understanding and not enough concern about the 'realities' of competition, careers and the creation of wealth. Neither of us totally approves of the present system, but we would improve things in totally opposed ways. The debate is a real one.

At this historical moment (late 1983) there is little doubt that the economic utility model, supported by the government and the Manpower Services Commission as well as by powerful agencies of industry and commerce, is winning the power struggle if not the debate. The reason it is winning is mainly to do with the strength and alignment of political forces, but a powerful subsidiary factor is the failure of professional educators to first articulate, and then defend, a coherent view of liberal education.

There are those who would say that what is happening is no more than forces already and always at work in a capitalist democratic society becoming open about what they are always trying to do. The liberal education I am advocating would never stand a chance, these critics would say, because it could not be divorced from the productive and social relationships obtaining in a capitalist society. These critics raise profound problems about the relativity of knowledge, and about the relationship between knowledge and ideology, and to these difficult questions we must now turn.

References and Notes

1 Mr James Callaghan, then Prime Minister, made such charges in his speech at Ruskin College Oxford, on 18 October 1976. The charge that schools pay insufficient attention to respect for industry and wealth creation was made by Mrs Shirley Williams, then Secretary of State for Education, in 1977 and more stridently by Conservative politicians and by groups like Understanding British Industry ever since.
2 Department of Education and Science (1982) *Teacher Training and Preparation for Working Life*. London: HMSO, p. 1.
3 Council for Science and Society (1981) *New Technology: Society, Employment and Skill*. London: CSS.
4 To confirm this brief assertion, readers might look at: J. Rawls (1972) *A Theory of Justice*. Oxford: Clarendon Press; A. Gewirth (1978) *Reason and Morality*. Chicago: University of Chicago Press; and B. Ackerman (1980) *Social Justice in the Liberal State*. New Haven: Yale University Press.
5 E. Fromm (1956) *The Sane Society*. London: Allen & Unwin.
6 R. S. Peters (1966) *Ethics and Education*. London: Allen & Unwin, pp. 225-6.
7 Council for Science and Society, op. cit., p. 89.

8 Department of Education and Science (1981) *The School Curriculum*. London: HMSO, p. 3.

9 Council for Science and Society, op. cit., p. 77.

10 Schools Council, Working Paper 70 (1981) *The Practical Curriculum*. London: Methuen Educational, p. 22.

11 Ibid., p. 22.

12 Ibid., p. 22.

13 Council for Science and Society, op. cit., pp. 23–4.

14 R. Jonathan (1983) 'The manpower service model of education', in *Cambridge Journal of Education*, 13(2), p. 9.

15 C. Bailey (1984) *Beyond the Present and Particular*. London: Routledge & Kegan Paul.

16 Schools Council, op. cit., p. 23.

17 Ibid., p. 23.

18 R. Jonathan, op. cit., pp. 8–9.

19 B. Davies (1979) *From Social Education to Social and Life Skills Training: In Whose Interest?* Leicester: National Youth Bureau, p. 11.

20 Ibid., p. 10

21 R. Jonathan, op. cit., p. 8.

22 Ibid., p. 9. The whole of Ruth Jonathan's paper is an excellent case against the trends criticized in this chapter. For another form of criticism against skills approaches see P. Atkinson, T.L. Rees, D. Shore and H. Williamson (1982) 'Social and Life Skills: The Latest Case of Compensatory Education', in T. Rees and P. Atkinson (eds) *Youth Unemployment and State Intervention*. London: Routledge & Kegan Paul.

4.3 Schooling for Inequality? Ordinary Kids in School and the Labour Market
Phillip Brown

Introduction

The institutionally arranged passage into adulthood has been seriously disrupted for large numbers of school-leavers due to the collapse of the transition from 'school to work'. Many pupils are delaying entry into the labour market by opting to stay-on in full-time education; many are being forced on to government schemes for unemployed youth in order to bridge the gap between school and work; and many are experiencing long periods of unemployment.

The collapse of occupational opportunities for school-leavers has generated what C. Wright Mills (1971) has called 'private problems of milieu' and 'public issues of social structure'. In this chapter I will consider the private troubles confronting 'ordinary' (Kahl, 1961) working-class boys and girls as they prepare to leave school and enter the labour market.[1] It will be argued that the changing relationship between the reward structures of the school and the labour market signals a major threat to the ordinary kids' understanding of their *being* in school and of what they hope to *become* when they leave.

The public issues which will be addressed concern the production and reproduction of educational and social inequalities. More specifically, it examines the way in which the state has defined the problem of youth unemployment and what it is doing about it. This is a public issue because as Mills tells us in a well-known passage from *The Sociological Imagination* (1971):

> When, in a city of 100,000, only one man is unemployed, that is his personal trouble, and for its relief we properly look to the character of the man, his skills, and his immediate opportunities. But when in a nation of 50 million employees, 15 million men are unemployed, that is an issue, and we may not hope to find its solution within the range of opportunities open to any one individual. The very structure of the problem and the range of possible solutions require us to consider the economic and political institutions of the society, and not merely the personal situation and character of a scatter of individuals (Mills, 1971, p. 15).

The question of youth employment therefore, is a public issue because the state has sought vocational solutions to the problem, which I will argue, represents an attempt to maintain existing patterns of educational and social inequalities, and to avert an impending legitimation crisis both in and outside the school.

Class, Culture and Schooling

Considerable interest has been shown in the transition from 'school to work' in the post-war period, and more recently, the consequences of youth unemployment, partly because the passage into adulthood has been seen to depend on acquisition of employment. In the 1970s some writers were concerned with finding ways of 'smoothing the transition' (Bazelgette, 1978; Clarke, 1980), while others were more concerned with revealing the processes which ensure the reproduction of educational and economic inequalities (Willis, 1977; Corrigan, 1979). Despite such differences in emphasis, British research has consistently found that the school has been very successful in regulating the ambitions of school leavers so that they fit the available opportunities in the labour market (Carter, 1966; Roberts, 1974; Ashton, 1986).

In the 1980s similar studies have examined the personal and social consequences of youth unemployment (Kelvin and Jarrett, 1985; Ashton, 1986). The main concern of this discussion, however, is to evaluate the likely consequences of youth unemployment for working-class responses to the school, and particularly those of the ordinary kids. One confronts a major problem when attempting such an endeavour in that contemporary theories of schooling the working class have failed to provide an adequate account of the range of working-class orientations to school and the labour market. The ordinary kids have remained invisible from such accounts (with some important exceptions: Kahl, 1961; Ashton and Field, 1976; Jenkins, 1983), because of a tendency for sociologists to *describe* variations in working-class responses in terms of pupil acceptance or rejection; conformity or non-comformity (Hargreaves, 1967; Willis, 1977; Corrigan, 1979), and because of a failure to include female pupils in such analyses.

Moreover, those differences in working class responses which have been acknowledged are usually explained in terms of what will be called a process of *educational* or *cultural* differentation. Consideration of ordinary kids reveals that both these approaches are singularly inadequate, because if an adequate explanation of working-class responses to the school and occupational structure is to be developed, it is the interplay between the processes of *educational* and *cultural* differentiation which needs to be understood.

My reason for identifying the problem with existing sociological accounts is not to lead into a description of what an alternative explanation would look like. This task is undertaken elsewhere (Brown, 1987a). What I do want to show is that because sociologists have studied working-class responses to the school in terms of pupil acceptance and rejection, and as a result of explaining differences in pupil orientations to school and the occupational structure in terms of a process of *educational* and *cultural* differentiation, they have failed to provide an adequate account of working class responses to the school which would provide a basis for evaluating the likely impact of changing labour market conditions for schooling working-class pupils in the 1980s.

Explanations in terms of the process of *educational* differentiation have emphasized the school's role as a sifting and sorting mechanism which ensures that pupils from middle and working-class backgrounds arrive at educational and occupational destinations appropriate to their class membership. The apparent acquiescence of working-class pupils as they move into the market for working-class jobs is seen as a by-product of their educational location, given the apparent success of the school in its role of 'cooling out' unrealistic expectations. Therefore, both Marxists (Bourdieu and Passeron, 1977; Bowles and Gintis, 1976) and non-Marxists (Hopper, 1971; Roberts, 1974) who seek to explain working class experiences in school in terms of the process of *educational* differentiation identify the school as performing a central role in determining differences in educational attainment and give it an important role in the pre-occupational socialization of working-class school-leavers.

Alternatively, there are a number of writers who have challenged this orthodoxy, and have attempted to explain working-class educational and labour market experiences in terms of class *cultural* differences in attitudes and aspirations. Explanations couched in terms of a process of *cultural* differentiation correctly emphasize cultural differences in the *demand* for education and in the definition of desirable occupational goals. For example, in Willis's (1977) book *Learning to Labour* he argues that the difficult thing to explain about how working-class kids get working-class jobs is not how the school allocates working class kids to the lower bands, but why working-class kids voluntarily 'fail' themselves. Rather than attempt to explain educational failure in terms of the available *means* to succeed within the school, Willis views middle and working-class pupils as already culturally distinct. What happens in the school is simply an expression of cultural differences originating outside it. Working-class kids do not evaluate their relationship with the school in terms of what the school might offer given their location in the academic order, but in terms of the consequence of academic success for *being* a working-class adult as understood in their 'parent' culture. It is the class cultural definition of a future in manual labour offering little intrinsic reward, he argues, which leads to the basic exchanges on offer within the school – 'Knowledge for qualifications, qualified activity for high pay and pay for goods and services' (p. 64) – being rejected. Despite recognizing class culture as important for understanding pupil responses to school and the transition into the labour market, a major difficulty with *cultural* explanations such as Willis's is how to explain why large numbers of working-class pupils do *not* develop an anti-school subculture. This difficulty results from a characterization of middle and working-class pupils as culturally distinct, and the assumption that the development of pro- and anti-school subcultures is a manifestation of these cultural differences. This leads Willis to understand the counter-school subculture as the *normal* working-class response to the school. And it is because the counter-school culture is assumed to be the *normal* working-class response to the school that he is led to lump together other working-class responses as *conformist* responses, and to an explanation of the working-class conformists (ear'oles) in terms of the school's success in ideologically incorporating these working-class kids into bourgeois modes of thought. However, the range of working-class responses to the school cannot be explained simply in terms of working-class culture because pupil responses to the school will, at least in part, reflect a *selection* from that culture, unless we regress to a form of explanation which relies on differences in working class family 'types' (Carter, 1966; Ashton and Field, 1976) or, like Willis, condemn the majority of working-class kids to the status of ideological dupes as the price for celebrating 'the lads' as cultural heroes.

Ordinary Kids

The study of comprehensive schooling which I conducted in Middleport, South Wales, revealed that a simple bi-polar distinction between those who accept or reject the school is a misleading oversimplification of classroom life (Brown, 1987a). Within the informal pupil culture found in the two working class comprehensive schools, pupils recognized three different ways of *being* a working class pupil in school. These were commonly recognized in terms of the rems, swots and ordinary kids. While it is legitimate to identify the rems as those pupils who reject the school, and the swots as those who accept the school the ordinary kids (who comprise the largest category of pupils from both schools), neither simply accept or reject the school, but nevertheless comply with it. The ordinary kids' compliance with school is not based upon the premise that if they worked hard in lessons they could 'get out' of the working class, seduced by the knowledge that a few do succeed, but on their own class cultural desire to become a working-class adult in a respectable fashion. The ordinary kids believed that modest levels of endeavour and attainment (usually leading to CSEs) would help them 'get on' which, in the working class neighbourhoods of Middleport, typically meant boys entering craft apprenticeships and girls low-level clerical and personal service occupations. The educational incorporation of ordinary working class girls and boys was based on an *'alienated instrumental'* orientation which led the ordinary kids to reject much of the academic curriculum which was believed to be irrelevant to their present and future lives.

> *Martin:* We got maths lessons, they're putting in, like, all different things like algebra, cross-sections and trigonometry and all that. But like me, I want to be a welder, won't need none of it. Might have somethin' like adding up, to measure a piece of metal to which you're goin' to weld to it. But you don't need nothin' like statistics like, things like that ... like science, you don't want to know all the different things.
> *Mark:* History, with history now, say somebody wants to be a motor

> mechanic say, I can't see where history comes into it, you know, I can't really see what history has got to do with school, you know... with learnin' 'cos history is... it... just deals with the past.

Despite their resistance to the school's definition of 'useful knowledge' and 'success', the ordinary kids were willing to make an effort in school because limited commitment and modest levels of attainment were seen to offer the opportunity to 'get on' in working-class terms. If this interpretation of the ordinary kids' compliance to school is correct, then it needs to be understood to be as much a working-class response as that which leads to a rejection of the school. It also raises serious objections to the way Willis and others restrict the possibility of a 'truly' working-class response to the 'cultural few' whom he identified as adopting a counter-school subculture, thus denying the existence of any other form of class culture/school structure mechanisms which acts to reproduce or threaten class and/or school stability.

The most important point to note about the ordinary kids' compliance with school is that it has depended upon certain historical conditions in which the reward structure of the school and labour market have corresponded sufficiently to allow pupils to predict the likely outcomes of efforts in school. The problem this generates for schooling ordinary kids in the 1980s is that unless they perceive a clear relationship between the products of 'making an effort' in school and rewards in the labour market these pupils will see little point in bothering to comply, because their interest in much of what is taught is limited to those 'practical' subjects which are believed to have some relevance and interest to them. Any situation where the ordinary kids can no longer predict rewards in the labour market for efforts in school, therefore, not only threatens the social order of the school but also presents personal troubles for the ordinary kids.

THE PERSONAL TROUBLES OF MILIEU

C. Wright Mills (1971) suggests that *troubles* concern the personal problems confronting the individual and those areas of social life of which he or she is directly and personally aware. 'A trouble is a private matter: values cherished by an individual are felt by him to be threatened' (p. 15), the personal troubles which threaten the ordinary kids stem from the fact that their future frame of reference reflects past processes and practices rather than present circumstances. Inherited beliefs, attitudes and values, including an understanding of the school and their future place in society are becoming a less adequate basis for maintaining personal dignity in the school and personal survival in the labour market.

AT SCHOOL

Between the time the ordinary kids were deciding what examination subjects to study for CSE in the fourth year and the time they reached school-leaving age, their chances of finding 'any' job declined to a quarter and their chances of finding an apprenticeship declined to an eighth of the proportion of those who had left school three years earlier. The responses of the ordinary kids to this changing situation have not been uniform. Some of them now believe that there are few opportunities and little point bothering to make an effort in school.

Amy: All the teachers are the same, they say 'oh you should get this, you could pass in this', but they're no good to you, when you're leavin'. I don't see the point in havin' em... people these days have got qualifications but they still haven't got jobs.

However, over two-thirds of the 225 ordinary kids still believed that they could get a job if they made an effort to find one. The need to maintain a sense of purpose and predictability in their life provided a powerful *raison d'être* for continuing to believe that they could find suitable employment. It also provided a compelling reason for continuing to 'make an effort' in school. Therefore despite questioning its 'value' there are a number of reasons why the ordinary kids compliance with the school has not been completely withdrawn.

First, the rapid decline in occupational opportunities occurred when the ordinary kids were in secondary education. It was only as they approached school leaving age that they began to realize how difficult it might be to get a job, by which time it seemed pointless to 'give up' completely, because qualifications gave them something to show for their years at school. 'Havin' you somethin' to show for your years at school' was believed to convey the 'right' attitude to employers, and therefore improve the chances of getting any job. Among younger working-class pupils who are entering secondary education with a knowledge that there is little hope of them getting a job when they leave school, 'making an effort' will refer to a much longer time-span. Were they to ask themselves whether it is worth 'making an effort' for five years when there is little chance of a job at the end of it, the answer from a large proportion of working-class pupils would probably be 'No'. In these circumstances there is likely to be a fundamental change in the attitudes of even junior school pupils in the direction of an alienated orientation.

Secondly, although qualifications were seen to be of little help in getting the jobs they wanted, making an effort in school was now justified as a way of improving their chances of getting 'any' job,

Liz: When you leave school with no qualifications and the unemployment is as it is now, you won't be able to get a job, they're looking for school leavers with, you know, qualifications.

Mark: Well the job situation... well it's worse now and there's not much chance of you gettin' jobs because of the situation, but if you've got qualifications behind you, the employers will take somebody who's got qualifications before someone who hasn't got qualifications.

Thirdly, the way the ordinary kids understood the relationship between employment and 'being' in school provided them with a sense of personal dignity because academic success had never been necessary to 'get on' in working-class terms. The ordinary kids could achieve their occupational ambitions without being like pupils whom they identified as the 'swots' and who were seen as spending all their time doing school work and 'never going out in the nights', or like the 'rems' who had not bothered to 'make an effort' in school and who condemned themselves to a life in unskilled jobs or government schemes.

> [Talking about the rems]
> *Amanda:* They spent all these years at school haven't they, you know. They could have tried, if they had CSEs at least it's something '... at least they're tryin' ent they?
> *Mark:* I don't really have no disrespect for 'em, but if you want to be a layabout, job creation and all that, what's the future in that, diggin' a garden... what security for your family is that, you know. What prospects have you got for the future, right 'I'll be famous [imitating some of the rems], you see 'em out of school... 'Oh I've got a job, I've got forty quid a week in Burgerland', what's the point in that?

To 'give up' and leave school without qualifications would be an extraordinary act, which would make them little better than rems, forfeiting any legitimate claim to what occupational opportunities now remain for school-leavers.

IN THE LABOUR MARKET[2]

Despite the ordinary kids' efforts in school, Table 4.3.1 shows that under 20 per cent found employment within three months of attaining school-leaving age. Twice this proportion of ordinary kids stayed in full-time education, while others entered government schemes or became unemployed. Over a year later the proportion of ordinary kids in employment had more than doubled, but remained at under 40 per cent. The proportion of unemployed ordinary kids has also more than doubled to almost a fifth, but the percentage of ordinary kids on government schemes had declined by two-thirds to under 10 per cent. Almost a third of the ordinary kids opted for a second year of additional study. The large proportion of ordinary kids opting to stay in full-time study signals the failure of these pupils in their attempt to find suitable employment at the time they had intended to leave school. The primary motivator for the ordinary kids' staying in education was their perceived chances of finding employment and a desire to avoid having to go on a government scheme or on the dole.

The majority of ordinary kids (57 per cent) did enter the labour market and almost two-thirds (62 per cent) of these went on at least one government scheme (a third had been on more than one scheme). This was despite finding that 40 per cent of those who entered a scheme did *not* state a willingness to do so while at school. A large proportion of ordinary kids have therefore been forced to bridge the gap between school and trying to find employment with the entry onto a scheme.

Jane: I was determined not to go on a scheme because, you know, the money for a start, £25 a week it's nothin' is it? The way that people were takin' advantage of them, I was determined not to go on one. But in the end it got so bad, you know, it was terrible, you know, you never realize it's going to be that bad ... when I came out of school, and no job, I thought it couldn't be that bad and I could get a job easy ... my mother she was havin' me up before nine every morning and goin' down to the job centre, but it was just useless, so I didn't have no alternative, it was either a government scheme or just you know, laze about on the dole and do nothin' about it.

4.3.1 *Destinations three months and eighteen months after attaining school leaving age (percentage)*

	Ordinary kids		Total	
	Three	*Eighteen*	*Three*	*Eighteen**
full-time employment	18	38	13	32
unemployment	9	19	6	16
government schemes	29	9	27	9
college/school	43	32	53	41
other	1	3	1	2
totals (number)	163	162	317	316

*Number of months after attaining school leaving age

The majority of ordinary kids, although hoping that a scheme would improve their chances of getting the sort of job they want, believe (particularly after the first scheme) that they were a means of making the most of no job. They were also a way of keeping in circulation and a demonstration that they were doing something rather than being on the dole. Yet some of the ordinary kids who left full-time study preferred to seek employment while they were on the dole and many of those who went on a scheme found themselves joining the dole queues.

Over a quarter of the ordinary kids with labour market experience had been unemployed for more than three months, and almost half of these for more than six months (not including time spent on government schemes). Responses to unemployment obviously depend upon its duration. If it is short-term it is unlikely to threaten social identity. However, despite the relatively short time the ordinary kids have been in the labour market it is the group of long-term unemployed whose social identity may be particularly out of tune with their understanding of what they *could* have become, or could now be becoming. The experience of long-term unemployment not only threatens the ordinary kids' chances of 'getting on', but indefinitely postpones their acquisition of the status of working class adult, previously arranged through the transition to employment and, eventually, marriage (Leonard, 1980; Jenkins, 1983). The social significance of engaging in paid employment in order to secure adult status is perhaps lessened for female school leavers (Gaskell and Lazerson, 1980). Yet, in the early years of post-school life, finding 'suitable' employment is important to both sexes (Griffin, 1985).

One of the concerns of this chapter has been to describe how the ordinary kids confront the personal troubles which have resulted from the collapse of the transition from 'school to work'. It has been shown that many of these young people have postponed their transition into the labour market or are now unemployed. It can also be shown (although not here) that most of those ordinary kids who have found employment are not in the jobs they want. A detailed analysis of the ordinary kids' responses to their labour market experiences is beyond the scope of this chapter (see Brown, 1987a), but what I want to show is that despite sharing a common understanding of *being* in school, it is possible to identify important differences between ordinary kids on the basis of labour market experiences. The ordinary kids who are unemployed, although registering a decline in the perceived importance they ascribe to school performance in finding jobs, remain more likely than those in jobs to emphasize *technical* differences in 'human capital' (i.e. having enough qualifications) as a reason for their failure to find jobs, rather than a *moral* failing involving a willingness to 'make an effort'. Alternatively, those *in* jobs emphasize that the reason why some of their peers are unemployed is not a *technical* but a *moral* issue. They are unemployed because they have not been willing to 'make an effort'.

The belief among the ordinary kids who are *in employment* that finding employment depends primarily upon a willingness to 'make an effort' is consistent with the way in which the ordinary kids *in school* legitimated their right to whatever jobs were available, compared with the rems who had not bothered to 'make an effort'. The same cultural understandings in school, which united the ordinary kids by distinguishing them from the morally inferior rems now threaten to divide the ordinary kids in the labour market.

Differences between jobs in terms of level of skills, training, working conditions and money, previously represented a division between 're-spectable' and 'rough' working class youth (Willmott, 1966; Jenkins, 1983). In a period of declining occupational opportunities, the manifestation of a willingness to 'make an effort' increasingly depends upon being in a job whether or not it is the one preferred. Sennet and Cobb (1977) have argued that there is no more urgent business in life than establishing a sense of personal dignity, and this certainly appears to underlie the attitudes of the ordinary kids who are in jobs. They may not be in the jobs they want, but at least they have made the effort to find a job rather than being on the dole. It is through employment that the ordinary kids can demonstrate their moral worth both to themselves and to others. The experience of unemployment therefore circularly reinforces the attitude that to be unemployed is not to show willing, because by definition you can only show willing once you are in a job.

As the duration of unemployment increases it is also increasingly difficult to do - and to be seen to be doing - something to demonstrate one's social worth: one is forced to leave the vagaries of the market to determine an increasingly uncertain and bleak future. A major problem in the experience of unemployment is the threat of falling to a position normally felt to be below one, and is not only a social descent but a moral descent.

Being unemployed *is* interpreted as a moral descent among the ordinary kids in jobs, but those on the dole are more likely to reject the view that their unemployment is the result of a failure to 'make an effort'. There was a substantial increase among the unemployed ordinary kids in the proportion who believed that there are no jobs regardless of how hard they try to find one, and it may well be that a small proportion of the ordinary kids who are currently unemployed may not be prepared to take jobs they do not want. However, although the ordinary kids recognize the lack of occupational opportunity for school-leavers, their response to unemployment is fatalistic (if only they had better qualifications, worked harder at school, or if only mum or dad could put a 'word in' for them). The crucial link between personal predicament and labour market conditions is rarely made in a consistent manner. However there may be a growing sense of alienation among the ordinary kids in employment as well as those on the dole. The ordinary kids have not simply accommodated previous understandings of who they are and what the future has to offer according to changing circumstances, or according to labour market conditions. Despite the tendency to understand personal experiences in individualistic and fatalistic terms, 'their apparent acquiescence should not be confused with contentment' (Runciman, 1966, p. 26). Sennett and Cobb (1977) have also noted that the psychological motivation instilled by a class society is aimed at healing a doubt about the self rather than creating more power over things and other persons in the outer world. Despite the fact that what has happened to many of the ordinary kids since leaving school directly challenges their sense of social justice based on a willingness to 'make an effort', their transition from school seems set to lead to increasing divisions amongst working-class youth, rather than to the creation of collective understanding of their collective problems.

Public Issues of Social Structure

In this section I will suggest that the personal troubles experienced by the ordinary kids are, in the main, a manifestation of public issues of social structure. A *public issue*, Mills tells us, is a public matter which often involves a crisis in institutional arrangements. The crisis in institutional arrangements which this chapter addresses concerns the political incorporation of large numbers of working-class people into the school and the reproduction of social and educational inequality. It will also be argued that:

1   The collapse of the transition from 'school to work' is not an educational problem but a problem for education (Watts, 1978; Roberts, 1984), and the main reason why working-class youth are unable to find employment is a result of a collapse in the *demand* for young workers.
2   The attempt to find vocational solutions to economic and social problems by restructuring secondary education is not only a justification for increasing inequality of opportunity, it is a blue-print for the future educational system of the 1990s which is as redundant as many of the jobs the Thatcher government now feels it needs to prepare school-leavers to enter.
3   There is an urgent need to establish a new politics of education if any semblance of social justice is to remain in British secondary schools. But changes in the educational system cannot compensate for society (Bernstein, 1969); broader changes will be necessary if a 'new deal' for Britain's youth is to be achieved.

EDUCATION AND ECONOMIC EFFICIENCY

In the era of the welfare state and continuing economic growth, the educational system was identified as holding the key to Britain's future prosperity. It was widely believed that the better educated the workforce, the greater the level of economic efficiency. Moreover, for the investment in education to yield its potential economic returns, it was argued (particularly by liberal reformers) that the educational system must be restructured in order to improve opportunities for pupils from a working-class background to draw upon an hitherto untapped 'pool of ability'. However, economic recession and the growth in youth unemployment are seen to undermine the view that investment in education will ensure continuing economic prosperity. By the middle of the 1970s the dual objective of equality of opportunity and economic efficiency could no longer be sustained as an argument for more investment in education. The liberal movement of the 1960s and 1970s were mortally wounded by their own two-edged sword. Investment in education did not prevent recession or unemployment, but was increasingly assumed to be a contributory factor to Britain's economic problems. The attempt to use the educational system as an instrument for orchestrating social reform was believed by conservative writers such as Boyson (1975) to have gone too far, too fast. There was growing anxiety, fuelled by the media, that the comprehensive reorganization of secondary education had led both to a decline in educational standards, and presented a growing threat to the very fabric of British society. Therefore, while Britain's economic prosperity was seen to depend on the school's ability to tap the 'pool of ability' in the 1960s, by the late 1970s such efforts were identified as a source of economic liability.

Despite such claims, the existence of *some* relationship between 'educated' labour power and economic efficiency has not been questioned. What has been questioned is any *simple* relationship between economic efficiency and investment in 'human' capital. It is because the school has given the wrong medicine, in the wrong dosage, to the wrong children, that a disproportionate number of school-leavers are now unemployed. As a result of this diagnosis the Thatcher government (partly under the guise of falling rolls) has performed major surgery on the educational budget. There have also been efforts to remedy the apparent mismatch between the needs of industry and the products of the school, by restructuring the secondary school curriculum. The Manpower Services Commission (MSC) (rather than the Department of Education and Science (DES)) has been provided with funds to introduce new forms of technical and vocational education. TVEI began during September 1983 in fourteen areas in England and Wales. The current total is now over 100. The main purpose of TVEI is to make the school curriculum more relevant to the world of work, and it is intended to be available for all pupils who want to take part regardless of sex or educational attainment (MSC, 1985).

THE LIMITS OF THE NEW VOCATIONALISM

Initiatives such as the TVEI, it can be argued, manifest a contradiction between the state's attempt to maintain existing patterns of educational and social inequalities, and the potential for social and educational change which is resulting from the restructuring of the economy. My reasons for this assertion are given below.

First, the argument that the current crisis in schools and the market for young workers results from the school engendering anti-industrial attitudes and unrealistic expectations of working life is not supported by the evidence (Bates *et al.*, 1984; Brown, 1987b). The study of school leavers in Middleport leads to the conclusion that the current crisis in schools results from the fact that there has been a decline in the type of employment opportunities through which the ordinary kids can 'get on' in working-class terms, and become adult in a respectable fashion. Its conclusion was *not* that these school-leavers must be educated once more to know their place; it is that they *do* know their place, that they see the school as a useful aid in attaining it, but have become increasingly frustrated and angry when they discover that there are insufficient places to accommodate them.[3]

Secondly, attempts to restructure the educational system in order to meet the 'needs' of industry must be treated with considerable scepticism. As long ago as 1947 the Central Advisory Council for Education stated:

Schools can prepare their pupils for industry only to a very limited degree, because it is in practice almost impossible to do more and would be highly undesirable on the grounds of educational principle. The practical objection to basing education on the needs of the scholar's future employment is the variety and frequent change of occupations, and rapidity of technical change (Policy Review Staff, 1947, p. 50).

Indeed when it comes to specifying what the 'needs' of industry are and how they can best be met, employers express considerable uncertainty (CPRS, 1980). What they do seem to agree about is the need for a flexible and adaptable workforce capable of responding to changes in the work process (Parsons, 1985; MSC, 1985). I will say more about this in a moment.

Thirdly, if there are anti-industrial attitudes harbouring among Britain's youth today, they are to be found not among ordinary kids but within the middle class (Wiener, 1981). Yet it will be middle-class parents and pupils who will resist any interference with the school curriculum which affects the acquisition of paper qualifications giving access to higher education and the professions. Therefore a likely outcome of the state's attempt to be seen to be 'doing something' about youth unemployment (given a definition of the problem as one of supply rather than demand), will be the use of such initiatives as TVEI to appeal to working-class pupils as part of the attempt by teachers to keep the post-war settlement (between large numbers of working class pupils and the school) alive.[4]

In the previous section I tried to show that the school compliance of the ordinary kids has depended upon certain historical conditions in which the reward structure of the school and labour market have corresponded sufficiently to allow pupils to predict the likely outcomes of efforts in school. The teachers I spoke to in Middleport acknowledged much of what is taught in comprehensive schools has always been irrelevant to the future lives of working class school leavers. Until recently they could justify what they were doing on the ground that modest levels of academic achievement appeared to provide access to the types of jobs these pupils wanted. This rationale for a far from satisfactory situation can no longer be sustained, and the realization of this fact is seriously affecting teacher morale and forcing teachers to find ways of justifying their day-to-day practices to both themselves and their pupils. Coupled with the prevailing climate of government cutbacks and falling school rolls, the financial incentives offered to local education authorities and schools makes TVEI an all too inviting innovation (Watts, 1983; Bates *et al.*, 1984). The TVEI offers teachers the opportunity of bolstering their own sense of purpose and pupil compliance by placing less emphasis on the value of qualifications which can be traded in the market for jobs, and more upon the *direct* relevance of school learning to employment. This emphasis upon the extrinsic value of school *learning*, rather than school certificates, is seen as providing the opportunity for making the move to increase the *practical* content of the curriculum more *intrinsically* meaningful and interesting. But if more involvement in practical endeavour is the carrot dangled in front of the ordinary kids, there is also a stick. The more sinister aspect of recent attempts to reform the educational system involves a shift from relatively impersonal and objective (although academic) systems of educational assessment, to one where the school increasingly emphasizes the 'personality market': where pupils' subjective attributes are assessed on a highly subjective basis. It is the whole person which is now on show and at stake in the market for jobs. It is the personality package (Fromm, 1962) which must be sold in the marketplace. This trend, epitomized by the growing popularity of 'pupil profiles', emphasizes – as the kids do themselves – that it is not only 'what you know' which gets one a job.

This response by teachers is not surprising because we would expect teachers and careers officers to advance what they see to be in the best interests of *their* pupils or clients in the hope that it is they who will get a job (Kirton, 1983). Yet a consequence of teachers attempting to resolve their personal and professional troubles, and having to work within the constraints imposed by the 'chalk face', is that the question of school leaver 'employability' is not defined as it should be, as relative to the *demand* for labour, but as a personal trouble which can only be overcome at the expense of other teachers' equally deserving (or undeserving) pupils.[5]

The important point here, is that the absence of an alternative politics of education to Thatcherism – which emphasizes the freedom of the individual to be unemployed as a price of market competition, and the restoration of *social* rather than educational authority and discipline *through* the classroom (Hall, 1983, p. 3) – amounts to a roaring silence. One of the reasons why the teaching profession and others concerned with the present trends in British education have failed to mobilize popular support for an alternative politics of education results from an apparent inability to counter the argument that the school has failed to meet the 'needs' of industry and consequently needs to be trimmed and restructured. The issue of the relationship between the educational system and the economy must be confronted head on if an alternative educational strategy is to gain credibility and 'work'! There are at least three reasons for this.

First, the reduction of social and educational inequality is a political, not an educational goal. It has to be set *for* education, not just *in* education (Hall, 1983, p. 6).

Secondly, popular support for educational reform and investment in education has always been couched in terms of its beneficial impact for Britain's economic development (Halsey, Floud and Anderson, 1961; Vaizey, 1962).

Thirdly, many of those whom the school serves will evaluate being in school with an eye to their future economic and social roles beyond the school gates (Ashton and Field, 1976; Griffin, 1985).

The real issue is *not* whether any connection should exist between education and industry but *how* the connection is made. There is a considerable difference between teaching *about* industry and teaching *for* industry (Jamieson and Lightfoot, 1981). Moreover, if we are going to meet the social and economic demands of an advanced capitalist democracy, we will require young women and men to be capable of responding to new opportunities, which will include periods of retraining, but also allow them to benefit constructively from a shorter working week and a shorter working life (Watts, 1983; Handy, 1984; Williams, 1985). If Britain is to meet these demands it is not more *vocational* education which is required during the compulsory school years, but a more *general* education of *all* pupils.[6] The way to ensure the provision of a workforce to meet the *social* and economic needs of the late twentieth century requires that we *break down class and gender inequalities, not impose them, which I believe will be the result of the TVEI in many schools.*

The reason why I believe this to be the case, partly stems from the unsurprising finding that pupils construct their social identities (to which occupational identity is central), in class and gender specific ways. For example, although the ordinary kids shared a frame of reference towards the future in terms of 'getting on' in working-class terms, the types of employment and ways in which they can become adults in a respectable fashion varied between the sexes. If we are genuinely interested in producing the 'labour force of the future', the educational system must attempt to breakdown sexism in schools which operates against both boys and girls and fosters the development of gender specific occupational preferences and expectations by, for example, *reinforcing* the processes through which boys enter metalwork, woodwork, and design, craft and technology and, for girls, home economics, childcare and office practice (Whyte *et al.,* 1985).

A study of the ordinary kids in Middleport also shows that because categories of pupils are so closely related to class cultural understandings of being a working class adult, it is only when the school offers an 'out' both subjectively and objectively that the costs and benefits of being defined as a swot and 'getting out' of the working class are truly posed for the majority of these pupils.[7] Conservatives such as Hampson (1980) however have argued that:

> Young people's perception of jobs are often outdated and their aspirations circumscribed by social and cultural factors. The problem is to overcome the pupil's family, background and peer group influences (Hampson, 1980 p. 93.).

This lack of openness to new possibilities Hampson considers to be a problem of 'ignorance' to be overcome by better careers advice and sources of occupational information. But when ordinary kids discuss school and adulthood they are not expressing attitudes based on an *ignorance* of alternatives; they are expressing collective *knowledge* of ways of being a working-class pupil and an adult in Middleport. Their orientations are grounded in the material practices of working-class people, transmitted from generation to generation, and are the basis for establishing personal dignity,[8] social identity and social status in a class society. They will not easily give up understandings which serve to define who they are, and to maintain a sense of social dignity, unless there are genuine opportunities to make a *new* future. The importance of this point reminds us that the educational system cannot compensate for society (Bernstein, 1969), and so long as sexual discrimination is practised by employers against any application for employment which does not conform to appropriate gender specification, or as long as the attempt to encourage the ordinary kids to conceptualize their future in 'new' ways is not supported by equal access to a comprehensive education or genuine opportunities beyond the school gate, the school's impact on pupil attitudes and preferences will be small.

Conclusion

The scenario of the educational system I have briefly sketched in the latter part of this chapter is far removed from the current trend in secondary education, and from the problems of 'growing up' if one is a working-class teenager in the 1980s. In the present political climate the stage is set for increasing inequalities of educational opportunity (Dale, 1983). I have argued that efforts to find vocational solutions to social and economic problems are part of an attempt (for whatever reason, or indeed lack of reason), to maintain the existing patterns of social and educational inequalities. The burden of the growing contradiction within capitalist Britain – which in Marxist terms can be expressed as a contradiction between the forces and relations of production – has fallen heavily on working-class youth.

It remains unclear what will be the long-term consequences of contemporary economic and social change. What we can conclude is that it is not only the political consensus concerning the role of the educational system which has collapsed (and awaits appropriate political responses to Thatcherism): it is also a working class understanding of being in school and becoming adult. The personal problems this has caused have been defined as private problems which the individual must look to him or herself to resolve, rather than as a public issue of social structure which raises uncomfortable questions about the sort of society we have and the sort of society we want.

It has also been show that ordinary boys and girls usually define these personal troubles in individualistic and fatalistic ways. However, the inability of the labour market to provide them with a means of maintaining a sense of personal dignity and achieving adult status challenges their sense of social justice. The allocation of middle-class kids to middle-class jobs has not led to working-class revolts; the schools' attempt to determine who gets a job and who is unemployed on the basis of school performance may meet with far greater resistance. For the first time in British history the school will become an ideological battle ground where the legitimation of educational outcomes – as much as the school's day-to-day practices – must be won among working-class youth, because it is no longer a matter of educational outcomes determining the type of jobs pupils will enter, but increasingly, of determining who gets any job. The new battle over 'education', like the ordinary kids' fight to become adult in a respectable fashion, is only just beginning.

Acknowledgment

I would like to thank Chris Harris for his comments on an earlier draft of this chapter.

Notes

1 The data which inform this study were collected between 1981 and 1984. All fifth-form pupils from two coeducational working-class schools were given a self-completion questionnaire, along with selected classes of mainly 'academic' pupils from a third school catering for pupils from a middle-class background. 451 fifth-form pupils (223 males and 228 females) completed the questionnaire. A subsample of 120 pupils were then interviewed. On the basis of these interviews and observations in Thomas High School (one of the working-class schools) it was clear that pupils distinguished three ways of *being* in school, which were characterized as being like 'rems', 'swots' or 'ordinary kids'. These are not the author's terms but those of the pupils. The term rem is taken from the term 'remedial'. However, it is important to note that although the term remedial is used with reference to non-examination pupils by teachers, when the term rem is used by the ordinary kids it has moral connotations. It is not that the rems are believed to be 'thick', but that they are unwilling to 'make an effort'. It was the members of the conspicuous male anti-school subculture in Thomas High School who were most likely to be referred to as rems. The swots are alternatively those pupils located in the upper bands of the school and who were identified as spending all their time working and never having a laugh or getting into trouble with teachers. In Thomas High School to be studying for O-levels was almost by definition to be a swot. The ordinary kids stand between the rems and swots. They are defined with reference to what they are not, rems or swots, rather than what they are, 'ordinary' or 'average'.

   The questionnaire data were used in an attempt to quantify how many rems, swots and ordinary kids there were, because these different ways of being in school were closely related to different pupil orientations. On the basis of pupils' attitudes to school, future educational plans, occupational preferences, and school performance, it was possible to distinguish 49 rems; 177 swots; and 225 ordinary kids (see Brown, 1987a).

2 The main source of information was a postal questionnaire administered 18 months after attaining school leaving age. Three hundred and eighteen of the 451 young people in the original sample responded.

3 However, these are still expressed in individualistic and fatalistic terms.

4 In some circumstances TVEI may overcome this problem by linking into the academic studies which will exclude many of the rems and ordinary kids from participating. The point is that it is not for *all* pupils.

5 And there is evidence that by continuing to tie teacher authority closely to the exchange value of school learning for jobs, it highlights rather than resolves contradictions in the school's attempt to win the compliance of ordinary working class kids.

6 This is particularly appropriate given the time for skills training after the age of 16 in colleges and on the extended two-year Youth Training Schemes.

7 Even then there is no guarantee that location in the upper-band will lead working class pupils to conceptualize their futures in this way.

8 Albeit frequently at the expense of other working class pupils who they define as morally inferior.

References

ASHTON, D. (1986) *Unemployment Under Capitalism*. Brighton: Wheatsheaf.

ASHTON D. and FIELD, D. (1976) *Young Workers: From School to Work.* London: Hutchinson.

BATES. I. *et al.* (1984) *Schooling for the Dole?* London: Macmillan.

BAZALGETTE, J. (1978) *School Life and Work Life.* London: Hutchinson.

BERNSTEING, B. (1969) *Class Codes and Control,* Vol. 2. London: Routledge & Kegan Paul.

BOURDIEU, P. and PASSERON. J.C. (1977) *Reproduction in Education, Society and Culture.* London: Sage.

BOWLES, S. and GINTIS, H. (1976) *Schooling in Capitalist America: Educational Reform and the Contradictions of Economic Life.* London: Routledge & Kegan Paul.

BOYSON, R. (1975) *The Crisis in Education.* London: Woburn Press.

BROWN, P. (1987a) *Schooling Ordinary Kids: Inequality, Unemployment and the New Vocationalism.* London: Tavistock.

BROWN, P. (1987b) 'The new vocationalism: A curriculum for inequality?', in COLES. B. *The Search for Jobs and the New Vocationalism.* Milton Keynes: Open University.

CARTER, M. (1966) *Into Work.* Harmondsworth: Penguin.

CENTRAL POLICY REVIEW STAFF (1980) *Education, Training and Industrial Performance.* London: HMSO.

CLARKE, L. (1980). *The Transition from School to Work: A Critical Review of Research in the United Kingdom.* London: HMSO.

CORRIGAN, P. (1979) *Schooling the Smash Street Kids.* London: Macmillan.

DALE, R. (1983) 'Thatcherism and education', in AHIER. J. and FLUDE. M. (eds) *Contemporary Education Policy.* London: Croom Helm, pp. 233–56.

FROMM, E. (1962) 'Personality and the market place', in NOSOW. S. and FORM. W.H. (eds) *Man, Work and Society.* New York: Basic Books, pp. 446–52.

GASKELL, J. and LAZERSON, M. (1980) 'Between school and work: Perspectives of working class youth', *Interchange,* 11, pp. 80–96.

GRIFFIN, C. (1985) *Typical Girls?: Young Women from School to the Job Market.* London: Routledge & Kegan Paul.

HALL, S. (1983) 'Education in crisis', in WOLPE. A.M. and DONALD. J. (eds) *Is There Anyone Here from Education.* London: Pluto, pp. 2–10.

HALSEY, A.H., FLOUD, J. and ANDERSON, C.A. (eds) (1961) *Education, Economy and Society.* New York: Free Press.

HAMPSON, K. (1980) 'Schools and work', in PLUCKROSE H. and WILBY. P. (eds) *Education 2000.* London: Temple Smith, pp. 85–94.

HANDY, C. (1984) *The Future of Work.* Oxford: Robertson.

HARGREAVES, D. (1967) *Social Relations in a Secondary School.* London: Routledge & Kegan Paul.

HOPPER, E. (1971) 'Notes on stratification, education and mobility in industrial societies', in HOPPER, E. (ed.) *Readings in the Theory of Educational Systems.* London: Hutchinson, pp. 13–37.

JAMIESON, I. and LIGHTFOOT, M. (1981) 'Learning about work', *Educational Analysis,* 2, pp. 37–51.

JENKINS, R. (1983) *Lads, Citizens and Ordinary Kids.* London: Routledge & Kegan Paul.

KAHL, J.A. (1961) 'Common man boys', in HALSEY, A.H. *et al.* (eds) *Education, Economy and Society.* New York: Free Press, pp. 348–66.

KELVIN, P. and JARRETT, J.E. (1985) *Unemployment: Its Social Psychological Effects.* Cambridge: Cambridge University Press.

KIRTON, D. (1983) 'The impact of mass unemployment on careers guidance, in the Durham coalfield', in FIDDY. R. (ed.) *In Place of Work.* Lewes: Falmer Press, pp. 99–112.

LEONARD, D. (1980) *Sex and Generation: A Study of Courtship and Weddings*. London: Tavistock.

MSC (MANPOWER SERVICES COMMISSION) (1985) *TVEI Review 1985*. Sheffield: Manpower Services Commission.

MILLS, C.W. (1971) *The Sociological Imagination*. Harmondsworth: Penguin.

MINISTRY OF EDUCATION (1947) *School and Life*. London: HMSO.

PARSONS, D. (1985) *Changing Patterns of Employment in Great Britain - A Context for Education*. Sheffield: Manpower Services Commission.

ROBERTS, K. (1974) 'The entry into employment: an approach towards a general theory', in WILLIAMS, W.M. (ed.) *Occupational Choice*. London: George Allen & Unwin, pp. 138-57.

ROBERTS, K. (1984) *School Leavers and their Prospects: Youth and the Labour Market in the 1980s*. Milton Keynes: Open Univerity.

RUNCIMAN, W.G. (1966) *Relative Deprivation and Social Justice*. London: Routledge & Kegan Paul.

SENNETT, R. and COBB, J. (1977) *The Hidden Injuries of Class*. Cambridge: Cambridge University Press.

VAIZEY, J. (1962) *Education for Tomorrow*. Harmondsworth: Penguin.

WATTS, A.G. (1978) 'The implications of school-leaver unemployment for careers education in schools', *Journal of Curriculum Studies*, 10, pp. 233-50.

WATTS, A.G. (1983) *Education, Unemployment and the Future of Work*. Milton Keynes: Open University.

WHYTE, J. et al. (eds) (1985) *Girl Friendly Schooling*. London: Methuen.

WIENER, M.J. (1981) *English Culture and the Decline of the Industrial Spirit, 1850-1980*. Cambridge: Cambridge University Press.

WILLIAMS, S. (1985) *A Job to Live*. Harmondsworth: Penguin.

WILLIS, P. (1977) *Learning to Labour*. Farnborough: Saxon House.

WILLMOTT, P. (1966) *Adolescent Boys of East London*. London: Routledge & Kegan Paul.

On the Dole
4.4 Frank Coffield, Carol Borrill and Sarah Marshall

Commentary

Youth unemployment is no stranger to the North East. Witness a speech of the Lord Mayor of Newcastle upon Tyne made in 1937:

> In this area there are thousands of young persons of both sexes who are now attaining the age of twenty without ever having done a day's work. They see no prospect of employment... (Quoted by Horne, 1983, p. 314.)

Most writers agree (see Jahoda, 1979; Watts, 1983; Warr, 1983a; and Roberts, 1984) that unemployment has adverse effects on adults. But there is still a debate about the effects of being on the dole on young people who, it is believed, are at 'the most vulnerable age emotionally' (Ridley, 1981). Jobless young adults, Roberts (1984) argued 'lack relevant aims and motives' and their mental health has been shown to deteriorate. Jackson *et al.* (1983), for example, found that compared with those in jobs, young adults on the dole are 'less satisfied with life, have lower self-esteem, suffer greater depression and anxiety, and have lower social and family adjustment scores'. Additionally, Roberts commented there are fears that the lack of an 'adult wage' at sixteen, which until recently compensated those who had failed at school, will lead to young adults rejecting society. There is concern that the consequences may be an increase in crime, policing problems and 'embittered young adults, available for mobilization by extremist political movements' (p. 72).

Roberts' discussion of the effects of unemployment on young people also considered the alternative argument 'that unemployment is far less devastating for young people than adults'. This view is shared by Watts (1983, p. 103) who argued, 'some school leavers who have not experienced much occupation socialization, and who are not impressed by the employment opportunities open to them, will not be as adversely affected by unemployment as most older adults'. Warr's (1983a, p. 308) comments are in the same vein:

> Teenagers who are unemployed tend to have fewer financial problems than other unemployed people, for instance because they may be living reasonably cheaply with parents. They carry forward from school a network of friends and leisure activities, and the social stigma of unemployment may be less for them than for unemployed middle-aged people.

Our fieldwork challenges the ideas of Roberts, Watts and Warr on a number of points. We found that unemployment tended not to be seen as a problem by young people when they first left school, and so as Watts and Warr suggested, they were not adversely affected at that time. But this was *only* during their early days on the dole. As periods of unemployment lengthened the women and men in our study began to experience real and substantial financial problems, particularly if they took on the financial responsibilities of marriage and children. The majority of young women and men in our study did 'carry forward from school a network of friends', but at most they could afford to socialize with them once or twice a week when on the dole and often tended to sink into social isolation. Rather than the social stigma being less for unemployed young adults we believe that they are doubly stigmatized: not only are they on the dole, but they are also in the no man's land of adolescence without the status accorded to either adults or children.

Roberts (1984) presented additional evidence to support the idea that 'young people can cope' with unemployment. First, he suggested they have families who can support them and, as it is now more usual for young women and men to remain financially dependent on their parents, 'adult independence can be achieved without wage-earning status'. Our fieldwork suggested that families would have difficulty supporting young adults indefinitely. Parents should not be expected to, nor should the young be denied the opportunity to become financially independent. How can full adult status be achieved while women and men depend on their parents to buy their clothes and pay for their entertainment? We wish to add to Robert's suggestion that young adults no longer see the dole as charity. Those in our study who received social security benefit saw it as their right, but they still felt like scroungers because of their treatment by older adults, social security officials and the media.

Roberts also reported that young people suffer less while unemployed because they have 'no occupational identities to shatter, and... their personalities cannot be assaulted in quite the same way as life-long steel workers and dockers' (p. 73). We believe their position is much worse than this suggests: young adults who never have had a job have no occupational identity at all – they are not even an unemployed shop assistant or joiner, they are simply *unemployed*.

We do not hold much faith either in the argument put forward by Roberts that young adults can cope with unemployment because, by virtue of their youth, they can 'realistically expect their prospects to improve'. A more accurate scenario for the future was painted in *Economic Prospects for the North* (Robinson, 1982, p. 123) where the conclusion was reached that: 'Some of the older members of the workforce are clearly destined never to work again and some young people may never work.' Finally, Roberts suggested that young people can adapt to unemployment particularly in areas where it has persisted throughout the 1950s and 1960s. The trend, he argued, is for young adults to get used to being unemployed and to cope rather than to 'fester and eventually explode' into political action. In addition, survival skills that have been passed down through generations can be taught to young adults by their parents: how to claim their rights and how to survive on low incomes. It is also in areas of persistent unemployment, Roberts claimed, that leisure activities and social contacts are usually available to help pass the time.

We found some evidence to support these arguments. The women and men in our study were not involved in political action as a response to unemployment, and a few young adults seemed to have given up all hope of finding a job. But we would agree with Hirsch (1983) who commented that it is a mistake to view passive *acceptance* of unemployment as an indication that people judge their unemployment as *acceptable*. We want to stress that unemployment was reluctantly and gradually accepted by young adults – because there was no other option available. This acceptance, however, did not always occur in areas where unemployment was most persistent. Some of the young adults who suffered the most lived in such areas.

Roberts' discussion of unemployment considered evidence which supported two opposing views: that young adults in unemployment suffer either more or less because of their age. Our evidence suggested, however, that attempting to discuss one global reaction to unemployment is unproductive as young adults' responses varied considerably: the young unemployed are not an homogeneous group, self-contained and hermetically sealed off from the rest of the population. For the same reasons attempts at isolating the psychological characteristics of the unemployed are doomed to failure. There is no sharp division between the employed and the unemployed. The most common pattern followed by school-leavers and young adults in our study was to move from government scheme to unemployment, then back to government scheme, and on to a further period of unemployment with occasional breaks when in a job.

We were left in no doubt after our two-and-a-half years of contact with young adults who were regularly on the dole, that with only the one exception we mention they all wanted employment and were prepared to take almost any kind of proper job. We were also left in no doubt that much of the time most young adults were adversely affected by unemployment, but there were exceptions. We found that their reactions varied, and moreover an individual's feelings about being on the dole changed markedly during a single period of unemployment.

Our evidence suggested a complex interaction between individual factors such as abilities and character and other moderating variables identified by Warr (1983a) and Roberts (1984) such as family support, finances and social contact. Our extended period of contact with them, however, has emphasized the extent to which all these factors can change with time. The detrimental effect of unemployment does not, as Warr (1983a, 1983b) has suggested, simply increase the longer a person is on the dole. Changes such as the government deciding to reduce social security by £3.10, or quarrels with parents about moping round the house or friends finding employment were all likely to increase young adults' suffering, but such changes occurred to different people at different times during periods on the dole. Other changes, such as meeting a new partner or finding a job on the side, made being on the dole more tolerable.

We found no simple connection between duration of unemployment and young adults' reactions to being on the dole, and therefore question Breakwell's (1984) very specific finding that young women and men become depressed around their sixth week of unemployment. This would seem to us to be an artefact of the questionnaire methods used rather than a reflection of either the variety of reactions *among* individuals or the variations *within* any one individual. The evidence discussed above also leads us to raise questions about the findings of researchers such as Powell and Driscoll (1973), Harrison (1976) and Hill (1978), who claimed that people go through the following clear stages when they become unemployed: shock, optimism, despair and finally resignation. While some young adults in our study *did* seem to give up hope, this response changed dramatically when they finally found employment and easily fitted into a full-time job.

We found that young adults blamed themselves for being unemployed. This has been confirmed time and again by researchers such as Norris (1978), Stirling (1982), and Cashmore (1984). Why was it that young adults blamed themselves even when they were aware that there were over three million unemployed and a scarcity of jobs? There were a number of interconnected reasons that reflect the way young people viewed society and not just their attitudes to the specific problem of unemployment.

Young adults (and presumably many older adults) did not make the connection between national statistics about the recession and their own subjective experiences, nor were they used to talking about their own lives except in personal terms. In addition, the young adults lived in a society where the political atmosphere sought to divide the populace – no longer into biblical sheep and goats – but into high fliers and lame ducks. The endless exhortations to individual effort and individual competition in the so-called enterprise society provoke intense feelings among those who lose (as some must) and who are then invited to consider their failure as a personal one. The widely held assumption is that, if young adults cannot find a job, then they have only their own lack of skills or lack of effort to blame, particularly if they have been introduced to all manner of job searching and interview techniques on a government training scheme. The media and conservative politicians alike perpetuate the myth that all can succeed through hard work by publicizing stories of the infrequent individuals who move from rags to riches. As a consequence, British society is prone to view unemployment as a personal trouble rather than as a public issue, to use the terms of Wright Mills (1970).

Two general themes emerge from this discussion. First, our evidence suggests strongly that we need to move from individual, psychological explanations of mass phenomena like unemployment to more sociological and collective interpretations. Secondly, the constant harping of the character or ability of those who happen to be unemployed is a good example of the fallacy of individualism. We use this term to refer to a general principle whereby young adults explain social mobility, financial success and failure, employment and unemployment by exclusive reference to the characteristics of the individuals concerned. We would agree with Richard Jenkins (1983, p. 132) who made the further point that 'power and inequality become transformed, as a result, into the expression and reflection of real differences in the qualities of individuals'.

In addition, Kelvin (1984) has pointed out that the very language we use in connection with unemployment stigmatizes people. For example, the unemployed receive 'allowances' and 'benefits' rather than payments which can be considered as rights, and these and other terms such as 'dole', 'assistance' and 'relief' are 'all redolent with images of charity to the inadequate' (p. 419).

One of the main observations of our research is that the unemployed are not a discrete group. As this chapter has illustrated, it was the same young adults, approximately half our sample, who during the relatively short period of two-and-a-half years when we knew them, had been in and out of shit jobs, on and off govvies and the dole. The present crisis of youth unemployment cannot be explained by a sudden decline in the standards of schooling nor by a lack of employable skills among school-leavers; it has been caused more than anything else by the virtual collapse of the job market which never showed much interest in training young adults anyway. The figures for Newcastle make the point: in 1974, 80 per cent of all school-leavers found full-time employment, which nine years later in 1983 was obtained by just 16.6 per cent. In Gateshead in one week in September 1982, more than 4,000 young people aged 16 to 18, who were either unemployed or on government schemes, were chasing the twelve jobs known to Careers Officers and Jobcentres. Such figures make nonsense of any attempt to establish the personal characteristics of the unemployed. We examined our own data to see whether – in a particular month – we could differentiate between those in a job and those who were not. Neither educational qualifications, nor physical attributes, nor enthusiasm for employment, nor any other personal quality that we could think of explained the difference. Having relatives, friends or local connections who notified you in advance about possible vacancies explained more of the variation than any other factor.

While youth unemployment is no stranger to the North East, long-term unemployment for young adults is a new phenomenon and no one as yet is sure what effect this will have on the present generation of school-leavers. How will they feel in the year 2000 when they look back on sixteen years of unemployment and look forward to a further thirty plus years of unemployment before 'retiring' at the ages of 60 or 65? If we are to see the emergence of a new subclass of young adults who are state pensioners from the age of 17, then political discussion must turn from the provision of a minimum *wage* to the guarantee of a minimum *income*.

References

BREAKWELL, G. (1984) 'Knowing Your Place; Finding Your Place', *ESRC Newsletter*, 52, 29-30.

CASHMORE, E.E. (1984) *No Future - Youth and Society*, Heinemann, London.

HARRISON, R. (1976) 'The demoralising experience of prolonged unemployment', *Department of Employment Gazette*, 84, 339-48.

HILL, J. (1978) 'The psychological impact of unemployment', *New Society*, 118-20.

HIRSCH, D. (1983) *Youth Unemployment: a background paper*, Youthaid, London.

HORNE, J. (1983) 'Youth Unemployment Programmes: a historical account of the development of dole colleges', in GLEESON, D. (ed.), *Youth Training and the Search for Work*, Routledge and Kegan Paul, London.

JACKSON, P.K., STAFFORD, E.M., BANKS, M.H. and WARR, P.B. (1983) 'Unemployment and Psychological Distress in Young People', *Journal of Applied Psychology*, 3, 525-35.

JAHODA, M. (1979) 'The impact of unemployment in the 1930s and the 1970s', *Bulletin of the British Psychological Society*, 32, 309-14.

JENKINS, R. (1983) *Lads, Citizens and Ordinary Kids: Working-class Youth Life-styles in Belfast*, Routledge and Kegan Paul, London.

KELVIN, P. (1984) 'The Historical dimensions of social psychology, the case of Unemployment', in TAUFEL, H. (ed.) *The Social Dimension*, Vol, 2., Cambridge University Press, 405-24.

NORRIS, G.M. (1978) 'Unemployment, subemployment and personal characteristics', (A) 'The inadequacies of traditional approaches to unemployment', *Sociological Review*, 26, 1, 89-108. (B) 'Job separation from work historics: the alternative approach', *Sociological Review*, 26, 2, 327-47.

POWELL, P.H., and DRISCOLL, P.E. (1973) 'Middle-class professionals face unemployment', *New Society*, 10, 2, 18-26.

RIDLEY, F.F. (1981) 'View from a disaster area: unemployed youth in Merseyside', *Political Quarterly*, 52, 16-27.

ROBERTS, K. (1984) *School Leavers and their Prospects*, Open University Press, Milton Keynes.

ROBINSON, F. (1982) *Economic Prospects for the North*, Centre for Urban and Regional Development Studies, University of Newcastle-upon-Tyne.

STIRLING, A. (1982) 'Preparing school leavers for unemployment', *Bulletin of the British Psychological Society*, 35, 421-22.

WARR, P. (1983a) 'Work, jobs and unemployment', *Bulletin of the British Psychological Society*, 36, 305-11.

WARR, P. (1983b) 'Job Loss, Unemployment and Psychological Well Being', in ALLEN, V. and VAN DE VLIERT, E. (eds) *Role Transition*, Plenum Press, New York.

WATTS, A.G. (1983) *Education, Unemployment and the Future of Work*, Open University Press, Milton Keynes.

WRIGHT MILLS, C. (1970) *The Sociological Imagination*, Penguin, Harmondsworth.

**ESRC – Young People
in Society
Ken Roberts**

This article plots a sociological starting point for the Economic and Social Research Council (ESRC) 16–19 Initiative. It surveys current socio-economic trends, summarizes findings and conclusions from recent and, in some cases, on-going enquiries, and thereby defines our present state of knowledge about the situations of young people.

The exercise is sociological in focusing on youth's social context. Successive sections sketch recent trends in the economy, education and the family that are restructuring young people's situations. Sociology's special interest in youth in the 1980s concerns the interrelationships between these trends, the various configurations – the youth situations currently being forged, and the implications for young people's political behaviour and orientations, peer relationships, leisure activities, self-concepts and other socio-psychological processes.

This review concentrates on trends and investigations in the 1980s. Ten years ago a review of sociological youth research would have been very different and possibly much closer to the ESRC initiative's focal concerns. In the mid-1980s British sociology has more research in process among young people, but may appear to have lost sight of youth cultures. Young people are now being studied to clarify trends and to test theories about the organization of labour markets, gender and whether leisure can compensate for unemployment. Theories about youth cultures, youth as a developmental process and life-stage, the transition to adulthood and the reproduction of social patterns have been set aside. However, the older concerns and theories have not been abandoned or eclipsed so much as placed in abeyance while investigators take stock of the effects of broader social and economic changes on young people's situations.

The Sociology of Youth Culture

The sociology of youth was born between the wars when Mead (1935), Reuter (1937), and their contemporaries claimed youth as a social phenomenon, a product of specific types of society rather than an inevitable stage in bio-psychological maturation. In post-Second World War British and American sociology the study of youth culture became a major research area. It was theoretically lively, sensitive to and often in the vanguard of broader intellectual fashions, and attracted scores of empirical enquiries. At the time, in the 1950s, the main issue in youth research was the extent to which youth cultures were rebellious, at war with mainstream society (Coleman, 1961).

Youth culture was a social issue as well as a sociological problem. Delinquency research and the investigation of youth culture became virtually synonymous. Functionalism was then sociology's leading theory, particularly in North America. The theory's defenders tried to explain how, despite surface appearances, adolescent rebellion and dissent could be processes of continuing socialization, how this aided the emancipation of young people from childhood roles and restrictions, taught independence and other qualities required for eventual entry into adult roles, and reconciled inconsistencies between values inculcated during childhood and the adult prospects that awaited teenagers (Elkin and Westley, 1955; Parsons, 1954; Smith, 1962).

During the 1960s functionalism was jettisoned, and youth research gained a fresh impetus alongside a new ascendant brand of deviance theory. Youth and delinquency research remained intimately related. They were not only influenced by broader theoretical fashions – phenomenology, ethnomethodology and symbolic interactionism, but became major vehicles for popularizing these theories in British sociology. New deviance theorists taught that delinquents were simply different and that their deviance was only relative to other groups' norms. Explaining delinquent behaviour, it was argued, required a transcendence of official definitions. Youth and delinquency researchers, therefore, endeavoured to appreciate their subjects. The latter's conduct was related to and explained, in the first instance, by their own values, beliefs and definitions of their situations. Official statistics were dismissed or treated as just one of many possible definitions of social reality. Ethnography became the orthodox type of youth research. Fieldworkers sought to 'get inside' youth cultures, much as social anthropologists had once 'gone native' before returning to 'tell it as it really happens' (Cohen, 1971; Parker, 1974; Young, 1971).

For a time youth and deviance theory abandoned not just functionalism but the entire vocabulary of social structure. The idea of society existing 'out there' as a system of interrelated institutions and roles awaiting actors was dismissed as an unhelpful metaphor. Deviance theorists insisted that social reality was fluid, not rigidly structured; that what had previously been treated as 'social facts' were ultimately beliefs and values. However, before long the new deviance theorists were proposing a newer criminology that resurrected society (Taylor *et al.*, 1973). A theory of social structure appeared necessary to explain the sources of, or young people's susceptibility to certain values and beliefs in preference to the alternatives, and to account for societal reactions. It also became evident that attempted cultural revolutions could encounter external realities that refused to crumble when challenged by unorthodox beliefs. Hence the argument for situating youth cultures, analysing them within and refusing to abstract them from their wider social contexts.

By the mid-1970s British sociology had a 'new wave' theory of youth cultures. The new wave retained deviance theory's insistence upon appreciating its subjects and support for ethnography, but incorporated a model of social structure derived from sociology's conflict tradition (Hall and Jefferson, 1976; Mungham and Pearson, 1976). After their release from the structural restrictions of childhood, young people were seen as heirs to cultures handed down through their families and neighbourhoods. In addition, they had access to cultural resources offered by the entertainment industries that had developed alongside post-war youth cultures. Young people were seen as beset by contradictions whose sources, however obscure to the actors, were attributed to wider social conflicts. The particular contradictions with which youth had to contend were seen as varying with family and neighbourhood backgrounds, educational attainments, gender, ethnic origins and labour market situations. Youth cultures, according to the new wave, were to be understood as collective attempts to generate solutions by young people facing common contradictions. The solutions were essentially cultural and imaginary, rather than material. They usually proved temporary and were eventually abandoned in preference for conventional adult roles (Cohen, 1976; Hebdige, 1979). But the new wave refused to accept this abandonment as functionally inevitable and insisted that, given some favourable historical situation, youth cultures could become genuinely radical, even revolutionary instruments (Willis, 1977).

The language was different, but this sociological theory of youth culture had similar preoccupations to those of social psychologists who were, for example interested in the development of young people's self-identities and social representations. The research encouraged by the new wave sociology of youth explored young people's understanding of their societies, their own positions, and their attempts to negotiate then enact identities (Jenkins, 1983).

The new wave was always more of an agenda for, rather than a programme of accomplished research. The class model of society that the theory incorporated was asserted, then used to interpret, rather than tested by ethnographic evidence. Investigators never employed replicable measurements of their subjects' self-concepts and social beliefs. The theory was applied selectively. The investigations that it inspired dealt mainly with male, working-class youth. Girls were ignored or treated as appendages to male peer groups and youth cultures. This treatment would be justified and inevitable if, as Brake (1985) claims, all recent youth cultures have been masculine. However, some female and feminist followers of the new wave have attempted to apply its ideas and methods in studying the lives of female teenagers (McRobbie and Garber, 1976; Griffin, 1985).

The new wave and the preceding sociological literature on youth cultures are examined fully elsewhere (Smith, 1981; Brake, 1980, 1985; Roberts, 1983). It is unnecessary for this review to recapitulate in detail, but it is important to stress that sociology has not abandoned the ideas. They are prominent in the main recent textbooks and present day courses though the research itself has dried to a trickle. The sociologists who generated the new wave have probably grown too old to remain credible ethnographers of youth cultures and the generation has not been replaced. By the late-1970s the findings from ethnographic research among young working-class males had become predictable. Since then the literature has been overwhelmed by changes in the situations of working-class teenagers, and these changes themselves have preoccupied sociological investigations in the 1980s.

Throughout the 1960s and early 1970s the main 'facts' about teenagers' situations were well known and agreed. The vast majority of working-class teenagers finished school at 15 or 16. Most boys entered unskilled manual jobs or obtained apprenticeships. Girls were recruited into offices, factories and shops. The transition from school to work was soon followed by courtship and marriage. Trajectories and destinations were not in doubt. The main problems for theory and research concerned how young people became reconciled to their destinies, whether because of or in spite of the various youth cultures in which they became involved. Since the mid-1970s trajectories and outcomes have become doubtful. Hence the preoccupation of researchers in the 1980s with the effects of changes in employment, vocational training and education on young people's situations. As the effects of recent trends become clearer, the older genre could merit revival, possibly in the ESRC initiative.

The following sections discuss the main trends affecting young people that recent research has exploited, together with some questions about the trends' implications that are posed but so far unanswered, and which could be pursued in the type of fieldwork envisaged for the ESRC initiative – a set of longitudinal studies in different areas combining quantitative surveys with qualitative ethnographic methods. There remain serious gaps in our knowledge about the impact of recent trends in education and the labour market on young people's situations. Most of these gaps could be at least part filled by the ESRC enquiries. However, an even stronger case for a new research initiative can be made in terms of a need to revive the type of youth research that has fallen into abeyance, by exploring how young people are now coping, and the identities and understandings of their society that they are formulating in the new youth situations of the 1980s.

The Economy

The decine of youth employment. This is undoubtedly the most dramatic single development affecting young people and possibly the main reason why a new research initiative is deemed necessary. Jobs accessible to young people with just basic education have declined rapidly. In 1974, 61 per cent of 16 years olds were in employment: in 1984, only 18 per cent held jobs. Hence the talk of a 'vanishing youth labour market' (Ashton and Maguire, 1983).

Postponing work entry is a long-term historical trend. Throughout the twentieth century it has been making young people into 'age segregated outsiders' (President's Science and Advisory Committee, 1974). However, since the mid-1970s the trend has accelerated at a pace that was neither planned nor predicted. Various explanations have been offered and disputed.

Is the recent decline of youth employment due mainly to recession, to sector and occupation shifts, to new technologies, or to the internationalization of production and distribution? Is contemporary youth unemployment structural? If so, does this make it intractable? Would market forces clear unemployment if allowed to operate freely? Or does persistent unemployment reflect British governments' social and economic priorities?

A series of investigations have examined variations in unemployment rates between regions, males and females, with different educational levels, and from different ethnic groups. The ESRC enquiry will need to take account of these differences, but there is no need for a new initiative into these matters. The initiative will probably be ill-advised to attempt to participate in, let alone resolve debates about sources of and cures for youth unemployment. The enquiry envisaged will be better equipped to explore social and psychological implications rather than causes of the decline of youth employment.

Schemes have replaced jobs in most early school-leavers' immediate prospects. The current generation of special measures began with Job Creation Projects in 1975, from which a Work Experience Programme for young people was separated in 1976. In 1978 work experience was absorbed into a larger Youth Opportunities Programme, which was superseded by the Youth Training Scheme (YTS) in 1983. In 1983 and 1984, most 16 year old school-leavers entered the YTS (Employment Gazette, 1984) and in 1986 the scheme was extended from 12 to 24 months.

Successive special measures have been subjected to detailed investigation by the MSC (Bedeman and Courtenay, 1983) and independent researchers (Fiddy, 1983; Varlaam, 1984). As a result, we are well informed about who has entered the various programmes, the types of training, work experience and continuing education offered, and what happened to the young people subsequently.

Some of the more interesting findings have emerged incrementally rather than from single enquires. For instance, when special measures were first introduced to cater for a minority of school-leavers, the training and work experience overcame some disadvantages associated with lack of qualifications. Schemes have now become normal preludes to orthodox employment and, in the process, have ceased to compensate. The effects of social class, ethnic and educational backgrounds are now surviving the programmes (Bedeman and Courtenay, 1983; Greaves, 1983).

From the point of view of the ESRC initiative, the most interesting consequences of schemes may not be the immediate implications for trainees' prospects, but their cumulative impact on the process of work entry. School-leavers used to make smooth and rapid transitions into the workforce, along trajectories leading to adult jobs. The majority settled quickly. Those who changed jobs were mostly learning patterns of mobility associated with their occupations.

Transitions are now protracted. New transition systems are being created from training schemes and educational programmes (see below). The normal progression is now from school, to schemes to employment, often punctuated by periods of joblessness. It has been argued that these changes amount to a 'new curriculum' for the less able, the young people who used to be called 'Newson children' (Edwards, 1984).

Some commentators argue that this new curriculum is best understood in terms of social control (Loney, 1979; Rees and Atkinson, 1982). Young people are kept off the streets. The provision of training, hopefully leading to good jobs, secures their compliance. Yet the real functions of the new curriculum, it is argued, are to conceal the true level of unemployment, to shift the blame to the victims, to preserve young people's labour power, their willingness and ability to work while, simultaneously, deflating occupational aspirations and wage expectations into line with what, in most cases, are objectively limited prospects.

Quantitative decline has been accompanied by a deterioration in the quality of youth employment. From the Second World War until the end of the 1970s there was a trend towards narrower pay differentials between young and adult males, though not females (Wells, 1983). Subsequently age differentials have widened. Youth employment has become relatively lower paid, and less secure (Jones, 1983, 1984).

These trends are products of market conditions reinforced by government measures – the allowance fixed for youth trainees, and the Young Workers Scheme (which was replaced by the New Workers Scheme when the YTS was extended to two years). One body of opinion considers a further erosion in the terms of young people's employment desirable, to be achieved, possibly, by removing the protection of Wages Councils, and by further reductions in young adults' welfare rights.

The above trends have not been uniform throughout the country, in all business sectors, and have not affected all young people to the same extent. A side effect of the changes therefore has been to create or deepen divisions among out-of-school youth. Youth recruitment by some sectors has remained relatively buoyant. Banking and insurance, hotels and catering, and new technology firms are leading examples. Demand for better qualified young people has proved far more resilient than the less qualified's opportunities. School-leavers in areas with relatively low unemployment, and with business mixes in which growth sectors are well represented, have been protected from the general deterioration in opportunities.

The result has been widening gulfs – between regions, including the South and the rest, then within regions between young people who obtain primary employment, those left in secondary labour markets, others who are catered for in a new 'tertiary' sector created by special programmes, and an unemployed residue.

The above trends set the context and define problems for further research.

1   We need to identify and distinguish different career patterns that are being established among different groups of young people in different parts of the country. It was once sufficient to locate school leavers' destinations within the Registrar General's social classes or similar classifying schemes

conventionally used to grade adult occupations. Such members have ceased to describe the process of work entry. New typologies of early career patterns are required (Roberts *et al.*, 1982a; McDermott and Dench, 1983).

The following scheme is provisional. It may serve as a starting point, but the fieldwork could suggest a more satisfactory typology:

a   *Traditional transitions,* straight from school into primary occupations which can be practised into adulthood. Some young people still make such transitions which were the norm for most school-leavers in all parts of Britain until the mid 1970s.
b   *Protracted transitions,* which lead to primary adult employment via various combinations of schemes, youth jobs and periods of joblessness.
c   Early careers in which young people become trapped in special programmes, youth jobs and secondary labour markets.
d   Careers in which young people descend into *long-term unemployment.* Government measures that have reduced unemployment among 16–18 year olds have been accompanied by a rise in unemployment among the 19–25s. In some parts of the country, substantial numbers of young people are now proceeding from school through youth training, then becoming long-term unemployed. By age 20, with no substantial work experience, they have joined the 'hardcore', as employment service staff often describe them. Employers prefer 'nice fresh school-leavers' to young adults who have grown accustomed to idleness and settled into claimant roles. There is evidence of the long term young unemployed gravitating into separate social networks, becoming a new underclass in which social pressures to find work and individuals' commitment to employment are relaxed (Banks *et al.*, 1984).

2   We need to investigate the social-psychological implications of youth unemployment – long term, transitory, and repeated short episodes. The effects may vary considerably depending on the types of young people involved and the career patterns within their unemployment is located.

Recent investigations confirm that employment remains a crucial aid and symbol in becoming an adult (DES, 1983). The occupations in which they establish themselves or hope to enter are foundations for young people's social identities and self-concepts. So what happens when individuals leave school or training schemes then cannot obtain employment, or wish to protect their real selves from, rather than to identify or be identified with secondary occupations? Investigators have found that unemployment reduces young people's mental health scores. Work experience, YOP and now (presumably) the YTS can preserve well-being while individuals are on the programmes, but these benefits do not persist into subsequent periods of unemployment (Graves, 1983; Banks *et al.*, 1984). The findings from enquiries that have administered standardised tests of mental health are unambiguous, but they do not describe exactly how different groups of young people feel, flounder or cope.

3   The preceding passages have referred to a deterioration in young people's prospects, which is the popular, common sense view and the dominant academic interpretation of recent trends. However, there is an alternative diagnosis. It can be argued that youth labour markets in the 1980s are offering better vocational preparation than school-leavers received in previous decades.

Most youth unemployment consists of short episodes. The exceptionally high level of youth compared with adult unemployment is explicable partly in terms of young workers' mobility. Many appear willing to face and are able to cope with short spells out of work. As youth unemployment rises, periods between jobs lengthen, but rates of job-changing do not appear to diminish (Ashton and Maguire, 1984). The proportion of involuntary departures increases (Jones, 1983), but some young people seem not only able to cope, but actually prefer intermittent employment to continuous work in low paid, unskilled jobs (Roberts *et al.*, 1982b). The levels to which youth unemployment in Europe has now risen have been normal since the Second World War in North America where a period of 'milling around' is commonly regarded as a healthy preparation for life in a competitive, dynamic economy (Gaskell and Lazerson, 1980; Gordon, 1979; Freeman and Wise, 1982).

It can be argued that British school-leavers' former smooth and rapid transitions into the labour force involved hidden but heavy long-term costs – that decisive choices had to be made prematurely, and that vocational development was often stunted. If so, the more flexible youth labour markets of the 1980s could be offering new opportunities for experiment and self-assessment, and could be allowing young people to formulate, then set themselves en route towards realistic goals. Alongside current educational developments (see below), recent changes in youth labour markets could be nurturing 'enterprise cultures' among certain groups of young people, and the ESRC initiative should be aware of, and prepared to check out this possibility.

4   If youth unemployment is not the time-bomb once imagined, a source of discontent and frustration that will eventually explode, the main reasons may have less to do with young people discovering opportunities for growth and development in the new bracing conditions than their capacity to 'survive'. The ESRC initiative should examine the extent to which different groups of young people are using different resources and strategies to 'keep afloat':

a   *Work in 'alternative economies'* – self-employment, cooperatives and community projects. Are there any signs of youth unemployment being drained by the development of work outside orthodox employment? (Watts, 1983).

b   *Work in the 'black economy'* – illegal, and legal but undeclared.

c   *Voluntary work* – is an expansion of voluntary service a plausible solution to youth unemployment (Marsland, 1984), or should proposals for 'youth conscription' be resisted (Jeffs, 1982)?

d *Mobility* – to what extent do young people still insist on working close to their homes? Is high unemployment in certain regions leading to more youth migration?

Education

There has been little recent change at the top – in curricula, teaching methods or the proportions of young people gaining five O-levels, three A-levels, then proceeding to higher education. University and polytechnic expansion during the 1970s only kept pace with the size of school-leaving cohorts. The contraction in higher education in the mid-1980s has not been as sharp as the decline in the numbers reaching the normal age of entry. The major recent changes in education have involved the other 80 per cent.

More are staying on beyond 16. These students are becoming 'new sixth formers', and less than 14 per cent of school leavers are now completely unqualified. In 1974, 35 per cent of 16 year olds continued in education. By 1982, 48 per cent were staying on. This trend appears to have been checked by the introduction of the YTS. In 1984, 31 per cent of 16 year olds remained at school, and another 14 per cent transferred to full time further education. Girls are more likely than boys to stay on (50 per cent and 40 per cent).

If the financial implications for young people were neutral, if it was not financially advantageous to leave school and join the YTS or even remain unemployed, staying on would almost certainly become the majority choice. Already the issue of whether to leave or continue has become a matter of choice for virtually all young people. This is a novel situation in Britain.

Many educational institutions have become entrepreneurial, keen to enrol and to retain young people. Their efforts are likely to increase as the size of the age group declines. Schools sometimes fail to notice when sixth formers 'sign on'. Colleges design courses so that students can meet the 21 hour or whatever other rules are intended to prevent the abuse of social security in lieu of student grants.

Many young people who stay on obtain part-time jobs. Students have become a major source of labour in certain growth sectors, particularly catering and distribution. Educational institutions often ignore their own rules when full-time students take part-time jobs. Private finance, raised through part time employment, is playing an enlarged role in supporting students who remain at school, then proceed to college.

Traditional careers education is being engulfed by a 'new vocationalism' (Bates *et al.*, 1984). Since the 'Great Debate' there have been renewed attempts to promote work experience for secondary school pupils. Virtually all schools are now equipped with computers. Courses in information technology have multiplied. Many of these developments are supported under the MSC's Technical and Vocational Education Initiative (TVEI). By 1984 two-thirds of LEAs were involved. Simultaneously, the MSC's role in further education, as financier and arbiter of course content, is being strengthened. Young people are being prepared more thoroughly for employment that has become scarcer than ever.

Enrolments in part-time further education have risen. Off-the-job training, which often means college, is mandatory on the YTS. In 1974, 47 per cent of 16 year olds left school, obtained employment and severed connections with education. In 1984 only 24 per cent (13 per cent unemployed, and 11 per cent in jobs) had lost contact. These trends offer further support for claims that far from their prospects deteriorating, school leavers are now being given better than ever starts in working life.

Educational developments, like economic trends, raise a series of issues for investigation.

Why are more young people staying on despite the financial disincentives? Are they 'human capitalists', anticipating or hoping for vocational returns? Are they motivated by the intrinsic satisfactions? Or are they simply afraid of dropping out and entering the labour market? Are the identities and statuses associated with the student role attractive or repellent?

Do recent educational developments yield vocational returns? Up to now, education has played a major role in fixing and producing consistency between levels of occupational aspiration and attainment (Ryrie, 1983). In general, qualifications and years of schooling are still positively related to grades of employment and, indeed, to young people's chances of obtaining any jobs. Whether current developments are strengthening or eroding these relationships is less clear.

In the past, the returns from vocational courses have been no greater than from academic syllabuses (Freeman and Wise, 1982). So, do work experience, computing and other technical subjects that are being strenuously promoted within the TVEI and MSC-backed further education yield greater returns than students could expect from conventional studies?

Can Britain's new sixth formers, particularly those who leave after one year without taking A-levels, expect any vocational return? Even before the recent expansion, there was talk of over-inflated school systems, of young people being over educated and sickened by a 'diploma disease' (Dore, 1976), and of credentials failing to measure the true value of their holders' labour power (Berg, 1973). Evidence from the Scottish school-leavers surveys suggests that staying on may actually damage some young people's prospects (Raffe, 1984). Ashton and Maguire (1984) have found, among 18–24 year olds, that the unemployed are equally qualified as individuals in non-skilled jobs.

Some countries with generations of experience in mass post-compulsory education have long-running debates on the inherent dangers. One fear is that over-qualified employees will be dissatisfied and frustrated. Italian evidence links this syndrome with political radicalism (Barbagli, 1982). In contrast, in the USA Burris (1983) claims no major repercussions from over-education because the effects on job satisfaction are so marginal.

A new underclass? Europe's earlier elitist educational regimes distinguished successful minorities from the mass of young people. Today, in Britain and elsewhere, majorities can gain qualifications and stay on beyond the statutory requirements. Unqualified early leavers are now a minority. Enlarged and democratized school systems blur former divisions beneath elites while, simultaneously, separating minorities of failures from the mainstreams.

Coleman and Husen (1985) argue that these new educational practices are *helping to create a new underclass.* They claim that, within secondary schools, a tail-end abandons hope and effort, and sometimes attendance, long before the official leaving date. The majority of young people now leave school with qualifications, *so the failures are a disadvantaged minority.*

Whether their disadvantages persist will depend on labour market conditions. In times of high unemployment, as at present, when employers have scope for choice, it is possible that *current educational practices are creating or perpetuating an underclass,* and the ESRC initiative should test this possibility.

The enterprise culture. Aitken and Fasano (OECD, 1983) argue that educating workforces of the future will require flexible institutions which can offer opportunities for individualized learning. Economic recovery in Britain, according to one school of thought, requires the promotion of an enterprise culture in which, instead of being spoonfed, individuals learn to accept responsibility for equipping themselves with the education, training, skills and qualifications required for occupational success or even survival. A report from the National Economic Development Office (Hayes, *et al.,* 1984) claims that education and training in Japan, the USA and the Federal Republic of Germany, albeit in very different ways, nurture enterprise cultures, and that Britain must follow suit or fall further behind her competitors.

Some recent educational trends could be construed as movements in the right direction. More 16 year olds are choosing to stay on and the decision is becoming a matter of choice for all. Approximately a third of those who stay on transfer to further education. Some young people are pioneering their own forms of alternation - moving from education into training or employment, then back to college. Current educational trends could be creating an underclass at the bottom, and a more enterprising younger generation in the middle layers.

The Family

The economic and educational trends just described can hardly avoid influencing processes of family disengagement and formation, but the character of the implications remains unclear. Indeed, different groups of young people appear to be responding to objectively similar predicaments in opposite ways.

Some general trends in family patterns are well known and predate the recent changes in young people's situations.

PARENT–CHILD RELATIONSHIPS.

Child-rearing families are now an economically disadvantaged minority. They have become a minority as child-rearing has been compresed into a smaller part of a lengthening lifespan. The birth rate fell from 1965 until 1977. One result has been a further reduction in the proportion of child-rearing households, and there are still no signs of the birth rate returning to earlier levels.

Child-rearing families' economic disadvantages have mounted alongside labour market participation by married women. This has increased the opportunity costs of rearing children. Mothers of young children are disadvantaged in the search for work. They are less likely to be employed than other women. When obtained, their employment is typically low paid and part-time.

The direct costs of parenthood have risen more rapidly than welfare benefits. This is especially so with teenage children. The latter are remaining longer in education, and parental contributions to the maintenance of those entering higher education have been increased. Early school-leavers can no longer expect a rapid transition to affluence. They face immediate futures on training allowances, supplementary benefit and/or low wages. Welfare payments to the young unemployed have been reduced. Sixteen year old summer school-leavers' entitlement to benefit has been postponed until September. Housing and lodging allowances have already been reduced. Further cuts are now proposed.

These trends must have implications for teenagers' relationships with parents, for their roles and statuses in their families of orientation. As yet, however, the character of these implications is unclear. There are various possibilities and, probably, different trends among different groups.

Current trends could be 'strengthening the family' by confirming parental responsibilities and young people's dependence. There is evidence of some families and neighbourhoods reviving that traditional virtue, 'looking after your own', (Allat and Yeandle, 1984). Where they exist, strong family relationships appear to cushion and thereby limit the psychological damage otherwise inflicted by unemployment (Donovan and Oddy, 1982).

Alternatively, or in different families, current trends could be weakening and, in some cases, provoking breakdowns in parent-teenager relationships. Both parties may resent the burden of teenagers' dependence (Fagin and Little, 1984). According to Cusack and Roll (1985), the spread of unemployment and simultaneous cut-backs in the young unemployed's welfare rights, are contributing to a growing problem of teenage homelessness.

There are additional longer term trends, which, in some families, may have weakened parent–child relationships. Divorce and separation rates have risen. More teenagers now live with step-parents and in lone-parent households. Parents' sense of competence may have been undermined by the growth and professionalization of education, the influence of the mass media and, in recent years, by their inability to assist school leavers into employment (Coleman and Husen, 1985).

FAMILY FORMATION

Once again, the evidence is sparse and contradictory. On the one hand, there is support for a deceleration theory, of unemployment obstructing and delaying processes of growing up, going out, feeling adult and establishing heterosexual liaisons (Gurney, 1980; Hendry *et al.*, 1984). Other evidence supports an acceleration theory. Girls' first responses to employment difficulties sometimes include more strenuous efforts to 'get a man' (Griffin, 1985). For young women, marriage and parenthood have always been an alternative route, arguably their primary route to adult status. Unemployment must make this route appear more attractive than ever.

National trends in marriage and fertility among teenagers offer some support for both theories.

1   There is no teenage baby boom. Birth rates among the married under 20s have fallen since the mid-1970s. There are fewer teenage marriages and legitimate births, which is consistent with the deceleration theory.

2   However, illegitimate birth rates among under 20 years old women (and in older age groups) have risen. There are now more illegitimate than legitimate births to the under 20s. The majority of these births appear to be unplanned and unwanted, but two-fifths of teenage mothers say that they intended or did not mind having babies (Francome, 1983; Simms and Smith, 1985). Most sexually active teenagers are now controlling their fertility successfully. The rise in illegitimate births, therefore, may be cited in support of the acceleration theory. The stigma of illegitimacy has probably lessened and, in some communities, 'precipitous routes' to parenthood and marriage have been accepted for generations (Klein, 1964; Wallace, 1985).

3   Cohabiting, often but not always in pre-marital relationships, has become more prevalent. This suggests that current trends may not be fully comprehensible in terms of the acceleration or deceleration of older transition processes. New strategies and routes to family formation are probably being developed, by some young people. Getting married and leaving the parental home are no longer the indivisible steps that they appeared to earlier generations, particularly in working-class communities (Leonard, 1980).

National trends can conceal numerous, sometimes conflicting tendencies. There is plentiful scope for the ESRC initiative to contribute to knowledge:

1   It should aim to clarify the sexual and domestic careers that are taking shape in different sections of the population.

2   It should examine how these career opportunities are structured by trends in education and employment, plus the operation of housing markets and welfare rights (Ineichen, 1981).

3   It should distinguish the implications of current trends for males and females. There is no evidence of unemployment propelling males into marriage and paternity. Quite the reverse: unemployed males appear condemned to perpetual adolescence, and to sexual exploits in fantasy (Wallace, 1985). This may limit girls' escapes from the labour market to lone-parenthood, and the attractions or stigma probably vary considerably between different sections of the population.

Politics

There has been relatively little research into youth and politics. Unemployment has been the dominant issue and, contrary to some earlier forecasts, fears and hopes, it has not elevated young people's political behaviour into 'a problem'. Unemployed young people have not been successfully mobilized by any political party, moderate or extreme. Youth in the 1980s are politically acquiescent, probably more so than in the 1960s. This is why the literature on 'Young Radicals' and 'The Making of a Counter-Culture' is not being revived.

It used to be said that the return of mass unemployment would drain support from moderate democratic parties and swell extremist movements. A 1980 UNESCO report anticipated mass unemployment creating a new radical generation. From time to time there are reports of Britain's young unemployed being recruited by the National Front and kindred organizations, but there is really nothing that counts as evidence of the extreme right carrying any greater appeal or threat than in the 1960s.

Throughout the western world in general, the spread of unemployment in the late 1970s and early 1980s was accompanied by a shift of political opinion towards the 'moderate' right of Reagan, Thatcher and Kohl. This trend may now be arrested. While it was underway, young people were sensitive to the drift, but they did not lurch to any political extreme, or in a contrary direction to general political opinion.

The majority of young people currently at risk and, in many cases, actually unemployed, display little overt interest in politics. Many are vehement in proclaiming disinterest. Needless to say, an apolitical younger generation is not a new phenomenon. Radical activists in the 1960s were a minority, even on campuses. Political socialization by families, schools and the media is simply continuing to produce disinterested school-leavers.

This lack of political interest, young people's apathy despite all attempts to mobilize their support, is politically significant. It helps to explain the persistence of inferior stereotypes of the unemployed, and why so many blame (and thereby police) themselves (Breakwell, 1983; Walsgrove, 1984). It suggests that most young people will seek solutions individually, or within families and local peer groups rather than in broader industrial or political movements. The ESRC initiative must check and take account of young people's political indifference, assuming that it is not due to be shattered, but disinterest is not a new teenage phenomenon, and we already possess convincing explanations (Dowse and Hughes, 1971a, 1971b; Stradling and Zurick, 1971).

Some people are politically active, and the initiative could attempt to identify political youth. Questions on political knowledge, interest, activity and partisanship will suffice for these purposes. However, an issue that deserves at least equal attention is whether unemployment, a sign that politicians have broken their side of an unwritten contract, is eroding the state's legitimacy (Turner, 1984) thereby creating the conditions for social disorder which erupts intermittently, but maybe more frequently than during previous decades, on the streets, picket lines and football terraces. The ESRC initiative might miss the point if pre-occupied with the opinions, attitudes and party loyalties that are regularly polled to predict election results. Young people's attitudes towards dealings with various civil authorities - the police, courts, government, parliament and managements - could prove far more interesting.

Leisure

Youth researchers and theoreticians have written extensively about young people's leisure activities. Leisure has been impossible to ignore. After all, youth cultures are constructed and celebrated primarily during leisure time, through leisure pursuits. The importance of leisure in nurturing and maintaining peer relationships, gender roles, adolescent and adult identities has always been recognized. Unfortunately, youth researchers have never developed instruments to measure and typify young people's ways of life systematically and comprehensively. The time may be ripe for youth investigations to incorporate ways of collecting and analysing information about uses of time, income and expenditure, social networks and contacts, and participation in leisure activities that have been developed in other areas of leisure research.

Recent studies of youth at leisure have been pre-occupied with the effects of unemployment. What are the implications for social relationships, leisure activities and spending? Can leisure compensate for lack of work? It is necessary to stress some limitations in most studies. (a) The subjects have usually been recent school-leavers. We know far less about older young people. (b) Many studies have compared young people in education, jobs and/or on schemes with 'the unemployed'. There have been few attempts to distinguish the effects of different types of unemployment. (c) Virtually all the evidence is of short, rather than long-term effects. (d) Some results are from very small samples. (e) Investigators have focused on specimen activities, which is easier and cheaper than more comprehensive measurements of young people's ways of life.

Despite the above limitations, the following conclusions are quite firmly established.

Few young people respond proactively to unemployment (Fryer and Payne, 1984). The experience is usually considered 'an ordeal' (Hendry *et al.*, 1984). Unemployed young people are the more anxious and prone to worry about clothes, appearance and money (DES, 1983). According to one study, long-term youth unemployment is related to suicidal tendencies (Francis, 1984). Unemployment among school-leavers appears to delay growing up, going out, developing 'mature' relationships, acquiring adult tastes and spending patterns (Gurney, 1980; Hendry *et al.*, 1984). As previously mentioned, unemployed young people have lower health scores than those in work (Breakwell, 1983; Banks *et al.*, 1984).

Participation in leisure activities lessens, but does not eliminate the socio-psychological damage of unemployment (Stokes, 1983; Warr, 1983). At best, leisure is a 'palliative' rather than a substitute for work (Kelvin *et al.*, 1984).

The (short-term) social and psychological effects of unemployment among young people are less pronounced than among adults (Warr, 1983). In general, modifications in leisure patterns are undramatic. Unemployment does not isolate young people. Unlike adults, they spend more, not less time with friends than when in employment (Kelvin *et al.*, 1984). Unemployment does not reduce the frequency or range of young people's leisure activities. Leisure is simply 'scaled-down' (Willis, 1979). It becomes cheaper, localized, and less commercial (Sandhu, 1984). Unemployment appears to have led to greater use of the Youth Service (DES, 1983) and reversed the former situation where the educationally successful, usually from middle class homes, were the main beneficiaries.

The effects of unemployment are not identical for boys and girls. The latter appear the more restricted, and are rendered less adaptable by the availability of a domestic role (Banks *et al.*, 1984). Girls are more isolated than unemployed boys who, when frustrated and depressed, may act out their problems on the streets. Girls' problems seem more likely to be bottled up, and they display more evidence of psychological disturbances (DES, 1983; Donovan and Oddy, 1982).

Future research needs to build on the above findings and transcend the limitations listed earlier. In particular, if possible, the research initiative should attempt comprehensive assessments of the ways of life of different groups of young people, not just the unemployed but the larger numbers in education youth training and jobs.

There are two additional issues, so far the subject of mere speculation, that the initiative could engage. First, it is frequently suggested that youth unemployment, and the associated despair and desperation, are parts of the backgrounds that breed crime against property, drug abuse, violence on streets, soccer terraces, against girl friends and ethnic minorities (Scarman,

1981). However, causal links have not been demonstrated. The initiative could aim to clarify any connections.

Secondly, many young people are affected directly by unemployment. Other effects will be indirect, transmitted through households with unemployed parents. Previous studies have found many parents doing their utmost to ensure that out-of-school children do not suffer when unable to find work. Families can offer moral and material support, but the price of acceptance often includes more pressure to find employment, plus prolonged dependence (Wallace, 1985). Some working teenagers, especially those with unemployed parents, may lead more impoverished life-styles, but enjoy greater independence. What happens when both generations are un-employed? Parents' ability to support teenage children may have become a key factor in decisions on whether to remain in education. Even transitions to unemployment mean a rise in personal income.

Since 1975 the amounts of pocket money received by 14–16 year olds have lagged behind rising prices. This may be because many families are poorer, but average living standards have risen, and 5–7 year olds' pocket money has kept well ahead of inflation. Parents may be adjusting the sums given to young people in their final school years in response to the postponement of, and/or the lower incomes now expected after leaving. If so, young people will still be experiencing a gradual rise in personal income as they move from school, through schemes and unemployment, then towards adult jobs. This could be a reason why the short term effects of unemployment on teenage leisure are undramatic.

The value of the ESRC initiative will be enhanced if parents or, even better still, entire households can be studied. The effects of unemployment will sometimes be transmitted through, and may also be mediated and blunted by changes in parents' behaviour.

Young People In Society

A research initiative that addresses the questions outlined above, about the implications of current trends for young people in education, the labour market, the family and leisure will interface with broader sociological debates about changes in the pattern of stratification, the shape of society in the 1980s.

It has been hypothesized that, in some respects, recession then persistent unemployment are accentuating rather than reversing trends that began during the post-war decades of economic growth and affluence. For example, it is suggested that conflicts are increasingly distributional, that privatisation is spreading, and that a pecuniary instrumentalism is becoming more pronounced than ever (Newby and Vogler, 1983). One study reports that young people place even more stress than their parents on economic rewards from employment (Turner *et al.*, 1983).

The British working class has long regarded the macro-economic structure, the contours of inequality and the labour market as 'beyond control'

(Blackburn and Mann, 1979). Hence workers' renowned fatalism and stoicism. Apolitical responses may be explicable in terms of the experience of unemployment being assimilated within this prior frame of reference.

Newby and Vogler (1983) suggest that, in the 1980s, class divisions are becoming more opaque, and that boundaries are less easily discerned. This may be true of the middle-working class schism, but unemployment and occupational restructuring appear to be creating other clearer divisions. It has been argued that primary and secondary economies and labour markets are to become more distinct (Craig *et al.*, 1983). There are several indications:

1   wider income inequalities;
2   firms distinguishing core workforces from temporary and casual staff. High unemployment creates a reserve army, some of whom are prepared to accept exceptionally low wages and/or to work 'off the record' (Morris, 1984);
3   some firms are making greater use of internal, and extended internal labour markets, recruiting by word-of-mouth (Jenkins *et al.*, 1983). Jobcentres have retained their market share, but firms are making less use of newspaper adverts and fee-charging agencies (MSC, 1984);
4   some households are participating in a virtuous circle in which work breeds work. Primary employment supplies contacts and skills that enable individuals to take second jobs, and provides the income necessary for self-provisioning. Meanwhile, other households are trapped in a vicious circle, excluded from all types of work (Pahl, 1984).

Many of the issues for the 16–19 initiative outlined above are closely related to problems being addressed in the parallel ESRC enquiries into social change and economic life. The latter investigations will examine the implications of parents' employment and unemployment for children's economic socialization, attitudes towards technical change, trade unions and other work-related issues, and the impact of on-going economic changes on family patterns, community integration, physical and psychological well-being.

The economic life fieldwork is concentrating on over-20 year olds only because young people are being treated in separate existing and proposed investigations, including the ESRC initiative. Young people are especially sensitive to current rather than peripheral economic trends. Hence the inevitability of overlap and the case for collaboration between the two ESRC initiatives. This collaboration could involve fieldwork in the same areas, which would supply the 16–19 initiative with information about the local labour markets and adult populations. In addition or in any event, each initiative could benefit from standardized questions on, for example, family relationships, work attitudes, and well-being.

The economic life research is already underway, so the 16–19 initiative cannot become a major influence on the design of these enquiries. Collaboration may necessarily mean the 16–19 enquiries using areas and research instruments already selected by the economic life investigators. The 16-19 investigators are likely to resist becoming mere adjuncts, and quite rightly, for the issues to be investigated in the two initiatives overlap but are not identical. At this stage, therefore, the 16-19 initiative will probably benefit by treating collaboration as a potential opportunity rather than a constraint. If the 16-19 researchers can decide, initially, which methods they would prefer given the issues they define for investigation, the ways and extent to which collaboration with the economic life teams might be mutually advantageous can then be considered.

The Core Issues

It has been impossible to prevent this review of recent trends and investigations being dominated by unemployment since the issue has pervaded virtually all recent youth research. Enquiries into other spheres of teenagers' lives, including their fertility and leisure, have tended to concentrate on the implications of joblessness.

Unemployment remains far too important an issue to ignore in the ESRC initiative, but it needs to be set in context:

1 The majority of young people are still making transitions to employment.
2 Other young people, apart from those unemployed at any point in time, will be affected by the socio-economic trends reviewed in previous passages.
3 The assumption of economic determinism implicit in much recent research needs to be challenged, or at least investigated. Gender divisions, family behaviour, leisure patterns and educational trends can have a momentum of their own. Everything else does not necessarily hinge on whether young people are employed and, if so, their types of jobs. Work or its absence is not always the central, determining feature in individuals' life-styles. As previously explained, strong family relationships and/or leisure interests appear capable of lessening the damage of unemployment. There is evidence of marriage fostering different attitudes towards work. Males feel that it becomes more important to hold a job. Some become less selective and stress instrumental at the expense of intrinsic satisfactions (Wallace, 1985).

The questions left by gaps in, and posed by ambiguous results from recent research define two sets of core issues for the ESRC initiative. First, an initiative is required to identify comprehensively the main outcomes of recent trends - the emergent patterns in young people's careers in education, employment, the family and leisure, and to explain how these careers differ between various groups of young people.

Sociologists routinely divide the population into middle and working classes. It would be amazing if the ESRC enquiries ignored this schism. The investigators will be aware that previous youth researchers have emphasized the significance of a cleavage within the manual working class, separating the skilled from the rest, or the respectable from the rough, or the aspiring from the indifferent (Carter, 1962), or those who anticipate and experience career progression from the careerless (Ashton and Field, 1976), or 'lads' from 'ear oles','citizens and ordinary kids' (Willis, 1977; Jenkins, 1983). ESRC investigators will want to discover whether these are still major divisions. Do they apply among girls? Are there equally significant divisions among middle class youth?

Secondly, an initiative is needed to examine how careers in education, the labour market, the family and leisure interact. Patterns of interaction may vary considerably between different groups of young people. Education and employment are unlikely to have exactly the same meaning for males and females, whatever their qualifications.

The ESRC initiative must build upon, but in some respects it will be intentionally different from recent investigations in its concern for all aspects of young people's situations, and with developmental processes and patterns from age 16 or earlier to 19 or older. It will want to separate, not in order to isolate, but eventually to interrelate young people's experiences in employment, education, the family and leisure. The initiative will want to engage young people's attempts, successful or otherwise, to make sense of and to exercise some control over their total situations. The research will be attempting to identify typical configurations formed by the interaction between careers in different domains, and young people's own attempts to understand their predicaments, and to create and sustain identities from the consistencies and contradictions that they encounter.

A fresh research initiative is required partly because recent enquiries have left many of their own questions unanswered, but equally because these studies have been preoccupied, for excellent reasons, with the impact of specific trends, particularly the spread of unemployment, and have thereby submerged an older genre of youth theory and research which now needs resuscitating in order to assess the overall impact of recent trends on youth cultures and transitions towards adulthood. In conceptualizing its problems, the ESRC initiative must be sensitive to the changes in young people's situations wrought by the trends on which recent research has focused, but the initiative will also be able to draw upon the type of sociological theory and research on youth culture that was interrupted after the rise of 'the new wave' in the 1970s. When reviving this older genre, a synthesis with social psychological concepts and findings may be productive. The different vocabularies are grappling with similar problems. Cross-fertilization could facilitate solutions.

References and Notes

ALLAT, P. and YEANDLE, S. M. (1984) *Family structure and youth unemployment*. Paper presented to British Sociological Association Conference, Bradford.

ASHTON, D. N. and FIELD, D. (1976) *Young Workers*. Hutchinson.

ASHTON, D. and MAGUIRE, M. (1983) *The Vanishing Youth Labour Market*. Youthaid Occasional Paper 3. London.

ASHTON, D.N. and MAGUIRE, M.J. (1984) *Labour market segmentation and the work experience of young adults*. Paper presented at conference on 'The Young Persons Labour Market'. University of Warwick.

BANKS, M., ULLAH, P. and WARR, P. (1984) 'Unemployed and less qualified urban young people', *Employment Gazette*, August, pp. 343–46.

BARBAGLI, M. (1982) *Educating for Unemployment*. Columbia University Press.

BATES, I., CLARKE, J., COHEN, P., FINN, D., MOORE, R., WILLIS, P. (1984) *Schooling for the Dole*. Macmillan.

BEDEMAN, T. and COURTENAY, G. (1983) *One in Three*, MSC Research and Development Series, 13.

BERG, I. (1973) *Education and Jobs*, Penguin.

BLACKBURN, R. M. and MANN, M. (1979) *The Working Class in the Labour Market*. Macmillan.

BRAKE, M. (1980) *The Sociology of Youth Culture and Youth Sub-Cultures*. Routledge.

BRAKE, M. (1985) *Comparative Youth Culture*. Routledge.

BREAKWELL, G. M. (1983) *Young people in and out of work*. Paper presented at SSRC Labour Markets Workshop. Manchester.

BURRIS, V. (1983) 'The Social and Political Consequences of Over-education', *American Sociological Review*, 48, pp. 454–67.

CARTER, M. P. (1962) *Home School and Work*, Pergamon.

COHEN, P. (1976) 'Sub-cultural conflicts and working class community', in HAMMERSLEY, M. and WOODS, P. (eds) *The Process of Schooling*, Routledge.

COHEN, S. (1976) (ed.) *Images of Deviance*, Penguin.

COLEMAN, J. S. (1961) *The Adolescent Society*, Free Press.

COLEMAN, J. and HUSEN, T. (1985) *Becoming Adult in a Changing Society*, OECD.

CRAIG, C., RUBERY, J., TARLING, R. and WILKINSON, F. (1983) *How labour markets operate: views developed from our research*. Paper presented at SSRC Labour Markets Workshop, Manchester.

CUSACK, S. and ROLL, J. (1985) *Families Rent Apart*. Child Poverty Action Group.

DES (DEPARTMENT OF EDUCATION AND SCIENCE.) (1983) *Young People in the 80s: a survey*. HMSO.

DONOVAN, A. and ODDY, M. (1982) 'Psychological aspects of unemployment: an investigation into the emotional and social adjustment of school-leavers', *Journal of Adolescence*, 5, pp. 15–30.

DORE, R. (1976) *The Diploma Disease*. Allen and Unwin.

DOWSE, R. E. and HUGHES, A. J. (1971a) 'Boys, girls and politics'. *British Journal of Sociology*, 22, p. 53–67.

DOWSE, R. E. and HUGHES, J. A. (1971b) 'The family, the school and the political socialisation process. *Sociology*, 5, pp. 21–45.

EDWARDS, T. (1984) *The Youth Training Scheme: a New Curriculum? Episode One*. Falmer.

ELKIN, F. and WESTLEY, W. A. (1984) 'The myth of the adolescent culture'. *American Sociological Review*, 20, pp. 680–4. 'First employment of young people'. *Employment Gazette* October 1984. pp. 445–8.

FAGIN, L. and LITTLE, M. (1983) *The Forsaken Families*. Penguin.

FIDDY, R. (ed.) (1983) *In Place of Work*. Falmer.

FRANCIS, L. J. (1984) *Young and Unemployed*. Costello.

FRANCOME, C. (1983) 'Unwanted pregnancies among teenagers'. *Journal of Biosocial Science*, 15, pp. 139–43.

FREEMAN, R. B. and WISE, D. A. (eds) (1982) *The Youth Labour Market Problem*. University of Chicago Press.

FRYER, D. and PAYNE, R. (1984) 'Proactive behaviour in unemployment: findings and implications'. *Leisure Studies*, 3, pp. 273–95.

GASKELL, J. and LAZERSON, M. (1980) *Between School and Work*. Faculty of Education, University of British Columbia, Vancouver, Mimeo.

GEAVES, K. (1983) *The Youth Opportunities Programme in Contrasting Local Areas*. MSC Research and Development Series, 16.

GORDON, M. S. (1979) *Youth Education and Unemployment Problems*. Carnegie Council, Berkeley.

GRIFFIN, C. (1985) *Typical Girls?* Routledge.

GURNEY, M. (1980) The effects of unemployment on the psycho-social development of school-leavers'. *Occupational Psychology*, 53, pp. 205–13.

HALL, S. and JEFFERSON, T. (eds) (1976) *Resistance Through Rituals*. Hutchinson.

HAYES, C., ANDERSON, A. and FONDA, N. (1984) *Competence and Competition*. NEDC/MSC. London.

HEBDIGE, D. (1979) *Sub-culture – the Meaning of Style*. Methuen.

HENDRY, L. B., RAYMOND, M. and STEWART, C. (1984) 'Unemployment, school and leisure: an adolescent study'. *Leisure Studies*, 3, pp. 175–87.

INEICHEN, B. (1981) 'The housing decisions of young people'. *British Journal of Sociology*, 32, pp. 252–8.

JEFFS, T. (1982) *Youth Conscription*. Youthaid Occasional Paper 1.

JENKINS, R. (1983) *Citizens, Lads and Ordinary Kids*. Routledge.

JENKINS, R., BRYMAN, A., KEIL, T. and BEARDSWORTH, A. (1983) 'Information in the labour market: the impact of recession'. *Sociology*, 17, pp. 260–7.

JONES, P. (1983) 'Effects of rising unemployment on school-leavers'. *Employment Gazette*, 91, pp. 13–16.

JONES, P. (1984) *What Opportunities for Youth?* Youthaid Occasional Paper 4.

KELVIN, P., DEWBERRY, C. and MORELEY-BUNKER, N. (1984) *Unemployment and Leisure*. University College, London, Mimeo.

KLEIN, J. (1964) *Samples from English Cultures*, Vol. II. Routledge.

LEONARD, D. (1980) *Sex and Generation*. Tavistock.

LONEY, M. (1979) 'The politics of job creation', in CRAIG, G., MAYO, M. and SHARMAN, N. (eds) *Jobs and Community Action*. Routledge.

McDERMOTT, K. and DENCH, S. (1983) *Youth Opportunities in a Rural Area*. MSC Research and Development Series 14.

McROBBIE, A. and GARBER, J. (1976) 'Girls and Sub-cultures', in HALL, S. and JEFFERSON, T. (eds) op. cit.

MSC (MANPOWER SERVICES COMMISSION) (1984) 'Employers' recruitment practices'. *Labour Market Quarterly Report*, February, pp. 5–6.

MARSLAND, D. (1984) *Work to be Done*. Youth Call.

MEAD, M (1935) *Sex and Temperament in Three Primitive Societies*. Routledge.

MORRIS, L. D. (1984) 'Patterns of social activity and post-redundancy labour market experience'. Sociology, 18, pp. 339–52.

MUNGHAM, G. and PEARSON, G. (eds) (1976) *Working Class Youth Cultures*. Routledge.

NEWBY, H. and VOGLER, C.(1983)   *From class structure to class action: a critique of recent theories*. Paper presented at SSRC Labour Markets Workshop, Manchester.

OECD (ORGANISATION FOR ECONOMIC CO-OPERATION AND DEVELOPMENT) (1983) *Report on a Conference on the Transition from Compulsory Education to Active Life*. Paris.

PAHL, R. E. (1984) *Divisions of Labour*. Blackwell.

PARKER, H. J. (1974) *View from the Boys*. David and Charles.

PARSONS, T. (1954) 'Age and sex in the social structure of the United States', in *Essays in Sociological Theory*. Free Press.

PRESIDENT'S SCIENCE AND ADVISORY COMMITTEE (1974) *Panel on Youth: Transition to Adulthood*. University of Chicago Press.

RAFFE, D. (1984) *The transition from school to work and the recession: evidence from the Scottish school-leavers surveys, 1977–83*. Paper 84/10. Proceedings of the Standing Conference on the Sociology of Further Education. Coombe Lodge, Blagdon.

REES, T. L. and ATKINSON, P. (eds) (1982) *Youth Unemployment and State Intervention*. Routledge.

REUTER, E. B. (1937) 'The sociology of adolescence'. *American Journal of Sociology*, 43, pp. 414–27.

ROBERTS, K. (1983) *Youth and Leisure*. Allen and Unwin.

ROBERTS, K. (1984) *School-leavers and their Prospects*. Open University Press.

ROBERTS, K., NOBLE, M. and DUGGAN, J. (1982a) Unregistered Youth Unemployment and Outreach Careers Work, Part II, Outreach Careers Work. Research Paper 32, Department of Employment.

ROBERTS, K., NOBLE, M. and DUGGAN, J. (1982b) 'Youth unemployment: an old problem or a new life-style'. *Leisure Studies*, 1, pp. 171–82.

RYRIE, A. C. (1983) *On Leaving School*. Hodder and Stoughton.

SANDHU, R. (1984) Young and unemployed in Wolverhampton: provisions and facilities. Paper presented at Conference of Unemployment. Wolverhampton Polytechnic.

SCARMAN, LORD (1981) *The Brixton Disorders, 10–12 April 1981*. Cmnd 8427. HMSO.

SIMMS, M. and SMITH, C. (1985) 'Why teenage mothers say they did not use birth control'. *Family Planning*. First Quarter.

SMITH, D. M. (1987) 'New movements in the sociology of youth: a critique'. *British Journal of Sociology*, 32, pp. 239–51.

SMITH, E. A. (1962) *American Youth Culture*. Free Press.

STOKES, G. (1983) 'Work, leisure and unemployment'. *Leisure Studies*, 2, pp. 269–86.

STRADLING, R. and ZURICK, E. (1971) 'Political and non-political ideals of English primary and secondary school-children'. *Sociological Review*, 19, pp. 203–27.

TAYLOR, I., WALTON, P. and YOUNG, J. (1973) *The New Criminology*. Routledge.

TURNER, R., BOSTYN, A. M. and WIGHT, D. (1983) *The work ethic in a Scottish town with declining employment*. Paper presented to XIth International Congress of Anthropological and Ethnological Sciences. Vancouver.

TURNER, S. (1984) *Bursting the balloon*. Paper presented to British Sociological Association Conference. Bradford.

UNESCO (1981) *Youth in the 1980s*. Unesco Press.

VARLAAM, C. (ed.) (1984) *Rethinking Transition: Educational Innovation and the Transition to Adult Life*. Falmer.

WALLACE, C. (1985) *Growing Apart: Unemployment, Polarisation and Family Formation Amongst Young People*. University of Kent at Canterbury, Mimeo.

WARR, P. (1983) 'Work, jobs and unemployment', *Bulletin of the British Psychological Society,* 36, pp. 305–11.

WASLGROVE, D. *Policing yourself: youth unemployment, individualism and amplification of normality.* Paper presented to British Sociological Association Conference, Bradford.

WATTS, A. G. (1983) *Education, Unemployment and the Future of Work.* Open University Press.

WELLS, W. (1983) *The Relative Pay and Employment of Young People.* Research paper 42, Department of Employment.

WILLIS, M. (1977) *Youth Unemployment and Leisure Opportunities.* Department of Education and Science, London, Mimeo.

WILLIS, P. (1977) *Learning to Labour,* Saxon House.

YOUNG, J. (1971) *The Drugtakers.* Paladin.

Index

academic research, independent 159–65
accountability 26, 44, 48–9, 95, 114, 120–2, 136
accreditation of teacher training courses 24, 52, 56; *see also* Council for
achievement 22, 42, 87; enhanced definitions of 196; *see also* records of achievement
Adult Training Centres 202
American Educational Research Association (AERA) 111–12
Apple, M. 145, 156
appraisal, teacher 24, 142–4
apprenticeships 227, 232
Archer, M.S. 198
Aristotle 170, 183
Ashton, D. 206, 208–10, 216–17
Aspects of Secondary Education (HMI) 18, 98
assessment 3, 43–8, 95–9; graded 47, 81–5, 91, 99; side effects of 76–84
Assessment of Performance Unit (APU) 22–3, 96
attainment: and social class 184–8, 189–94; and gender 219–20; and race 219–20; statement of 99
Australia 97, 121
autonomy: of educational institutions 163–5; licensed to regulated 136; pupil 228, 235; teacher 31–2, 49, 69, 151–2, 155, 164

Baker, Kenneth 31, 45
Basis for Choice, A (ABC) (FEU) 90
Bennett, N. 138
Better Schools 20, 36, 52, 54, 55
Blackburn, R. 216
Booth, A. 196
Boyd, W.L. 136–7
Boyson, R. 248
Brereton, J.I. 78
Brookover, W.B. *Elementary School Climate and School Achievement* 105
Burt, Cyril 197

Caldwell, B. 121
California, study of school effectiveness 104–5
Callaghan, James: Ruskin College speech (1976) 14–15, 34
Cambridgeshire 114, 115, 116, 118, 119
Canada 117, 121
Central Advisory Council for Education 249–50
centralization of power in education 138–9, 155: limitations of 157–9
Certificate of Pre-Vocational Education (CPVE) 50, 88, 89, 91, 141–2
Certificate of Secondary Education (CSE) 7, 23
certification procedures 186, 187; attitudes to 92–3; consensus, 85–6
child-centred education 31, 202–3
Clark, L. 215–16
class: in the classroom 184–8; culture and schooling 239–41; inequalities 6–7, 174–5
Clignet, Remi 77
Cobb, J. 246–7
Cockcroft Report 13, 98
Coleman, J.S. 103, 109, 273
competition: and assessment 76–81; or cooperation 226–7, 236; open 6, 179; and testing 98

comprehensive schools: Scottish 7, 189–94; and special needs 199–200; standards and equality 184–8, 192–3
consensus: assumption of economic utility 224–7; on certification procedures 85–6; collapse of political on role of education system 253
Conservatives 24, 26, 138, 184, 225
control issue 142, 154–68: in classrooms 58–61, 71
Council for the Accreditation of Teacher Education (CATE) 162
Council for Science and Society Report (1981) 224–5, 227, 229, 230
Cox, Roy 79
criterion referencing 23, 45, 86, 93, 94, 96, 98
Crompton, R. 220
culture, class and schooling 239–41; *see also* youth culture
Cumin, D. 206, 207
Curriculum 11–16 (HMI) 18, 19–20, 36
curriculum: central influence on 12–33; continuity and 49–50; history 12–14; national 1, 34–51; framework 18–21, 32; legislating for 25–8; resistance to 31–2; as a whole 42
Curriculum and Assessment in Scotland: a policy for the 90s 30
curriculum development 'cascade' model 30
Curriculum from 5 to 16, The (HMI) 18
curriculum planning 138
Cusack, S. 274

Davies, Bernard 116, 231–2
Dawson, Jean 22–3
delinquency research 264, 278
democracy 5, 155, 157, 158, 161, 165–7, 194, 226, 236
Department of Education and Science (DES): curriculum documents 16–17, 34–6; and LMS 114; objectives in areas of curriculum 20; and teaching quality 54
Department of Employment 25
Detroit, Model Cities Neighborhood 108
differentiation 42; cultural or educational 239–40
domination, relations of 53, 60, 202
Dunning report (1977) 2, 28, 29

Eccles, David 14
economic efficiency, education and 248–9
Economic and Social Research Council (ESRC) 16–19; Initiative 263–86
economy, and youth unemployment 266–71
Edmonton, Alberta 117, 121
Educating our Children: Four Subjects for Debate (DES) 15
Education Acts: (1944) 12, 187; Scotland (1945) 13; (1980) 63; 1981) 199; (1986) 27
Education Reform Bill (1987) 1, 2, 4, 26, 27, 37, 50nl, 114
Education in Schools: a Consultative Document (1977 Green Paper) 16, 34, 225
educational problems 155–7
educational studies, politics and control of 159–63
employers: educational standards and young workers 210–17; and qualifications 8, 207–8